Washington. US. of Americ[a]

[...]out to undertake for the [...]

[...]most convenient water c[...]

[...] being small, it is to be e[...]

[...]from the Indian inhabit[...]

[...]Pacific ocean, you may [...]

[...] I be forced to seek a pa[...]

[...]he Western coast. but [...]

[...]; as a sufficient supp[...]

[...]e in that case can on[...]

[...]authorise you to draw on the Secretaries

[...] Navy of the US.. according as you may find

[...]le [...] the purpose of obtaining money or

[...] I solemnly pledge the faith of the

[...]be paid punctu[...] late they

Consuls, agents, merch[...] [...]ens of any

The Founding Fathers

Pencil sketch by Benjamin H. Latrobe, drawn from life in Philadelphia, c. 1799

The Founding Fathers

THOMAS JEFFERSON

A Biography in His Own Words

By
THE EDITORS OF NEWSWEEK BOOKS

With an Introduction by
JOSEPH L. GARDNER

JOAN PATERSON KERR
Picture Editor

Published by NEWSWEEK, New York
Distributed by HARPER & ROW, PUBLISHERS, INC.

We dedicate this series of books to the memory of
Frederick S. Beebe
friend, mentor, and "Founding Father" of Newsweek Books

Thomas Jefferson, A Biography in His Own Words,
has been produced by Newsweek Books:

Joseph L. Gardner, Editor

Janet Czarnetzki, Art Director

Judith Bentley, Copy Editor

Susan Storer, Picture Researcher

S. Arthur Dembner, President

This book is based on Volumes 1–19 of *The Papers of Thomas Jefferson,*
edited by Julian P. Boyd and others, published by Princeton University Press,
and copyright Princeton University Press.
The texts of documents published in this edition have been obtained
from photocopies in the files of *The Papers of Thomas Jefferson,*
made from original manuscripts located in various public repositories.
Specific sources are acknowledged on page 409.

For information address Harper & Row, Publishers, Inc.
10 East 53rd Street, New York, N.Y. 10022
Published simultaneously in Canada by Fitzhenry & Whiteside Limited, Toronto.

Contents

Introduction

by Joseph L. Gardner
Editor, Newsweek Books

The American Colonies were at a crossroads in May, 1776. George Washington, in the field for a year, had at last forced the British to evacuate Boston, but a colonial expedition to Canada had ended in a rout. In Congress, John Adams was calling for the Colonies to establish their own governments; "Every Post and every Day rolls in upon Us Independence like a Torrent," he wrote in excitement. Acting upon the unanimous instruction of the Virginia Convention, Richard Henry Lee introduced a resolution of independence on June 7. Although debate was postponed until July 1, a committee was appointed to draft an appropriate declaration should Lee's resolution be carried. The chairman and actual draftsman of the declaration was to be thirty-three-year-old Thomas Jefferson, who had just resumed his seat as a delegate. Absent since December but a regular attendant the previous year, he had sat silent through most earlier congressional sessions; nonetheless, the tall, lanky, red-haired Virginian—his envious colleague Adams conceded—"had the reputation of a masterly Pen."

Working at a small portable writing desk of his own design, in his second-floor lodgings in a private home, Jefferson produced over the next seventeen days the ringing statement with which his name will forever be linked—indeed, it was one of the three accomplishments of his life he asked to have memorialized on his tombstone. The Declaration of Independence, Jefferson later claimed, was drafted without recourse to book, pamphlet, or previous writing of any kind. Instead, this rarely gifted man drew upon the vast reservoir of his brilliant, uniquely trained intellect to produce a timely and timeless "expression of the American mind."

An early biographer described the Jefferson of this period as a man "who could calculate an eclipse, survey an estate, tie an artery, plan an edifice, try a cause, break a horse, dance a minuet, and play the violin." Despite the incongruity of such a statement, a later scholar, Julian P. Boyd, has stated that this gives only a partial picture. Of his contemporaries, only Benjamin Franklin approached him in the extent and variety of his interests. "To catalogue the areas of his explorations," writes Boyd, "is to list most of the principal categories of knowledge—law, government, history, mathematics, architecture, medicine, agriculture, languages and literature, education, music, philosophy, religion, and almost every branch of the natural sciences from astronomy through meteorology to zoology." The attempt to capture such a life has been the tantalizing task and elusive goal of numerous biographers since Jefferson's death a century and a half ago.

Jefferson himself shied away from such an undertaking, producing only a fragmentary *Autobiography* in 1821; the work ended with his taking office as Secretary of State in March, 1790. "To become my own biographer is the last thing in the world I would undertake," he had stated in his seventy-second year. "No. If there has been anything in my course worth the public attention, they are better judges of it than I can be myself, and to them it is my duty to leave it." He thus bequeathed to posterity the obligation to reconstruct his life; fortunately, he also left the means to do so.

"The letters of a person, especially of one whose business has been chiefly transacted by letters," Jefferson observed toward the end of his remarkably long and active career, "form the only full and genuine journal of his life." In the case of the third President such a "genuine journal" runs to 60,000 items—a correspondence with thousands of people stretching over a period of seven decades. "I wonder how Mr. Jefferson made out to answer everybody who wrote to him . . . ?" an awed contemporary asked. Even in retirement, Jefferson complained that "My greatest oppression is a correspondence afflictingly laborious." To Adams he confided in 1817 that from sunrise to two o'clock and often from dinner to dark, "I am drudging at the writing table." Answering letters, even from people he did not know, was "the burthen of my life, a very grievous one indeed, and one I must get rid of." But, of course, he continued to write.

Jefferson took extraordinary pains to be precise and felicitous in his writing, Boyd has concluded. It was therefore not merely his insatiable curiosity about technical improvements that led him to experiment with such methods of preserving his letters as the letterpress and the polygraph—only with such aids could his hours at the desk be spent creatively and not be consumed in the drudgery of copying. But with his selfless perception of the role he was playing in history and with his clear vision of future generations' interest in that role, Jefferson faithfully preserved an unrivaled and invaluable record of his life. From 1783 until 1826 he kept an "epistolary ledger" of his correspondence, a neat, precise listing in parallel columns of virtually every letter he wrote or received. This extraordinary 656-page document reveals Jefferson's love of system and order; for those who would study his life, Boyd claims, it is "an authoritative device for establishing the dates of undated or mutilated letters, for ascertaining the author's whereabouts, and for unlocking some of the mysteries of postal communication during his time." All his other papers—law cases, bank accounts, plantation records, state documents, drafts for *Notes on Virginia*—were also once systematically arranged.

A few months before his death on July 4, 1826—the fiftieth anniversary of the Declaration of Independence—Jefferson signed a will that named his beloved grandson, Thomas Jefferson Randolph, the executor of his estate and recipient of his papers. It was the principal legacy that the nearly bankrupt ex-President could convey, and for a quarter century Randolph was the faithful guardian of this treasure.

Although Jefferson had left no specific request that his papers be published, Randolph undertook to select and edit the documents he had received from his grandfather and in 1829 published a four-volume work, *Memoirs, Correspondence, and Miscellanies from the Papers of Thomas Jefferson.* Within a year the 6,000 printing was sold out; subsequent editions were printed in London, Boston, and Paris. "Have you seen Mr. Jefferson's *Works?* . . ." the jurist Joseph Story wrote a colleague. "It is the most precious melange of all sorts of scandals you ever read. It will elevate your opinion of his talents, but lower him in point of principle and morals not a little." The *Memoirs* — containing uncensored quotes from letters and a journal called the *Anas* — fanned political flames, and Jefferson was soon being "quoted on any side of almost any question." Many expressed shock over the candor revealed in Jefferson's writings about his contemporaries and criticized his grandson for not being more judicious in his selection. But Randolph had been acting in good faith, fully aware of the obligation imposed by the family legacy. "Short of wanton mutilation and distortion," a modern historian has stated, "no editor of the papers could have steered Jefferson's reputation into a safe harbor."

Perhaps realizing the inadequacy of his edition, Randolph next gave St. George Tucker access to the papers, and in 1837 Tucker published *The Life of Thomas Jefferson,* a sympathetic account that was criticized as "ice trying to represent fire!" Meanwhile, the federal government had acquired papers of both George Washington and James Madison. A national responsibility for safeguarding the record of the past was only beginning to receive widespread acceptance. Indeed, not until 1848 did Congress authorize the purchase of the Jefferson papers from Randolph — and then in an appropriations bill that ironically put the same price tag of $20,000 on the papers of Jefferson's archrival, Alexander Hamilton.

In due course Randolph deposited his grandfather's papers at the Department of State in Washington, D. C. There, it might be assumed, they were safe for posterity. Instead, the carefully assembled and systematically arranged collection was subjected to a bizarre "trial-by-editing" that prevented even a partial restoration of its unity for half a century.

The congressional appropriation of 1848 had also provided funds for editing and publishing the papers, and this task was assigned to Professor Henry Augustine Washington of the College of William and Mary. Preoccupied with his academic duties, Professor Washington prevailed upon Congress to ship its priceless new acquisition to Williamsburg, where he felt he could work more comfortably and efficiently. He next proposed sending certain Jefferson documents directly to the printer to save the expense of making new transcriptions, and he did not hesitate to trace over faded lines to make them more legible. His assignment completed and a ten-volume edition of *Writings* ready for printing by early 1854, Washington had 130 volumes of Jefferson's papers selected, arranged, indexed, and bound for return to the government. This left in his hands "a mass of refuse matter nearly twice as large as that which has been selected for preservation. . . ." Three boxes of papers deemed too personal for publication were returned to the Department of State, while the "mass of refuse matter" was separately turned over to Congress.

Sixteen more years, during which the nation was sundered by civil war, passed before Congress fully evaluated its collection and finally got around to returning to the family the private papers exempted from the sale of 1848. Five years after that, in 1875, Thomas Jefferson Randolph died and the remaining papers were gradually dispersed among his heirs. These eventually came to such repositories as the University of Virginia, the Massachusetts Historical Society, and the Library of Congress—though one portion was tragically lost in a fire. Apparently St. George Tucker and Henry Augustine Washington had retained some Jefferson papers after completing their editorial endeavors, and a descendant of both acquired 2,500 documents early in the twentieth century; the largest portion of this lot went to the Missouri Historical Society. Incredibly, the federal government did not actually gather under one roof all the papers it owned until 1905, more than half a century after the original acquisition. Two years later a misplaced box of 2,000 items was found in a Library office.

By that date two more editions of Jefferson papers had been published: a ten-volume work by Paul Leicester Ford (1892–99) and a twenty-volume one by A. A. Lipscomb and A. E. Bergh (1903–4). Although competently edited, the Ford edition was too restrictive in length and reflected the editor's main preoccupation with Jefferson's political career. The Lipscomb-Bergh edition, following too closely Randolph's and Washington's works of the preceding century, a critic has noted, "reflected the inexact scholarly standards of that day." The inaccuracies, distortions, and omissions of all previous editions of Jefferson papers were increasingly recognized by twentieth-century scholars, but not until the bicentennial of the statesman's birth approached in 1943 was a solution proposed to this problem. In a report to the Bicentennial Commission, Julian P. Boyd, then librarian of Princeton University, proposed a new, comprehensive edition of Jefferson's writings.

In March, 1943, Boyd was directed by the Commission to make a study that would analyze the scope, probable cost, and length of time required for the preparation of the new edition. When his report was completed that September, Princeton proposed to sponsor the edition, with the aid of a gift of $200,000 from The New York Times Company. Despite wartime austerity, Datus C. Smith, Jr., Director of the Princeton University Press, made a courageous and farsighted commitment to publish the work. In the spring of 1944 Boyd established his editorial offices at Princeton University Library and began the time-consuming chore of gathering from all over the world photoduplicates of all known Jefferson documents. Eventually a staggering 60,000 documents in facsimile—from 425 different sources in thirty-eight states, the District of Columbia, and several foreign countries—were assembled at Princeton. The range of subjects covered in the documents astonished even the editors. "There are," wrote Associate Editor L. H. Butterfield, "mathematical calculations, designs for machines and furniture and landscape details; recipes for macaroni and other dishes; itineraries; agricultural and meteorological data; tables of useful information; book lists, and notes and memoranda on an incredible variety of subjects, from the use of Archimedes' screw at Kew to snuff, Sophocles, and specific gravity."

There was no implication in his original report, Boyd later claimed, that "a new dimension of documentary editing had been projected or that new techniques for carrying the work forward had been discovered." His modestly stated but heroically ambitious aim was to prepare "a sort of comprehensive documentary biography, not narrated, not fully analyzed, not integrated, but set forth as the whole written corpus of one individual in its totality." Once this was accomplished for Jefferson, it would never have to be undertaken again. It was to be the final, definitive record of the man and his times "in all its discoverable fullness," addressed to an unforeseeable audience in the future.

Boyd's first major decision was to publish not only letters by Jefferson but also letters to him, "for the simple reason that Jefferson's own letters can scarcely achieve the fullest degree of meaning unless it is known what points in his correspondents' letters he chose to comment upon and what he chose to ignore." Although perhaps a third of the estimated 19,000 letters written by Jefferson had been previously published, less than a fifteenth of the much larger number of letters written to him had ever appeared in print. The new edition would embrace not only letters but also messages, speeches, reports, legislative bills, state papers, memoranda, travel journals, resolutions, petitions, minutes of proceedings—all "documents that were written by Jefferson or had a direct relationship with him." The highest degree of textual fidelity (consistent with modern understanding) was to be maintained; each document was to be fully annotated; all would be cross-referenced and indexed.

Publication in 1950 of the first volume of Boyd's *The Papers of Thomas Jefferson* brought paeans of praise from the scholarly world—"This is the most monumental editorial task ever undertaken in this country," wrote Louis B. Wright in the *Yale Review;* Adrienne Koch said in *The New Republic* that the first volume "gives evidence of the astonishing breadth and exacting scholarship that will characterize the entire work." Boyd and his staff, wrote Daniel Boorstin, "seem to have developed successfully a new genre of historical writing." As each volume appeared—there were nineteen by 1974—new light was shed on the historical Jefferson and renewed appreciation was expressed for Boyd's pioneering scholarship. In frank and appreciative imitation, definitive editions of the papers of the other Founding Fathers were launched—Benjamin Franklin (American Philosophical Society and Yale, 1954), John Adams (Massachusetts Historical Society and Harvard, 1954), Alexander Hamilton (Columbia University, 1955), James Madison (University of Chicago and University of Virginia, 1956), and George Washington (Mount Vernon Ladies Association of the Union and University of Virginia, 1966).

"There is properly no history, only biography," Ralph Waldo Emerson stated in a famous aphorism. And thus the Editors of Newsweek Books have sought to present in the series concluded with this work a sweeping panorama of American history through the lives of six ever-illustrious founders of the Republic. A century and a quarter elapsed between the birth of Benjamin Franklin and the death of James Madison—almost as much time as has passed since the departure from the historical stage of that last Father and the present day. There was a vast difference between the rude colonial world into which Franklin was born in 1706 and the lusty young nation facing its great test of Union that Madison left in 1836. In between, as described by the men who lived them, are some of the memorable moments of early American history—the six biographies forming a virtual library of the Revolutionary period.

The runaway apprentice printer Ben Franklin arrives in Philadelphia to make his fortune; grown up and serving his country as a diplomat abroad, the same man, fifty-two years later, leaves England for home—in the sad realization that the end to empire is at hand. George Washington takes command of the "mixed multitude...under very little discipline" that he is to shape into the Continental Army. John Adams exalts to his "dearest friend" and wife, Abigail, in the Declaration of Independence he has just signed—an event to be celebrated "from this Time forward forever more." The illegitimate merchant's clerk in the West Indies, Alexander Hamilton, dreams of military glory and finds it at the side of his hero, Washington, at Yorktown. The diminutive thinker James Madison helps shape one of mankind's most noble statements, the United States Constitution, during a sultry Philadelphia summer—and later as an unhappy President sees his capital burned and looted by the British in the War of 1812.

And finally there is the many-faceted Jefferson, colleague, friend, or adversary of all the others, a man whose life was inextricably entwined with theirs and with the destiny of the nation he helped bring to birth. He sat with Franklin in the Second Continental Congress and later joined the venerable patriot in delicate diplomacy abroad. He was a fellow delegate to Congress and diplomatic partner of John Adams as well, and later an uneasy Vice President to the Massachusetts statesman. To Madison he was a lifelong friend, partner in the most enduring and fruitful intellectual collaboration in American history. Jefferson served Washington wisely and faithfully as Secretary of State but later came to a parting of the ways with his fellow Virginian—largely because of the bitterly contested philosophies that separated him from his Cabinet rival, Alexander Hamilton.

"Thomas Jefferson survives," Adams gasped on his deathbed. He was wrong, for his great contemporary had expired earlier that same day. But he was also right, for Jefferson does indeed triumphantly survive in the words he left his grateful and admiring descendants, the American people.

EDITORIAL NOTE

Most of the Jefferson writings reprinted in this biography have been excerpted from the longer original documents being published in their entirety by Princeton University Press. Omissions at the beginning or ending of a document are indicated by ellipses only if the extract begins or ends in the middle of a sentence; omissions within a quoted passage are also indicated by ellipses. The original spellings have been retained; editorial insertions are set within square brackets.

Chronology of Jefferson and His Times

Thomas Jefferson born April 13 (April 2 Old Style) at Shadwell in Albemarle County, Virginia	1743	
	1754	French and Indian War, 1754–63
Father dies; classical studies with the Rev. James Maury	1757	
Enrolls at College of William and Mary	1760	Reign of George III of England, 1760–1820
Leaves college, begins law and general studies with George Wythe	1762	
Travels to Annapolis, Philadelphia, New York	1766	Stamp Act repealed
Admitted to Virginia bar, manages farms	1767	Townshend Acts; nonimportation movement
Begins construction at Monticello; elected to House of Burgesses	1769	Virginia Resolves and Association
Shadwell burns; moves to Monticello	1770	Boston Massacre
Marries Martha Wayles Skelton; daughter Martha born, first of six children; only two live past childhood	1772	
Appointed to committee of correspondence	1773	
Drafts Albemarle resolutions; *Summary View of the Rights of British America* published	1774	Coercive Acts; First Continental Congress
Delegate to Second Continental Congress; drafts Declaration of Causes	1775	Lexington and Concord skirmishes
Writes Declaration of Independence; drafts constitution for Virginia; leads state reform in House of Delegates	1776	Dunmore burns Norfolk; Virginia introduces independence resolution in Congress
Report of the Committee of Revisors; elected governor	1777	Battle of Saratoga
Directs war preparations in Virginia	1780	Fall of Charleston; Battle of Camden
Retires from governorship; completes *Notes on Virginia;* refutes charges in assembly	1781	Cornwallis invades Virginia; British defeat at Yorktown; Articles of Confederation ratified
Wife dies; appointed to peace commission	1782	
Released from commission; elected to Congress	1783	Congress ratifies peace treaty
Report on plan of government for Northwest Territory; joins Franklin and Adams as minister plenipotentiary in Paris	1784	Netherlands-Austria dispute over Scheldt
Succeeds Franklin as Minister to France; draws plans for Virginia state capitol	1785	Balloon craze in Paris
Visits London, tours English gardens; romance with Maria Cosway	1786	Shays' Rebellion; Statute for Religious Freedom passed by Virginia Assembly; Annapolis Convention
Trip to southern France and northern Italy; corresponds with Madison and others on Constitution	1787	Federal Convention; Louis XVI dissolves the Assembly of Notables; Northwest Ordinance adopted
Negotiates new loans; tour of Holland and Germany; *Observations on the Whale-Fishery*	1788	Constitution ratified
Urges bill of rights; advises Lafayette on	1789	Meeting of Estates General; storming of the

Declaration of the Rights of Man; returns home		Bastille; Washington elected President
Accepts appointment as Secretary of State; aids funding-assumption compromise; *Report on Weights and Measures*; first conflict with Alexander Hamilton in the Cabinet	1790	Hamilton's *Report on the Public Credit*; war threatens between Spain and Britain over Nootka Sound
Argues unconstitutionality of national bank; *Report on Fisheries*; tour of New England and New York with Madison; begins *Anas*	1791	Thomas Paine's *The Rights of Man* printed in Philadelphia; Freneau starts publishing *National Gazette*; First Bank of the United States established
Increases opposition to Hamiltonian policies	1792	
Submits resignation; *Report on Commerce*	1793	Louis XVI guillotined; Citizen Genêt affair; Proclamation of Neutrality
Retires to Monticello; declines mission to Spain	1794	Whisky Rebellion; Jay Treaty signed
New construction at Monticello; correspondence with Washington ends; elected Vice President	1796	Pinckney's Treaty; Washington's Farewell Address; Adams elected President
Elected president of American Philosophical Society; becomes leader of the opposition	1797	XYZ affair; Mazzei letter published
Drafts Kentucky Resolutions; begins to emerge as Republican party leader	1798	Quasi war with France; Alien and Sedition Acts
Elected President by House after electoral tie; appoints James Madison Secretary of State; fills vacancies with Republicans; annual message urges repeal of Naturalization and Judiciary Acts; promulgates economy in government	1801	Appointment of "midnight" judges; capital moved to Washington; Spain cedes Louisiana to France; Tripolitan War begins
Initiates Lewis and Clark expedition; Louisiana Purchase	1803	*Marbury* v. *Madison*; Ohio admitted to Union; renewal of Napoleonic wars
Reelected with George Clinton, Vice President; daughter Mary dies	1804	Hamilton-Burr duel; Napoleon crowned Emperor
Treaty with Tripoli; plans Floridas purchase	1805	War of the Third Coalition
Rejects Monroe-Pinkney treaty; urges embargo	1807	Burr acquitted of treason; *Chesapeake-Leopard* affair; Embargo Act
Address to Albemarle neighbors on retirement	1809	Presidency of James Madison, 1809–1817
Correspondence with John Adams resumed	1812	War declared with Great Britain
Drafts plan for Central College; sells library to Congress	1814	Washington, D.C. burned; Treaty of Ghent; severe economic depression; Congress of Vienna
Appointed member of Board of Visitors for college	1816	Second Bank of the United States
	1817	Presidency of James Monroe, 1817–25
Successfully urges Charlottesville as site for college	1818	
Appointed Rector of state university; assumes debt in Nicholas bankruptcy	1819	Financial panic
	1820	Missouri Compromise
Writes *Autobiography*	1821	
	1823	Monroe Doctrine
Recruits faculty for University of Virginia	1824	Lafayette visits the United States
	1825	University of Virginia opens; Presidency of John Quincy Adams, 1825–29
Thomas Jefferson dies July 4 at Monticello	1826	John Adams dies July 4 at Quincy

A Declaration by the Representatives of the UNITED STATES OF AMERICA, in General Congress assembled.

When in the course of human events it becomes necessary for ~~one~~ people to dissolve the political bands which have connected them with another, and to ~~take among the powers of the earth the~~ as -sume among the powers of the earth the separate and equal ~~station~~ station to which the laws of nature & of nature's god entitle them, a decent respect to the opinions of mankind requires that they should declare the causes which impel them to ~~the change~~ the separation.

We hold these truths to be self-evident; ~~sacred & undeniable~~ that all men are created equal ~~& independent~~, that ~~from that equal creation they derive~~ ~~rights~~ they are endowed by their creator with ~~equal~~ [inherent &] inalienable rights; that ~~among which~~ among these are the ~~preservation of~~ life, & liberty, & the pursuit of happiness; that to secure these rights ~~ends~~, go -vernments are instituted among men, deriving their just powers from the consent of the governed; that whenever any form of government ~~shall~~ becomes destructive of these ends, it is the right of the people to alter or to abolish it, & to institute new government, laying it's foundation on such principles & organising it's powers in such form, as to them shall seem most likely to effect their safety & happiness. prudence indeed will dictate that governments long established should not be ~~changed~~ for light & transient causes: and accordingly all experience hath shewn that mankind are more disposed to suffer while evils are sufferable, than to right themselves by abolishing the forms to which they are accustomed. but when a long train of abuses & usurpations [begun at a distinguished period, &] pursuing invariably the same object, evinces a design to ~~subject~~ reduce them ~~to arbitrary power~~ + under absolute ~~Despotism~~, it is their right, it is their duty, to throw off such ~~government~~ + & to provide new guards for their future security. such has been the patient sufferance of these colonies; & such is now the necessity which constrains them to [expunge] their former systems of government. the history of ~~his~~ the present king of Great Britain is a history of [unremitting] injuries and usurpations, [among which, appears no solitary fact ~~to prove the contrary~~ to contra -dict the uniform tenor of the rest [all of which have] but all have] in direct object the establishment of an absolute tyranny over these states. to prove this, let facts be submitted to a candid world, [for the truth of which we pledge a faith yet unsullied by falsehood.]

Chapter **1**

Formative Years

The American Revolution and the nation created by that Revolution owed their existence both to men who could have looked forward to ease and advancement under the British colonial system and to men who despaired of success or recognition under the empire. Thomas Jefferson clearly belonged to the first group. At his birth on April 13, 1743, at Shadwell, the family estate on the Rivanna River in Albemarle County, he was heir to part of the seventy-five hundred acres of Jefferson land in the Virginia Piedmont. There his father had established a family reputation for ability and public service to the Crown on the expanding frontier. But Thomas Jefferson did not use the lands and position bequeathed to him to perpetuate the traditions of the Virginia planters. Instead he directed his own talents to revolution and the abolition of legal privileges and social attitudes maintaining that way of life; he fought not only for the end of the old, but for the creation of a distinctly new society.

Jefferson's character, as formed in his first twenty years, made that choice inevitable. "An honest heart being the first blessing," he advised his nephew in 1785, "a knowing head is the second." The story of his early life is an account of the influences that gave him an honest heart, which would not allow him to violate the principles in which he believed, and of his own careful cultivation of a knowing head, which made him a champion of the original, experimental, and radical dream of creating a new nation. Jefferson's terse account of his family background, recorded in the *Autobiography* he wrote when he was seventy-seven, displays his impatience with those who were preoccupied with the past.

Autobiography, 1821

The tradition in my father's family was that their ancestor came to this country from Wales, and from near the mountain of Snowden, the highest in Gr. Br. I noted once a case from Wales in the law reports where a person

Thomas Jefferson's draft of the Declaration of Independence, written when he was thirty-three

15

*Cartouche of the map drawn by
Joshua Fry and Peter Jefferson
of "inhabited part of Virginia"*

of our name was either pl[aintiff] or def[endant] and one of the same name was Secretary to the Virginia company. These are the only instances in which I have met with the name in that country. I have found it in our early records, but the first particular information I have of any ancestor was my grandfather who lived at the place in Chesterfield called Ozborne's and ownd. the lands afterwards the glebe of the parish. He had 3. sons, Thomas who died young, Field who settled on the waters of Roanoke and left numerous descendants, and Peter my father, who settled on the lands I still own called Shadwell adjoining my present residence. He was born Feb. 29. 1707/8 and intermarried in 1739. with Jane Randolph of the age of 19. daur of Isham Randolph one of the seven sons of that name & family settled at Dungeness in Goochld. They trace their pedigree far back in England & Scotland, to which let every one ascribe the faith & merit he chuses.

[If Jefferson scoffed at the Randolphs' claims to distinguished lineage, he expressed deep respect for his father, a tall, self-educated man who had pioneered in settling the foothills of the Blue Ridge Mountains.]

My father's education had been quite neglected; but being of a strong mind, sound judgment and eager after information, he read much and improved himself insomuch that he was chosen with Joshua Fry professor of Mathem. in W[illiam] & M[ary] college to continue the boundary line between Virginia & N. Carolina which had been begun by Colo. [William] Byrd, and was afterwards employed with the same Mr. Fry to make the 1st. Map of Virginia which had ever been made, that of Capt [John] Smith being merely a conjectural sketch. They possessed excellent materials for so much of the country as is below the blue ridge; little being then known beyond that ridge. He was the 3d. or 4th. settler of the part of the country in which I live, which was about 1737.

Peter Jefferson took care that his son's education would not be as neglected as his own. This task was made easier in 1745 when the family moved from Shadwell to Tuckahoe fifteen miles to the east. Jane Jefferson's cousin William Randolph died that year and named Peter Jefferson as one of the executors of his estate, including Tuckahoe. For seven years Jefferson managed the house and supervised the education of the four Randolph orphans and his own children in what Thomas later described as the "English school." After the family's return to Shadwell, the boy was sent to study with William Douglas, the Scot cleric at Dover Church in Northam. There he received more lessons in English grammar and an introduction to Latin, Greek, and French. Although Thomas Jefferson later questioned the quality of instruction at Douglas's small school, there were many advantages to growing up in frontier Albemarle. His letter to John Adams in 1812 described another variety of education at Shadwell.

Monticello June 11. 1812.

Indians of North America by Samuel Drake, 1841

So much in answer to your enquiries concerning Indians, a people with whom, in the very early part of my life, I was very familiar, and acquired impressions of attachment and commiseration for them which have never been obliterated. Before the revolution they were in the habit of coming often, and in great numbers to the seat of our government, where I was very much with them. I knew much the great Outassete [Outacity], the warrior and orator of the Cherokees. He was always the guest of my father, on his journies to and from Williamsburg. I was in his camp when he made his great farewell oration to his people, the evening before his departure for England. The moon was in full splendor, and to her he seemed to address himself in his prayers for his own safety on the voyage, and that of his people during his absence. His sounding voice, distinct articulation, animated action, and the solemn silence of his people at their several fires, filled me with awe and veneration, altho' I did not understand a word he uttered.

Outacity, chief of the Cherokee

At the age of fourteen, Jefferson abruptly assumed heavy responsibilities that ended his boyish excitement over events like the Cherokees' visits. In August, 1757, Peter Jefferson died, leaving Thomas the oldest child in a family consisting of his mother, six sisters, and an infant brother. At twenty-one Thomas would inherit the lands at Shadwell, his father's estate at Snowden going to his younger brother. Even more important were the instructions Peter Jefferson had left that his son was to receive a thorough classical education. Thomas Jefferson recalled this legacy with gratitude. "I have often heard him say," his grandson later declared, "that if he had to decide between pleasure derived from the classical education which his father had given him, and the estate left him, he would decide in favor of the former."

After three years as a student of the Reverend James Maury, "a correct classical scholar," Jefferson carefully considered the next step in his education. A few months before his seventeenth birthday, he wrote to one of his guardians, John Harvie, carefully marshaling his arguments for attending William and Mary College. The letter reveals Jefferson's growing impatience with life at Shadwell and his eagerness to find intellectual stimulation.

Shadwell, Jan. 14, 1760

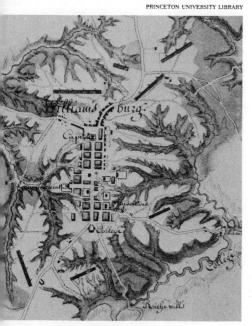

PRINCETON UNIVERSITY LIBRARY

Map of Williamsburg and surrounding country during Jefferson's time

Sir

I was at Colo. Peter Randolph's about a Fortnight ago, and my Schooling falling into Discourse, he said he thought it would be to my Advantage to go to the College, and was desirous I should go, as indeed I am myself for several Reasons. In the first place as long as I stay at the Mountain the Loss of one fourth of my Time is inevitable, by Company's coming here and detaining me from School. And likewise my Absence will in a great Measure put a Stop to so much Company, and by that Means lessen the Expences of the Estate in House-Keeping. And on the other Hand by going to the College I shall get a more universal Acquaintance, which may hereafter be serviceable to me; and I suppose I can pursue my Studies in the Greek and Latin as well there as here, and likewise learn something of the Mathematics. I shall be glad of your opinion, and remain Sir Yr most humble Servant,

THOMAS JEFFERSON, JR.

Harvie evidently agreed, and not long after writing this letter Jefferson left Shadwell for Williamsburg, the provincial capital. The 120-mile journey brought him not to a bustling, commercial city but to a quiet town with a population of about one thousand whites and blacks. Despite its small size, Williamsburg was Virginia's social and cultural center as well as the seat of government. William and Mary College, at the head of the Duke of Gloucester Street, had been founded in 1693 and was the second oldest college in the Colonies. At seventeen, Jefferson must certainly have been impressed by the town, but some twenty years later, in his famous volume *Notes on Virginia*, he revealed a cool sophistication in describing two Williamsburg landmarks.

Notes on Virginia, 1782

The only public buildings worthy mention are the Capitol, the Palace, the College, and the Hospital for Lunatics, all of them in Williamsburg, heretofore the seat of our government. The Capitol is a light and airy structure, with a portico in front of two orders, the lower of which, being Doric, is tolerably just in its proportions and ornaments, save only that the intercolonnations are too large. The upper is Ionic, much too small for that on which it is mounted, its ornaments not proper to the order, nor proportioned within themselves. It is crowned with a pediment, which is too high for its span. Yet on the whole, it is the most pleasing piece of architecture we have. The Palace is not handsome without: but it is spacious and commodious within, is prettily situated, and, with the grounds annexed to it, is capable of being made an elegant seat. The College and Hospital are rude, mis-shapen piles, which, but that they have roofs, would be taken for brick-kilns....

[In retrospect, Jefferson was no kinder to the education he received at William and Mary than he was to the architecture of the college town.]

The admission of the learners of Latin and Greek filled the college with children. This rendering it disagreeable and degrading to young gentlemen already prepared for entering on the sciences, they were discouraged from resorting to it, and thus the schools for Mathematics and Moral philosophy, which might have been of some service became of very little. The revenues too were exhausted in accomodating those who came only to acquire the rudiments of science.

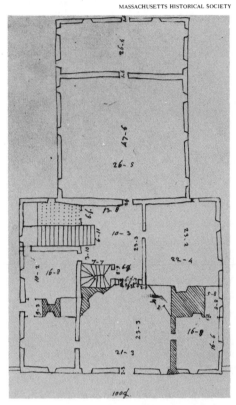

Jefferson's plan, with measurements, of the Governor's Palace, c. 1779

Fortunately Williamsburg had more to offer Jefferson than the courses at William and Mary. Soon after being admitted to the college in March, 1760, he came under the influence of two remarkable men, William Small and George Wythe. The first to befriend Jefferson was Small, a professor of natural philosophy who encouraged his budding interest in mathematics and science. Jefferson never hesitated to acknowledge his debt to the Scot scholar, who was the only faculty member at William and Mary not a member of the clergy. He easily recognized Thomas's gifts and potential for learning.

Autobiography, 1821
It was my great good fortune, and what probably fixed the destinies of my life that Dr. Wm. Small of Scotland was then professor of Mathematics, a man profound in most of the useful branches of science, with a happy

19

talent of communication correct and gentlemanly manners, & an enlarged & liberal mind. He, most happily for me, became soon attached to me & made me his daily companion when not engaged in the school; and from his conversation I got my first views of the expansion of science & of the system of things in which we are placed. Fortunately the Philosophical chair became vacant soon after my arrival at College, and he was appointed to fill it per interim: and he was the first who ever gave in that college regular lectures in Ethics, Rhetoric & Belles lettres.

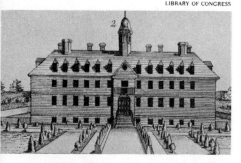

Page from bursar's book at College of William and Mary listing fees for Jefferson's room and board

Small not only shared his liberal mind with Jefferson in the classroom; he also shared his influential and stimulating friends in the town. Among these was George Wythe, a thirty-three-year-old member of the House of Burgesses who became a prominent jurist in Virginia. Responding to a request from a biographer many years later, Jefferson described this learned gentleman who, he said, "continued until death my most affectionate Friend."

Monticello Aug. 31. [18]20.

No man ever left behind him a character more venerated than G[eorge] Wythe. His virtue was of the purest tint; his integrity flexible, and his justice exact; of warm patriotism, and, devoted as he was to liberty, and the natural and equal rights of man, he might truly be called the Cato of his country, without the avarice of the Roman; for a more disinterested person never lived. Temperance and regularity in all his habits gave him general good health, and his unaffected modesty and suavity of manners endeared him to every one.

He was of easy elocution, his language chaste, methodical in the arrangement of his matter, learned and logical in the use of it, and of great urbanity in debate. Not quick of apprehension, but with a little time profound in penetration, and sound in conclusion. In his philosophy he was firm, and neither troubling, nor perhaps trusting, any one with his religious creed, he left to the world the conclusion that that religion must be good which could produce a life of such exemplary virtue.

His stature was of the middle size, well formed and proportioned and the features of his face manly, comely and engaging. Such was George Wythe, the honor of his own, and the model of future times.

Mid-eighteenth century engraving of the College of William and Mary

Jefferson recognized his good fortune in having found advisers like Small and Wythe who encouraged the very traits Peter Jefferson might have nurtured in his son, questioning habits of mind and self-discipline. Much later, Thomas described to his grandson how he avoided an easy, aimless life in Williamsburg.

Washington Nov. 24. [18]08.
When I recollect that at 14. years of age, the whole care & direction of myself was thrown on myself entirely without a relation or friend qualified to advise or guide me, and recollect the various sorts of bad company with which I associated from time to time, I am astonished I did not turn off with some of them, & become as worthless to society as they were. I had the good fortune to become acquainted very early with some characters of very high standing, and to feel the incessant wish that I could ever become what they were. Under temptations & difficulties, I would ask myself what would Dr. Small, Mr. Wythe, Peyton Randolph [his mother's cousin] do in this situation? What course in it will insure me their approbation? I am certain that this mode of deciding on my conduct, tended more to its correctness than any reasoning powers I possessed. Knowing the even & dignified line they pursued, I could never doubt for a moment which of two courses would be in character for them. Whereas seeking the same object through a process of moral reasoning, & with the jaundiced eye of youth, I should often have erred. From the circumstances of my position I was often thrown into the society of horseracers, cardplayers, foxhunters, scientific & professional men, and of dignified men; and many a time have I asked myself, in the enthusiastic moment of the death of a fox, the victory of a favorite horse, the issue of a question eloquently argued at the bar or in the great council of the nation, well, which of these kinds of reputation should I prefer? That of a horse jockey? a foxhunter? an Orator? or the honest advocate of my country's rights? Be assured my dear Jefferson, that these little returns into ourselves, this self-catechising habit, is not trifling, nor useless, but leads to the prudent selection & steady pursuit of what is right.

George Wythe as an older man

The self-catechizing habit instilled early in Jefferson by his mentors in Williamsburg can be seen in his later intellectual development. Neither Small nor Wythe was bound by religious orthodoxy, but they were both profoundly moral men in a sense the Enlightenment would soon make popular. Jefferson absorbed their lessons well. In a letter to his nephew Peter Carr in 1787, Jefferson outlined his own very pragmatic philosophy of social morality and justice, a philosophy obviously influenced by his father, early teachers, and the circle at Williamsburg.

Paris Aug. 10. 1787.
Man was destined for society. His morality therefore was to be formed to this object. He was endowed with a sense of right and wrong merely relative to this. This sense is as much a part of his nature as the sense of hearing, seeing, feeling; it is the true foundation of morality, and not the...truth, &c., as fanciful writers have imagined. The moral sense, or conscience, is as much a part of man as his leg or arm. It is given to all human beings in a stronger or weaker degree, as force of members is given them in a greater or less degree. It may be strengthened by exercise, as may any particular limb of the body. This sense is submitted indeed in some degree to the guidance of reason; but it is a small stock which is required for this: even a less one than what we call Common sense. State a moral case to a ploughman and a professor. The former will decide it as well, and often better than the latter, because he has not been led astray by artificial rules.

Governor Francis Fauquier

Wythe and Small did not confine their tutelage of Jefferson to moral values; they broadened his social experience as well by introducing him to Francis Fauquier, Virginia's able and popular governor. When Fauquier learned of Jefferson's abilities as a violinist he invited him to join himself and several other amateurs in weekly concerts at the Governor's Palace. The tall, rather shy boy from Albemarle was soon part of Williamsburg society, which he later described as "the finest school of manners and morals that ever existed in America." At Fauquier's dinner table, Jefferson said, "I have heard more good sense, more rational and philosophical conversations, than in all my life besides. They were truly Attic societies."

Jefferson's education outside the college soon outstripped the instruction he gained in its classrooms, and it is not surprising that he left William and Mary at the age of nineteen. In an autobiographical memorandum written about 1821, he noted tersely after the year 1762: "Quitted College and began study of Law." His legal studies allowed him to remain in the same congenial circles in Williamsburg, however, for he entered the law office of George Wythe. For the next five years, Jefferson pored over Wythe's books, not limiting himself to law but embarking on a vigorous program of self-education and laying the groundwork of his own schooling in statecraft.

Jefferson was better equipped than most for this task; his self-discipline was the envy of his friends. John Page recalled that his own studies had suffered "for I was too sociable, and fond of the conversation of my friends, to study as Mr. Jefferson did, who could tear himself away from his dearest friends, to fly to his studies." According to family tradition, Jefferson devoted no less than fifteen hours a day to academic work at college. A letter he wrote in his old age to Dr. Vine Utley gives a notion of the strength and physical stamina that allowed him to maintain a similar schedule throughout his life.

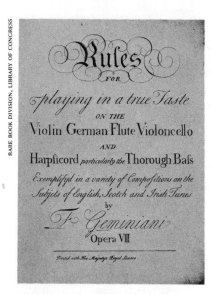

Title page of a rule book, from Jefferson's library, for playing the violin and other instruments

Monticello Mar. 21. [18]19.

Your letter of Feb. 18. came to hand on the 1st. instant; and the request of the history of my physical habits would have puzzled me not a little, had it not been for the model with which you accompanied it, of Doctor [Benjamin] Rush's answer to a similar enquiry. I live so much like other people, that I might refer to ordinary life as the history of my own. Like my friend the Doctor, I have lived temperately, eating little animal food, and that, not as an aliment so much as a condiment for the vegetables, which constitute my principal diet. I double, however, the Doctor's glass and a half of wine, and even treble it with a friend; but halve its effects by drinking the weak wines only. The ardent wines I cannot drink, nor do I use ardent spirits in any form. Malt liquors and cyder are my table drinks, and my breakfast, like that also of my friend, is of tea and coffee. I have been blest with organs of digestion which accept and concoct, without ever murmuring whatever the palate chuses to consign to them, and I have not yet lost a tooth by age. I was a hard student until I entered on the business of life, the duties of which leave no idle time to those disposed to fulfill them; and now, retired, and at the age of 76. I am again a hard student. Indeed my fondness for reading and study revolts me from the drudgery of letter writing. And a stiff wrist, the consequence of an early dislocation, makes writing both slow and painful. I am not so regular in my sleep as the Doctor says he was, devoting to it from 5. to 8. hours, according as my company or the book I am reading interests me; and I never go to bed without an hour, or half hour's previous reading of something moral, whereon to ruminate in the intervals

A "recipe," consisting of six grains of calomel, which Jefferson used to treat his "periodical headache"

of sleep. But whether I retire to bed early or late, I rise with the sun. I use spectacles at night, but not necessarily in the day, unless in reading small print. My hearing is distinct in particular conversation, but confused when several voices cross each other, which unfits me for the society of the table. I have been more fortunate than my friend in the article of health. So free from catarrhs that I have not had one, (in the breast, I mean) on an average of 8. or 10. years through life. I ascribe this exemption partly to the habit of bathing my feet in cold water every morning for 60. years past. A fever of more than 24. hours I have not had above 2. or 3. times in my life. A periodical headache has afflicted me occasionally, once perhaps in 6. or 8. years, for 2. or 3. weeks at a time, which seems now to have left me; and, except on a late occasion of indisposition, I enjoy good health. . . .

But in 1762, Jefferson had not quite perfected the regimen he followed in later years. His letters to John Page reveal a restless young man who rebelled at the drudgery of a law clerk's life and weighed a dozen alternative plans for his future. His life became even more unbearable when he fell in love with the pious and wealthy Rebecca Burwell. On Christmas Day he wrote Page of his disaster-filled holiday at Fairfield, not far from Shadwell, where a rainstorm had ruined a treasured silhouette of his beloved "Belinda."

Fairfeilds Dec: 25. 1762.

Dear Page

This very day, to others the day of greatest mirth and jollity, sees me overwhelmed with more and greater misfortunes than have befallen a descendant of Adam for these thousand years past I am sure; and perhaps, after excepting Job, since the creation of the world. I think his misfortunes were somewhat greater than mine: for although we may be pretty nearly on a level in other respects, yet I thank my God I have the advantage of brother Job in this, that Satan has not as yet put forth his hand to load me with bodily afflictions. You must know, dear Page, that I am now in a house surrounded with enemies, who take counsel together against my soul and when I lay me down to rest they say among themselves Come let us destroy him. I am sure if there is such a thing as a devil in this world, he must have been here last night and have had some hand in contriving what happened to me. Do you think the cursed rats (at his instigation I suppose) did not eat up my pocket-book which was in my pocket within a foot of my head? And not contented with plenty for the present they carried away my Jemmy worked silk garters and half a dozen new minuets I had just got, to serve I suppose as provision for the winter. But of this I should not have accused the devil (because you know rats will be rats, and hunger without the addition of his instigations might have urged them to do this) if something worse and from a different quarter had not happened. You know it rained last night, or if you do not know it I am sure I do. When I went to bed I laid my watch in the usual place, and going to take her up after I arose this morning I found her, in the same place it's true but! Quantum mutatus ab illo [how changed from what it was]! all afloat in water let in at a leak in the roof of the house, and as silent and still as the rats that had eat my pocket-book. Now you know if Chance had had any thing to do in this matter, there were a thousand other spots where it might have chanced to leak as well as at this one which was perpendicularly over my watch. But I'll tell you: It's my opinion that the Devil came and bored the hole over it on purpose. Well as I was saying, my poor watch had lost her speech: I should not have cared much for this, but something worse attended it: the subtle particles of the water with which the case was filled had by their penetration so overcome the cohesion of the particles of the paper of which my dear picture and watch paper were composed that in attempting to take them out to dry them Good God! mens horret referre [the mind shudders to recall it]! my cursed fingers gave them such a rent as I fear I never shall get over. This, cried I, was the last stroke Satan had in reserve for me: he knew I cared not for any thing else he could do to me, and was determined to try this last most fatal expedient....I would have cryed bitterly, but I thought it beneath the dignity of a man....However whatever misfortunes may attend the picture or lover, my hearty prayers shall be that all the health and happiness which heaven can send may be the portion of the original, and that so much goodness may ever meet with what may be most agreeable in this world, as I am sure it must in the next. And now although the picture be defaced there is so lively an image of her imprinted in

Portrait by John Wollaston of John Page, Jefferson's lifelong friend

my mind that I shall think of her too often I fear for my peace of mind, and too often I am sure to get through Old Cooke [Coke] this winter: for God knows I have not seen him since I packed him up in my trunk in Williamsburgh.

Well, Page, I do wish the Devil had old Cooke, for I am sure I never was so tired of an old dull scoundrel in my life. What! are there so few inquietudes tacked to this momentary life of ours that we must need be loading ourselves with a thousand more? Or as brother Job sais (who by the bye I think began to whine a little under his afflictions) 'Are not my days few? Cease then that I may take comfort a little before I go whence I shall not return, even to the land of darkness and the shadow of death.' But the old-fellows say we must read to gain knowledge; and gain knowledge to make us happy and be admired. Mere jargon! Is there any such thing as happiness in this world? No: And as for admiration I am sure the man who powders most, parfumes most, embroiders most, and talks most nonsense, is most admired. Though to be candid, there are some who have too much good sense to esteem such monkey-like animals as these ... and since these are the only persons whose esteem is worth a wish, I do not know but that upon the whole the advice of these old fellows may be worth following.

You cannot conceive the satisfaction it would give me to have a letter from you: Write me very circumstantially everything which happened at the wedding. Was SHE there? Because if she was I ought to have been at the devil for not being there too. If there is any news stirring in town or country, such as deaths, courtships and marriages in the circle of my acquaintance let me know it. Remember me affectionately to all the young ladies of my acquaintance, particularly the Miss Burwells and Miss Potters, and tell them that though that heavy earthly part of me, my body, be absent, the better half of me, my soul, is ever with them, and that my best wishes shall ever attend them. Tell Miss Alice Corbin that I verily believe the rats knew I was to win a pair of garters from her, or they never would have been so cruel as to carry mine away.... I would fain ask the favor of Miss Becca Burwell to give me another watch paper, of her own cutting which I should esteem much more though it were a plain round one, than the nicest in the world cut by other hands: however I am afraid she would think this pre-

The Raleigh Tavern in Williamsburg

sumption after my suffering the other to get spoiled. If you think you can excuse me to her for this I should be glad if you would ask her....

... that I may not tire your patience by further additions I will make but this one more that I am sincerely and affectionately Dr Page your friend and servant,

T: JEFFERSON

For months Jefferson agonized over proposing to Rebecca. Page was subjected to letter after letter describing his friend's poignant indecision. Jefferson's visits to the Governor's Palace had apparently not given him the poise and assurance needed to express his feelings to the sixteen-year-old heiress. In October, 1763, he told Page of his latest embarrassment at the Apollo Room of the Raleigh Tavern.

Apollo Room of the Raleigh Tavern where Jefferson danced with Rebecca

Williamsburg, October 7, 1763.
In the most melancholy fit that ever any poor soul was, I sit down to write to you. Last night, as merry as agreeable company and dancing with Belinda in the Apollo could make me, I never could have thought the succeeding sun would have seen me so wretched as I now am! I was prepared to say a great deal: I had dressed up in my own mind, such thoughts as occurred to me, in as moving language as I knew how, and expected to have performed in a tolerably creditable manner. But, good God! When I had an opportunity of venting them, a few broken sentences, uttered in great disorder, and interrupted with pauses of uncommon length, were the too visible marks of my strange confusion! The whole confab I will tell you, word for word, if I can, when I see you, which God send may be soon.... The court is now at hand, which I must attend constantly, so that unless you come to town, there is little probability of my meeting with you any where else. For God's sake come.

This encounter was apparently one of the last between Jefferson and Miss Burwell; her engagement to another the following spring ended any hopes he had for his first love. Shortly after learning of his loss, Jefferson wrote his college friend William Fleming.

Wmsburgh. March 20. 1764.
11. o'clock at night.
With regard to the scheme which I proposed to you some time since, I am sorry to tell you it is totally frustrated

*Jefferson's friend William Fleming
in a portrait of a later date*

by Miss R. B's marriage with Jacquelin Ambler which the people here tell me they daily expect: I say, the people here tell me so, for (can you beleive it?) I have been so abominably indolent as not to have seen her since last October, wherefore I cannot affirm that I know it from herself, though am as well satisfied that it is true as if she had told me.... You say you are determined to be married as soon as possible: and advise me to do the same. No, thank ye; I will consider of it first. Many and great are the comforts of a single state, and neither of the reasons you urge can have any influence with an inhabitant and a young inhabitant too of Wmsburgh.

Jefferson used his single state to good advantage and returned to his studies with his usual determination. Like many students of the time, he compiled several commonplace books in which he made notes of his readings and comments on his studies in law, equity, history and government, and parliamentary history and procedure. Throughout his life, Jefferson gave advice on the study of law. A letter responding to a young student in 1772 was revised in later years to answer similar requests, with the addition of new texts as they were published. From the beginning, Jefferson emphasized that the intellectual foundations must be broad, and his outline of study probably mirrors the very one he had painstakingly worked out for himself in Williamsburg.

[c. 1772]

Before you enter on the study of the law a sufficient ground-work must be laid. For this purpose an acquaintance with the Latin and French languages is absolutely necessary. The former you have; the latter must now be acquired. Mathematics and Natural philosophy are so useful in the most familiar occurrences of life, and are so peculiarly engaging & delightful as would induce every person to wish an acquaintance with them. Besides this, the faculties of the mind, like the members of the body, are strengthened & improved by exercise. Mathematical reasonings & deductions are therefore a fine preparation for investigating the abstruse speculations of the law....

This foundation being laid, you may enter regularly on the study of the Law, taking with it such of it's kindred sciences as will contribute to eminence in it's attainment. The principal of these are Physics, Ethics, Religion, Natural law, Belles lettres, Criticism, Rhetoric and Oratory. The carrying on several studies at a time is attended with advantage. Variety relieves the mind, as well as the eye, palled with too long attention to a single object. But with both, transitions from one object to another may be so frequent and transitory as to leave no impression. The mean is therefore to be steered and a competent space of time allotted to each branch of study. Again, a great inequality is observable in the vigor of the mind at different periods of the day. It's powers at these periods should therefore be attended to in marshalling the business of the day. For these reasons I should recommend the following distribution of your time.

Till VIII o'clock in the morning employ yourself in Physical studies, Ethics, Religion, natural and sectarian, and Natural law....

From VIII. to XII. read law. The general course of this reading may be formed on the following grounds. Ld. Coke has given us the first view of the whole body of law worthy now of being studied.... Coke's Institutes are a perfect Digest of the law as it stood in his day. After this, new laws were added by the legislature, and new developments of the old laws by the Judges, until they had become so voluminous as to require a new Digest. This was ably executed by Matthew Bacon, altho' unfortunately under an Alphabetical instead of Analytical arrangement of matter. The same process of new laws & new decisions on the old laws going on, called at length for the same operation again, and produced the inimitable Commentaries of Blackstone....

In reading the Reporters [reports of contemporary cases], enter in a Common-place book every case of value, condensed into the narrowest compass possible which will admit of presenting distinctly the principles of the case. This operation is doubly useful, inasmuch as it obliges the student to seek out the pith of the case, and habituates him to a condensation of thought, and to an acquisition of the most valuable of all talents, that of never using two words where one will do. It fixes the case too more indelibly in the mind.

From XII to I. read Politics... Locke on Government, Sidney on Government, Priestley's First Principles of Government, Review of Montesquieu's Spirit of Laws.... The Federalist [inserted in 1814]....

In the Afternoon read History....

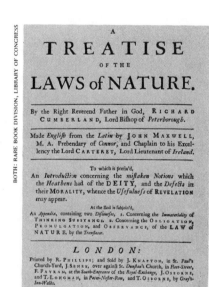

A

TREATISE

OF THE

LAWS of NATURE.

By the Right Reverend Father in God, RICHARD CUMBERLAND, Lord Bishop of *Peterborough*.

Made *English* from the *Latin* by JOHN MAXWELL, M. A. Prebendary of *Connor*, and Chaplain to his Excellency the Lord CARTERET, Lord Lieutenant of *Ireland*.

To which is prefix'd,
An *Introduction* concerning the *mistaken Notions* which the *Heathens* had of the DEITY, and the *Defects* in their MORALITY, whence the *Usefulness* of REVELATION may appear.

At the End is subjoin'd,
An *Appendix*, containing two *Discourses*, 1. Concerning the *Immateriality* of THINKING SUBSTANCE. 2. Concerning the OBLIGATION, PROMULGATION, and OBSERVANCE, of the LAW of NATURE, by the *Translator*.

LONDON:

Printed by R. PHILLIPS; and Sold by J. KNAPTON, in St. *Paul's* Church-Yard, J. SENEX, over against St. *Dunstan's* Church, in *Fleet-Street*, F. FAYRAM, at the *South-Entrance* of the *Royal-Exchange*, J. OSBORNE, and T. LONGMAN, in *Pater-Noster-Row*, and T. OSBORNE, by *Gray's-Inn-Walks*.

Jefferson's own reading was various; his library included A Treatise of the Laws of Nature *(above) and a book on* Elements of Conchology *from which the plate below is taken.*

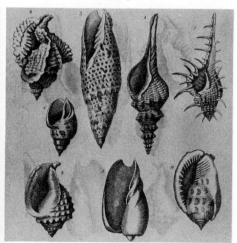

From Dark to Bedtime—Belles Lettres; Criticism;
Rhetoric; Oratory....
NOTE.   Under each of the preceding heads, the books
are to be read in the order in which they are named.
These by no means constitute the whole of what might
be usefully read in each of these branches of science.
The mass of excellent works going more into detail is
great indeed. But those here noted will enable the student to select for himself such others of detail as may
suit his particular views and dispositions. They will give
him a respectable, an useful, & satisfactory degree of
knolege in these branches, and will themselves form a
valuable and sufficient library for a lawyer, who is at
the same time a lover of science.

Jefferson's self-discipline was tested repeatedly, for his
years in Wythe's law office coincided with the opening of the revolutionary
movement in the Colonies, and Virginia's burgesses were leaders in this
battle. In the spring of 1765, Jefferson stood at the door of the House of
Burgesses' chamber where he heard the "splendid display of Mr. [Patrick]
Henry's talents as a popular orator. They were great indeed," Jefferson
recalled, "such as I have never heard from any other Man. He appeared to
me to speak as Homer wrote." Jefferson never aspired to Henry's dazzling
oratorical eloquence, but he genuinely admired the other's talents. Many
years later he wrote this biographical sketch of Henry for William Wirt.

[Monticello, c. 1810–11]
My acqce with Mr. Henry commenced in the winter of
1759–60. On my way to college I passed the Xmas holi-
days at Colo. [Nathaniel West] Dandridge's in Hanover,
to whom Mr. Henry was a near neighbor. During the
festivity of the season I met him in society every day, &
we became well acquainted, altho' I was much his junior,
being then in my 17th. year, & he a married man. The
spring following he came to Wmsbg to obtain a license as
a lawyer, & he called on me at College. He told me he
had been reading law only 6. weeks....
   The next great occasion on which he signalised himself was that which may be considered as the dawn of
the revoln in March 1774 [1764]. The British parliament
had passed resolns. preparatory to the levying a revenue
on the Colonies by a Stamp tax. The Virginia assembly,
at their next session, prepared & sent to England very
elaborate representns addressed in separate forms to

A primitive painting shows Henry arguing one of his most famous cases, the Parson's Cause, in 1763.

the King, Lords, and Commons, against the right to impose such taxes. The famous Stamp act was however passed in Jan. 1765. and in the session of the Virgi assembly of May following, Mr. Henry introduced the celebrated resolns of that date. These were drawn by George Johnston, a lawyer of the Northern neck, a very able, logical and correct Speaker. Mr. Henry moved, and Johnston seconded these resolns successively. They were opposed by Randolph, Bland, Pendleton, Nicholas, Wythe & all the old members whose influence in the house had, till then, been unbroken. They did it, not from any question of our rights, but on the ground that the same sentiments had been, at their preceeding session, expressed in a more conciliatory form, to which the answers were not yet received. But torrents of sublime eloquence from Mr. Henry, backed up by the solid reasoning of Johnston, prevailed. The last however, & strongest resoln was carried but by a single vote. The debate on it was most bloody. I was then but a student, and was listening at the door of the lobby (for as yet there was no gallery) when Peyton Randolph, after the vote, came out of the house and said, as he entered the lobby 'By god, I would have given 500. guineas for a single vote.' For as this would have divided the house, the vote of Robinson, the Speaker, would have rejected the resolution....

I found Mr. Henry to be a silent & almost unmeddling member in Congress. On the original opening of that body, while general grievances were the topics, he was in his element & captivated all with his bold & splendid eloquence. But as soon as they came to specific matters, to sober reasoning and solid argumentation, he had the good sense to perceive that his declamation, however excellent in it's proper place, had no weight at all in such an assembly as that, of cool-headed, reflecting, judicious men. He ceased therefore in a great measure to take any part in the business....

A year later, the twenty-three-year-old Jefferson made his first trip outside the borders of his native province. In a three-month-long journey, undertaken for inoculation against smallpox by a Philadelphia physician, Jefferson first viewed his fellow Americans in the Middle Colonies. His journey had an unpleasant beginning, as he reported from Maryland to John Page.

Annapolis May. 25. 1766.

Surely never did small hero experience greater misadventures than I did on the first two or three days of my travelling. Twice did my horse run away with me and greatly endanger the breaking my neck on the first day. On the second I drove two hours through as copious a rain as ever I have seen, without meeting with a single house to which I could repair for shelter. On the third in going through Pamunkey, being unacquainted with the ford, I passed through water so deep as to run over the cushion as I sat on it, and to add to the danger, at that instant one wheel mounted a rock which I am confident was as high as the axle, and rendered it necessary for me to exercise all my skill in the doctrine of gravity, in order to prevent the center of gravity from being left unsupported....I confess that on this occasion I was seised with a violent hydrophobia....

[Well versed in parliamentary proceedings and the knowledge of how a deliberative body ought to proceed, Jefferson was appalled at the way the Maryland General Assembly conducted business.]

But I will now give you some account of what I have seen in this Metropolis. The assembly happens to be sitting at this time. Their upper and lower house, as they call them, sit in different houses. I went into the lower, sitting in an old courthouse, which, judging from it's form and appearance, was built in the year one. I was surprised on approaching it to hear as great a noise and hubbub as you will usually observe at a publick meeting of the planters in Virginia. The first object which struck me after my entrance was the figure of a little old man dressed but indifferently, with a yellow queüe wig on, and mounted in the judge's chair. This the gentleman who walked with me informed me was the speaker, a man of a very fair character, but who by the bye has very little the air of a speaker. At one end of the justices' bench stood a man whom in another place I should from his dress and phis [physiognomy] have taken for Goodall the lawyer in Williamsburgh, reading a bill then before the house with a schoolboy tone and an abrupt pause at every half dozen words. This I found to be the clerk of the assembly. The mob (for such was their appearance) sat covered on the justices' and lawyers' benches, and were divided into little clubs amusing themselves in the common chit chat way. I was surprised to see them address the speaker without rising from their seats, and three, four, and five at a time without being checked. When [a motion was] made, the speaker instead of putting the question in the usual form only asked the gentlemen whether they chose that such or such a thing should be done, and was answered by a yes sir, or no sir: and tho' the voices appeared frequently to be divided, they never would go to the trouble of dividing the house, but the clerk entered the resolutions, I supposed, as he thought proper. In short every thing seems to be carried without the house in general's knowing what was proposed. The situation of this place is extremely beautiful, and very commodious for trade having a most secure port capable of receiving the largest vessels, those of 400 hh'ds [hogsheads] being able to brush against the sides of the dock. The houses are in general better than those in Williamsburgh, but the gardens more indifferent. The two towns seem much of a size. They have no publick buildings worth mentioning except a governor's house, the hull of which after being nearly finished, they have suffered to go to ruin. I would give you an account of the rejoicings here on the repeal of the stamp act but this you will probably see in print before my letter can reach you. I shall proceed tomorrow to Philadelphia where I shall make the stay necessary for inoculation, thence going on to New York. I shall return by water to Williamsburgh, about the middle of July....

Town of Annapolis, which Jefferson thought was beautifully situated

There are no records of Jefferson's impressions of Philadelphia and New York. He returned home in the summer to complete his legal apprenticeship and early the next year was admitted to the bar. His career as a lawyer continued, in his own words, "until the revolution shut up the courts of justice." By the time that Revolution came Jefferson had become a candidate for leadership of the rebels in his own province and in what was to become his own nation.

Chapter 2

Eloquent Revolutionary

Thomas Jefferson used the years before the Revolution to broaden his intellectual and cultural interests as well as to establish a successful legal practice. The man who left Virginia to join other patriots in Philadelphia at the Continental Congress in 1775 was a far more sophisticated and cultured traveler than the twenty-three-year-old visitor of 1766. The self-discipline that served him so well in George Wythe's office never disappeared, and Jefferson applied it to educating himself in such fields as literature, music, architecture, and botany.

A young attorney in provincial Virginia needed such diversions, for there was little excitement and much drudgery in the practice of law. Indeed, even after six years in the profession, Jefferson was forced to resort to such unpleasant strategies as the notice he and five fellow attorneys placed in the *Virginia Gazette* in hopes of forcing clients to pay their fees.

Virginia Gazette, May 20, 1773

On serious Consideration of the present State of our Practice in the General Court, we find it can no longer be continued on the same Terms. The Fees allowed by Law, if regularly paid, would barely compensate our incessant Labours, reimburse our Expenses, and the Losses incurred by Neglect of our private Affairs; yet even these Rewards, confessedly moderate, are withheld from us, in a great Proportion, by the unworthy Part of our Clients. Some Regulation, therefore, is become absolutely requisite to establish Terms more equal between the Client and his Counsel. To effect this, we have come to the following Resolution, for the invariable Observance of which we mutually plight our Honour to each other: "That after the 10th Day of *October* next we will not give an Opinion on any Case stated to us but on Payment of the whole Fee, nor prosecute or defend any Suit or Motion unless the Tax, and one Half the Fee, be previously advanced, excepting those Cases only where we choose to act *gratis:*" and we hope no Person whatever will think of applying to us in any other Way.

Jefferson seemed to realize that the law could not satisfy his needs for personal fulfillment and often seemed to belittle his own profession. "I was bred to the law," he once remarked, "and that gave me a view of the dark side of humanity. Then I read poetry to qualify it with a gaze upon its bright side." When he sent his friend Joseph Cabell the draft of a bill for establishing elementary schools in 1817, Jefferson commented on the literary standards of his chosen profession.

Poplar Forest. Sep. 9. [18]17.
I should apologize perhaps for the style of this bill. I dislike the verbose and intricate style of the English statutes....You however can easily correct this bill to the taste of my brother lawyers, by making every other word a 'said' or 'aforesaid,' and saying every thing over 2. or 3. times, so as that nobody but we of the craft can untwist the diction, and find out what it means; and that too not so plainly but that we may conscientiously divide, one half on each side.

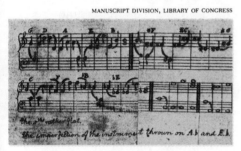

A musical pattern used by Jefferson to tune a harpsichord

Jefferson's new appreciation of poetry did not prevent him from pursuing his old interest in music. In 1768 he purchased a violin for five pounds and played it most of his life. Even in his hobbies he was an eminently frugal and practical man. During the Revolution he wrote to his friend Giovanni Fabbroni, an Italian musician, to complain of the "barbarism" that prevented him from enjoying music as fully as he wished and to propose an ingenious solution to his problem.

Williamsburgh in Virginia June. 8. 1778
If there is a gratification which I envy any people in this world, it is to your country it's music. This is the favorite passion of my soul, and fortune has cast my lot in a country where it is in a state of deplorable barbarism....The bounds of an American fortune will not admit the indulgence of a domestic band of musicians. Yet I have thought that a passion for music might be reconciled with that œconomy which we are obliged to observe. I retain for instance among my domestic servants a gardener (Ortolano) a weaver (Tessitore di lino e lana) a cabinet maker

35

THE FOUNDING FATHERS

AMERICAN ANTIQUARIAN SOCIETY

Engraving by twelve-year-old Horace Doolittle illustrates Jefferson's advice to nephew on carrying a gun.

(Stipettaio) and a stonecutter (scalpellino lavorante in piano) to which I would add a Vigneron. In a country where, like yours, music is cultivated and practised by every class of men, I suppose there might be found persons of those trades who could perform on the French horn, clarinets and hautboys, and a bassoon. So that one might have a band of two French horns, two clarinets or hautboys, and a bassoon, without enlarging their domestic expences. A certainty of employment for a half dozen years, and at the end of that time to find them a conveyance to their own country if they chose to return might induce them to come here on reasonable wages. Without meaning to give you trouble, perhaps it might be practicable for you in your ordinary intercourse with your people to find out such men, disposed to come to America. Sobriety and good nature would be desireable parts of their characters.

Balancing his interest in the arts, Jefferson developed a simultaneous passion for agriculture. Returning to Shadwell after his years in Williamsburg, he began to keep a garden book whose first entry on March 30, 1766, was merely that the "purple hyacinth begins to bloom." His concern for agriculture and botany grew naturally from his love for the outdoors—a love reinforced by his conviction that only a carefully planned program of exercise would sustain his physical strength and mental alertness. In 1785 he described this regimen to his nephew.

MANUSCRIPTS DEPARTMENT, ALDERMAN LIBRARY, UNIVERSITY OF VIRGINIA

Jefferson's specifications for and drawing of a partridge snare

Paris Aug. 19. 1785.

A strong body makes the mind strong. As to the species of exercise, I advise the gun. While this gives a moderate exercise to the body, it gives boldness, enterprize, and independance to the mind. Games played with the ball and others of that nature, are too violent for the body and stamp no character on the mind. Let your gun therefore be the constant companion of your walks. Never think of taking a book with you. The object of walking is to relax the mind. You should therefore not permit yourself even to think while you walk. But divert your attention by the objects surrounding you. Walking is the best possible exercise. Habituate yourself to walk very far. The Europeans value themselves on having subdued the horse to the uses of man. But I doubt whether we have not lost more than we have gained by the use of this animal. No one has occasioned so much the degener-

36

acy of the human body. An Indian goes on foot nearly as far in a day, for a long journey, as an enfeebled white does on his horse, and he will tire the best horses. There is no habit you will value so much as that of walking far without fatigue. I would advise you to take your exercise in the afternoon. Not because it is the best time for exercise for certainly it is not: but because it is the best time to spare from your studies; and habit will soon reconcile it to health, and render it nearly as useful as if you gave to that the more precious hours of the day. A little walk of half an hour in the morning when you first rise is adviseable also. It shakes off sleep, and produces other good effects in the animal œconomy. Rise at a fixed and an early hour, and go to bed at a fixed and early hour also. Sitting up late at night is injurious to the health, and not useful to the mind.

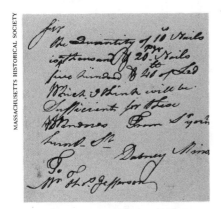

An estimate from Dabney Minor, a lowlands builder, of the nails and lead required for Monticello

Pleasant as life at Shadwell was, with the work of a lawyer and a planter to occupy his days and music, poetry, and good company to fill the evenings, Jefferson became enmeshed in another all-consuming project—one that would eventually encompass all the others. About a year after he had been admitted to the bar, he began to clear the summit of a hill across the river from his mother's home at Shadwell—a hill he had dubbed "Monticello," Italian for "little mountain." Here Jefferson, the self-educated architect, would build a mansion perfectly suited to Jefferson the agriculturist, the student of literature, and the musician. The beautiful Palladian structure would not be completed for more than twenty years, but by the fall of 1769 a single, one-room outbuilding had been erected. This proved a fortunate coincidence, for on February 1, 1770, Shadwell burned to the ground. Jefferson wrote to John Page of his most important personal loss—his books.

Charlottesville Feb. 21. 1770.
My late loss may perhaps have reac[hed y]ou by this time, I mean the loss of my mother's house by fire, and in it, of every pa[per I] had in the world, and almost every book. On a reasonable estimate I calculate th[e cost o]f t[he b]ooks burned to have been £200. sterling. Would to god it had been the money [; then] had it never cost me a sigh! To make the loss more sensible it fell principally on m[y books] of common law, of which I have but one left, at that time lent out. Of papers too of every kind I am utterly destitute. All of these, whether public or private, of business or of amusement have perished in

37

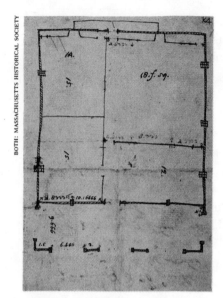

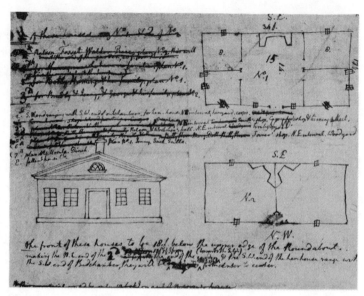

Jefferson's earliest plan for Monticello (above) was of a square wooden house divided into four rooms; above right, his sketches and notes for the slave quarters.

the flames. I had made some progress in preparing for the succeeding general court, and having, as was my custom, thrown my thoughts into the form of notes, I troubled my head no more with them. These are gone, and 'like the baseless fabric of a vision, Leave not a trace behind.' The records also and other papers, which furnished me with states of the several cases, having shared the same fate, I have no foundation whereon to set out anew.

In November, 1770, Jefferson moved to the lone building at Monticello, leaving his mother and her family at Shadwell where they made their quarters in structures that had survived the flames in the main house. After a few months in his new residence, Jefferson wrote cheerfully to James Ogilvie.

Virginia Gazette, FEBRUARY 22, 1770; RARE BOOK DIVISION, N.Y. PUBLIC LIBRARY

WILLIAMSBURG, Feb. 22.

WE hear from Albemarle that about a fortnight ago the house of Thomas Jefferson, Esq; in that county, was burnt to the ground, together with all his furniture, books, papers, &c. by which that Gentleman sustains a very great loss. He was from home when the accident happened.

The smallpox, we learn, has for some time past been very prevalent in Cumberland and Amelia, and that there is great reason to apprehend the contagion will spread to several of the adjoining counties; that many Gentlemen have had their families inoculated, and from the success which has attended that practice it is thought it will be generally adopted.

Notice in the Virginia Gazette *of the fire that destroyed Shadwell*

Monticello Feb. 20 1771

I have lately removed to the mountain from whence this is dated, and with which you are not unacquainted. I have here but one room, which, like the cobler's, serves me for parlour for kitchen and hall. I may add, for bed chamber and study too. My friends sometimes take a temperate dinner with me and then retire to look for beds elsewhere. I have hopes however of getting more elbow room this summer. But be this as may happen, whether my tenements be great or small homely or elegant they will always receive you with a hearty welcome.

A life of splendidly isolated bachelorhood at Monticello was not Jefferson's plan. Despite Rebecca Burwell's indifference, he had not turned his back on love. In the same letter in which he told John Page of Shadwell's destruction, Jefferson reminded his friend of his fondness for the company of women.

Charlottesville Feb. 21. 1770.

[I r]efl[ect of]ten with pleasure on the philosophical evenings I passed at Rosewell in my last [visit]s there. I was always fond of philosophy even in it's dryer forms, but from a ruby [lip] it comes with charms irresistible. Such a feast of sentiment must exhilarate and lengthen life at least as much as the feast of the sensualist shortens it. In a word I prize it so highly that if you will at any time collect the same Belle assemblèe on giving me three days previous notice, I shall certainly repair to my place as a member of it.

Later that year Jefferson began to visit The Forest, the estate of John Wayles near Williamsburg. Here he courted Wayles's attractive, widowed daughter, Martha Wayles Skelton. By June, 1771, he was sure enough of Martha's affection to order his London agent to purchase a pianoforte for her.

Monticello. June 1. 1771.

As it was somewhat doubtful when you left the country how far my little invoice delivered you might be complied with till we should know the fate of the association [the Virginia Nonimportation Association], I desired you to withhold purchasing the things till you should hear further from me. The day appointed for the meeting of the associates is not yet arrived, however from the universal sense of those who are likely to attend it seems reduced to a certainty that the restrictions will be taken off everything but the dutied articles. I will therefore venture to desire that branch of my invoice may be complied with in which were some shoes and other prohibited articles; since if contrary to our expectations the restrictions should be continued I can store, or otherwise dispose of them as our committees please. I must alter one article in the invoice. I wrote therein for a Clavichord. I have since seen a Forte-piano and am charmed with it. Send me this instrument then instead of the Clavichord. Let the case be of fine mahogany, solid, not vineered. The compass from Double G. to F. in alt. a plenty of spare

Frontispiece of The Compleat Tutor for the Harpsichord or Spinnet, *a book in Jefferson's library*

strings; and the workmanship of the whole very handsome, and worthy the acceptance of a lady for whom I intend it.

By August he had apparently made his intentions known to the Wayles family, for he concluded a letter to Martha's brother-in-law, Robert Skipwith, with this injunction.

Monticello. Aug. 3. 1771.

Offer prayers for me too at that shrine to which, tho' absent, I pay continual devotion. In every scheme of happiness she is placed in the fore-ground of the picture, as the principal figure. Take that away, and it is no picture for me.

On New Year's Day, 1772, Jefferson and Martha Skelton were married at The Forest. His *Autobiography* included those details Jefferson thought would be of public interest.

Autobiography, 1821

On the 1st. of January 1772. I was married to Martha Skelton widow of Bathurst Skelton, & daughter of John Wayles, then 23. years old. Mr. Wayles was a lawyer of much practice, to which he was introduced more by his great industry, punctuality & practical readiness, than to eminence in the science of his profession. He was a most agreeable companion, full of pleasantry & good humor, and welcomed in every society. He acquired a handsome fortune, died in May. 1773. leaving three daughters, and the portion which came on that event to Mrs. Jefferson, after the debts should be paid, which were very considerable, was about equal to my own patrimony, and consequently doubled the ease of our circumstances.

Virginia Gazette, JULY 15, 1773;
RARE BOOK DIVISION, N.Y. PUBLIC LIBRARY

TO BE SOLD,

TWO Thousand five Hundred and twenty Acres of LAND in Cumberland, commonly known by the Name of SAINT JAMES's; one Thousand four Hundred and twenty Acres in the Counties of Goochland and Cumberland, on both Sides of James River, opposite to Elk Island; and one Thousand four Hundred and eighty Acres on Herring Creek, in Charles City County. The above Tracts of Land were of the Estate of the late John Wayles, deceased, devised to the Subscribers, and are now offered for Sale. Persons disposed to purchase may be informed of the Terms, on Application to any one of the Subscribers; and the Times of Payment will be made easy, on giving Bond and Security to

(tf). 　　　　　THOMAS JEFFERSON.
　　　　　　　　FRANCIS EPPES.
　　　　　　　　HENRY SKIPWITH.

After the death of John Wayles, this advertisement for the sale of part of his estate appeared in the Gazette.

Marriage, the fascinating details of supervising the construction of Monticello, the less fascinating details of his legal practice— these occupied Jefferson's time for the first year after he brought Martha to her new home in Albemarle County. Politics, however, remained foremost. He had been elected to the House of Burgesses in 1769 but had not found the legislature a particularly congenial body.

Autobiography, 1821

In 1769. I became a member of the legislature by the

Reverse silhouette thought to be of young Martha Wayles Jefferson; no authentic likeness of her is known.

choice of the county in which I live, & continued in that until it was closed by the revolution. I made one effort in that body for the permission of the emancipation of slaves, which was rejected: and indeed, during the regal government, nothing liberal could expect success. Our minds were circumscribed within narrow limits by an habitual belief that it was our duty to be subordinate to the mother country in all matters of government, to direct all our labors in subservience to her interests, and even to observe a bigotted intolerance for all religions but hers. The difficulties with our representatives were of habit and despair, not of reflection & conviction. Experience soon proved that they could bring their minds to rights on the first summons of their attention. But the king's council, which acted as another house of legislature, held their places at will & were in most humble obedience to that will: the Governor too, who had a negative on our laws held by the same tenure, & with still greater devotedness to it: and last of all the Royal negative closed the last door to every hope of amelioration.

In his fifth year as a burgess, Jefferson began to question the mother country's authority more openly and to demonstrate more resourcefulness in circumventing conservative burgesses, councilors, and governors. When the House was convened in the spring of 1773, relations with the Crown had again become strained. Episodes such as the burning of the British customs schooner the *Gaspee* in Rhode Island threatened the comparative peace established between the mother country and the Colonies by the repeal of the Townshend duties. Jefferson recalled how he and his allies had devised a method of rallying public opinion and coordinating resistance to the Crown during that session at Williamsburg.

Autobiography, 1821

Not thinking our old & leading members up to the point of forwardness & zeal which the times required, Mr. Henry, R[ichard] H[enry] Lee, Francis L. Lee, Mr. [Dabney] Carr & myself agreed to meet in the evening in a private room of the Raleigh to consult on the state of things. There may have been a member or two more whom I do not recollect. We were all sensible that the most urgent of all measures was that of coming to an understanding with all the other colonies to consider the British claims as a common cause to all, & to produce

41

TO all to whom these Presents shall come, Greeting: Know ye, that we the President and Masters of the College of William and Mary in Virginia, by Virtue of a royal Grant from their late Majesties King William and Queen Mary, of the Office of Surveyor General of the Colony of Virginia to the said College, have constituted and appointed, and by these Presents do constitute and appoint _ _ _ _ *Thomas Jefferson* _ _ _ _ _ Surveyor of *Albemarle County* during Pleasure, in the Place and Stead of

In Witness whereof we have hereunto set our Hands, and caused the Seal of the said College to be affixed, this *sixth Day of* _ *June* _ _ _ _ _ in the *fourteenth* Year of the Reign of our Sovereign Lord *George*, King of *Great Britain, France,* and *Ireland, &c.* And in the Year of our Lord God one thousand seven hundred and seventy three.

John Camm Pr

T Gwatkin

James Madison

Jefferson's appointment as surveyor of Albemarle County, June 6, 1773

an unity of action: and for this purpose that a commee of correspondce in each colony would be the best instrument for intercommunication: and that their first measure would probably be to propose a meeting of deputies from every colony at some central place, who should be charged with the direction of the measures which should be taken by all. We therefore drew up the resolutions. . . . The consulting members proposed to me to move them, but I urged that it should be done by Mr. Carr, my friend & brother in law [his sister Martha's husband], then a new member to whom I wished an opportunity should be given of making known to the house his great worth & talents. It was so agreed; he moved them, they were agreed to nem. con. [unanimously] and a commee of correspondence appointed of whom Peyton Randolph, the Speaker, was chairman. The Govr. (then Ld. Dunmore) dissolved us, but the Commee met the next day, prepared a circular letter to the Speakers of the other colonies, inclosing to each a copy of the resolns and left it in charge with their chairman to forward them by expresses.

By the time the House was called again in 1774, even more effective methods of resistance were necessary. Boston had greeted the new tea tax with her tea party, and the Crown had retaliated with the notorious Boston Port Act. Again Jefferson left a record of the developing strategy of the defiant group in Williamsburg that met in private to work out a protest plan.

Autobiography, 1821

The next event which excited our sympathies for Massachusets was the Boston port bill, by which that port was to be shut up on the 1st. of June 1774. This arrived while we were in session in the spring of that year. The lead in the house on these subjects being no longer left to the old members, Mr. Henry, R. H. Lee, Fr. L. Lee, 3. or 4. other members, whom I do not recollect, and myself, agreeing that we must boldly take an unequivocal stand in the line with Massachusetts, determined to meet and consult on the proper measures in the Council chamber, for the benefit of the library in that room. We were under conviction of the necessity of arousing our people from the lethargy into which they had fallen as to passing events; and thought that the appointment of a day of general fasting & prayer would be most likely to call up & alarm their attention.... To give greater emphasis to our proposition, we agreed to wait the next morning on Mr. [Robert Carter] Nicholas, whose grave & religious character was more in unison with the tone of our resolution and to sollicit him to move it. We accordingly went to him in the morning. He moved it the same day. The 1st of June was proposed and it passed without opposition. The Governor dissolved us as usual. We retired to the Apollo as before, agreed to an association, and instructed the Commee of correspdce to propose to the corresponding commees of the other colonies to appoint deputies to meet in Congress at such place, *annually*, as should be convenient to direct, from time to time, the measures required by the general interest: and we declared that an attack on any one colony should be considered as an attack on the whole.... We returned home, and in our several counties invited the clergy to meet assemblies of the people on the 1st. of June, to perform the ceremonies of the day, & to address to them discourses suited to the occasion. The people met generally, with anxiety & alarm in their countenances, and the effect of the day thro' the whole colony was like a shock of electricity, arousing every man & placing him erect & solidly on his center.

Cyclopedia of United States History BY BENSON J. LOSSING, 1893

Seal of Lord Dunmore, Governor of Virginia prior to the Revolution

Virginians responded as Jefferson had thought they would in the latest confrontation with the governor. Dunmore, having dissolved the House of Burgesses in the hope that a newly elected House would be less troublesome, found that the counties had not only reelected the same men but designated them to meet in convention to choose delegates to a proposed Continental Congress. Jefferson outlined a plan of action for the Congress in these resolutions he drafted for signing by the freeholders of Albemarle.

[July 26, 1774]

RESOLVED, that the inhabitants of the several states of British America are subject to the laws which they adopted at their first settlement, and to such others as have been since made by their respective legislatures, duly constituted and appointed with their own consent; that no other legislature whatever may rightfully exercise authority over them, and that these privileges they hold as the common rights of mankind, confirmed by the political constitutions they have respectively assumed, and also by several charters of compact from the crown.

Resolved, that these their natural and legal rights have in frequent instances been invaded by the parliament of Great Britain, and particularly that they were so by an act lately passed to take away the trade of the inhabitants of the town of Boston, in the province of Massachusetts Bay, that all such assumptions of unlawful power are dangerous to the rights of the British empire in general, and should be considered as its common cause, and that we will ever be ready to join with our fellow subjects, in every part of the same, in exerting all those rightful powers, which God has given us, for the re-establishing and guaranteeing such their constitutional rights, when, where, and by whomsoever invaded.

It is the opinion of this meeting, that the most eligible means of effecting these purposes will be to put an immediate stop to all imports from Great Britain (cotton, oznabrigs [osnaburg—coarse cotton], striped duffil [duffel—heavy wool], medicines, gunpowder, lead, books and printed papers, the necessary tools and implements for the handycraft arts and manufactures excepted for a limited time) and to all exports thereto after the 1st day of October, which shall be in the year of our Lord, 1775; and immediately to discontinue all commercial intercourse with every part of the British empire which shall not in like manner break off their commerce with Great Britain.

It is the opinion of this meeting, that we immediately cease to import all commodities from every part of the world which are subjected by the British parliament to the payment of duties in America.

It is the opinion of this meeting that these measures should be pursued until a repeal be obtained of the act for blocking up the harbour of Boston, of the acts prohibiting or restraining internal manufactures in America, of the acts imposing on any commodities duties to be paid in America, and of the acts laying restrictions on the American trade; and that on such repeal it will be reasonable to grant to our brethren of Great Britain such privileges in commerce as may amply compensate their fraternal assistance, past and future.

Proclamation by House of Burgesses setting June 1, 1774, as the day of fasting Jefferson and others had urged "to take an unequivocal stand in the line with Massachusetts"

Jefferson said that an attack of dysentery prevented him from attending the convention that met in Williamsburg on August 1, 1774, but he prepared additional resolutions to be adopted as instructions to the congressmen chosen there. He described the background of this draft.

Autobiography, 1821

They chose universally delegates for the Convention. Being elected one for my own county I prepared a draught of instructions to be given to the delegates whom we should send to the Congress, and which I meant to propose at our meeting. In this I took the ground which, from the beginning I had thought the only one orthodox or tenable, which was that the relation between Gr. Br. and these colonies was exactly the same as that of England & Scotland after the accession of James & until the Union ... having the same Executive chief but no other necessary political connection; and that our emigration from England to this country gave her no more rights over us, than the emigrations of the Danes and Saxons gave to the present authorities of the mother country over England. In this doctrine however I had never been able to get any one to agree with me but Mr. Wythe.... Our other patriots [Peyton] Randolph, the Lees, Nicholas, [Edmund] Pendleton stopped at the half-way house of John Dickinson who admitted that England had a right to regulate our commerce, and to lay duties on it for the purposes of regulation, but not of raising revenue. But for this ground there was no foundation in compact, in any acknoleged principles of colonization, nor in reason: expatriation being a natural right, and acted on as such, by all nations, in all ages. I set out for Wmsbg some days before that appointed for our meeting, but was taken ill of a dysentery on the road, & unable to proceed. I sent on therefore to Wmsbg two copies of my draught, the one under cover to Peyton Randolph, who I knew would be in the chair of the convention, the other to Patrick Henry. Whether Mr. Henry disapproved the ground taken, or was too lazy to read it (for he was the laziest man in reading I ever knew) I never learnt: but he communicated it to nobody. Peyton Randolph informed the Convention he had received such a paper from a member prevented by sickness from offering it in his place, and he laid it on the table for perusal. It was read generally by the members, approved by many, but thought too bold for the present state of things; but they printed it in pamphlet form under the title of 'A Summary view of the rights of British America.'

Although Jefferson explained that there were "some uncertainties and inaccuracies of historical facts" in the *Summary View* that he "neglected at the moment, knowing they could be readily corrected at the meeting," it is possible that he never intended to attend the convention and introduce the instructions himself. He knew he did not have the oratorical eloquence necessary to sway the delegates to such an advanced legal argument and he may have employed an indirect means of achieving his goal, a method thoroughly characteristic of his political style. In this case, he sent a copy of the arguments to Patrick Henry who had so impressed him with his persuasive abilities. He may have hoped Henry would introduce and move them, perhaps employing some of the ardent revolutionary rhetoric Jefferson had provided. Jefferson's dysentery may in fact have been a "diplomatic" illness; his account books show no record of an attempt to get to Williamsburg in time for the convention.

Even though the resolutions were not adopted, they more than served Jefferson's purpose. Published as a twenty-three page pamphlet, the *Summary View* gained wide circulation and brought Jefferson recognition outside his own colony. Ostensibly a guideline for Virginia's delegates to Congress, Jefferson's document went far beyond its avowed goal, setting forth specific grievances that had brought the Congress into existence. It even contained a veiled warning that unless those grievances were remedied, the King might lose the allegiance of his American subjects. Although Jefferson couched his threat in terms of advice to the King, there was no doubt of what he expected to happen if that advice was ignored.

A Summary View of the Rights
of British America [July, 1774]

Resolved that it be an instruction to the said deputies when assembled in General Congress with the deputies from the other states of British America to propose to the said Congress that an humble and dutiful address be presented to his majesty begging leave to lay before him as chief magistrate of the British empire the united complaints of his majesty's subjects in America; complaints which are excited by many unwarrantable incroachments and usurpations, attempted to be made by the legislature of one part of the empire, upon those rights which god and the laws have given equally and independently to all. To represent to his majesty that these his states have often individually made humble application to his imperial throne, to obtain thro' it's intervention some redress of their injured rights; to none of which was ever an answer condescended. Humbly to hope that this their joint address, penned in the language of truth, and divested of those expressions of servility which would persuade his majesty that we are asking favors and not rights shall obtain from his majesty a more respectful acceptance. And this his majesty will think we have reason to expect when he reflects that he is no more than the chief officer of the people, appointed by the laws, and circumscribed with definite powers, to assist in working the great machine of government erected for their use, and consequently to their superintendance. And in order that these our rights, as well as the invasions of them, may be laid more fully before his majesty, to take a view of them from the origin and first settlement of these countries.

To remind him that our ancestors, before their emigration to America, were the free inhabitants of the British dominions in Europe, and possessed a right, which nature has given to all men, of departing from the country in which chance, not choice has placed them, of going in quest of new habitations, and of there establishing new societies, under such laws and regulations as to them shall seem most likely to promote public happiness. That their Saxon ancestors had under this universal law, in like manner, left their native wilds and woods in the North of Europe, had possessed themselves of the island of Britain then less charged with inhabitants, and had established there that system of laws which has so long been the glory and protection of that country. Nor was ever any claim of superiority or dependance asserted over them by that mother country from which they had migrated: and were such a claim made it is beleived his majesty's subjects in Great Britain have too firm a feeling of the rights derived to them from their ancestors to bow down the sovereignty of their state before such visionary pretensions. And it is thought that no circumstance has occurred to distinguish materially the British from the Saxon emigration. America was conquered, and her settlements made and firmly established, at the expence of individuals, and not of the British public. Their own blood was spilt in acquiring lands for their settlement, their own fortunes expended in making that settlement effectual. For themselves they fought, for themselves they conquered, and for themselves alone they have right to hold. No shilling was ever issued from the public treasures of his majesty or his ancestors for their assistance, till of very late times, after the colonies had

Title page of the twenty-three page Summary View, *with Jefferson's name filled in as the author*

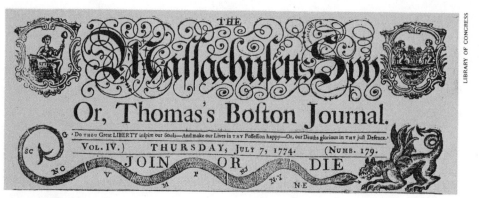

In July, 1774, as Jefferson was writing the Summary View, The Massachusetts Spy *carried this engraving by Paul Revere of a snake made up of the various colonies defying Great Britain's griffin.*

become established on a firm and permanent footing....

[Jefferson acknowledged the aid Britain had given the Colonies once they had become commercially valuable, but he said the help did not entitle Parliament to any arrogation of authority and could be repaid by granting exclusive trade privileges.]

That settlements having been thus effected in the wilds of America, the emigrants thought proper to adopt that system of laws under which they had hitherto lived in the mother country, and to continue their union with her by submitting themselves to the same common sovereign, who was thereby made the central link connecting the several parts of the empire thus newly multiplied.

But that not long were they permitted, however far they thought themselves removed from the hand of oppression, to hold undisturbed the rights thus acquired at the hazard of their lives and loss of their fortunes. A family of princes [the Stuarts] was then on the British throne, whose treasonable crimes against their people brought on them afterwards the exertion of those sacred and sovereign rights of punishment, reserved in the hands of the people for cases of extreme necessity, and judged by the constitution unsafe to be delegated to any other judicature. While every day brought forth some new and unjustifiable exertion of power over their subjects on that side the water, it was not to be expected that those here, much less able at that time to oppose the designs of despotism, should be exempted from injury. Accordingly that country [British North America]...was by these princes at several times parted out and distributed among the favorites and followers of their fortunes; and by an assumed right of the crown alone were erected into distinct and independent governments; a measure which it is beleived his majesty's prudence and understanding would prevent him from imitating at this day; as no exercise of such a power of dividing and dismembering a country has ever occurred in his majesty's realm of England....

That thus have we hastened thro' the reigns which preceded his majesty's, during which the violation of our rights were less alarming, because repeated at more distant intervals, than that rapid and bold succession of injuries which is likely to distinguish the present from all other periods of American story. Scarcely have our minds been able to emerge from the astonishment into which one stroke of parliamentary thunder has involved us, before another more heavy and more alarming is fallen on us. Single acts of tyranny may be ascribed to the accidental opinion of a day; but a series of oppressions, begun at a distinguished period, and pursued unalterably thro' every change of ministers, too plainly prove a deliberate, systematical plan of reducing us to slavery....

...Not only the principles of common sense, but the common feelings of human nature must be surrendered up, before his majesty's subjects here can be persuaded to beleive that they hold their political existence at the will of a British parliament[.] Shall these governments be dissolved, their property annihilated, and their people reduced to a state of nature, at the imperious breath of a body of men whom they never saw, in whom they never confided, and over whom they have no powers of punishment or removal, let their crimes against the American public be ever so great? Can any one reason be assigned why 160,000 electors in the island of Great Britain should give law to four millions in the states of America, every individual of whom is equal to every individual of them in virtue, in understanding, and in bodily strength? Were this to be admitted, instead of being a free people, as we have hitherto supposed, and mean to continue, ourselves, we should suddenly be found the slaves, not of one, but of 160,000 tyrants, distinguished too from all others by this singular circumstance that they are removed from the reach of fear, the only restraining motive which may hold the hand of a tyrant....

[Jefferson then traced the history of the Boston Port Bill and described other interferences with the Colonies' "glorious right of representation" such as the mother country's habit of dissolving American houses of representatives.]

But your majesty or your Governors have carried this power beyond every limit known or provided for by the laws. After dissolving one house of representatives, they have refused to call another, so that for a great length of time the legislature provided by the laws has been out of existence. From the nature of things, every society must at all times possess within itself the sovereign powers of legislation. The feelings of human nature revolt against the supposition of a state so situated as that it may not in any emergency provide against dangers which perhaps threaten immediate ruin. While those bodies are in existence to whom the people have delegated the powers of legislation, they alone possess and may exercise those powers. But when they are dissolved by the lopping off one or more of their branches, the power reverts to the people, who may use it to unlimited extent, either assembling together in person, sending deputies, or in any other way they may think proper. We forbear to trace consequences further; the dangers are conspicuous with which this practice is replete....

[He then discussed an "error in the nature of our land-holdings," that "all lands belong originally to the king." Instead, he said that allotting property was the right of a particular society through legislative action or that each individual "may appropriate to himself such lands as he finds vacant, and occupancy will give him title."]

That, in order to inforce the arbitrary measures before complained of, his majesty has from time to time sent among us large bodies of armed forces, not made up of the people here, nor raised by the authority of our laws. Did his majesty possess such a right as this, it might swallow up all our other rights whenever he should think proper. But his majesty has no right to land a single armed man on our shores; and those whom he sends here are liable to our laws for the suppression and punishment of Riots, Routs, and unlawful assemblies, or are hostile bodies invading us in defiance of law....To render these proceedings still more criminal against our laws, instead of subjecting the military to the civil power, his majesty has expressly made the civil subordinate to the military. But can his majesty thus put down all law under his feet? Can he erect a power superior to that which erected himself? He has done it indeed by force; but let him remember that force cannot give right.

That these are our grievances which we have thus laid before his majesty with that freedom of language and sentiment which becomes a free people, claiming their rights as derived from the laws of nature, and not as the gift of their chief magistrate. Let those flatter, who fear: it is not an American art. To give praise where it is not due, might be well from the venal, but would ill beseem those who are asserting the rights of human nature. They know, and will therefore say, that kings are the servants, not the proprietors of the people. Open your breast Sire, to liberal and expanded thought. Let not the name of George the third be a blot in the page of history. You are surrounded by British counsellors, but remember that they are parties. You have no ministers for American affairs, because you have none taken from among us, nor amenable to the laws on which they are to give you advice. It behoves you therefore to think and to act for yourself and your people. The great principles of right and wrong are legible to every reader: to pursue them requires not the aid of many counsellors. The whole art of government consists in the art of being honest. Only aim to do your duty, and mankind will give you credit where you fail. No longer persevere in sacrificing the rights of one part of the empire to the inordinate desires of another: but deal out to all equal and impartial right....This, Sire, is the advice of your great American council, on the observance of which may perhaps depend your felicity and future fame, and the preservation of that harmony which alone can continue both to Great Britain and America the reciprocal advantages of their connection. It is neither our wish nor our interest to separate from her. We are willing on our part to sacrifice every thing which reason can ask to the restoration of that tranquility for which all must wish. On their part let them be ready to establish union on a generous plan.

King George III

The State House in Philadelphia, after a drawing by C. W. Peale

Let them name their terms, but let them be just. Accept of every commercial preference it is in our power to give for such things as we can raise for their use, or they make for ours. But let them not think to exclude us from going to other markets, to dispose of those commodities which they cannot use, nor to supply those wants which they cannot supply. Still less let it be proposed that our properties within our own territories shall be taxed or regulated by any power on earth but our own. The god who gave us life, gave us liberty at the same time: the land of force may destroy, but cannot disjoin them. This, Sire, is our last, our determined resolution: and that you will be pleased to interpose with that efficacy which your earnest endeavors may insure to procure redress of these our great grievances, to quiet the minds of your subjects in British America against any apprehensions of future incroachment, to establish fraternal love and harmony thro' the whole empire, and that that may continue to the latest ages of time, is the fervent prayer of all British America.

The First Continental Congress did adopt a petition to the King, but it went on to employ more practical measures of protest: an association to be signed as a pledge to bar the importation of British goods. Economic boycotts had proved successful in the past, and Americans hoped for some good effect. Jefferson, who had ordered window glass from a London merchant in the summer of 1774, hastened to abide by the new agreement. On December 9 he wrote to the enforcement committees in counties along the James River where he expected his goods to arrive.

> Monticello Dec. 9. 1774.
>
> In order therefore that no proceedings of mine might give a handle for traducing our measures I thought it better previously to lay before your committee... a full state of the matter by which it might be seen under what expectations I had failed to give an earlier countermand and to shew that as they come within the prohibitions of the Continental Association (which without the spirit of prophecy could not have been foretold when I ordered them) so I mean they shall be subject to it's condemnation. To your committee therefore if landed within their county I submit the disposal of them, which shall be obeyed as soon as made known to their and your most humble servt.

In the spring of 1775, Jefferson was called on to sacrifice more than a few panes of glass for the American cause. As directed by the First Continental Congress at its adjournment in October, 1774, a second congress was to convene the following May, and Jefferson joined the Virginia delegation in June, replacing Peyton Randolph. A month before leaving for Philadelphia, Jefferson learned of the skirmishes at Lexington and Concord. As he began a letter to Dr. William Small, who had returned to England, he at first confined himself to the details of a shipment of Madeira he had sent his former teacher; but he soon spoke of the disturbing news from Massachusetts.

Virginia May 7. 1775.

Within this week we have received the unhappy news of an action of considerable magnitude between the king's troops and our brethren of Boston, in which it is said 500. of the former with Earl Piercy [Percy] are slain. That such an action has happened is undoubted, tho' perhaps the circumstances may not yet have reached us with truth. This accident has cut off our last hopes of reconciliation, and a phrenzy of revenge seems to have seized all ranks of people. It is a lamentable circumstance that the only mediatory power acknoleged by both parties, instead of leading to a reconciliation his divided people, should pursue the incendiary purpose of still blowing up the flames as we find him constantly doing in every speech and public declaration. This may perhaps be intended to intimidate into acquiescence, but the effect has been most unfortunately otherwise. A little knolege of human nature and attention to it's ordinary workings might have foreseen that the spirits of the people here were in a state in which they were more likely to be provoked than frightened by haughty deportment. And, to fill up the measure of irritation, proscription of individuals has been substituted in the room of just trial. Can it be believed that a grateful people will suffer those to be consigned to execution whose sole crime has been the developing and asserting their rights? Had the parliament possessed the liberty of reflection they would have avoided a measure as impotent as it was inflammatory. When I saw Lord Chatham's bill [a plan for imperial union presented in the House of Lords] I entertained high hope that a reconciliation could have been brought about. The difference between his terms and those offered by our congress might have been accomodated if entered on by both parties with a disposi-

A pencil sketch by Du Simitière, though identified as Jefferson in 1775, is more likely an anonymous British or colonial officer.

tion to accomodate. But the dignity of parliament it seems can brook no opposition to it's power. Strange that a set of men who have made sale of their virtue to the minister should yet talk of retaining dignity! —But I am getting into politics tho' I sat down only to ask your acceptance of the wine, and express my constant wishes for your happiness. This however seems secured by your philosophy and peaceful vocation. I shall still hope that amidst public dissension private friendship may be preserved inviolate, and among the warmest you can ever possess is that of Your obliged humble servt.,

TH. JEFFERSON

Unknown to Jefferson, Small had died some months before: the kindly scholar never learned of the war that split Virginia from Britain or the part his pupil played in the conflict. That role became more important on June 21, 1775, when Jefferson took his seat in the Second Continental Congress. At thirty-two he was one of the youngest members; only John Jay of New York was his junior. Unlike Jay, a veteran of the first congress, Jefferson was a stranger to most of the delegates at Philadelphia. With few skills as an orator he might have had to wait for recognition, but his reputation as a writer had spread quickly. John Adams's recollections of Jefferson as a congressman indicate that it was just as well that Jefferson chose to stay in the background.

Autobiography, 1802–7

Mr. Jefferson had been now about a Year a Member of Congress, but had attended his Duty in the House but a very small part of the time and when there had never spoken in public: and during the whole Time I satt with him in Congress, I never heard him utter three Sentences together. The most of a Speech he ever made in my hearing was a gross insult on Religion, in one or two Sentences, for which I gave him immediately the Reprehension, which he richly merited.

Despite his unorthodox views on religion, Jefferson made a good friend in Adams who confessed that the young Virginian "soon seized upon my heart." A few days after his arrival, Jefferson was added to the important committee charged with preparing a declaration to be issued by General George Washington, the new Commander in Chief of the Continental Army, at camp in Boston. Jefferson recalled the fate of the draft declaration he prepared.

John Dickinson in an engraving
after a drawing by Du Simitière

Autobiography, 1821

I prepared a draught of the Declaration committed to us. It was too strong for Mr. [John] Dickinson. He still retained the hope of reconciliation with the mother country, and was unwilling it should be lessened by offensive statements. He was so honest a man, & so able a one that he was greatly indulged even by those who could not feel his scruples. We therefore requested him to take the paper, and put it into a form he could approve. He did so, preparing an entire new statement, and preserving of the former only the last 4. paragraphs & half of the preceding one. We approved & reported it to Congress, who accepted it.

John Dickinson revised the Declaration of the Causes and Necessity for Taking Up Arms, but retained many of Jefferson's fiery phrases. He did not, despite what Jefferson wrote, just add on his last few paragraphs. Like Jefferson in *A Summary View,* he catalogued the unjust acts of the Crown and ministry and the patient response of the Americans in the past. The Declaration, as revised by Dickinson with Jefferson's phrases in italics, continued in this vein.

Declaration of the Causes and Necessity
for Taking Up Arms, July 6, 1775

But why should we enumerate our Injuries in detail?...

...[An] Administration sensible that we should regard these oppressive Measures as Freemen ought to do, sent over Fleets and Armies to enforce them. The Indignation of the Americans was roused, it is true; but it was the Indignation of a virtuous, loyal, and affectionate People. A Congress of Delegates from the United Colonies was assembled at Philadelphia, on the fifth Day of last September. We resolved again to offer an humble and dutiful Petition to the King, and also addressed our Fellow Subjects of Great-Britain. *We have pursued every temperate, every respectful Measure; we have even proceeded to break off our commercial Intercourse with our Fellow Subjects, as the last peaceable Admonition, that our Attachment to no Nation upon Earth should supplant our Attachment to Liberty. This, we flattered ourselves, was the ultimate Step of the Controversy: But subsequent Events have shewn, how vain was this Hope of finding Moderation in our Enemies.*

Several threatening Expressions against the Colonies

were inserted in His Majesty's Speech; our Petition, tho'
we were told it was a Decent one, and that his Majesty
had been pleased to receive it graciously, and to promise
laying it before his Parliament, was huddled into both
Houses among a Bundle of American Papers, and there
neglected. The Lords and Commons in their Address,
in the Month of February, said, that "a Rebellion at that
Time actually existed within the Province of Massachusetts-Bay.... Soon after, the commercial Intercourse
of whole Colonies, with foreign Countries, and with
each other, was cut off by an Act of Parliament; by
another, several of them were intirely prohibited from
the Fisheries in the Seas near their Coasts, on which
they always depended for their Sustenance; and large
Re-inforcements of Ships and Troops were immediately
sent over to General Gage.

Fruitless were all the entreaties, arguments, and eloquence of an Illustrious Band of the most distinguished
Peers, and Commoners, who nobly and strenuously asserted the Justice of our Cause, to stay, or even to miti-
gate the heedless fury with which these accumulated and
unexampled Outrages were hurried on. Equally fruitless
was the interference of the City of London, of Bristol,
and many other respectable Towns in our Favour. Parliament adopted an insidious Manoeuvre calculated to
divide us, to establish a perpetual Auction of Taxations
where Colony should bid against Colony, all of them
uninformed what Ransom would redeem their Lives;
and thus to extort from us, at the point of the Bayonet,
the unknown sums that should be sufficient to gratify,
if possible to gratify, ministerial Rapacity, with the miserable indulgence left to us of raising, in our own Mode,
the prescribed Tribute. What Terms more rigid and humiliating could have been dictated by remorseless Victors
to conquered Enemies? In our circumstances to accept
them, would be to deserve them.

*Soon after the Intelligence of these proceedings arrived
on this Continent, General Gage, who in the course of
the last Year had taken Possession of the Town of Boston, in the Province of Massachusetts-Bay, and still occupied it as a Garrison, on the 19th day of April, sent
out from that Place a large detachment of his Army, who
made an unprovoked Assault on the Inhabitants of the
said Province, at the Town of Lexington, as appears by*

*A view of the green in Lexington,
where British troops first clashed
with Americans in April, 1775*

*A French engraving by F. Godefroy
of the infamous day at Lexington*

the Affidavits of a great Number of Persons, some of whom were Officers and Soldiers of that detachment, murdered eight of the Inhabitants, and wounded many others. From thence the Troops proceeded in warlike Array to the Town of Concord, where they set upon another Party of the Inhabitants of the same Province, killing several and wounding more, until compelled to retreat by the country People suddenly assembled to repel this cruel Aggression. Hostilities, thus commenced by the British Troops, have been since prosecuted by them without regard to Faith or Reputation. . . .

The General, further emulating his ministerial Masters, by a Proclamation bearing date on the 12th day of June, after venting the grossest Falsehoods and Calumnies against the good People of these Colonies, proceeds to "declare them all, either by Name or Description, to be Rebels and Traitors, to supersede the course of the Common Law, and instead thereof to publish and order the use and exercise of the Law Martial." His Troops have butchered our Countrymen, have wantonly burnt Charlestown, besides a considerable number of Houses in other Places; our Ships and Vessels are seized; the necessary supplies of Provisions are intercepted, and he is exerting his utmost Power to spread destruction and devastation around him. . . .

. . . We are reduced to the alternative of chusing an unconditional Submission to the tyranny of irritated Ministers, or resistance by Force. The latter is our choice. We have counted the cost of this contest, and find nothing so dreadful as voluntary Slavery. Honour, Justice, and Humanity, forbid us tamely to surrender that Freedom which we received from our gallant Ancestors, and which our innocent Posterity have a right to receive from us. We cannot endure the infamy and guilt of resigning succeeding Generations to that wretchedness which inevitably awaits them, if we basely entail hereditary Bondage upon them.

Our cause is just. Our union is perfect. Our internal Resources are great, and, if necessary, foreign Assistance is undoubtedly attainable. We gratefully acknowledge, as signal Instances of the Divine Favour towards us, that his Providence would permit us to be called into this severe Controversy, until we were grown up to our present strength, had been previously exercised in warlike Operation, and possessed of the means of defending ourselves. With hearts fortified with these animating Reflections, *we most solemnly, before God and the World, declare, that, exerting the utmost Energy of those Powers, which our beneficent Creator hath graciously bestowed upon us, the Arms we have been compelled by our Enemies to assume, we will, in defiance of every Hazard, with unabating Firmness and Perseverence, employ for the preservation of our Liberties;* being with one Mind resolved to die Freemen rather than to live Slaves.

Lest this Declaration should disquiet the Minds of our Friends and Fellow-Subjects in any part of the Empire, we assure them that we mean not to dissolve that Union which has so long and so happily subsisted between us, and which we sincerely wish to see restored. Necessity has not yet driven us into that desperate Measure, or induced us to excite any other Nation to War against them. We have not raised Armies with ambitious Designs of separating from Great-Britain, and establishing Independent States. *We fight not for Glory or for Conquest. We exhibit to Mankind the remarkable Spectacle of a People attacked by unprovoked Enemies, without any imputation or even suspicion of Offence.* They boast of their Privileges and Civilization, and yet proffer no milder Conditions than Servitude or Death.

In our own native Land, in defence of the Freedom that is our Birthright, and which we ever enjoyed till the late Violation of it—for the protection of our Property, acquired solely by the honest Industry of our fore-fathers and ourselves, *against Violence actually offered, we have taken up Arms. We shall lay them down when Hostilities shall cease on the part of the Aggressors, and all danger of their being renewed shall be removed, and not before.*

With an humble Confidence in the Mercies of the supreme and impartial Judge and Ruler of the Universe, *we most devoutly implore his Divine Goodness to protect us happily through this great Conflict, to dispose our Adversaries to reconciliation on reasonable Terms, and thereby to relieve the Empire from the Calamities of civil War.*

Washington had assumed command of the army on July 3, an event depicted in this stylized woodcut.

Jefferson may have felt a literary artist's sensitivity to criticism when his draft declaration was rewritten. Certainly he did not care for Dickinson's cautious ways. Two days after the adoption of the Declaration on July 6, Dickinson's draft of a second petition to the King, the Olive Branch Petition, was approved by Congress. Jefferson happily recalled Benjamin Harrison's tart comment on the Pennsylvania conservative's handiwork.

Autobiography, 1821

Congress gave a signal proof of their indulgence to Mr. Dickinson, and of their great desire not to go too fast for any respectable part of our body, in permitting him to draw their second petition to the King according to his own ideas, and passing it with scarcely any amendment. The disgust against it's humility was general; and Mr. Dickinson's delight at its passage was the only circumstance which reconciled them to it. The vote being past, altho' further observn on it was out of order, he could not refrain from rising and expressing his satisfaction and concluded by saying 'there is but one word, Mr. President, in the paper which I disapprove, & that is the word *Congress*,' on which Ben Harrison rose and said 'there is but one word in the paper, Mr. President, of which I approve, and that is the word *Congress*.'

When Congress recessed in early August, Jefferson returned to Virginia with a clearer vision of his and America's future. His work with other leaders from the Colonies had given him a chance to exchange ideas with stimulating men and had helped him refine his own views. Still, he had not abandoned hope for reconciliation. Shortly after arriving at Monticello, Jefferson—in an attempt to influence British opinion more directly—wrote to his kinsman John Randolph, a Loyalist who had fled from Virginia to England.

Monticello. Aug. 25. 1775

I am sorry the situation of our country should render it not eligible to you to remain longer in it. I hope the returning wisdom of Great Britain will e'er long put an end to this unnatural contest. There may be people to whose tempers and dispositions Contention may be pleasing, and who may therefore wish a continuance of confusion. But to me it is of all states, but one, the most horrid. My first wish is a restoration of our just rights; my second a return of the happy period when, consistently with duty, I may withdraw myself totally from the public stage and pass the rest of my days in domestic ease and tranquillity, banishing every desire of afterwards even hearing what passes in the world. Perhaps ardour for the latter may add considerably to the warmth of the former wish. Looking with fondness towards a reconciliation with Great Britain, I cannot help hoping you may be able to contribute towards expediting this good work. I think it must be evident to yourself that the ministry have been deceived by their officers on this side the water, who (for what purposes I cannot tell) have constantly represented the American opposition as that of a small faction, in which the body of the people took little part. This you can inform them of your own knolege to be untrue. They have taken it into their heads too that we are cowards and shall surrender at discretion to an armed force. The past and future operations of the war must confirm or undeceive them on that head. I wish they were thoroughly and minutely acquainted with every circumstance relative to America as it exists in truth. I am persuaded this would go far towards disposing them to reconciliation. Even those in parliament who are called friends to America seem to know nothing of our real determinations. I observe they pronounced in the last parliament that the Congress of 1774 did not mean to insist rigorously on the terms they held out, but kept something in reserve to give up; and in fact that they would give up everything but the article of taxation. Now the truth is far from this, as I can affirm, and put my honor to the assertion; and their continuance in this error may perhaps have very ill consequences. The Congress stated the lowest terms they thought possible to be accepted in order to convince the world they were not unreasonable. They gave up the monopoly and regulation of trade, and all the acts of parliament prior to 1764. leaving to British generosity to render these at some future time as easy to America as the interest of Britain would admit. But this was before blood was spilt. I cannot affirm, but have reason to think, these terms would not now be accepted. I wish no false sense of honor, no ignorance of our real intentions, no vain hope that partial concessions of right will be accepted may induce the ministry to trifle with accomodation till it shall be put even out of our own power to accomodate. If indeed Great Britain, disjoined from her colonies, be a match for the most potent nations of Europe with the colonies thrown into their scale, they may go on securely. But if they are not assured of this, it would be certainly unwise, by trying the event of another campaign, to risque our accepting a foreign aid which perhaps may not be obtainable but on a condition of everlasting avulsion from Great Britain. This would be thought a hard condition to those who still wish for reunion with their parent country. I am sincerely one of those, and would rather be in dependance of Great Britain, properly limited, than on any nation upon earth, or than on no nation. But I am one of those too who rather than submit to the right of legislating for us assumed by the British parliament, and which late experience has shewn they will so cruelly exercise, would lend my hand to sink the whole island in the ocean.

If undeceiving the minister as to matters of fact may change his dispositions, it will perhaps be in your power by assisting to do this, to render service to the whole empire, at the most critical time certainly that it has ever seen. Whether Britain shall continue the head of the greatest empire on earth, or shall return to her original station in the political scale of Europe depends perhaps on the resolutions of the succeeding winter. God send they may be wise and salutary for us all!

But by the time of Jefferson's return to Congress in late September, it was clear that Parliament's resolutions would not lead to peace. Armed resistance to the Crown had broken out in Virginia; Congress had sent out a military expedition to win over Canada. When Jefferson wrote John Randolph in November his tone was far more bitter, and he launched a merciless attack on the "sceptered tyrant" he had once acknowledged as his sovereign.

Philadelphia Nov. 29. 1775.
You will have heard before this reaches you that Ld. Dunmore has commenced hostilities in Virginia. That people bore with every thing till he attempted to burn the town of Hampton. They opposed and repelled him with considerable loss on his side and none on ours. It has raised our country into perfect phrensy. It is an immense misfortune to the whole empire to have a king of such a disposition at such a time. We are told and every thing proves it true that he is the bitterest enemy we have. His minister is able, and that satisfies me that ignorance or wickedness somewhere controuls him. In an earlier part of this contest our petitions told him that

Jefferson's notes on proceedings in the Congress on June 7, 1776, the day Virginia's call for a declaration of independence was moved

from our king there was but one appeal. The admonition was despised and that appeal forced on us. To undo his empire he has but one truth more to learn, that after colonies have drawn the sword there is but one step more they can take. That step is now pressed upon us by the measures adopted as if they were afraid we would not take it. Beleive me Dear Sir there is not in the British empire a man who more cordially loves a Union with Gr. Britain than I do. But by the god that made me I will cease to exist before I yeild to a connection on such terms as the British parliament propose and in this I think I speak the sentiments of America. We want neither inducement nor power to declare and assert a separation. It is will alone which is wanting and that is growing apace under the fostering hand of our king. One bloody campaign will probably decide everlastingly our future course; I am sorry to find a bloody campaign is decided on. If our winds and waters should not combine to rescue their shores from slavery, and General Howe's reinforcement should arrive in safety we have hopes he will be inspirited to come out of Boston and take another drubbing: and we must drub you soundly before the sceptered tyrant will know we are not mere brutes, to crouch under his hand and kiss the rod with which he deigns to scourge us.

A month later Jefferson left Philadelphia to spend the winter at Monticello with Martha and their three-year-old daughter Martha, called Patsy. He found little peace at home. Dunmore had fled the province and now directed naval and military operations against Virginia; Norfolk was burned by Dunmore's forces on New Year's Day and slaves were urged to revolt and join the Crown's forces. Jefferson's mother died at the end of March and his own health was poor.

When he rejoined Congress in early May, he found that independence was no longer a theory to be discussed at leisure. In most colonies royal government had disintegrated as Crown officials prudently withdrew. Provision had to be made for self-government or anarchy would follow. On May 15, the day after Jefferson reached Philadelphia, Congress passed a resolution calling on the colonies to establish new forms of government. But this was not enough. In April John Page had written Jefferson: "For God's sake declare the Colonies independant at once, and save us from ruin." A resolution of the Virginia Convention in May opened the way for debate. Jefferson recorded his delegation's role in Congress on June 7.

Notes of Proceedings in the
Continental Congress, 1776

Friday June 7. 1776. the Delegates from Virginia moved in obedience to instructions from their constituents that the Congress should declare that these United colonies are & of right ought to be free & independant states, that they are absolved from all allegiance to the British crown, and that all political connection between them and the state of Great Britain is & ought to be totally dissolved; that measures should be immediately taken for procuring the assistance of foreign powers, and a Confederation be formed to bind the colonies more closely together.

The house being obliged to attend at that time to some other business the propostition was referred to the next day....

Historical Collections of Virginia, BY HENRY HOWE, 1856

A view of Norfolk, which was burned by the British in January, 1776

When debate resumed, a sectional division was apparent. Richard Henry Lee, George Wythe, and John Adams pressed for adoption of the resolutions; James Wilson and John Dickinson of Pennsylvania, Robert R. Livingston of New York, and Edward Rutledge of South Carolina argued for caution. The Middle Colonies and South Carolina stood against New England, Virginia, and Georgia in the debates that lasted until Monday, June 10. Congress then hit on a compromise that would win time for public opinion to fall behind independence: a decision on the resolutions themselves would be postponed until July 1, but in the meantime a committee was to draft a declaration of the reasons "which impelled us to this mighty resolution." Jefferson, Adams, Livingston, Benjamin Franklin, and Roger Sherman were appointed to the committee June 11, and the task of actually drafting the declaration fell to Jefferson. In the following seventeen days, Jefferson worked at a desk in his parlor in Graaf's boardinghouse. In years to come, he insisted that his was not a particularly original composition, that the truths he recited were so self-evident that he was merely a reporter rather than a formulator of any new doctrine. He repeated this view in a letter to Henry Lee in 1825.

Monticello May 8. 1825.

But with respect to our rights, and the acts of the British government contravening those rights, there was but one opinion on this side of the water. All American Whigs thought alike on these subjects....Not to find out new principles, or new arguments, never before thought of, not merely to say things which had never been said before; but to place before mankind the common sense of

Jefferson's writing desk
CULVER PICTURES, INC.

Jacob Graff's boardinghouse

the subject, [in] terms so plain and firm as to command their assent, and to justify ourselves in the independant stand we [were] compelled to take. Neither aiming at originality of principle or sentiment, nor yet copied from any particular and previous writing, it was intended to be an expression of the American mind, and to give to that expression the proper tone and spirit called for by the occasion. All it's authority rests then on the harmonizing sentiments of the day, whether expressed in conversation, in letters, printed essays or in the elementary books of public right, as Aristotle, Cicero, Locke, Sidney, &c.

Not until July 2 was the question of independence finally met. The original resolution presented by Richard Henry Lee was adopted, and Congress then considered Jefferson's draft declaration itself, which had received some minor revisions in committee. Jefferson recorded his reactions as the delegates debated the declaration for the next three days.

Notes of Proceedings in the Continental Congress, 1776

Committee of Franklin, Jefferson, Adams, Livingston, and Sherman consulting on the Declaration

Congress proceeded the same day to consider the declaration of Independance.... the pusillanimous idea that we had friends in England worth keeping terms with, still haunted the minds of many. for this reason those passages which conveyed censures on the people of England were struck out, lest they should give them offence. the clause too, reprobating the enslaving the inhabitants of Africa, was struck out in complaisance to South Carolina & Georgia, who had never attempted to restrain the importation of slaves, and who on the contrary still wished to continue it. our Northern brethren also I believe felt a little tender under those censures; for tho' their people have very few slaves themselves yet they had pretty considerable carriers of them to others. the debates having taken up the greater parts of the 2d. 3d. & 4th. days of July were, in the evening of the last closed. The declaration was reported by the commee., agreed to by the house, and signed by every member present except Mr. Dickinson.

John Adams steadfastly defended every word of the draft in floor debate, while Jefferson—as the inevitable alterations were made—sat by listening to Franklin's anecdotes.

Monticello Dec. 4. [18]18.

When the Declaration of Independence was under the consideration of Congress, there were two or three unlucky expressions in it which gave offence to some members.... Altho' the offensive expressions were immediately yielded, these gentlemen continued their depredations on other parts of the instrument. I was sitting by Dr. Franklin who "percieved" that I was not insensible to these mutilations. 'I have made it a rule, said he, whenever in my power, to avoid becoming the draughtsman of papers to be reviewed by a public body. I took my lesson from an incident which I will relate to you. When I was a journeyman printer, one of my companions, an apprentice Hatter, having served out his time, was about to open shop for himself. His first concern was to have a handsome sign-board, with a proper inscription. He composed it in these words 'John Thompson, *Hatter, makes* and *sells hats for*

Page two of Jefferson's four-page draft of the Declaration; marginal notes identify alterations made by John Adams and Benjamin Franklin.

THIRTEEN

UNITED COLONIES.

United, we stand---Divided, we fall.

In May, Alexander Purdie's Virginia Gazette *had replaced its ancient seal of the colony with the new, simple logo shown above.*

ready money,' with a figure of a hat subjoined. But he thought he would submit it to his friends for their amendments. The first he shewed it to thought the word 'Hatter' tautologous, because followed by the words 'makes hats' which shew he was a Hatter. It was struck out. The next observed that the word *'makes'* might as well be omitted, because his customers would not care who made the hats. If good & to their mind, they would buy, by whomsoever made. He struck it out. A third said he thought the words *'for ready money,'* were useless as it was not the custom of the place to sell on credit. Every one who purchased expected to pay. They were parted with, and the inscription now stood 'John Thompson sells hats.' *'sells hats'* says his next friend? 'Why nobody will expect you to give them away. What then is the use of that word?' It was stricken out, and *'hats'* followed it, the rather, as there was one painted on the board. So his inscription was reduced ultimately to 'John Thompson' with the figure of a hat subjoined.

Of the deletions Congress made in Jefferson's draft one, which involved several passages in a long indictment of George III, probably improved the document; but Congress also left out several phrases that might well have been preserved, such as "we must endeavor to forget our former love for them...." and "we might have been a free & a great people together; but a communication of grandeur & of freedom it seems is below their dignity." Jefferson would certainly have preferred to omit the final appeal to Divine Providence. Despite these minor revisions, the basic nobility of his Declaration remained, and it is still one of the most influential political documents of modern times. He had turned philosophic principles into self-evident truths coupled with impassioned pleas for justice similar to those he had presented in the *Summary View* and in his draft of the Declaration of Causes. Finally on July 4 twelve states (New York abstaining) agreed to the amended Declaration, and it was printed that night.

In Congress, July 4, 1776.
A DECLARATION
By the Representatives of the
United States of America
In General Congress Assembled
When in the Course of human events, it becomes necessary for one people to dissolve the political bands which have connected them with another, and to assume

done by M. Jefferson — Paris 1786 to convey
an Idea of the Room in which congress
sat, at the Declaration of Independence
on the groundfloor of the Old State house in
Philadelphia — lefthand of entering

When John Trumbull began a painting of the Declaration's presentation by the Committee of Five, Jefferson drew this floor plan to show him the layout of the room in the State House.

among the powers of the earth, the separate and equal station to which the Laws of Nature and of Nature's God entitle them, a decent respect to the opinions of mankind requires that they should declare the causes which impel them to the separation. We hold these truths to be self-evident, that all men are created equal, that they are endowed by their Creator with certain unalienable Rights, that among these are Life, Liberty and the pursuit of Happiness. That to secure these rights, Governments are instituted among Men, deriving their just powers from the consent of the governed, That whenever any Form of Government becomes destructive of these ends, it is the Right of the People to alter or to abolish it, and to institute new Government, laying its foundation on such principles and organizing its powers in such form, as to them shall seem most likely to effect their Safety and Happiness. Prudence, indeed, will dictate that Governments long established should not be changed for light and transient causes; and accordingly all experience hath shewn, that mankind are more disposed to suffer, while evils are sufferable, than to right themselves by abolishing the forms to which they are accustomed. But when a long train of abuses and usurpations, pursuing invariably the same Object evinces a design to reduce them under absolute Despotism, it is their right, it is their duty, to throw off such Government, and to provide new Guards for their future security. Such has been the patient sufferance of these Colonies; and such is now the necessity which constrains them to alter their former Systems of Government. The history of the present King of Great Britain is a history of repeated injuries and usurpations, all having in direct object the establishment of an absolute Tyranny over these States. To prove this, let Facts be submitted to a candid world. He has refused his Assent to Laws, the most wholesome and necessary for the public good. He has forbidden his Governors to pass Laws of immediate and pressing importance, unless suspended in their operation till his Assent should be obtained; and when so suspended, he has utterly neglected to attend to them. He has refused to pass other Laws for the accommodation of large districts of people, unless those people would relinquish the right of Representation in the Legislature, a right inestimable to them and formidable to tyrants only. He has called together legislative bodies at places unusual, uncomfortable, and distant from the depository of their public Records, for the sole purpose of fatiguing them into compliance with his measures. He has dissolved Representative Houses repeatedly, for opposing with manly firmness his invasions on the rights of the people. He has refused for a long time, after such dissolutions, to cause others to be elected; whereby the Legislative powers, incapable of Annihilation, have returned to the People at large for their exercise; the State remaining in the mean time exposed to all the dangers of invasion from without, and convulsions within. He has endeavoured to prevent the population of these States; for that purpose obstructing the Laws for Naturalization of Foreigners; refusing to pass others to encourage their migrations hither, and raising the conditions of new Appropriations of Lands. He has obstructed the Administration of Justice, by refusing his Assent to Laws for establishing Judiciary powers. He has made Judges dependent on his Will alone, for the tenure of their offices, and the amount and payment of their salaries. He has erected a multitude of New Offices, and sent hither swarms of Officers to harrass our people, and eat out their substance. He has kept among us, in times of peace, standing Armies without the Consent of our legislatures. He has affected to render the Military independent of and superior to the Civil power. He has combined with others to subject us to a jurisdiction foreign to our constitution, and unacknowledged by our laws; giving his Assent to their Acts of pretended Legislation: For Quartering large bodies of armed troops among us: For protecting them, by a mock Trial, from punishment for any Murders which they should commit on the Inhabitants of these States: For cutting off our Trade with all parts of the world: For imposing Taxes on us without our Consent: For depriving us in many cases of the benefits of Trial by Jury: For transporting us beyond Seas to be tried for pretended offences: For abolishing the free System of English Laws in a neighbouring Province, establishing therein an Arbitrary government, and enlarging its Boundaries so as to render it at once an example and fit instrument for introducing the same absolute rule into these Colonies: For taking away our Charters, abolishing our most valuable Laws, and altering fundamentally the Forms of our

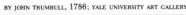

Trumbull's pencil sketch, made in 1786, of his original idea for a depiction of the presentation

Final version of Trumbull's The Declaration of Independence, *which was completed in 1797 in London*

Governments: For suspending our own Legislatures, and declaring themselves invested with power to legislate for us in all cases whatsoever. He has abdicated Government here, by declaring us out of his Protection and waging War against us. He has plundered our seas, ravaged our Coasts, burnt our towns, and destroyed the Lives of our people. He is at this time transporting large Armies of foreign Mercenaries to compleat the works of death, desolation and tyranny, already begun with circumstances of Cruelty & perfidy scarcely paralleled in the most barbarous ages, and totally unworthy the Head of a civilized nation. He has constrained our fellow Citizens taken Captive on the high Seas to bear Arms against their Country, to become the executioners of their friends and Brethren, or to fall themselves by their Hands. He has excited domestic insurrections amongst us, and has endeavoured to bring on the inhabitants of our frontiers, the merciless Indian Savages, whose known rule of warfare, is an undistinguished destruction of all ages, sexes and conditions. In every stage of these Oppressions We

69

have Petitioned for Redress in the most humble terms: Our repeated Petitions have been answered only by repeated injury. A Prince, whose character is thus marked by every act which may define a Tyrant, is unfit to be the ruler of a free people. Nor have We been wanting in attentions to our Brittish brethren. We have warned them from time to time of attempts by their legislature to extend an unwarrantable jurisdiction over us. We have reminded them of the circumstances of our emigration and settlement here. We have appealed to their native justice and magnanimity, and we have conjured them by the ties of our common kindred to disavow these usurpations, which, would inevitably interrupt our connections and correspondence. They too have been deaf to the voice of justice and of consanguinity. We must, therefore, acquiesce in the necessity, which denounces our Separation, and hold them, as we hold the rest of mankind, Enemies in War, in Peace Friends.

We, therefore, the Representatives of the united States of America, in General Congress, Assembled, appealing to the Supreme Judge of the world for the rectitude of our intentions, do, in the Name, and by Authority of the good People of these Colonies, solemnly publish and declare, That these United Colonies are, and of Right ought to be Free and Independent States; that they are Absolved from all Allegiance to the British Crown, and that all political connection between them and the State of Great Britain, is and ought to be totally dissolved; and that as Free and Independent States, they have full Power to levy War, conclude Peace, contract Alliances, establish Commerce, and to do all other Acts and Things which Independent States may of right do. And for the support of this Declaration, with a firm reliance on the protection of divine Providence, we mutually pledge to each other our Lives, our Fortunes and our sacred Honor.

The official text of the Declaration was printed and circulated among the Thirteen Colonies and read to a crowd in the State House yard in Philadelphia on July 8. New York's delegates received instructions allowing them to give their assent a week later, and an elaborately engrossed parchment copy was prepared by Timothy Matlack. When it arrived on August 2 those members present added their signatures. Not

PROPOSALS
BY JOHN TRUMBULL,
FOR
PUBLISHING BY SUBSCRIPTION
A PRINT
FROM THE ORIGINAL PICTURE, PAINTED BY HIM,
BY ORDER OF THE GOVERNMENT OF THE UNITED STATES, AND
TO BE PLACED IN THE CAPITOL,
REPRESENTING THE
DECLARATION OF INDEPENDENCE,
AND CONTAINING
PORTRAITS
OF MOST OF THE MEMBERS PRESENT IN CONGRESS,
ON THAT MEMORABLE OCCASION.

Trumbull's proposals for raising funds to install a print of his famous painting in the Rotunda of the Capitol, which was done in 1824; subscribers of twenty dollars were to receive copies of the print.

until November had all those who voted for independence attended and signed their names, which were not made public until January, 1777.

Even though Jefferson remained in Congress until September, serving on several important committees, his attention wandered more and more to his home province. Only two days after his return to Philadelphia in May, he had written to Thomas Nelson in Williamsburg.

Scribner's Monthly JULY, 1876

Philadelphia May. 16. 1776

Should our Convention propose to establish now a form of government perhaps it might be agreeable to recall for a short time their delegates. It is a work of the most interesting nature and such as every individual would wish to have his voice in. In truth it is the whole object of the present controversy; for should a bad government be instituted for us in future it had been as well to have accepted at first the bad one offered to us from beyond the water without the risk and expence of contest. But this I mention to you in confidence, as in our situation, a hint to any other is too delicate however anxiously interesting the subject is to our feelings....

P.S. In the other colonies who have instituted government they recalled their delegates leaving only one or two to give information to Congress of matters which might relate to their country particularly, and giving them a vote during the interval of absence.

Tradition has it that a few days after the Declaration's adoption Jefferson and others had a private celebration in this garden house in nearby Frankford, Pennsylvania.

Throughout the spring and summer, Jefferson urged his friends to call him back in time to work in the Virginia Convention. The challenge of creating a state government was tantalizing; indeed, Jefferson had found another lifelong preoccupation. He drafted a constitution himself and sent it to Williamsburg with George Wythe in June, but it arrived too late in the convention's sessions to be considered as a whole and it was drawn on only for amendments to the version George Mason presented. If he could have no part in drawing the plan for Virginia's government, Jefferson was nevertheless determined to return home to correct the faults of the newly adopted constitution and to see Virginia launched safely in statehood. He was reelected to Congress but resigned. Reports that his wife was ill prompted him to write Richard Henry Lee, who was to succeed him in Philadelphia: "For God's sake, for your country's sake, and for my sake, come." At last, on September 3, he was able to return to Virginia, a new state with a new, untested frame of government.

Chapter 3

Virginia Reformer

A month after Jefferson's return to Virginia in September, 1776, he was offered a diplomatic appointment by the Continental Congress. Officially he declined this post in Paris because of "circumstances very peculiar in the situation of my family." Certainly his concern for his wife's health was enough to keep him in Virginia, but he confided in his *Autobiography*, "I saw too, that the laboring oar was really at home." The work of transforming Virginia from a colony into a state had begun with the new constitution. Although there seemed to be no marked differences between the political framework suggested by Jefferson and that adopted by the convention on June 29, his version had provided broader citizen participation in government. His property qualifications for voting were so low that they would have resulted in something very close to universal suffrage for white males. In addition, his draft emphasized freedom from maintaining religious establishments, more independence and appointive power for the executive, and a greater portion of legislative control to the more representative lower house of the assembly. Jefferson objected to the fact that the constitution had not been referred to the electorate for approval. He viewed the Declaration of Rights adopted before the constitution, however, as a proper philosophical basis for a government that valued individual liberties.

Even if the constitution was more conservative than Jefferson might have wished, there was still much he could do to implement reforms. For the next three years he worked constantly to enact more democratic laws, beginning in October when he took his seat in the House of Delegates, the successor to the House of Burgesses, at Williamsburg. He would look back upon this period in his life with great satisfaction; for, though many of his proposals were defeated and as many others simply ignored, he was able to begin destroying the vestiges of aristocracy and laying the foundations for a free society. In his *Autobiography*, he recorded the background of his first major campaign that fall, a move to abolish entails and primogeniture.

*Part of page one from Jefferson's
draft of his "first ideas" for a
Virginia constitution, June, 1776*

Autobiography, 1821

On the 12th. [of October] I obtained leave to bring [in] a bill declaring tenants in tail to hold their lands in fee simple. In the earlier times of the colony when lands were to be obtained for little or nothing, some provident individuals procured large grants, and, desirous of founding great families for themselves, settled them on their descendants in fee-tail. The transmission of this property from generation to generation in the same name raised up a distinct set of families who, being privileged by law in the perpetuation of their wealth were thus formed into a Patrician order, distinguished by the splendor and luxury of their establishments. From this order too the king habitually selected his Counsellors of State, the hope of which distinction devoted the whole corps to the interests & will of the crown. To annul this privilege, and instead of an Aristocracy of wealth, of more harm and danger, than benefit, to society, to make an opening for the aristocracy of virtue and talent, which nature has wisely provided for the direction of the interests of society, & scattered with equal hand through all it's conditions, was deemed essential to a well ordered republic. To effect it no violence was necessary, no deprivation of natural right, but rather an enlargement of it by a repeal of the law. For this would authorise the present holder to divide the property among his children equally, as his affections were divided; and would place them, by natural generation on the level of their fellow citizens. . . . The repeal of the laws of entail would prevent the accumulation and perpetuation of wealth in select families, and preserve the soil of the country from being daily more & more absorbed in Mortmain. The abolition of primogeniture, and equal partition of inheritances removed the feudal and unnatural distinctions which made one member of every family rich, and all the rest poor, substituting equal partition, the best of all Agrarian laws.

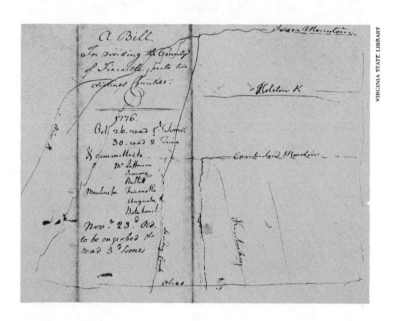

George Rogers Clark sketched this map of western Virginia on the cover of a bill to divide Fincastle County. Jefferson sponsored the bill at the request of settlers of the region; it passed despite the opposition of land speculators.

Edmund Pendleton, Speaker of the House, led the opponents of Jefferson's bill. Unlike Jefferson, Pendleton had not embarked on revolution in order to create a society in which he might lose his traditional position, and he defended the status quo brilliantly. Jefferson admired an able foe and left this account of Pendleton's part in the debates.

Autobiography, 1821

But this repeal was strongly opposed by Mr. Pendleton, who was zealously attached to ancient establishments;

and who, taken all in all, was the ablest man in debate I have ever met with. He had not indeed the poetical fancy of Mr. Henry, his sublime imagination, his lofty and overwhelming diction; but he was cool, smooth and persuasive; his language flowing, chaste & embellished, his conceptions quick, acute and full of resource; never vanquished; for if he lost the main battle, he returned upon you, and regained so much of it as to make it a drawn one, by dexterous maneuvres, skirmishes in detail, and the recovery of small advantages which, little singly, were important all together. You never knew when you were clear of him, but were harrassed by his perseverance until the patience was worn down of all who had less of it than himself.

In the House of Delegates Jefferson was more active as a leader in floor debates than he had been in the Continental Congress. Nevertheless, in Williamsburg, as in Philadelphia, he valued the aid of friends who helped present and support his views. The first of these "coadjutors in debate" was George Mason.

Autobiography, 1821

In giving this account of the laws of which I was myself the mover & draughtsman, I by no means mean to claim to myself the merit of obtaining their passage. I had many occasional and strenuous coadjutors in debate, and one most steadfast, able, and zealous; who was himself a host. This was George Mason, a man of the first order of wisdom among those who acted on the theatre of the revolution, of expansive mind, profound judgment, cogent in argument, learned in the lore of our former constitution, and earnest for the republican change on democratic principles. His elocution was neither flowing nor smooth, but his language was strong, his manner most impressive, and strengthened by a dash of biting cynicism when provocation made it seasonable.

George Wythe was another ally in the House that autumn, one whose "pure integrity, judgment and reasoning powers gave him great weight." He became the Speaker in 1777. Jefferson also found a new associate in twenty-five-year-old James Madison of Orange County. In 1821 Jefferson paid tribute to the man who had been his closest personal friend and his most able political collaborator for nearly half a century.

*Miniature by Charles W. Peale of
James Madison, who still looked
very young at the age of thirty-two*

Autobiography, 1821

Mr. Madison came into the House in 1776. a new member and young; which circumstances, concurring with his extreme modesty, prevented his venturing himself in debate before his removal to the Council of State in Nov. 77. From thence he went to Congress, then consisting of few members. Trained in these successive schools, he acquired a habit of self-possession which placed at ready command the rich resources of his luminous and discriminating mind, & of his extensive information, and rendered him the first of every assembly afterwards of which he became a member. Never wandering from his subject into vain declamation, but pursuing it closely in language pure, classical, and copious, soothing always the feelings of his adversaries by civilities and softness of expression, he rose to the eminent station which he held in the great National convention of 1787. And in that of Virginia which followed, he sustained the new constitution in all it's parts, bearing off the palm against the logic of George Mason and the fervid declamation of Mr. Henry. With these consummate powers were united a pure and spotless virtue which no calumny has ever attempted to sully. Of the powers and polish of his pen, and of the wisdom of his administration in the highest office of the nation, I need say nothing. They have spoken, and will for ever speak for themselves.

Passage of the bills to abolish entail and primogeniture was only the beginning of Jefferson's program to legislate an opening for an aristocracy of virtue and talent. The same day he proposed those changes, Jefferson had introduced a bill calling for a revision of Virginia's code of laws; in November he was named to a committee charged with carrying it out. The legislators doubtlessly expected the committee to correct inequities and discard archaic statutes; few shared Jefferson's conviction that the code "should be corrected, in all its parts, with a single eye to reason, and the good of those for whose government it was framed."

The five members of the committee of revisors conferred at Fredericksburg in January, 1777. George Mason and Thomas Ludwell Lee immediately disqualified themselves from the actual drafting of statutes because they were not lawyers. The other three—Jefferson, George Wythe, and Edmund Pendleton—assumed the monumental task of reworking Virginia's entire legal structure. Jefferson's assignment was to review the common law and English statutes passed before 1607. British laws enacted after the founding of Virginia were committed to Wythe; Pendleton undertook the revision of all laws passed in the colony of Virginia itself. The three worked independently until February, 1779. The report they presented in June, which became known as the *Revisal,* drew little immediate attention from the wartime legislators. But the legislature dipped into what Madison called "a mine of Legislative wealth" over the next few years, and by 1786 fifty-six of the original bills, with amendments, had been adopted. Jefferson described the *Revisal's* history in his *Autobiography.*

In the 1777 cartoon above, "Poor old England" was still trying to "reclaim wicked American Children"; that year the committee of revisors began working on its report (below).

REPORT

OF THE

COMMITTEE of REVISORS

APPOINTED BY THE

GENERAL ASSEMBLY

of *VIRGINIA*

In MDCCLXXVI.

PUBLISHED BY ORDER
OF THE
GENERAL ASSEMBLY,
AND
PRINTED BY DIXON & HOLT,
In the CITY of RICHMOND,
NOVEMBER MDCCLXXXIV.

Autobiography, 1821

In the execution of my part I thought it material not to vary the diction of the antient statutes by modernizing it, nor to give rise to new questions by new expressions. The text of these statutes had been so fully explained and defined by numerous adjudications, as scarcely ever now to produce a question in our courts. I thought it would be useful also, in all new draughts, to reform the style of the later British statutes, and of our own acts of assembly, which from their verbosity, their endless tautologies, their involutions of case within case, and parenthesis within parenthesis, and their multiplied efforts at certainty by *saids* and *aforesaids*, by *ors* and by *ands,* to make them more plain, do really render them more perplexed and incomprehensible, not only to common readers, but to the lawyers themselves. We were employed in this work from that time to Feb. 1779, when we met at Williamsburg, that is to say, Mr. Pendleton, Mr. Wythe & myself, and meeting day by day, we examined critically our several parts, sentence by sentence, scrutinizing and amending until we had agreed on the whole. . . . We had in this work brought so much of the Common law as it was thought necessary to alter, all the British statutes from Magna charta to the present day, and all the laws of Virginia, from the establishment of our legislature, in [1607] to the present time, which we thought should be retained, within the compass of 126 bills, making a printed folio of 90 pages only. Some bills were taken out occasionally, from time to time, and past; but the main body of the work was not entered on by the legislature until after the general peace, in 1785. when by the unwearied exertions of Mr. Madison, in opposition to the endless quibbles, chicaneries, perversions, vexations and delays of lawyers and demi-lawyers, most of the bills were passed by the legislature, with little alteration.

Many of the statutes Jefferson revised required little work, merely the deletion of references to the authority of the Crown and the substitution of references to state authority. But legislation in four areas was especially important to him. He hoped to introduce two humanitarian reforms in Virginia: the abolition of slavery and the modernization of the criminal codes. Jefferson had spent his life in a slave-owning society, and in his *Notes on Virginia* he offered a now famous indictment of this way of life and its tragic consequences for both master and slave.

Notes on Virginia, 1782

There must doubtless be an unhappy influence on the manners of our people produced by the existence of slavery among us. The whole commerce between master and slave is a perpetual exercise of the most boisterous passions, the most unremitting despotism on the one part, and degrading submissions on the other. Our children see this, and learn to imitate it; for man is an imitative animal. This quality is the germ of all education in him. From his cradle to his grave he is learning to do what he sees others do. If a parent could find no motive either in his philanthropy or his self-love, for restraining the intemperance of passion towards his slave, it should always be a sufficient one that his child is present. But generally it is not sufficient. The parent storms, the child looks on, catches the lineaments of wrath, puts on the same airs in the circle of smaller slaves, gives a loose to his worst of passions, and thus nursed, educated, and daily exercised in tyranny, cannot but be stamped by it with odious peculiarities. The man must be a prodigy who can retain his manners and morals undepraved by such circumstances. And with what execration should the statesman be loaded, who permitting one half the citizens thus to trample on the rights of the other, transforms those into despots, and these into enemies, destroys the morals of the one part, and the amor patriæ of the other. For if a slave can have a country in this world, it must be any other in preference to that in which he is born to live and labour for another: in which he must lock up the faculties of his nature, contribute as far as depends on his individual endeavours to the evanishment of the human race, or entail his own miserable condition on the endless generations proceeding from him. With the morals of the people, their industry also is destroyed. For in a warm climate, no man will labour for himself who can make another labour for him. This

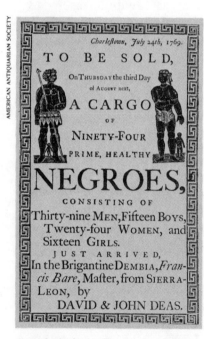

Broadside for a slave auction held at Charleston in August, 1769

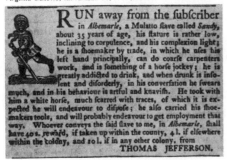

In 1769 Jefferson advertised for a runaway slave in the Gazette.

is so true, that of the proprietors of slaves a very small proportion indeed are ever seen to labour. And can the liberties of a nation be thought secure when we have removed their only firm basis, a conviction in the minds of the people that these liberties are of the gift of god? That they are not to be violated but with his wrath? Indeed I tremble for my country when I reflect that God is just: that his justice cannot sleep for ever: that considering numbers, nature and natural means only, a revolution of the wheel of fortune, an exchange of situation, is among possible events: that it may become probable by supernatural interference! The Almighty has no attribute which can take side with us in such a contest.

Jefferson was also convinced, however, that if the slaves were freed, there would be no hope for their integration into American society as full citizens.

Notes on Virginia, 1782

Deep rooted prejudices entertained by the whites; ten thousand recollections, by the blacks, of the injuries they have sustained; new provocations; the real distinctions which nature has made; and many other circumstances, will divide us into parties, and produce convulsions, which will probably never end but in the extermination of the one or the other race.

Thus, instead of advocating the simple abolition of slavery, Jefferson favored gradual emancipation and a carefully planned program to establish colonies for the freed slaves in areas distant from their former places of bondage. In 1779 public opinion in Virginia seemed ready to accept some modifications in the system; the assembly had already passed a law barring the further importation of slaves. Jefferson moved cautiously for more extensive reform and forty years later recalled the fate of the revisors' plan for an amendment to the bill they recommended.

Autobiography, 1821

The bill on the subject of slaves was a mere digest of the existing laws respecting them, without any intimation of a plan for a future & general emancipation. It was thought better that this should be kept back, and attempted only by way of amendment whenever the bill should be brought on. The principles of the amendment however were agreed on, that is to say, the freedom of

Louisiana slaves cutting sugar cane

all born after a certain day, and deportation at a proper age. But it was found that the public mind would not yet bear the proposition, nor will it bear it even at this day. Yet the day is not distant when it must bear and adopt it, or worse will follow. Nothing is more certainly written in the book of fate than that these people are to be free. Nor is it less certain that the two races, equally free, cannot live in the same government. Nature, habit, opinion has drawn indelible lines of distinction between them. It is still in our power to direct the process of emancipation and deportation peaceably and in such slow degree as that the evil will wear off insensibly, and their place be pari passu filled up by free white laborers. If on the contrary it is left to force itself on, human nature must shudder at the prospect held up.

Jefferson's other projected reform proved equally unsuccessful. He had anticipated opposition to his plan to end slavery, but he does not seem to have realized how controversial his program for a revised system of criminal law would be. His work on the portion of the Virginia code dealing with "the scale of punishments" probably took more of his time than any other statute assigned to him. His letter to George Wythe, written shortly before their final conference with Pendleton on the *Revisal*, not only gives Jefferson's views on criminal justice but also shows the system worked out by the committee for cooperating on their report.

Monticello Nov. 1. 1778.

I have got thro' the bill 'for proportioning crimes and punishments in cases heretofore capital,' and now inclose it to you with a request that you will be so good as scrupulously to examine and correct it, that it may be presented to our committee with as few defects as possible. In it's style I have aimed at accuracy, brevity and simplicity, preserving however the very words of the established law, wherever their meaning had been sanctioned by judicial decisions, or rendered technical by usage....And I must pray you to be as watchful over what I have not said as what is said; for the omissions of this bill have all their positive meaning. I have thought it better to drop in silence the laws we mean to discontinue, and let them be swept away by the general negative words of this, than to detail them in clauses of express repeal. By the side of the text I have written the notes I made, as I went along, for the benefit of my

Report of the Committee of Revisors, 1786; BEINECKE RARE BOOK AND MANUSCRIPT LIBRARY, YALE UNIVERSITY

Portion from a printed version of the "Bill for proportioning crimes and punishments" in the Revisal

own memory. They may serve to draw your attention to questions to which the expressions or the omissions of the text may give rise. . . .

I have strictly observed the scale of punishments settled by the Committee, without being entirely satisfied with it. The lex talionis [the law of punishment equivalent to the offense], altho' a restitution of the Common law, to the simplicity of which we have generally found it so advantageous to return will be revolting to the humanised feelings of modern times. An eye for an eye, and a hand for a hand will exhibit spectacles in execution whose moral effect would be questionable; and even the . . . punishment of the offending member, altho' long authorised by our law, for the same offence in a slave, has you know been not long since repealed in conformity with public sentiment. This needs reconsideration.

The committee apparently chose not to reconsider its decision on the principle of *lex talionis,* and this produced an odd dichotomy in Jefferson's final Bill for Proportioning Crimes and Punishments. His bill, in general, provided for less severe punishments than those dictated in old statutes, the death penalty being exacted only in cases of treason and murder. Other offenses that had been capital crimes would now be punished by hard labor. Grafted onto this modern, realistic bill was the committee's proposal that the rule of "an eye for an eye" be revived. When Jefferson's bill was finally considered by the legislature in 1784, however, it was not the *lex talionis* that drew criticism, but the plan for limiting crimes punishable by death. After the bill was defeated, James Madison wrote sadly, "Our old bloody code is . . . fully restored."

Neither slaves nor felons were to benefit from Jefferson's work on the revised statutes; public opinion had blocked reform in both areas. Jefferson believed, however, in the wisdom of Solon's remark, "that no more good must be attempted than the nation can bear." In later years he cited two other sections of the *Revisal* as his most important contributions: those on religious freedom and public education. They would lay the groundwork, he hoped, for an informed electorate.

Jefferson saw the alliance between Church and State as the enemy of personal freedom and a barrier to free inquiry. Thus, the protection of an individual's right to his own beliefs was essential to the enlightened society he hoped to see in Virginia. "In every country and in every age," he wrote, "the priest has been hostile to liberty. He is always in alliance with the despot, abetting his abuses in return for protection of his own." His determination to destroy the alliance already existing in his own state and his contempt for those who sought to control the thoughts of others were expounded in the book he wrote three years later.

Notes on Virginia, 1782

The error seems not sufficiently eradicated, that the operations of the mind, as well as the acts of the body, are subject to the coercion of the laws. But our rulers can have no authority over such natural rights, only as we have submitted to them. The rights on conscience we never submitted, we could not submit. We are answerable for them to our god. The legitimate powers of government extend to such acts only as are injurious to others. But it does me no injury for my neighbor to say there are twenty gods, or no god. It neither picks my pocket nor breaks my leg. If it be said his testimony in a court of justice cannot be relied on; reject it then, and be the stigma on him. Constraint may make him worse by making him a hypocrite, but it will never make him a truer man. It may fix him obstinately in his errors, but will not cure them. Reason and free enquiry are the only effectual agents against error. Give a loose to them, they will support the true religion by bringing every false one to their tribunal, to the test of their investigation. They are the natural enemies of error, and of error only. Had not the Roman government permitted free enquiry, Christianity could never have been introduced. Had not free enquiry been indulged, at the æra of the reformation, the corruptions of Christianity could not have been purged away. If it be restrained now, the present corruptions will be protected and new ones encouraged. Was the government to prescribe to us our medicine and diet, our bodies would be in such keeping as our souls are now. Thus in France the emetic was once forbidden as a medicine and the potatoe as an article of food. Government is just as infallible too when it fixes systems in Physics. Galileo was sent to the inquisition for affirming that the earth was a sphere: the government had declared it to be as flat as a trencher, and Galileo was obliged to abjure his error. This error however at length prevailed, the earth became a globe, and Descartes declared it was whirled round it's axis by a vortex. The government in which he lived was wise enough to see that this was no question of civil jurisdiction or we should all have been involved by authority in vortices. In fact, the vortices have been exploded, and the Newtonian principle of gravitation is now more firmly established on the basis of reason than it would be were the government to step in and to make it an article of necessary faith. Reason and experiment have been indulged, and error has fled before them. It is error alone which needs the support of government. Truth can stand by itself. Subject opinion to coercion: whom will you make your inquisitors? Fallible men; men governed by bad passions, by private as well as public reasons. And why subject it to coercion? To produce uniformity. But is uniformity of opinion desireable? No more than of face and stature. Introduce the bed of Procrustes then, and as there is danger that the large men may beat the small, make us all of a size by lopping the former and stretching the latter. Difference of opinion is advantageous in religion. The several sects perform the office of a Censor morum over each other. Is uniformity attainable? Millions of innocent men, women and children since the introduction of Christianity have been burnt, tortured, fined, imprisoned. Yet have we not advanced one inch towards uniformity. What has been the effect of coercion? To make one half the world fools and the other half hypocrites. To support roguery and error all over the earth. . . .

But every state, says an inquisitor, has established some religion. No two, say I, have established the same. Is this a proof of the infallibility of establishments? Our sister states of Pennsylvania and New York however have long subsisted without any establishment at all. The experiment was new and doubtful when they made it.

Virginia, HOWE

The legislature met in the old capitol in Williamsburg until 1780.

It has answered beyond conception. They flourish infinitely. Religion is well supported; of various kinds, indeed, but all good enough; all sufficient to preserve peace and order: or if a sect arises whose tenets would subvert morals, good sense has fair play and reasons and laughs it out of doors, without suffering the state to be troubled with it. They do not hang more malefactors than we do. They are not more disturbed with religious dissensions. On the contrary, their harmony is unparalleled, and can be ascribed to nothing but their unbounded tolerance, because there is no other circumstance in which they differ from every nation on earth. They have made the happy discovery that the way to silence religious disputes, is to take no notice of them. Let us too give this experiment fair play, and get rid while we may, of those tyrannical laws.

In Virginia an especially inequitable system had developed. In Jefferson's *Autobiography* he recited the history of religion in the colony. The first settlers, colonial Anglicans, had simply transplanted their homeland's established church, with all its legal privileges and special status. Soon, however, new immigrants had come: English dissenters, Scotch Presbyterians, and German Lutherans who resented contributing to the support of a faith to which they did not subscribe.

Autobiography, 1821

By the time of the revolution, a majority of the inhabitants had become dissenters from the established church, but were still obliged to pay contributions to support the Pastors of the minority. This unrighteous compulsion to maintain teachers of what they deemed religious errors was grievously felt during the regal government, and without a hope of relief. But the first republican legislature which met in 76. was crouded with petitions to abolish this spiritual tyranny. These brought on the severest contests in which I have ever been engaged. Our great opponents were Mr. Pendleton & Robert Carter Nicholas, honest men, but zealous churchmen. The petitions were referred to the Commee of the whole house on the state of the country; and after desperate contests in that Committee, almost daily from the 11th. of Octob. to the 5th. of December, we prevailed so far only as to repeal the laws which rendered criminal the maintenance of any religious opinions, the forbearance of repairing

THE COLLEGE OF WILLIAM AND MARY

Colonial Anglicans established churches such as the one above in Williamsburg's Bruton Parish.

to church, or the exercise of any mode of worship: and further, to exempt dissenters from contributions to the support of the established church; and to suspend, only until the next session levies on the members of that church for the salaries of their own incumbents. For altho' the majority of our citizens were dissenters, as has been observed, a majority of the legislature were churchmen. Among these however were some reasonable and liberal men, who enabled us, on some points, to obtain feeble majorities. But our opponents carried in the general resolutions of the Commee of Nov. 19. a declaration that religious assemblies ought to be regulated, and that provision ought to be made for continuing the succession of the clergy, and superintending their conduct. And in the bill now passed was inserted an express reservation of the question Whether a general assessment should not be established by law, on every one, to the support of the pastor of his choice; or whether all should be left to voluntary contributions; and on this question, debated at every session from 76. to 79. (some of our dissenting allies, having now secured their particular object, going over to the advocates of a general assessment) we could only obtain a suspension from session to session until 79. when the question against a general assessment was finally carried, and the establishment of the Anglican church entirely put down.

The disestablishment of the Church, however, was only a necessary first step, for the end of one state religion did not protect free inquiry for future generations. To protect his fellow citizens in their right to worship, or not to worship, as they chose, Jefferson drafted a Bill for Establishing Religious Freedom, which appeared as the eighty-second bill in the *Revisal*. The preamble opened with a sweeping declaration of man's right to freedom from coercion in matters of conscience. The bill went far beyond advocates of toleration and proclaimed full religious liberty. (The italicized words were not part of the version adopted by the legislature.)

A Bill for Establishing Religious Freedom [1779]

Well aware that the opinions and belief of men depend not on their own will, but follow involuntarily the evidence proposed to their minds; that Almighty God hath created the mind free, *and manifested his supreme will that free it shall remain by making it altogether insusceptible of restraint;* that all attempts to influence it by temporal punishments, or burthens, or by civil incapacitations, tend only to beget habits of hypocrisy and meanness, and are a departure from the plan of the holy author of our religion, who being lord both of body and mind, yet chose not to propagate it by coercions on either, as was in his Almighty power to do, *but to extend it by its influence on reason alone;* that the impious presumption of legislators and rulers, civil as well as ecclesiastical, who, being themselves but fallible and uninspired men, have assumed dominion over the faith of others, setting up their own opinions and modes of thinking as the only true and infallible, and as such endeavoring to impose them on others, hath established and maintained false religions over the greatest part of the world and through all time: That to compel a man to furnish contributions of money for the propagation of opinions which he disbelieves *and abhors,* is sinful and tyrannical; that even the forcing him to support this or that teacher of his own religious persuasion, is depriving him of the comfortable liberty of giving his contributions to the particular pastor whose morals he would make his pattern, and whose powers he feels most persuasive to righteousness; and is withdrawing from the ministry those temporary rewards, which proceeding from an approbation of their personal conduct, are an additional incitement to earnest and unremitting labours for the instruction of mankind; that our civil rights have no dependance on our religious opinions, any more than our opinions in physics or geometry; that therefore the proscribing any citizen as unworthy the public confidence by laying upon him an incapacity of being called to offices of trust and emolument, unless he profess or renounce this or that religious opinion, is depriving him injuriously of those privileges

Earliest printed text of the "Bill for establishing Religious Freedom"

and advantages to which, in common with his fellow citizens, he has a natural right; that it tends also to corrupt the principles of that *very* religion it is meant to encourage, by bribing, with a monopoly of worldly honours and emoluments, those who will externally profess and conform to it; that though indeed these are criminal who do not withstand such temptation, yet neither are those innocent who lay the bait in their way; *that the opinions of men are not the object of civil government, nor under its jurisdiction*; that to suffer the civil magistrate to intrude his powers into the field of opinion and to restrain the profession or propagation of principles on supposition of their ill tendency is a dangerous falacy, which at once destroys all religious liberty, because he being of course judge of that tendency will make his opinions the rule of judgment, and approve or condemn the sentiments of others only as they shall square with or differ from his own; that it is time enough for the rightful purposes of civil government for its officers to interfere when principles break out into overt acts against peace and good order; and finally, that truth is great and will prevail if left to herself; that she is the proper and sufficient antagonist to error, and has nothing to fear from the conflict unless by human interposition disarmed of her natural weapons, free argument and debate; errors ceasing to be dangerous when it is permitted freely to contradict them.

[The heart of the bill followed, concluding with an attempt to safeguard religious liberty from incursions by future legislators.]

We the General Assembly of Virginia do enact that no man shall be compelled to frequent or support any religious worship, place, or ministry whatsoever, nor shall be enforced, restrained, molested, or burthened in his body or goods, nor shall otherwise suffer, on account of his religious opinions or belief; but that all men shall be free to profess, and by argument to maintain, their opinions in matters of religion, and that the same shall in no wise diminish, enlarge, or affect their civil capacities.

And though we well know that this Assembly, elected by the people for the ordinary purposes of legislation only, have no power to restrain the acts of succeeding

Assemblies, constituted with powers equal to our own, and that therefore to declare this act irrevocable would be of no effect in law; yet we are free to declare, and do declare, that the rights hereby asserted are of the natural rights of mankind, and that if any act shall be hereafter passed to repeal the present or to narrow its operation, such act will be an infringement of natural right.

W hen this bill was first introduced in 1779, many Virginians saw it as a diabolical scheme, and it, too, waited several years for passage, aided by the "unwearied exertions" of James Madison. Jefferson was in France when his friend informed him that the bill had at last been approved, and he reported to Madison the enthusiasm aroused in the Old World by news of the statute. "It is honorable for us," he wrote Madison, "to have produced the first legislature which had the courage to declare that the reason of man may be trusted with the formation of his own opinions."

The reason of man, left in ignorance, would be imprisoned as cruelly as it had been by religious bigotry. Jefferson's Bill for the More General Diffusion of Knowledge, along with two others in the *Revisal*—one for a reform of William and Mary College and another for the creation of a public library—would have established an educational system designed to ensure an enlightened commonwealth of free men. In the Bill for the More General Diffusion of Knowledge, Jefferson proposed a pyramidal plan of educational opportunities. At the broad base, elementary schooling would be offered to all, regardless of ability to pay; higher levels of the system would be open to those selected for their outstanding performance in the lower levels.

Notes on Virginia, 1782

Another object of the Revisal is to diffuse knowledge more generally through the mass of the people. This bill proposes to lay off every county into small districts of five or six miles square called hundreds, and in each of them to establish a school for teaching reading, writing and arithmetic. The tutor to be supported by the hundred, and every person in it entitled to send their children three years gratis, and as much longer as they please, paying for it. These schools to be under a visitor, who is annually to chuse the boy, of best genius in the school, of those whose parents are too poor to give them further education, and to send him forward to one of the Grammar schools, of which twenty are proposed to be erected in different parts of the country, for teaching Greek, Latin,

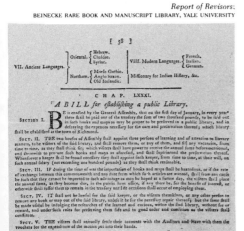

An important part of Jefferson's educational plan was the "Bill for establishing a public Library."

geography, and the higher branches of numerical Arithmetic. Of the boys thus sent in any one year, trial is to be made at the grammar schools one or two years, and the best genius of the whole selected and continued six years, and the residue dismissed. By this means twenty of the best geniusses will be raked from the rubbish annually, and be instructed, at the public expence so far as the Grammar schools go. At the end of six years instruction, one half are to be discontinued (from among whom the Grammar schools will probably be supplied with future masters); and the other half, who are to be chosen for the superiority of their parts and disposition, are to be sent and continued three years in the study of such sciences as they shall chuse, at William and Mary college, the plan of which is proposed to be enlarged, as will be hereafter explained, and extended to all the useful sciences. The ultimate result of the whole scheme of education would be the teaching all children of the state reading, writing, and common arithmetic: turning out ten annually, of superior genius, well taught in Greek, Latin, geography, and the higher branches of arithmetic: turning out ten others annually, of still superior parts, who, to those branches of learning, shall have added such of the sciences as their genius shall have led them to: the providing to the wealthier part of the people convenient schools, at which their children may be educated, at their own expence. — The general objects of this law are to provide an education adapted to the years, to the capacity, and the condition of every one, and directed to their freedom and happiness.... By that part of our plan which prescribes the selection of the youths of genius from among the classes of the poor, we hope to avail the state of those talents which nature has sown as liberally among the poor as the rich, but which perish without use, if not sought for and cultivated. — But of all the views of this law none is more important, none more legitimate, than that of rendering the people safe, as they are the ultimate, guardians of their own liberty. For this purpose the reading in the first stage, where *they* will receive their whole education, is proposed, as has been said, to be chiefly historical. History by apprising them of the past will enable them to judge of the future; it will avail them of the experience of other times and other nations; it will qualify them as judges of the actions

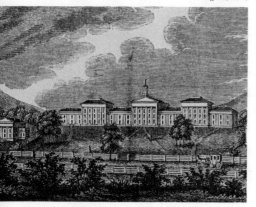

Virginia, HOWE

Liberty Hall, one of the oldest literary academies south of the Potomac, received an endowment and a new name—Washington Academy—in honor of George Washington in 1796; that year part of Jefferson's plan for public education was finally adopted.

and designs of men; it will enable them to know ambition under every disguise it may assume; and knowing it, to defeat its views. In every government on earth is some trace of human weakness, some germ of corruption and degeneracy, which cunning will discover, and wickedness insensibly open, cultivate, and improve. Every government degenerates when trusted to the rulers of the people alone. The people themselves therefore are its only safe depositories. And to render even them safe their minds must be improved to a certain degree.... The influence over government must be shared among all the people. If every individual which composes their mass participates of the ultimate authority, the government will be safe; because the corrupting the whole mass will exceed any private resources of wealth: and public ones cannot be provided but by levies on the people. In this case every man would have to pay his own price. The government of Great-Britain has been corrupted, because but one man in ten has a right to vote for members of parliament. The sellers of the government therefore get nine-tenths of their price clear. It has been thought that corruption is restrained by confining the right of suffrage to a few of the wealthier of the people: but it would be more effectually restrained by an extension of that right to such numbers as would bid defiance to the means of corruption.

Seven years after submitting the bill, Jefferson had come to believe that it was the most important bill in the *Revisal,* and he wrote to George Wythe from France concerning his hopes for its passage. His experience in Europe had confirmed his belief that no democracy could survive without an educated public.

Paris Aug. 13. 1786.
I think by far the most important bill in our whole code is that for the diffusion of knowlege among the people. No other sure foundation can be devised for the preservation of freedom, and happiness. If any body thinks that kings, nobles, or priests are good conservators of the public happiness, send them here. It is the best school in the universe to cure them of that folly. They will see here with their own eyes that these descriptions of men are an abandoned confederacy against the happiness of the mass of people. The omnipotence of their effect

cannot be better proved than in this country particularly, where notwithstanding the finest soil upon earth, the finest climate under heaven, and a people of the most benevolent, the most gay, and amiable character of which the human form is susceptible, where such a people I say, surrounded by so many blessings from nature, are yet loaded with misery by kings, nobles and priests, and by them alone. Preach, my dear Sir, a crusade against ignorance; establish and improve the law for educating the common people. Let our countrymen know that the people alone can protect us against these evils, and that the tax which will be paid for this purpose is not more than the thousandth part of what will be paid to kings, priests and nobles who will rise up among us if we leave the people in ignorance.

Virginians were not yet ready for public responsibility for education in the Confederation period. In 1796 a modified and fairly ineffective version of his plan for elementary schools was finally adopted, but the other provisions of the bill were ignored, as were his proposals for the reorganization of William and Mary and for the creation of a state-supported library.

Jefferson's early attempts to shape the development of Virginia government had met with little immediate success. His draft constitution had been all but ignored, and the most important sections of his contribution to the *Revisal* would be adopted piecemeal over the succeeding years or defeated. Shortly before the committee of revisors submitted its report on June 18, 1779, however, Jefferson's legislative efforts were rather abruptly curtailed. The assembly chose him to succeed Patrick Henry as Virginia's second governor. Henceforth, fundamental reform would be temporarily shelved as Jefferson concentrated all of his energy on meeting the daily crises of a wartime government.

List of articles purchased for the Governor's Palace at Williamsburg by Patrick Henry on May 29, 1779

Chapter 4

Wartime Governor

Jefferson certainly did not seek the opportunity to serve as Virginia's second governor. Under the constitution, the office had narrowly defined powers that would limit the executive's ability to implement any personal program for state policy. The thirty-six-year-old legislator probably did no more than allow his name to be put in nomination; he did not campaign among the assembly members who made the final selection in June, 1779. Any reluctance Jefferson may have felt over assuming the responsibilities of the governorship was justified. The next two years were to be an ordeal no one would have chosen to undergo, and the generally accepted view of Jefferson as a wartime governor is a critical one. It has been charged that he did not anticipate the problems that arose; that he was a poor administrator; that he hesitated to exceed the limits of his constitutional powers; that he exposed his state to invasion, humiliation, and the collapse of civil authority; in short, that he left office thoroughly discredited.

But the documentary record of his two one-year terms shows determined efforts to meet a military situation that would have strained the limits of the best equipped civil government. Despite the limits of his office, Jefferson devised a strategy for the defense of Virginia's frontier in the Northwest and an early warning system of communications in eastern Virginia. Despite the poor quality and inexperience of much of the military leadership sent to the Southern Department, Jefferson used his own knowledge of methods of frontier fighting and the ways of militia to organize what human and material resources Virginia did have. But he was continually hampered by the unwillingness and inability of Congress to provide adequate support and military leadership for the state's defense. Virginia had contributed to the "common cause," as Jefferson described it, with a flow of men, money, and supplies northward when the war centered in New England and the Middle States; but when British strategy shifted to the South in 1778, there seemed to be no reciprocal reinforcement. With scant assistance, the new governor was called on to preside over the most extensive territory in the new nation, bounded by a weakly defended western frontier and a particularly vulnerable coastline.

His term began with some personal embarrassment. On the first ballot in the legislature, he had received only a plurality of the votes; his two friends John Page and Thomas Nelson had won the rest. On the second ballot Jefferson narrowly defeated Page by a vote of sixty-seven to sixty-one. Both candidates were chagrined by this appearance of political rivalry, and Page immediately wrote to assure the governor-elect that he was not "influenced by some low dirty feelings" and promised to "do every thing in my Power to make your Administration easy and agreeable to you." Jefferson responded with equal warmth.

[Williamsburg, June 3, 1779]

It had given me much pain that the zeal of our respective friends should ever have placed you and me in the situation of competitors. I was comforted however with the reflection that it was their competition, not ours, and that the difference of the numbers which decided between us, was too insignificant to give you a pain or me a pleasure [had] our dispositions towards each other been such as to have admitted those sensations.

Jefferson's first message to the assembly seemed to reflect modest confidence as he assumed office.

[June 2, 1779]

In a virtuous and free state, no rewards can be so pleasing to sensible minds, as those which include the approbation of our fellow citizens. My great pain is, lest my poor endeavours should fall short of the kind expectations of my country; so far as impartiality, assiduous attention, and sincere affection to the great American cause, shall enable me to fulfill the duties of any appointment, so far I may, with confidence undertake; for all beyond, I must rely on the wise counsels of the General Assembly. . . .

In a letter to Richard Henry Lee two weeks later, however, Jefferson betrayed his fears of what the governorship might hold for him. Virginia was not threatened by British arms in the summer of 1779, but her economy, like those of all the other states, was endangered by depreciation of the Continental currency and by the assembly's desperate efforts to curb inflation with new and higher taxes.

Memorandum in Governor Jefferson's handwriting of "our forces supposed to be now in field," October, 1779

Williamsburgh June 17 1779

In a virtuous government, and more especially in times like these, public offices are, what they should be, burthens to those appointed to them which it would be wrong to decline, though foreseen to bring with them intense labor and great private loss....

It is a cruel thought that when we feel ourselves standing on the firmest ground in every respect, the cursed arts of our secret enemies combining with other causes, should effect, by depreciating our money, what the open arms of a powerful enemy could not. What is to be done? Taxation is become of no account, for it is foreseen that notwithstanding it's increased amount there will still be a greater deficiency than ever. I own I see no assured hope but in peace or a plentiful loan of hard money.

Three months after Jefferson took office, Congress voted to stop issuing new Continental currency. This was the first step in a program that would soon place the burden of supplying the army on individual states. Jefferson tried to cooperate fully with General Washington's requests for additional troops despite growing demands on the state.

Williamsburgh Nov. 28. 1779.

We have at present very pressing calls to send additional numbers of men to the Southward. No inclination is wanting in either the legislative or Executive powers to aid them, or to strengthen you: but we find it very difficult to procure men.

By the close of 1779, the state was hard pressed. Crops had failed, and for the first time Virginia had to import provisions. Jefferson and his Council of State sought relief by purchasing goods in Maryland, only to learn that their neighbor had seized the foodstuffs to insure adequate local supplies. On January 30 Jefferson made a vain appeal to Maryland authorities to release the desperately needed flour.

Wmsburg Jan. 30th. 1780.

A most distressing harvest in this State having reduced us to the necessity of either disbanding our military force or seeking subsistence for them else where we asked permission from Governor [Thomas] Johnson to purchase a quantity of flour in your State. He was pleased to grant it to the extent of two thousand Barrels. Mr. Smith who was intrusted with the purchase informed

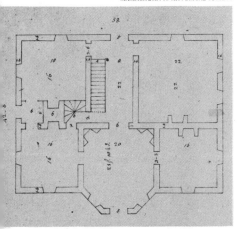

Jefferson made this plan, probably during 1779, for a proposed Governor's House in Richmond.

us at different times of purchases to the amount of sixteen hundred Barrels, of which about two hundred Barrels I believe have been forwarded.... we are now informed that the residue not forwarded has been seised by your State. Should it be detained we shall be in very great distress having absolutely no other means of supporting our military till harvest. The object of the act [of Maryland]...is patriotic and laudable. But I refer to your Excellency to consider whether the supply of the troops of the several states may not be considered as comprehended in the spirit of the act. The defence of the States severally makes up the general defence, no matter whether fed and paid at the generall or separate charge. Indeed I am induced to hope your Excellency will think our Stores not seizable within the Letter of the Law.... Accustomed at all other times to furnish Subsistence to others, it is the first instance wherein providence has exposed us to the necessity of asking leave to purchase it among our friends.

But as Jefferson's first term ended, Virginia's position became even more precarious. By April, 1780, when the state's capital was moved inland to Richmond, the British had opened a massive new campaign against Virginia's southern neighbors. A few days before Jefferson's reelection on June 2, he learned of the surrender of Charleston and the loss of the Virginia regiments garrisoned there. Adjusting quickly to his new role as leader of a state in danger of armed attack, he offered Washington a plan for improving the flow of military intelligence.

Richmond June 11th. 1780.

Our intelligence from the Southward is most lamentably defective. Tho' Charlestown has now been in the hands of the enemy a month, we hear nothing of their movements which can be relied on. Rumours are that they are penetrating Northward. To remedy this defect I shall immediately establish a line of expresses from hence to the neighborhood of their army, and send thither a sensible judicious gentleman to give us information of their movements.... There is really nothing to oppose the progress of the enemy Northward but the cautious principles of the military art. North Caroline is without arms. We do not abound. Those we have are freely imparted to them, but such is the state of their resources that they have not yet been able to move a single musket from this state

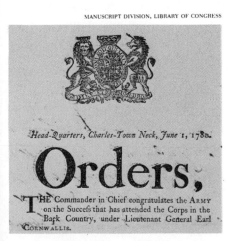

Sir Henry Clinton congratulates troops on South Carolina successes.

to theirs. All the waggons we can collect have been furnished to the Marquis de Kalb, and are assembling for the march of 2500 militia under Genl. Stevens of Culpeper who will move on the 19th, inst. I have written to Congress to hasten supplies of arms and military stores for the Southern states, and particularly to aid us with Cartridge paper and Cartridge boxes, the want of which articles, small as they are, renders our stores useless. The want of money cramps every effort.

By midsummer Lord Cornwallis's forces were camped near the North Carolina-Virginia border. With only the state militia left to guard Virginia, Jefferson had little reason to feel secure. Still he went about the routine of his office, acknowledging letters and searching for supplies for troops at the front. When the Chevalier de La Luzerne, the French minister at Philadelphia, announced the arrival of a French fleet, Jefferson replied that some force would be helpful in protecting Chesapeake Bay. But he kept the common cause uppermost, only hinting at the "temporary misfortunes" besetting the South.

Engraving of the Battle of Camden

Richmond August 31. 1780.

The interest of this State is intimately blended so perfectly the same with that of the others of the confederacy that the most effectual aid it can at any time receive is where the general cause most needs it. Of this yourself, Congress, and General Washington are so perfect judges that it is not for me to point it out. You can as well, and will as impartially judge whether the late disasters in the south call for any of those future aids so generously tendered in your Excellency's Letter. If their action in the north will have more powerful influence towards establishing our Independence, they ought not to be wished for in the south be the temporary misfortunes there what they will.

Among those "temporary misfortunes" was Horatio Gates's humiliating defeat at Camden, South Carolina, on August 16. The American commander's hurried retreat overshadowed his earlier triumphs in the war, and Virginia's troops had shared fully in the disgrace. Jefferson wrote ruefully to their commander, General Edward Stevens.

Richmond Septemr. 3rd. 1780

I sincerely condole with you on our late Misfortune which sits the heavier on my mind as being produced by my own Country Men. Instead of considering what is past, however, we are to look forward and prepare for the future.

The Continental government continued to demand reinforcements from Virginia but seemed disinclined to provide arms or supplies for these same troops. Vainly, Jefferson urged the president of Congress, Samuel Huntington, to come to terms with the situation.

Richmond Sep. 3. 1780.

Almost the whole of the small arms having been unfortunately lost in the last defeat, the men proposed for the feild will be unarmed, unless it is in your power to furnish arms. Indeed not only a sufficient number is wanting to arm the men now raising, but, as our stores will be exhausted in effecting that as far as they will go towards it, it seems indispensible that Congress should form a plentiful magazine of small arms, and other military stores that we may not be left an unarmed prey to the enemy, should our Southern misfortunes be not yet ended. Should any disaster like the late one, befal that army which is now collecting, and which will be so much weaker in regulars as that brave corps is lessened in the unequal conflict which was put upon them, the consequences will be really tremendous if we be found without arms. With a sufficiency of these, there can be no danger in the end. The losses of our brethren in the mean time may be great, the distresses of individuals in the neighborhood of the war will be cruel, but there can be no

Jefferson's responsibilities as war governor included commissioning an officer to recruit men (right) and urging Samuel Huntington (above) to replace the arms lost at Camden.

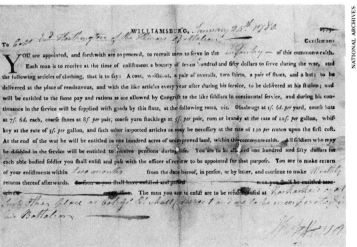

97

Richard Henry Lee by C. W. Peale

doubt of an ultimate recovery of the country. The scene of military operations has been hitherto so distant from these states, that their militia are strangers to the actual presence of danger. Habit alone will enable them to view this with familiarity, to face it without dismay; a habit which must be purchased by calamity, but cannot be purchased too dear. In the acquisition of this, other misfortunes may yet be to be incurred, for which we should be prepared. I am earnestly therefore to sollicit Congress for plentiful supplies of small arms, powder, flints, cartridge boxes and paper; and to pray that no moment may be lost in forwarding them.

In his public correspondence, Jefferson remained the determined, if hard-pressed, executive. But as he faced the autumn of 1780, he was privately near despair, and he confided his feelings to Richard Henry Lee.

> Richmond Sep. 13. 1780.
> The application requisite to the duties of the office I hold is so excessive, and the execution of them after all so imperfect, that I have determined to retire from it at the close of the present campaign. I wish a successor to be thought of in time who to sound whiggism can join perseverance in business, and an extensive knowlege of the various subjects he must superintend. Such a one may keep us above water even in our present moneyless situation.

Fortunately, Cornwallis was unable to take advantage of his position after his successes of the summer. His advance north from strongholds in South Carolina and Georgia was halted in the fall, and, except for a British coastal raid in October, Virginia would be safe for the rest of the year. In an effort to reorganize the shaken American army in the South, Washington named Nathanael Greene to replace Gates. Baron von Steuben, the famed drillmaster of Valley Forge, was left in charge of forces in Virginia for the winter.

In this comparatively stable situation, Jefferson found time to consider expanding military operations on another front; the lands claimed by Virginia to the north and west, a vast territory stretching to the Mississippi and the Great Lakes. Concerned by rumors of a secessionist movement in Kentucky and of a spring attack by Britain's Indian allies, Jefferson prepared instructions for young George Rogers Clark, Virginia's commander in the Northwest. Threatened by Cornwallis to the south and the British fleet to the east, Virginia would open a daring attack on the frontier.

George Rogers Clark (above) defended Virginia's western frontier while Lord Cornwallis (below) threatened from the south.

Richmond december 25th. 1780.

A powerful army forming by our enemies in the south renders it necessary for us to reserve as much of our militia as possible free to act in that quarter. At the same time we have reason to believe that a very extensive combination of British and Indian savages is preparing to invest our western frontier. To prevent the cruel murders and devastations which attend the latter species of war and at the same time to prevent it's producing a powerful diversion of our force from the southern quarter in which they mean to make their principal effort and where alone success can be decisive of their ultimate object, it becomes necessary that we aim the first stroke in the western country and throw the enemy under the embarrassments of a defensive war rather than labour under them ourselves. We have therefore determined that an expedition shall be undertaken under your command in a very early season of the approaching year into the hostile country beyond the Ohio, the principal object of which is to be the reduction of the British post at Detroit, and incidental to it the acquiring possession of Lake Erie....

...If that Post be reduced we shall be quiet in future on our frontiers, and thereby immense Treasures of blood and Money be saved; we shall be at leizure to turn our whole force to the rescue of our eastern Country from subjugation, we shall divert through our own Country a branch of commerce which the European States have thought worthy of the most important struggles and sacrifices, and in the event of peace on terms which have been contemplated by some powers we shall form to the American union a barrier against the dangerous extension of the British Province of Canada and add to the Empire of liberty an extensive and fertile Country thereby converting dangerous Enemies into valuable friends.

Jefferson's dreams of securing the Northwest were superseded a few days later when a British fleet commanded by the traitor Benedict Arnold was sighted in Chesapeake Bay. As the fleet moved up the James River, Jefferson called out the militia. It was obvious, however, that it was too late to organize a defense, and he arranged for the transfer of public stores and state records from Richmond. When he learned of the British landing at Westover on January 4, Jefferson took personal charge of these operations and then withdrew to await the next British move. In a report to Washington, he described the subsequent raid on the capital.

Richmond Jany 10. 1781.

They marched from Westover at 2 o Clock in the afternoon of the 4th. and entered Richmond at 1 o Clock in the afternoon of the 5th. A regiment of infantry and about 30 horse continued on without halting to the Foundery. They burnt that, the boring mill the magazine and two other houses, and proceeded to Westham, but nothing being in their power there they retired to Richmond. The next morning they burnt some buildings of public and some of private property, with what Stores remained in them, destroyed a great quantity of private Stores and about 12 o Clock retired towards Westover where they encamped within the neck the next day. The loss sustained is not yet accurately known. As far as I have been able to discover it consisted at this place in about 300 musquets, some soldiers clothing to a small amount some quarter masters Stores of which 120 sides of leather was the principal article, part of the artificers tools and 3 waggons, besides which 5 brass 4 [pounders] which we had sunk in the river were discovered to them, raised and carried off. At the Foundery we lost the greater part of the papers belonging to the auditors office, and of the books and papers of the Council office. About 5 or 6 tons as we conjecture of powder was thrown into the canal of which there will be a considerable saving by remanufacturing it. The roof of the foundery was burnt but the Stacks of Chimnies and furnaces not at all injured. The boring mill was consumed. Within less than 48 hours from the time of their landing and 19 from our knowing their destination they had penetrated 33 miles, done the whole injury and retired.

B Y

Brigadier-General ARNOLD,

A PROCLAMATION.

To the Officers and Soldiers of the Continental Army who have the real Interest of their Country at Heart; and who are determined to be no longer the Tools and Dupes of Congress, or of France.

Heading of a 1780 proclamation Benedict Arnold issued in New York inviting members of the Continental Army "to join His Majesty's Arms"

The Continental cause could survive the loss of some supplies and powder, but the reputation of Virginia and the state's new government was seriously damaged. After returning to Richmond, Jefferson conceived a plan for Arnold's capture. His letter outlining this scheme to General John Muhlenberg, second-in-command in Virginia, betrayed his feelings of personal humiliation at the turncoat general's hands. He deleted the material in italics before sending the instructions.

Richmond Jan. 31. 1781.

Acquainted as you are with the treasons of Arnold, I need say nothing for your information, or to give you a proper sentiment of them. You will readily suppose that it is above all things desireable to drag him from those under whose wing he is now sheltered. On his march to and from this place I am certain it might have been done with facility by men of enterprize and firmness. I think it may still be done though perhaps not quite so easily. Having peculiar confidence in the men from the Western side of the mountains, I meant as soon as they should come down to get the enterprize proposed to a chosen number of them, such whose courage and whose fidelity would be above all doubt. Your perfect knowlege of those men personally, and my confidence in your discretion, induce me to ask you to pick from among them proper characters, in such number as you think best, to reveal to them our desire, and engage them [to] undertake to seize and bring off this greatest of all traitors....*I shall be sorry to suppose that any circumstances may put it out of their power to bring him off alive after they shall have taken him and of course oblige them to put him to death. Should this happen, however, and America be deprived of the satisfaction of seeing him exhibited as a public spectacle of infamy, and of vengeance, I must give my approbation to their putting him to death. I do this considering him as a deserter from the American army, who has incurred the pain of death by his desertion, which we have a right to inflict on him and against which he cannot be protected by any act of our enemies. I distinguish him from an honourable enemy, who, in his station, would never be considered by me as a justifiable object of such an enterprize.*

German engraving of Arnold

Arnold remained at liberty while Jefferson did his best to meet Nathanael Greene's demands for men and supplies for the Southern Department. He hinted to Greene that the general might use his influence to gain aid from the other states.

Richmond Feb. 10. 1781.

Every moment however brings us new proofs that we must be aided by our Northern brethren. Perhaps they are aiding us, and we may be uninformed of it. I think near half the enemy's force are now in Virginia and the states South of that. Is half the burthen of opposition to rest on Virginia and N. Carolina? I trust you concur with us in crying aloud to Congress on this head.

A week later, Jefferson outlined the situation to Horatio Gates who had retired to his Berkeley County farm.

Broadside from Jefferson to county lieutenants in April, 1781, urged action against militia delinquents.

Richmond Feb. 17. 1781.

The situation of affairs here and in Carolina is such as must shortly turn up important events one way or the other. By letter from Genl. Greene dated Guilford C[ourt]house Feb. 10. Ld. Cornwallis rendered furious by the affair at the Cowpens [a British defeat] and surprise of George town [an American raid] had burnt his own waggons to enable himself to move with facility, had pressed on to the vicinities of the Moravian towns and was still advancing. The prisoners taken at the Cowpens were saved by a hair's breadth accident, and Greene was retreating. His force 2000 regulars and no militia, Cornwallis's 3000. Genl. [William] Davidson was killed in a skirmish. Arnold lies still at Portsmouth with 1500 men. A French 64. gun ship and 2 frigates of 36 each arrived in our bay three days ago. They would suffice to destroy the British shipping here (a 40., four frigates and a 20) could they get at them. But these are withdrawn up Elizabeth river which the 64. cannot enter. We have ordered about 700 riflemen from Washington Montgomery and Bedford and 500 common militia from Pittsylva. and Henry to reinforce Genl. Greene, and 500 new levies will march from Chestfd. C. H. in a few days. I have no doubt however that the Southwestern counties will have turned out in greater numbers before our orders reach them. I have been knocking at the door of Congress for aids of all kinds, but especially of arms ever since the middle of summer. The Speaker [of the House of Delegates, Benjamin] Harrison is gone to be heard on that subject. Justice indeed requires that we should be aided powerfully. Yet if they would repay us the arms we have lent them we should give the enemy trouble tho' abandoned to ourselves.

In March, as a response to Arnold's raid, the young Marquis de Lafayette was sent to Virginia in command of a detachment of the Continental Army. In a letter of welcome, Jefferson gave the French aristocrat fair warning of the problems he would face.

Richmond March 10th. 1781

Mild Laws, a People not used to war and prompt obedience, a want of the Provisions of War and means of procuring them render our orders often ineffectual, oblige us to temporize and when we cannot accomplish an object in one way to attempt it in another. Your knowledge of the Circumstances with a temper accomodated to them ensure me your Cooperation in the best way we can when we shall not be able to pursue the Way we would wish.

Lafayette adapted well to local customs and militiamen. At the end of April he helped turn back a British raid on Richmond, but his small force could not defend the capital against a major attack. Those members of the legislature who appeared for the May session promptly adjourned to the safety of Charlottesville. Jefferson remained in Richmond for a time, but any effective government ended in the face of Cornwallis's renewed march north from South Carolina. Added to this was the threat of another British force moving west from Petersburg. Even with invasion at hand, militia quotas were unfilled, and Jefferson gave Lafayette a discouraging report.

Richmond May 14th. 1781

I inclose you a State of the Counties who have been called on to come into the Field, some of them to perform a full Tour of Duty and others to make a present Opposition to the Junction of the two hostile Armies. The Delay and Deficiencies of the first are beyond all expectation and if the Calls on the latter do not produce sufficient Reinforcements to you, I shall candidly acknowledge that it is not in my power to do any thing more than to represent to the General Assembly that unless they can provide more effectually for the Execution of the Law it will be vain to call on Militia. I could perhaps do something by Reprimands to the County Lieutenants by repeating and even increasing the Demands on them by way of penalty, if you would be so good as to have returns made to me once a week or at any other stated periods of the particular number of men from each County. Without these we can never know what Counties obey our Calls or how long your men are to continue with you so as to provide in time.

Sketch by Dupré for a medal in honor of Daniel Morgan, who led the defeat of the British at Cowpens

The next day Jefferson joined his family at Tuckahoe. The legislature had failed to reorganize at Charlottesville, and in the last weeks of his governorship, Jefferson presided over a state without any effective legislative or executive program to meet Cornwallis's advance. On May 28 the assembly finally made a quorum, but in a letter to Washington of that date, Jefferson made it clear that Virginia could not survive without substantial aid from her kindred states and he pleaded for Washington himself to help defend his native state.

> Charlottsville May 28th. 1781.
>
> I make no doubt you will have heard, before this shall have the honour of being presented to Your Excellency, of the junction of Lord Cornwallis with the force at Petersburg under Arnold who had succeeded to the command on the death of Major General Philips. I am now advised that they have evacuated Petersburg, joined at Westover a Reinforcement of 2000 Men just arrived from New York, crossed James River, and on the 26th. Instant were three Miles advanced on their way towards Richmond.... Your Excellency will judge from this state of things and from what you know of your own Country what it may probably suffer during the present Campaign. Should the Enemy be able to produce no opportunity of annihilating the Marquis's Army a small proportion of their force may yet restrain his movements effectually while the greater part is employed in detachment to waste an unarmed Country and to lead the minds of the people to acquiesence under those events which they see no human power prepared to ward off. We are too far removed from the other scenes of war, to say whether the main force of the Enemy be within this State, but I suppose they cannot any where spare so great an Army for the operations of the field: Were it possible for this Circumstance to justify in Your Excellency a determination to lend us Your personal aid, it is evident from the universal voice that the presence of their beloved Countryman, whose talents have been so long successfully employed in establishing the freedom of kindred States, to whose person they have still flattered themselves they retained some right, and have ever looked up as their dernier resort in distress, that your appearance among them I say would restore full confidence of salvation, and would render them equal to whatever is not impossible.... A few days will bring to me that period of relief which the Constitution has prepared for those

oppressed with the labours of my office, and a long declared resolution of relinquishing it to abler hands has prepared my way for retirement to a private station: still however as an individual citizen I should feel the comfortable effects of your presence. . . .

Five days later Jefferson's second term as governor expired. The legislature neglected to choose a successor, and he remained in Charlottesville to finish up official business before returning to nearby Monticello on Sunday, June 3. That same day Banastre Tarleton, Cornwallis's brilliant cavalry commander, began a forced march from Hanover to Charlottesville to execute a surprise attack that Cornwallis hoped would destroy what remained of Virginia's government. Colonel John Jouett happened on Tarleton's party and began a legendary ride to warn Jefferson and the assembly of the danger. Jouett outraced Tarleton, reaching Monticello before dawn on June 5, and then covered the three miles to Charlottesville to warn the drowsy assemblymen. All but seven made their escape to Staunton—still without a governor. Jefferson arranged for his family to take refuge at a friend's estate at Blenheim and followed them there that evening. Seven years later Jefferson gave his account of Tarleton's raid to the historian William Gordon.

Paris July 16. 1788.

You ask, in your letter of Apr. 24. details of my sufferings by Colo. Tarleton. I did not suffer by him. On the contrary he behaved very genteelly with me. On his approach to Charlottesville which is within 3. miles of my house at Monticello, he dispatched a troop of his horse under Capt. Mc.leod with the double object of taking me prisoner with the two Speakers of the Senate and Delegates who then lodged with me, and remaining there. in vedette, my house commanding a view of 10. or 12. counties round about. He gave strict orders to Capt. Mc.leod to suffer nothing to be injured. The troop failed in one of their objects, as we had notice so that the two speakers had gone off about two hours before their arrival at Monticello, and myself with my family about five minutes. But Captn. Mc.leod preserved every thing with sacred care during about 18. hours that he remained there. Colo. Tarleton was just so long at Charlottesville being hurried from thence by news of the rising of the militia, and by a sudden fall of rain which threatened to swell the river and intercept his return. In general he did little injury to the inhabitants on that short and hasty excur-

Silhouette of John Jouett

sion, which was of about 60. miles from their main army then in Spotsylvania, and ours in Orange.

[But Jefferson's admiration for Tarleton did not extend to Cornwallis, who joined the advance party of raiders a few days later.]

Lord Cornwallis then proceeded to the point of fork, and encamped his army from thence all along the main James river to a seat of mine called Elkhill, opposite to Elk island and a little below the mouth of the Byrd creek.... He remained in this position ten days, his own head quarters being in my house at that place. I had had time to remove most of the effects out of the house. He destroyed all my growing crops of corn and tobacco, he burned all my barns containing the same articles of the last year, having first taken what corn he wanted, he used, as was to be expected, all my stocks of cattle, sheep, and hogs for the sustenance of his army, and carried off all the horses capable of service: of those too young for service he cut the throats, and he burnt all the fences on the plantation, so as to leave it an absolute waste. He carried off also about 30. slaves: had this been to give them freedom he would have done right, but it was to consign them to inevitable death from the small pox and putrid fever then raging in his camp. This I knew afterwards to have been the fate of 27. of them. I never had news of the remaining three, but presume they shared the same fate. When I say that Lord Cornwallis did all this, I do not mean that he carried about the torch in his own hands, but that it was all done under his eye, the situation of the house, in which he was, commanding a view of every part of the plantation, so that he must have seen every fire. I relate these things on my own knowlege in a great degree, as I was on the ground soon after he left it. He treated the rest of the neighborhood somewhat in the same stile, but not with that spirit of total extermination with which he seemed to rage over my possessions. Wherever he went, the dwelling houses were plundered of every thing which could be carried off. Lord Cornwallis's character in England would forbid the belief that he shared in the plunder. But that his table was served with the plate thus pillaged from private houses can be proved by many hundred eye witnesses. From an

Banastre Tarleton

estimate I made at that time on the best information I could collect, I supposed the state of Virginia lost under Ld. Cornwallis's hands that year about 30,000 slaves, and that of these about 27,000 died of the small pox and camp fever, and the rest were partly sent to the West Indies and exchanged for rum, sugar, coffee and fruits, and partly sent to New York, from whence they went at the peace either to Nova Scotia, or England. From this last place I believe they have been lately sent to Africa. History will never relate the horrors committed by the British army in the *Southern* states of America. They raged in Virginia 6. months only, from the middle of April to the middle of October 1781. when they were all taken prisoners, and I give you a faithful specimen of their transactions for 10. days of that time and in one spot only.... I suppose their whole devastations during those 6. months amounted to about three millions sterling.

Thomas Nelson, Jr.

In later years Jefferson's enemies blamed him for the interruption in effective state government that occurred, and critics charged him with abdicating official duty in his last-minute escape from Monticello. But as one Jefferson biographer, Dumas Malone, has pointed out, "It would be nearer the truth to say that the government abandoned him than that he abandoned the government." Even after the legislators reached Staunton, they seemed in no hurry to choose a new executive: five days passed before they elected Thomas Nelson, Jr.

Jefferson was less concerned about attacks on his behavior during the crisis of June, 1781, than he was by another result of Tarleton's raid: a move in the assembly for the creation of a dictator. Many of Patrick Henry's supporters argued that only this resort would give Virginia the leadership her governors had failed to provide by constitutional methods. Jefferson had no patience with those who argued that democracy could not function in an emergency or that such a crisis justified suspending the constitution. His ideal of a free society was not one that could be casually abandoned in time of peril and effectively resurrected on the return of safety. In his *Notes on Virginia*, Jefferson recalled the history of the attempts to impose temporary tyranny in Virginia.

Notes on Virginia, 1782

In December 1776, our circumstances being much distressed, it was proposed in the house of delegates to create a *dictator*, invested with every power legislative, executive and judiciary, civil and military, of life and of

Listing of Jefferson's traveling expenses and payment for "13 days attendance" at the December, 1781, session of the House of Delegates

death, over our persons and over our properties: and in June 1781, again under calamity, the same proposition was repeated, and wanted a few votes only of being passed. — One who entered into this contest from a pure love of liberty, and a sense of injured rights, who determined to make every sacrifice, and to meet every danger, for the re-establishment of those rights on a firm basis, who did not mean to expend his blood and substance for the wretched purpose of changing this master for that, but to place the powers of governing him in a plurality of hands of his own choice, so that the corrupt will of no one man might in future oppress him, must stand confounded and dismayed when he is told, that a considerable portion of that plurality had meditated the surrender of them into a single hand, and, in lieu of a limited monarch, to deliver him over to a despotic one! ... Necessities which dissolve a government, do not convey its authority to an oligarchy or a monarchy. They throw back, into the hands of the people, the powers they had delegated, and leave them as individuals to shift for themselves. A leader may offer, but not impose himself, nor be imposed on them. Much less can their necks be submitted to his sword, their breath be held at his will or caprice. The necessity which should operate these tremendous effects should at least be palpable and irresistible. Yet in both instances, where it was feared, or pretended with us, it was belied by the event. ... The very thought alone was treason against the people; was treason against mankind in general; as rivetting for ever the chains which bow down their necks, by giving to their oppressors a proof, which they would have trumpeted through the universe, of the imbecility of republican government, in times of pressing danger, to shield them from harm. Those who assume the right of giving away the reins of government in any case, must be sure that the herd, whom they hand on to the rods and hatchet of the dictator, will lay their necks on the block when he shall nod to them. But if our assemblies supposed such a resignation in the people, I hope they mistook their character.

The scheme's narrow defeat did not end Jefferson's tribulations that summer. By late June he had moved his wife and daughters to Poplar Forest, an estate he had inherited from his father-in-law in Bedford County, so that he could recuperate there from a fall from a horse. One of his first tasks after his recovery was meeting a proposed inquiry "into the Conduct of the Executive of this State for the last twelve Months." He sent a curt note to young George Nicholas, who had introduced the inquiry resolution in the assembly.

> Monticello July 28, 1781.
>
> I am informed that a resolution on your motion passed the House of Delegates requiring me to render account of some part of my administration without specifying the act to be accounted for. As I suppose that this was done under the impression of some particular instance or instances of ill conduct, and that it could not be intended just to stab a reputation by a general suggestion under a bare expectation that facts might be afterwards hunted up to boulster it, I hope you will not think me improper in asking the favor of you to specify to me the unfortunate passages in my conduct which you mean to adduce against me, that I may be enabled to prepare to yield obedience to the house while facts are fresh in my memory and witnesses and documents are in existence.

Silhouette of George Nicholas

Nicholas did present some charges, but he did not even attend the House session in December when Jefferson presented his defense. The legislature closed the matter by passing a resolution of "sincere thanks" to Jefferson "for his impartial, upright, and attentive administration whilst in office." Despite this public vindication, Jefferson remained bitter, and he confided to a friend that he suspected Patrick Henry of having engineered the attack on his integrity.

> Richmond Dec. 24. [1781]
>
> You have heard probably of the vote of the H. of Delegates at the last session of assembly. I came here in consequence of it, and found neither accuser nor accusation. They have acknowledged by an express vote that the former one was founded on *rumours* only, for which no foundation can be discovered: they have thanked &c. The trifling body who moved this matter was below contempt; he was more an object of pity. His natural ill-temper was the tool worked with by another hand. He [Nicholas] was like the minners which go in and out of the fundament of the whale [Henry]. But the whale himself was discoverable enough by the turbulence of the water under which he moved.

Months before he was given a chance to defend his administration, Jefferson had decided to retire from public life. He confessed to Edmund Randolph in Congress that not even a diplomatic appointment could shake his determination to withdraw.

> Monticello Sep. 16. 1781.
>
> Were it possible for me to determine again to enter into public business there is no appointment whatever which would have been so agreeable to me. But I have taken my final leave of every thing of that nature, have retired to my farm, my family and books from which I think nothing will ever more separate me. A desire to leave public office with a reputation not more blotted than it has deserved will oblige me to emerge at the next session of our assembly and perhaps to accept of a seat in it, but as I go with a single object, I shall withdraw when that shall be accomplished.

Jefferson's withdrawal seemed justified. Five years of service to Virginia had brought him little gratitude or popular recognition. At the end of 1781, his efforts to reform the state's legal system had stalled and his wartime efforts had brought sharp criticism from his fellow Virginians. A man as conscientious as he could not excuse the apparent failure of his administration by citing the obvious fact that probably no one else could have done more to prepare Virginia for invasion or contribute to the common cause.

Indeed Jefferson's commitment to that cause doubtless irritated many who placed local above national interests. Jefferson did not see Virginia as an isolated political entity, divorced from the needs of the other states. He had hoped to give the commonwealth laws that would have made it a model of progressive ideas and liberal policies. But few had shared his vision, and too few other state leaders had acknowledged or acted on a community of interests. In the short-term view, Jefferson had failed as a state political leader more because of his commitment to his ideals than because he had forsaken his responsibilities.

A Picture Portfolio

America's Renaissance Man

SON OF VIRGINIA

No one who came into contact with Thomas Jefferson could fail to be impressed by the wide range of his interests and knowledge. The Marquis de Chastellux, after a visit to Monticello, summed it up: "No object had escaped Mr. Jefferson; it seemed as if from his youth he had placed his mind, as he had done his house, on an elevated situation, from which he might contemplate the universe." His classic *Notes on Virginia*, written in 1781, answered twenty-three specific questions about his native state and securely established Jefferson's reputation as a universal scholar and perhaps the most learned man in America. He presented a published copy with an inscription (below, left) to the Marquis de Barbé-Marbois who had originally posed the questions on behalf of the French government which was eager to learn about the new country. The subjects listed on the title page (below, right) reveal the vast scope of his knowledge. Among the natural wonders of Virginia, the Natural Bridge (right), rising 215 feet over Cedar Creek, was described as "the most sublime." Jefferson had owned it since 1773 and extolled it further: "so beautiful an arch, so elevated, so light, and springing, as it were, up to heaven, the rapture of the Spectator is really indiscribable!"

Th:Jefferson having had a few copies of these Notes printed to be offered to some of his friends and to some other estimable characters beyond that line, presents one to Monsr de Marbois, under the most just of all titles, his right to the original. unwilling to expose them to the public eye, he asks the favour of Monsr de Marbois to put them into the hands of no person on whose care & fidelity he cannot rely to guard them against publication.

NOTES on the state of VIRGINIA;

written in the year 1781, somewhat corrected and enlarged in the winter of 1782, for the use of a Foreigner of distinction, in answer to certain queries proposed by him respecting

1. Its boundaries	page 1
2. Rivers	3
3. Sea ports	27
4. Mountains	28
5. Cascades and caverns	33
6. Productions mineral, vegetable and animal	41
7. Climate	134
8. Population	151
9. Military force	162
10. Marine force	165
11. Aborigines	166
12. Counties and towns	171
13. Constitution	173
14. Laws	135
15. Colleges, buildings, and roads	275
16. Proceedings as to tories	285
17. Religion	287
18. Manners	298
19. Manufactures	301
20. Subjects of commerce	304
21. Weights, Measures and Money	311
22. Public revenue and expences	313
23. Histories, memorials, and state-papers	322

MDCCLXXXII.

HOME ON A MOUNTAINTOP

When Jefferson was twenty-six, he began a project that was to give him great pleasure throughout a long life. Picking the highest site on his Albemarle County land, he began to build; the sketch at right, above, is the first version of the house. "Of prospect I have a rich profusion...," he wrote: "mountains distant & near, smooth & shaggy, single & in ridges, a little river hiding itself among the hills so as to shew in lagoons only, cultivated grounds under the eye and two small villages." The watercolor above shows the view from the north front of the house he called Monticello, Italian for little mountain. Surrounding this summit home lay five thousand acres of Jefferson's land on which he lavished his agricultural and horticultural skills. The sketch at right is of a plan he made in 1772 of the house and garden; additions to it were continued after he retired from public office in 1809. He adored gardening and wrote to Charles Willson Peale in 1811 that "no occupation is so delightful to me as the culture of the earth, and no culture comparable to that of the garden.... though an old man, I am but a young gardener."

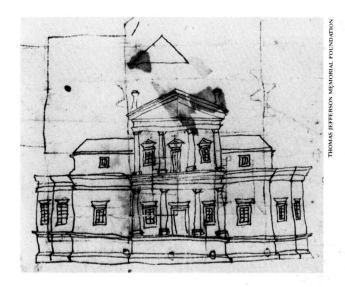

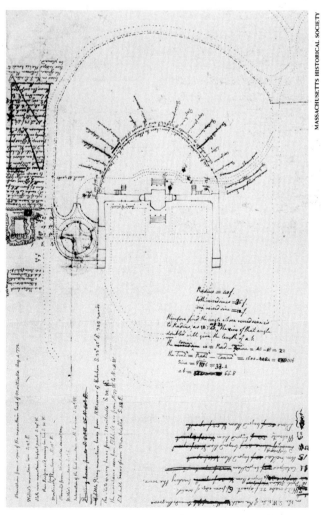

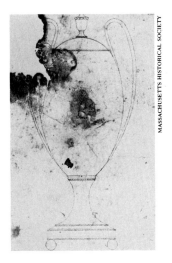

BEAUTY AND UTILITY

"Mr. Jefferson is the first American who has consulted the fine arts to know how he should shelter himself from the weather," observed a foreign visitor after seeing Monticello (right) for the first time. The interior, too, reflected Jefferson's appreciation for beautiful things, among them a magnificent silver coffee urn made from his own design (above). But Jefferson was also a highly practical man and loved to devise ways to improve the workings of things and thereby make life easier and more enjoyable. His house contained dumbwaiters that brought wine from the cellars and a wall panel with a revolving buffet from the kitchen to the dining room. Jefferson sat in a modified form of a swivel chair of his design with his feet on a chaise lounge over which a work table could be comfortably drawn. He had built for himself an adjustable music stand and architect's drafting desk. A notable improvement in moldboard plows resulted from his sketch at far right, bottom, of one "of least resistance." Above it are his designs for an apple mill and a fireplace that could be used to heat every apartment in a house. He even turned his fertile mind to the design of a "hominy beater," as shown in the detail at right from a letter to Charles Willson Peale. Inside and out, Monticello reflected to an extraordinary extent the taste and ingenuity of its architect, landscaper, builder, cabinetmaker, and proud owner.

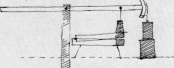

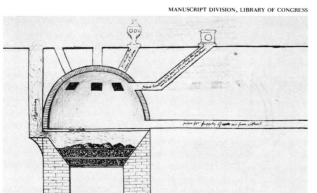

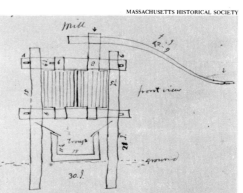

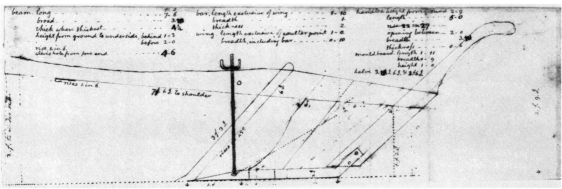

"ARCHITECTURE IS MY DELIGHT"

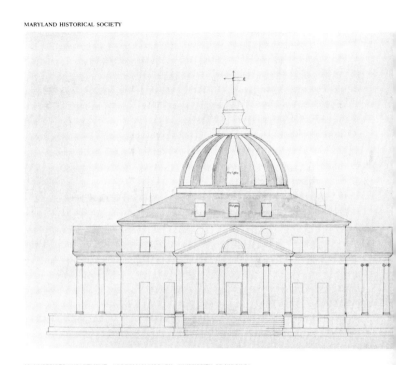

In the *Notes on Virginia* Jefferson had written that "the only public buildings worthy of mention are the capitol, the palace, the college, and the hospital for lunatics, all of them in Williamsburg." He became a one-man task force to rectify that situation and was the first in America, and indeed one of the first anywhere, to make use of classical models. While serving as a minister in Paris he was asked to submit a design for a state capitol in Richmond; he took for his model "what is called the Maison Quarré of Nismes [left, above], one of the most beautiful, if not the most beautiful and precious morsel of architecture left us by antiquity." When Benjamin Latrobe made the watercolor sketch at left of Richmond in 1796, Jefferson's graceful building dominated the landscape, and one could gaze at it "like a lover at his mistress," which is how Jefferson had described his first encounter with the Maison Carrée in 1787. Not all of Jefferson's designs were successful, however. When a national capital was planned on the banks of the Potomac, Jefferson anonymously submitted a design (right, above) in the competition for the President's House. But it lost out to the simpler one of James Hoban. "Architecture is my delight," Jefferson admitted, "and putting up and pulling down one of my favorite amusements." Near the end of his long life he planned and executed the beautiful University of Virginia at Charlottesville. The Rotunda (right, below) housed the library and was first used as a banquet hall to honor the Marquis de Lafayette when he visited America in 1824.

"ACADEMICAL VILLAGE"

Jefferson's election as Rector of the University of Virginia in 1819 capped four decades of his efforts to establish "a system of general instruction, which shall reach every description of our citizens from the richest to the poorest." The "academical village" (above) which he designed was only two miles from Monticello, visible on its mountaintop right of center.

Exhuming the First American Mastodon BY CHARLES WILLSON PEALE; THE PEALE MUSEUM, BALTIMORE

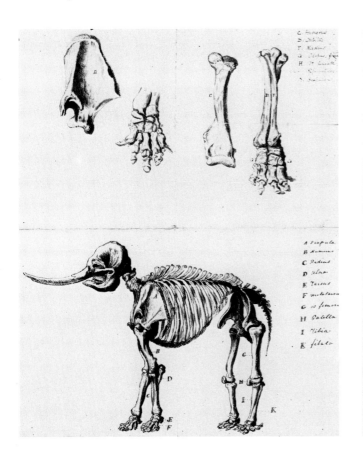

NATURAL HISTORIAN

In 1792, when Jefferson was Secretary of State, he had the honor of having a plant named for him, the *Jeffersonia diphylla* (above, right). The citation stated in part that "in botany and zoology, the information of this gentleman is equalled by that of few persons in the United States." He had been elected to membership in the prestigious American Philosophical Society in 1780 (the date on the copy of his certificate above, far left, is in error) and served as its third president for seventeen years. Jefferson succeeded David Rittenhouse (above, left), whom he considered "second to no astronomer living" and who, along with Washington and Franklin, he felt offered proof to doubting Europeans that America could indeed produce geniuses. While he was its head, the Society provided Charles Willson Peale with financial support to undertake the excavation of some mammoth bones in Ulster County, New York, a scene the versatile artist later put on canvas (left). The success of the venture can be surmised from the drawing (above) of the "first fossil skeleton ever mounted in America." Thirty feet long, it was displayed in Peale's Natural History Museum in Philadelphia and was an instant sensation.

123

BY MATHER BROWN, 1786; CHARLES FRANCIS ADAMS, BOSTON

MAN OF THE WORLD

Jefferson was appointed a minister plenipotentiary abroad in 1784 and Minister to France a year later. He had written Lafayette of his desire to see countries "whose improvements in science, in arts, and in civilization" he had long admired and he was not disappointed. He wrote from Paris of "how much I enjoy their architecture, sculpture, painting, music. . . . It is in these arts they shine." Jefferson also found romantic companionship for the first time since the death of his wife four years earlier. A vulnerable forty-three, he became infatuated with the lovely, talented, twenty-seven-year-old Maria Cosway (above, right) who was visiting France with her artist husband. For a blissful month Jefferson and Maria together enjoyed the wonders of Paris, including the superb domed market (above, far right) and the Tuileries gardens (right). Although this brief idyll was to contain no future, it revived Jefferson's spirit and lessened the pain so clearly revealed in the 1786 portrait by Mather Brown (above).

OBSERVANT TRAVELER

Jefferson's inquisitive mind was constantly rewarded during his years in France. Sitting on a balustrade of the Tuileries, he watched with fascination the building of the elegant Hôtel de Salm (above). Declaring himself "violently smitten," he filed away his impressions to recall when making additions to Monticello. He witnessed the balloon craze that swept Paris and reported on the first disaster when two Frenchmen tried to cross the English Channel only to have their balloon catch fire and fall, crushing them "to atoms" (above, right). Following his romance with Maria Cosway, during which he had dislocated his wrist in an accident, doctors advised a trip to Aix-en-Provence (right) to partake of the waters. Jefferson took this opportunity to make a three-month journey to southern France and northern Italy. He made detailed notes of his travels and wrote friends that "architecture, painting, sculpture, antiquities [such as the Roman aqueduct at Lyon (far right)], agriculture, the condition of the labouring poor fill all my moments."

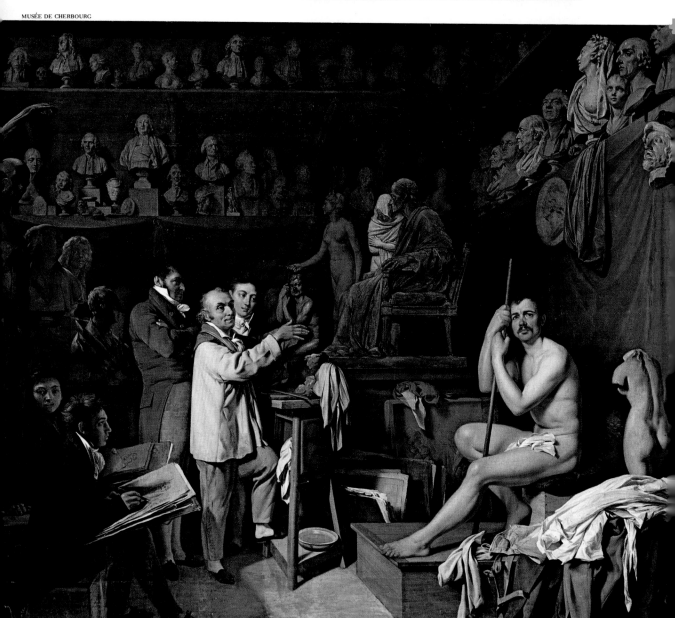

CONNOISSEUR OF THE ARTS

Although music for Jefferson was "the favorite passion of my soul" and the operas and concerts of Paris his delight, he derived considerable pleasure, too, in expanding his knowledge of the other fine arts in the magnificent museums and ateliers surrounding him. He was quick to recommend the sculptor Jean Antoine Houdon for the commission by the Virginia assembly to carve a heroic statue of Washington, for he considered him "unrivalled in Europe." Houdon, seen in his atelier (left), not only did Washington but also made the excellent bust of Jefferson himself (left, above) and, among many others, one of his predecessor as Minister to France, the venerable Benjamin Franklin. Jefferson's bust can be seen in the painting at left on the rear shelf; Franklin and a small bust of Washington, on the shelf to the right. Jefferson visited the biennial expositions held in the salon of the Louvre where paintings were exhibited from ceiling to floor (above), and he thoroughly enjoyed the soirées attended by the leading arbiters of artistic taste of this most cosmopolitan of cities. He wrote of France, after his five years packed full of experiences he was uniquely able to enjoy and absorb: "Ask the travelled inhabitant of any nation, in what country on earth would you rather live?—Certainly in my own, where are all my friends, my relations, and the earliest & sweetest affections and recollections of my life. Which would be your second choice? France."

Chapter 5

Public Service and Private Misery

By the summer of 1781, Jefferson's services to Virginia had apparently been repudiated and he returned to Albemarle to superintend Monticello in the company of his wife and daughters, who had often suffered by his absences in earlier years. Certainly he would eventually have overcome his resentment of the attacks by his political enemies, but had he been left to recover slowly from his harrowing experiences as governor and had his personal happiness at Monticello continued uninterrupted, he might well have been a figure of less imposing historical importance. Instead, his personal life was shattered by tragedy, and his deep-rooted impulse to serve "the holy cause of liberty" became dominant once again. His dedication to the new order was firm, stifled only momentarily by sorrow and disillusionment.

None of this could be foreseen in 1781, and Jefferson began his retirement by declining an appointment to the commission to negotiate peace with Britain, citing among other reasons his "indispensable obligation of being within this state till a later season of the present year" to defend himself in the assembly. Renouncing that diplomatic post caused him some personal anguish, however, as he revealed in a letter to the Marquis de Lafayette.

> Monticello Aug. 4. 1781.
> I thank you also for your kind sentiments and friendly offers on the occasion, which th[at] I cannot avail myself of has given me more mortification than al[most] any occurrence of my life. I lose an opportunity, the only one I ever had and perhaps ever shall have of combining public service with private gratification, of seeing count[ries] whose improvements in science, in arts, and in civilization it has been my fortune to [ad]mire at a distance but never to see and at the same

time of lending further aid to a cause which has been handed on from it's first origination to [its] present stage by every effort of which my poor faculties were capable. These however have not been such as to give satisfaction to some of my countrymen and [it] has become necessary for me to remain in the state till a later period in the present [year] . . . .

Shortly thereafter, Jefferson turned to a project which would keep that cause alive in his heart and mind and which helped him refine his ideas about America: his *Notes on the State of Virginia.* The project was set in motion at the end of the summer of 1780 when François de Barbé-Marbois, secretary of the French legation in Philadelphia, distributed twenty-two questions from his government on the government, economics, and customs of the thirteen states. Congressman Joseph Jones delivered a set to Governor Jefferson, who assigned himself the task of answering the questions for Virginia and began work as early as November, 1780. Wartime emergencies forced him to postpone his major research and writing, however, until the summer of 1781. At Poplar Forest, ninety miles west of Monticello, and later in his own library, Jefferson prepared the manuscript that would become the only full-length book he ever published. He explained some of his methods in his *Autobiography.*

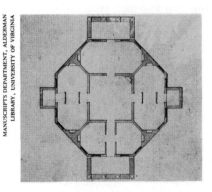

Floor plan of Poplar Forest

Autobiography, 1821

I had always made it a practice whenever an opportunity occurred of obtaining any information of our country, which might be of use to me in any station public or private, to commit it to writing. These memoranda were on loose papers, bundled up without order, and difficult of recurrence when I had occasion for a particular one. I thought this a good occasion to embody their substance, which I did in the order of Mr. Marbois' queries, so as to answer his wish and to arrange them for my own use.

By the end of the year, when he traveled to Richmond to answer Nicholas's charges, Jefferson had completed the manuscript. Marbois probably expected brief but useful answers that would give the French government a guide to local conditions. Instead, Jefferson's months of labor with his books and memoranda produced a profound study of the state's history and customs, detailed descriptions of its scenic beauty, and scholarly analyses of the political and economic factors that would shape the future not only of Virginia but of the United States as well. But Jefferson apologized to Marbois for troubling him with a manuscript so "imperfect." Although Jefferson did not intend to have the document publicized, he was too conscientious to allow its imperfections to remain. Over the next few years he revised and expanded the *Notes* until they had "swelled nearly to treble bulk" by mid-1784. In 1785 he arranged for the printing of two hundred copies, but his name did not appear on the title page and the books were only for distribution to carefully chosen friends and associates. Were the *Notes* "to go to the public at large," Jefferson feared that his frank comments might damage the political fortunes of two reforms he favored: the abolition of slavery and the revision of the state constitution. By the fall of 1785, he admitted that he might not long be able to keep the book secret. "I have been obliged to give so many...that I fear their getting published." Early in 1786, Jefferson found that his apprehensions were justified.

Autobiography, 1821

An European copy, by the death of the owner, got into the hands of a bookseller, who engaged it's translation, & when ready for the press, communicated his intentions & Manuscript to me, without any other permission than that of suggesting corrections. I never had seen so wretched an attempt at translation. Interverted, abridged, mutilated, and often reversing the sense of the original, I found it a blotch of errors from beginning to end. I corrected some of the most material, and in that form it was printed in French. A London bookseller, on seeing the translation, requested me to permit him to print the English original. I thought it best to do so to let the world see that it was not really so bad as the French translation had made it appear.

Early engraving of Natural Bridge

The book opened with a factual description of Virginia's geography, with subsequent topics following the order of Marbois's original queries. The Frenchman's question concerning "Cascades and Caverns" allowed Jefferson to depart from a discussion of rivers, mountains, and seaports to describe the famous Natural Bridge. Although this local wonder did not really fall under the question, Jefferson could not resist including it—especially since he was the proud owner of the land on which it stood.

Notes on Virginia, 1782

The *Natural bridge*, the most sublime of Nature's works, though not comprehended under the present head, must not be pretermitted. It is on the ascent of a hill, which seems to have been cloven through its length by some great convulsion....Though the sides of this bridge are provided in some parts with a parapet of fixed rocks, yet

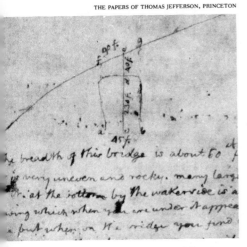

Jefferson's drawing, c. 1767

few men have resolution to walk to them and look over into the abyss. You involuntarily fall on your hands and feet, creep to the parapet and peep over it. Looking down from this height about a minute, gave me a violent head ach. This painful sensation is relieved by a short, but pleasing view of the Blue ridge along the fissure downwards, and upwards by that of the Short hills, which, with the Purgátory mountain is a divergence from the North ridge; and, descending then to the valley below, the sensation becomes delightful in the extreme. It is impossible for the emotions, arising from the sublime, to be felt beyond what they are here: so beautiful an arch, so elevated, so light, and springing, as it were, up to heaven, the rapture of the Spectator is really indiscribable!

Other selections from the *Notes on Virginia* reveal the work's breadth. It remains the most complete record of Jefferson's vision of America, not only of his home state, but also of his broader philosophical convictions. It was in reply to Marbois's question concerning "The present state of manufactures, commerce, interior and exterior trade," for example, that Jefferson outlined his theory of the moral superiority of agriculture as an occupation and hinted at his fear of the corrupting effects of a dependence on manufactures.

Notes on Virginia, 1782

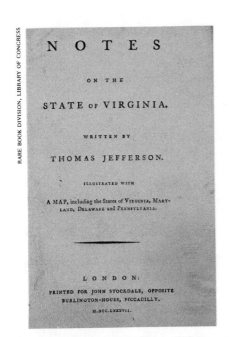

Authorized London edition of Notes, *printed in 1787 by John Stockdale*

Those who labour in the earth are the chosen people of god, if ever he had a chosen people, whose breasts he has made his peculiar deposit for substantial and genuine virtue. It is the focus in which he keeps alive that sacred fire, which otherwise might escape from the face of the earth. Corruption of morals in the mass of cultivators is a phænomenon of which no age nor nation has furnished an example. It is the mark set on those, who not looking up to heaven, to their own soil and industry, as does the husbandman, for their subsistance, depend for it on the casualties and caprice of customers. Dependance begets subservience and venality, suffocates the germ of virtue, and prepares fit tools for the designs of ambition. This, the natural progress and consequence of the arts, has sometimes perhaps been retarded by accidental circumstances: but, generally speaking, the proportion which the aggregate of the other classes of citizens bears in any state to that of its husbandmen, is the proportion of its unsound to its healthy parts, and is a good-enough

133

barometer whereby to measure its degree of corruption. While we have land to labour then, let us never wish to see our citizens occupied at a work-bench, or twirling a distaff. Carpenters, masons, smiths, are wanting in husbandry: but, for the general operations of manufacture, let our work-shops remain in Europe. It is better to carry provisions and materials to workmen there, than bring them to the provisions and materials, and with them their manners and principles.

Jefferson also used the opportunity to dispel myths that had grown up about America. He was particularly incensed by the theories of the French naturalist Buffon who had asserted that "the animals common both to the old and new world are smaller in the latter, that those peculiar to the new are in a smaller scale, that those which have been domesticated in both have degenerated in America." Another French author, the Abbé Raynal, had applied Buffon's theories to the descendants of European settlers in America. Jefferson not only debunked Raynal's charges, but claimed that the New World possessed boundless potential for development and even for attaining superiority to Europe.

Notes on Virginia, 1782

So far the Count de Buffon has carried this new theory of the tendency of nature to belittle her productions on this side of the Atlantic. Its application to the race of whites, transplanted from Europe, remained for the Abbé Raynal. '...l'Amerique n'ait pas encore produit un bon poëte...un homme de genie dans un seul art, ou seule Science....America has not yet produced one good poet.' When we shall have existed as a people as long as the Greeks did before they produced a Homer, the Romans a Virgil, the French a Racine and Voltaire, the English a Shakespeare and Milton, should this reproach be still true, we will enquire from what unfriendly causes it has proceeded, that the other countries of Europe and quarters of the earth shall not have inscribed any name in the roll of poets. But neither has America produced 'one able mathematician, one man of genius in a single art or a single science.' In war we have produced a Washington, whose memory will be adored while liberty shall have votaries, whose name will triumph over time, and will in future ages assume its just station among the most celebrated worthies of the world, when that wretched philosophy shall be forgotten which would have arranged

The Comte de Buffon

A Pictorial Geography BY S. G. GOODRICH, 1840

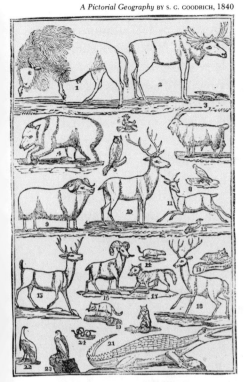

Comparative sizes of North American animals from A Pictorial Geography, *published in United States in 1840*

David Rittenhouse's observatory in Norriton, Pennsylvania, built to watch the transit of Venus in 1769

The History of Philadelphia
BY J. THOMAS SCHARF AND THOMPSON WESTCOTT, 1884

him among the degeneracies of nature. In physics we have produced a Franklin, than whom no one of the present age has made more important discoveries, nor has enriched philosophy with more, or more ingenious solutions of the phænomena of nature. We have supposed Mr. [David] Rittenhouse second to no astronomer living: that in genius he must be the first, because he is self-taught. As an artist he has exhibited as great a proof of mechanical genius as the world has ever produced. He has not indeed made a world; but he has by imitation approached nearer its Maker than any man who has lived from the creation to this day. As in philosophy and war, so in government, in oratory, in painting, in the plastic art, we might shew that America, though but a child of yesterday, has already given hopeful proofs of genius, as well of the nobler kinds, which arouse the best feelings of man, which call him into action, which substantiate his freedom, and conduct him to happiness, as of the subordinate, which serve to amuse him only. We therefore suppose, that this reproach is as unjust as it is unkind; and that, of the geniuses which adorn the present age, America contributes its full share. For comparing it with those countries, where genius is most cultivated, where are the most excellent models for art, and scaffoldings for the attainment of science, as France and England for instance, we calculate thus. The United States contain three millions of inhabitants; France twenty millions; and the British islands ten. We produce a Washington, a Franklin, a Rittenhouse. France then should have half a dozen in each of these lines, and Great-Britain half that number, equally eminent. It may be true, that France has: we are but just becoming acquainted with her, and our acquaintance so far gives us high ideas of the genius of her inhabitants. . . . The present war having so long cut off all communication with Great-Britain, we are not able to make a fair estimate of the state of science in that country. The spirit in which she wages war is the only sample before our eyes, and that does not seem the legitimate offspring either of science or of civilization. The sun of her glory is fast descending to the horizon. Her philosophy has crossed the Channel, her freedom the Atlantic, and herself seems passing to that awful dissolution, whose issue is not given human foresight to scan.

The dismemberment of the British Empire seemed near as Jefferson completed drafting his manuscript for Marbois. Two months before the finished *Notes* were sent to the French diplomat, Cornwallis's surrender at Yorktown brought peace to Virginia and the promise of peace and security to the United States. With the vindication of his administration by the legislature in December, 1781, Jefferson could more comfortably withdraw to the privacy for which he longed. He even declined a seat in the Virginia legislature as a representative from Albemarle, and his refusal of service prompted considerable criticism. James Monroe wrote from Richmond: "It is publickly said here that the people of your county inform'd you they had frequently elected you in times of less difficulty and danger than the present to please you, but that now they had call'd you forth into publick office to serve themselves." Jefferson's reply cited his need to repair the "disorder and ruin" of his private affairs and his obligations to his daughters and to the six children of his late brother-in-law Dabney Carr. But the letter showed, as well, that Jefferson was still bitter about the attacks from his political enemies.

Dutch cartoon of the surrender at Yorktown (in distance) has British lion howling in pain next to an Englishman on his knees in despair.

Monticello May 20. 1782.

I am much obliged by the kind wishes you express of seeing me also in Richmond, and am always mortified when any thing is expected from me which I cannot fulfill, and more especially if it relate to the public service. Before I ventured to declare to my countrymen my determination to retire from public employment I examined well my heart to know whether it were thoroughly cured of every principle of political ambition, whether no lurking particle remained which might leave me uneasy when reduced within the limits of mere private life. I became satisfied that every fibre of that passion was thoroughly eradicated. I examined also in other views my right to withdraw. I considered that I had been thirteen years engaged in public service, that during that time I had so totally abandoned all attention to my private affairs as to permit them to run into great disorder and ruin, that I had now a family advanced to years which require my attention and instruction, that to this was added the hopeful offspring of a deceased friend whose memory must be for ever dear to me..., that by a constant sacrifice of time, labour, loss, parental and friendly duties, I had been so far from gaining the affection of my countrymen which was the only reward I ever asked or could have felt, that I had even lost the small estimation I before possessed: that however I might have comforted myself under the dis-

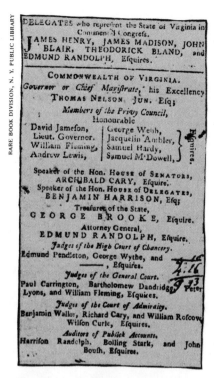

DELEGATES who represent the State of Virginia in Continental Congress.

JAMES HENRY, JAMES MADISON, JOHN BLAIR, THEODORICK BLAND, and EDMUND RANDOLPH, Esquires.

COMMONWEALTH OF VIRGINIA.

Governor or Chief Magistrate, his Excellency THOMAS NELSON, JUN. Esq;

Members of the Privy Council, Honourable

David Jamefon, Lieut. Governor. William Fleming, Andrew Lewis, | George Webb, Jacquelin Ambler, Samuel Hardy, Samuel M'Dowell, } Esquires.

Speaker of the Hon. HOUSE of SENATORS, ARCHIBALD CARY, Esquire.

Speaker of the Hon. HOUSE of DELEGATES, BENJAMIN HARRISON, Esq;

Treasurer of the State, GEORGE BROOKE, Esquire.

Attorney General, EDMUND RANDOLPH, Esquire.

Judges of the High Court of Chancery, Edmund Pendleton, George Wythe, and ————, Esquires.

Judges of the General Court. Paul Carrington, Bartholomew Dandridge, Peter Lyons, and William Fleming, Esquires.

Judges of the Court of Admiralty. Benjamin Waller, Richard Cary, and William Roscow Wilson Curle, Esquires.

Auditors of Publick Accounts, Harrifon Randolph, Bolling Stark, and John Bouth, Esquires.

Page from the Virginia Almanac *listing the members of government in 1782, one of the few years Jefferson held no public office*

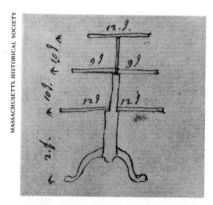

Jefferson's sketch for a circular stand with three shelves, probably designed for use at Monticello

approbation of the well-meaning but uninformed people yet that of their representatives was a shock on which I had not calculated: that this indeed had been followed by an exculpatory declaration, but in the mean time I had been suspected and suspended in the eyes of the world without the least hint then or afterwards made public which might restrain them from supposing I stood arraigned for treasons of the heart and not mere weaknesses of the head. And I felt that these injuries, for such they have been since acknowleged, had inflicted a wound on my spirit which will only be cured by the all-healing grave. If reason and inclination unite in justifying my retirement, the laws of my country are equally in favor of it.... Nothing could so completely divest us of ... liberty as the establishment of the opinion that the state has a *perpetual* right to the services of all it's members. This to men of certain ways of thinking would be to annihilate the blessing of existence; to contradict the giver of life who gave it for happiness and not for wretchedness, and certainly to such it were better that they had never been born. However with these I may think public service and private misery inseparably linked together, I have not the vanity to count myself among those whom the state would think worth oppressing with perpetual service. I have received a sufficient memento to the contrary. I am persuaded that having hitherto dedicated to them the whole of the active and useful part of my life I shall be permitted to pass the rest in mental quiet....I preferred a simple act of renunciation to the taking sanctuary under those many disqualifications (provided by the law for other purposes indeed but) which afford asylum also for rest to the wearied. I dare say you did not expect by the few words you dropped on the right of renunication to expose yourself to the fatigue of so long a letter, but I wished you to see that if I had done wrong I had been betrayed by a semblance of right at least.

[The closing paragraph of this long letter contained a further explanation of Jefferson's reluctance to leave Monticello.]

...Mrs. Jefferson has added another daughter to our family. She has been ever since and still continues very dangerously ill.

137

After visiting Jefferson in the spring of 1782, the Marquis de Chastellux had written of the master of Monticello: "it seemed as if from his youth he had placed his mind, as he had done his house, on an elevated situation, from which he might contemplate the universe." But his personal universe was shattered abruptly a few months later. The daughter born in May was Martha Jefferson's sixth child in ten years; a son and two daughters had died in infancy. Although Jefferson jealously guarded the details of his private life, it is clear that his wife had never enjoyed good health and she failed to recover from the delivery of Lucy Elizabeth. For four months Thomas Jefferson lived with the growing knowledge that his thirty-three-year-old wife was dying. His eldest daughter, Patsy, was only ten at the time, but nearly fifty years later she recalled that terrible summer and fall at Monticello.

"Reminiscences of Th. J. by MR," [c. 1832] As a nurse no female ever had more tenderness or anxiety; he nursed my poor Mother in turn with aunt Carr and her own sisters setting up with her and administring her medecines and drink to the last. For four months that she lingered he was never out of Calling. When not at her bed side he was writing in a small room which opened immediately at the head of her bed. A moment before the closing scene he was led from the room almost in a state of insensibility by his sister Mrs. Carr who with great difficulty got him into his library where he fainted and remained so long insensible that they feared he never would revive. The scene that followed I did not witness but the violence of his emotion, of his grief when almost by stealth I entered his room at night to this day I dare not trust myself to describe. He kept his room for three weeks and I was never a moment from his side. He walked almost incessantly night and day only lying down occasionally when nature was completely exhausted on a pallet that had been brought in during his long fainting fit. My Aunts remained constantly with him for some weeks, I do not remember how many. When at last he left his room he rode out and from that time he was incessantly on horseback rambling about the mountain in the least frequented roads and just as often through the woods; in those melancholy rambles I was his constant companion, a solitary witness to many a violent burst of grief, the remembrance of which has consecrated particular scenes of that lost home beyond the power of time to obliterate.

Martha Jefferson Carr,
Jefferson's widowed sister

There is a time in human suffering," Jefferson wrote in a small pocket notebook at the time, "when exceeding sorrows are but like snow falling on an iceberg." Despite his wife's long illness, he seemed unprepared for her death and the tragedy was too great for him to describe. His account book, usually reserved for the most impersonal notes, carried a simple entry: "September 6—My dear wife died this day at 11:45 A.M." He noted in his *Autobiography* that he had "lost the cherished companion of my life, in whose affections, unabated on both sides, I had lived the last ten years in unchequered happiness."

Even in preparing an epitaph, Jefferson tried to provide some privacy for his grief. A simple slab of white marble was placed over her grave in the family cemetery on the mountainside with a quotation from the *Iliad* in the original Greek. In Pope's translation it read:

If in the melancholy shades below,
The flames of friends and lovers cease to glow,
Yet mine shall sacred last; mine undecayed
Burn on through death and animate my shade.

Fortunately, Jefferson was not allowed to remain long at Monticello. His friends realized that he needed something to occupy his mind and new ideas and new surroundings to distract him from his grief. On November 12, 1782, he was unanimously reappointed to the peace commission. Madison noted that "the act took place in consequence of its being suggested that the death of Mrs. J. had probably changed the sentiments of Mr. J. with regard to public life, and that all the reasons which led to his original appointment still existed."

Jefferson's colleagues in Philadelphia had judged his mood with uncanny accuracy. He welcomed the opportunity to get away from his saddened home and fulfill his ambition to visit Europe. Jefferson himself best described his mood in one of the first letters he wrote after Martha's death, while visiting a friend's estate, to the Marquis de Chastellux.

Detail of a page from Jefferson's account book has entry of wife's death at 11:45 on September 6.

Ampthill Nov. 26. 1782.

[Your letter] found me a little emerging from that stupor of mind which had rendered me as dead to the world as she was whose loss occasioned it. Your letter recalled to my memory, that there were persons still living of much value to me. If you should have thought me remiss in not testifying to you sooner how deeply I had been impressed with your worth in the little time I had the happiness of being with you you will I am sure ascribe it to it's true cause the state of dreadful suspence in which I had been kept all the summer and the catastrophe which closed it. Before that event my scheme of life had been determined. I had folded myself in the arms of retirement, and rested all prospects of future happiness on domestic and literary objects. A single event wiped away all my plans and left me a blank which I had not the spirits to fill up. In this state of mind an appointment from Congress found me requiring me to cross the Atlantic, and that temptation might be added to duty I was informed at the same time from his Excy. the Chevalier de la Luzerne that a vessel of force would be sailing about the middle of Dec. in which you would be passing to France. I accepted the appointment and my only object now is so to hasten over those obstacles which would retard my departure as to be ready to join you in your voiage, fondly measuring your affections by my own and presuming your consent. It is not certain that by any exertions I can be in Philadelphia by the middle of December. The contrary is most probable. But hoping it will not be much later and counting on those procrastinations which usually attend the departure of vessels of size I have hopes of being with you in time. This will give me full Leisure to learn the result of your observations on the Natural bridge, to communicate to you my answers to the queries of Monsr. de Marbois, to receive edification from you on these and on other subjects of science, considering chess too as a matter of science.

Jefferson needed only a little more than three weeks to put his affairs in order in Virginia. His friends Francis Eppes and Nicholas Lewis would superintend his business interests in his absence, and Eppes and his wife Elizabeth, Martha's sister, also agreed to care for four-year-old Mary and the infant Lucy. Patsy would accompany her father and continue her education abroad under his direction.

On December 27, the Jeffersons arrived in Philadelphia. Patsy was put in school while her father made arrangements for their voyage. Bad weather delayed the sailing of the French vessel *Romulus*, however, and Jefferson waited out the delay in James Madison's company at a boarding-house owned by Mrs. Mary House. Mrs. House's daughter, Elizabeth Trist, befriended young Patsy and entertained her while Jefferson shopped for books and maps to take to Europe. At the end of January, Jefferson rode to Baltimore to confer with the captain of the ice-locked *Romulus*. The weather had improved, but a small British fleet had taken advantage of the thaw to station itself in Chesapeake Bay. Jefferson sought instructions from Congress since, "I must acknolege that they [the ships] appear such as to render a capture certain were we to hazard" a voyage. While Congress considered this new development, Jefferson amused himself in Baltimore as best he could by corresponding with his friends. In a letter to Madison, he considered the problems he might encounter serving as a minister plenipotentiary with John Adams in Paris.

Detail from unfinished painting by Benjamin West of commission: Jay, Adams, Franklin, Henry Laurens; William Temple Franklin, secretary

Baltimore Feb. 14. 1783.

I am nearly at a loss to judge how he will act in the negotiation. He hates Franklin, he hates Jay, he hates the French, he hates the English. To whom will he adhere? His vanity is a lineament in his character which had entirely escaped me. His want of taste I had observed. Notwithstanding all this he has a sound head on substantial points, and I think he has integrity. I am glad therefore that he is of the commission and expect he will be useful in it. His dislike of all parties, and all men, by balancing his prejudices, may give the same fair play to his reason as would a general benevolence of temper. At any rate honesty may be extracted even from poisonous weeds.

The next day Jefferson received word from Madison of unofficial reports that a preliminary peace treaty had already been concluded. Jefferson suspended his plans to sail and returned to Philadelphia. Not until April 1 did Congress release him from his commission so that he might return to Virginia. His journey to Monticello with Patsy was interrupted by a stop in Richmond where he conferred with members of the legislature. Two matters of great interest to Jefferson were to be considered at that session, and he probably used the opportunity to lobby on their behalf. The first proposal was for the states to grant Congress the right to impose an import tax or "impost" and to assume state debts which could then be met by this duty. The second was to call a popularly elected convention to revise the state constitution. After his return to Monticello on May 15, Jefferson prepared a draft constitution, drawing on the one he had written in 1776 and adding some new provisions. The convention was not called, but drafting the constitution and journeying to Philadelphia and Baltimore had helped bring Jefferson back to a full and active life. He would never forget his beloved wife, but he was beginning to learn to live with his loss. The assembly took notice of this fact in June, 1783, when they named him to the state's congressional delegation. The appointment would not take place until November, however, and Jefferson spent the summer and early autumn at home, superintending nine youngsters and organizing his personal library. His collection of 2,640 volumes, painstakingly assembled after the fire at Shadwell in 1770, was probably the finest of its kind in America. Arranging the items according to Lord Bacon's "table of sciences" was a labor of love for their owner.

The pleasant interlude at Monticello ended with Jefferson's departure in search of a wandering Congress, which had adjourned from Philadelphia when mutinous, unpaid troops threatened the State House. First leaving Patsy with Mrs. Trist in Philadelphia, Jefferson rode to New Jersey expecting to find his fellow delegates at Princeton, their most recent meeting place, but they had adjourned again to meet in Annapolis the following month. Jefferson returned to Philadelphia and spent the next few weeks attending to Patsy's education and care. Mrs. Trist was soon to leave the city, and he found a home for his eleven-year-old daughter with Mrs. Thomas Hopkinson, the mother of a congressional colleague of 1776. Determined to guide Patsy's development carefully, Jefferson continued to offer her stern fatherly lectures even after he left the city late in November. His letters combined deep affection with instructions on matters ranging from study habits to moral philosophy.

Annapolis Nov. 28. 1783.

My dear Patsy

After four days journey I arrived here without any accident and in as good health as when I left Philadelphia. The conviction that you would be more improved in the situation I have placed you than if still with me, has solaced me on my parting with you, which my love for you has rendered a difficult thing. The acquirements which I hope you will make under the tutors I have provided for you will render you more worthy of my love, and if they cannot increase it they will prevent it's diminution. Consider the good lady who has taken you under her roof, who has undertaken to see that you perform all your exercises, and to admonish you in all those wanderings from what is right or what is clever to which your inexperience would expose you, consider her I say as your mother, as the only person to whom, since the loss with which heaven has been pleased to afflict you, you can now look up; and that her displeasure or disapprobation on any occasion will be an immense misfortune which should you be so unhappy as to incur by any unguarded act, think no concession too much to regain her good will. With respect to the distribution of your time the following is what I should approve.

from 8. to 10 o'clock practise music.

from 10. to 1. dance one day and draw another

from 1. to 2. draw on the day you dance, and write a letter the next day.

from 3. to 4. read French.

from 4. to 5. exercise yourself in music.

D R A U G H T

OF A

FUNDAMENTAL CONSTITUTION

FOR THE

COMMONWEALTH OF VIRGINIA.

TO the citizens of the Commonwealth of Virginia, and all others whom it may concern, the Delegates for the said Commonwealth in Convention assembled, send greeting.

It is known to you and to the world, that the government of Great Britain, with which the American states were not long since connected, assumed over them an authority unwarrantable and oppressive; that they endeavored to enforce this authority by arms, and that the states of New Hampshire, Massachusets, Rhode island, Connecticut, New York, New Jersey, Pennsylvania, Delaware, Maryland, Virginia, North Carolina, South Carolina, and Georgia, considering resistance, with all its train of horrors, as a lesser evil than abject submission, closed in the appeal to arms. It hath pleased the sovereign disposer of all human events to give to this appeal an issue favourable to the rights of the states; to enable them to reject for ever all dependance on a government which had shewn itself so capable of abusing the trusts reposed in it; and to obtain from that government a solemn and explicit acknowledgment that they are free, sovereign, and independant states. During the progress of that war through which we had to labour for the establishment of our rights, the legislature of the commonwealth of Virginia, found it necessary to make a temporary organization of government for preventing anarchy, and pointing our efforts to the two important objects of war

First page of Jefferson's 1783 draft constitution, which he had printed and appended to some copies of the Notes on Virginia

Jefferson himself read widely in French as evidenced by books such as this history of Rome, translated from Lucius Florus, in his library.

from 5. till bedtime read English, write &c. Communicate this plan to Mrs. Hopkinson and if she approves of it pursue it. . . . I expect you will write to me by every post. Inform me what books you read, what tunes you learn, and inclose me your best copy of every lesson in drawing. Write also one letter every week either to your aunt Eppes, your aunt Skipwith [her mother's sister], your aunt Carr, or the little lady from whom I now inclose a letter, and always put the letter you so write under cover to me. Take care that you never spell a word wrong. Always before you write a word consider how it is spelt, and if you do not remember it, turn to a dictionary. It produces great praise to a lady to spell well. I have placed my happiness on seeing you good and accomplished, and no distress which this world can now bring on me could equal that of your disappointing my hopes. If you love me then, strive to be good under every situation and to all living creatures, and to acquire those accomplishments which I have put in your power, and which will go far towards ensuring you the warmest love of your affectionate father,

Th: Jefferson

P.S. keep my letters and read them at times that you may always have present in your mind those things which will endear you to me.

In a letter to Marbois, Jefferson explained his reasons for imposing this demanding schedule on Patsy. He hoped to prepare her for the heavy responsibilities she might face as a grown woman in America.

Annapolis Dec. 5. 1783.

Your very obliging letter of Nov. 22. was put into my hands just in the moment of my departure from Philadelphia, which put it out of my power to acknolege in the same instant my obligations for the charge you were so kind as to undertake of presenting a French tutor to my daughter. . . . The same cause prevented my procuring her the books you were so kind as to recommend, but this shall be supplied by orders from hence. . . . The plan of reading which I have formed for her is considerably different from what I think would be most proper for her sex in any other country than America. I am obliged in it to extend my views beyond herself, and consider her as possibly at the head of a little family of her own.

The chance that in marriage she will draw a blockhead I calculate at about fourteen to one, and of course that the education of her family will probably rest on her own ideas and direction without assistance. With the best poets and prosewriters I shall therefore combine a certain extent of reading in the graver sciences. However I scarcely expect to enter her on this till she returns to me. Her time in Philadelphia will be chiefly occupied in acquiring a little taste and execution in such of the fine arts as she could not prosecute to equal advantage in a more retired situation.

Jefferson was also determined that his motherless daughter would not lack guidance in the feminine graces or advice on the fashions that would most please the opposite sex.

Annapolis Dec. 22. 1783

I omitted in that [letter] to advise you on the subject of dress, which I know you are a little apt to neglect. I do not wish you to be gayly clothed at this time of life, but that what you wear should be fine of it's kind; but above all things, and at all times let your clothes be clean, whole, and properly put on. Do not fancy you must wear them till the dirt is visible to the eye. You will be the last who will be sensible of this. Some ladies think they may under the privileges of the dishabille be loose and negligent of their dress in the morning. But be you from the moment you rise till you go to bed as cleanly and properly dressed as at the hours of dinner or tea. A lady who has been seen as a sloven or slut in the morning, will never efface the impression she then made with all the dress and pageantry she can afterwards involve herself in. Nothing is so disgusting to our sex as a want of cleanliness and delicacy in yours. I hope therefore the moment you rise from bed, your first work will be to dress yourself in such a stile as that you may be seen by any gentleman without his being able to discover a pin amiss, or any other circumstance of neatness wanting.

The new State House in Annapolis

There was ample time for letter writing during Jefferson's first weeks in Annapolis. Although Congress was supposed to have opened sessions on November 26, only six states were represented by December 11. Under the Confederation, seven states were required to conduct the most routine business, and nine were necessary to consider extraordinary matters. Jefferson complained ruefully to James Madison who had retired temporarily to his home in Orange County.

> Annapolis Dec. 11. 1783.
>
> It is now above a fortnight since we should have met, and six states only appear. We have some hopes of Rhodeisland coming in to-day, but when two more will be added seems as insusceptible of calculation as when the next earthquake will happen.

It was essential that Congress be able to act quickly in December, 1783. The definitive treaty of peace, which ended the war and recognized American independence, had been signed in Paris on September 3, 1783. The treaty provided that ratifications be exchanged among the parties to the agreement within six months. Jefferson, as chairman of a committee charged with considering ratification, recommended approval of the articles on December 16, but by then more than half of the prescribed time had passed. A week later a seventh state had arrived; urgent appeals went out to governors of the unrepresented states warning that the delegates' absence might endanger the treaty. Jefferson recalled those tedious, frustrating weeks of arguing and waiting for a response.

Autobiography, 1821

HISTORICAL SOCIETY OF PENNSYLVANIA

Detail from ink sketch by Trumbull of presentation of the preliminary peace treaty in the House of Lords

Our body was little numerous, but very contentious. Day after day was wasted on the most unimportant questions. My colleague [John Francis] Mercer was one of those afflicted with the morbid rage of debate, of an ardent mind, prompt imagination, and copious flow of words, he heard with impatience any logic which was not his own. Sitting near me on some occasion of a trifling but wordy debate, he asked how I could sit in silence hearing so much false reasoning which a word should refute? I observed to him that to refute indeed was easy, but to silence impossible. That in measures brought forward by myself, I took the laboring oar, as was incumbent on me; but that in general I was willing to listen. If every sound argument or objection was used by some one or other of the numerous debaters, it was enough: if not, I thought it sufficient to suggest the omission, without going into a repetition of what had been already said by others. That this was a waste and abuse of the time and patience of the house which could not be justified. And I believe that if the members of deliberative bodies were to observe this course generally, they would do in a day

what takes them a week, and it is really more questionable, than may at first be thought, whether Bonaparte's
dumb legislature which said nothing and did much, may
not be preferable to one which talks much and does
nothing. I served with General Washington in the legislature of Virginia before the revolution, and, during it,
with Dr. Franklin in Congress. I never heard either of
them speak ten minutes at a time, nor to any but the
main point which was to decide the question. They laid
their shoulders to the great points, knowing that the
little ones would follow of themselves. If the present
Congress errs in too much talking, how can it be otherwise in a body to which the people send 150. lawyers,
whose trade it is to question everything, yield nothing,
& talk by the hour? That 150. lawyers should do business
together ought not to be expected.

At last, on January 14, delegates from New Jersey
and New Hampshire arrived to take their seats. Some members of Congress, to Jefferson's dismay, had been ready to ratify the treaty with only
seven states voting, but this desperate measure proved unnecessary. The
treaty was duly ratified, and congressmen soon began to find excuses to
leave: not until March would nine states again be represented. The problems that remained were those of peace, not war, but they were equally
vital for America's future. First was the question of western lands. After
years of argument over legal technicalities, Virginia's cession of the
Northwest Territory had been accepted in a form agreeable to the other
states. Jefferson was appointed to chair the committee that prepared a plan
for the area's temporary government. His final report of March 22, which
formed the basis for the Ordinance of 1784, was one of his most important
state papers. It provided a new legal structure for territorial expansion:
the formation not of subject colonies, but of territories with temporary
governments that would prepare them to join the older states as full partners.

[March 22, 1784]

Provided that both the temporary and permanent governments be established on these principles as their basis.
1. That they shall for ever remain a part of this confederacy of the United States of America. 2. That
in their persons, property and territory they shall be
subject to the government of the United states in Congress assembled, and to the articles of Confederation
in all those cases in which the original states shall be
so subject. 3. That they shall be subject to pay a part

The Critical Period of American History BY JOHN FISKE, 1897

*Copy of a map made in 1784 of
the proposed states in the Northwest*

of the federal debts...to be apportioned on them by Congress.... 4. That their respective governments shall be in republican forms, and shall admit no person to be a citizen who holds any hereditary title. 5. That after the year 1800. of the Christian æra, there shall be neither slavery nor involuntary servitude in any of the said states, otherwise than in punishment of crimes....

That whensoever any of the said states shall have, of free inhabitants, as many as shall then be in any one of the least numerous of the thirteen original states, such state shall be admitted...into the Congress of the United states, on an equal footing with the said original states: provided nine states agree to such admission according to the...11th of the articles of Confederation. And in order to adapt the said articles of confederation to the state of Congress when it's numbers shall be thus increased, it shall be proposed to the legislatures of the states originally parties thereto, to require the assent of two thirds of the United states in Congress assembled in all those cases wherein by the said articles the assent of nine states is now required....Until such admission by their delegates into Congress, any of the said states, after the establishment of their temporary government, shall have authority to keep a sitting member in Congress, with a right of debating, but not of voting.

Congress did not accept all of Jefferson's report: the sections barring slavery and citizenship for people holding hereditary titles were deleted. But by then Jefferson was accustomed to introducing reforms that were too radical for many of his colleagues. The fundamental provision of the report remained—the creation of self-governing territories that would be guaranteed republican government in all stages of their progress to full statehood. He had succeeded in giving America a form of territorial expansion appropriate to a democracy, not one borrowed from monarchical colonialism.

A variety of other projects occupied Jefferson during his six-month stint at Annapolis. He was placed on every important committee, served as chairman of most of them, and wrote almost all of the significant public papers to emerge from that session of Congress. In addition to his efforts in behalf of the peace treaty and the organization of governments in the Northwest, Jefferson arranged the state occasion for Washington's renunciation of his command, proposed canal routes, and developed a decimal system of coinage—making the Spanish dollar the base unit, with a gold piece worth ten dollars, a silver dime, and a copper cent. His insistence on this simplification earned for him the title "Father of the Dollar." Another matter had been of special interest to Jefferson: the plan to negotiate commercial treaties with European nations. In his *Notes*, Jefferson had written of the need not only to "cultivate the peace and friendship of every nation" but also "to throw open the doors of commerce."

Jefferson's expenses as a delegate to Congress, submitted to the Treasurer of Virginia, May 11, 1784

Notes on Virginia, 1782

Young as we are, and with such a country before us to fill with people and with happiness, we should point in that direction the whole generative force of nature, wasting none of it in efforts of mutual destruction. It should be our endeavour to cultivate the peace and friendship of every nation, even of that which has injured us most, when we shall have carried our point against her. Our interest will be to throw open the doors of commerce, and to knock off all its shackles, giving perfect freedom to all persons for the vent of whatever they may chuse to bring into our ports, and asking the same in theirs. Never was so much false arithmetic employed on any subject, as that which has been employed to persuade nations that it is their interest to go to war. Were the money which it has cost to gain, at the close of a long war, a little town, or a little territory, the right to cut wood here, or to catch fish there, expended in improving what they already possess, in making roads, opening rivers, building ports, improving the arts, and finding employment for their idle poor, it would render them much stronger, much wealthier and happier. This I hope will be our wisdom.

Commercial treaties, properly negotiated, would lay the foundations for free trade, and in May, 1784, Jefferson was named a commissioner with Franklin and Adams, who were already abroad, to accomplish this task. At last he would have his chance to visit Europe, not to negotiate an end to the war for political independence, but to help establish what he hoped would be the beginning of commercial independence for the young Republic.

Chapter 6

Seasoning of a Diplomat

On July 5, 1784, Jefferson and his daughter Patsy sailed from Boston for Paris, via West Cowes, England and Le Havre. America's newest minister plenipotentiary had carefully arranged his affairs to permit an absence of two years, the time limit placed on his joint commission with Franklin and Adams to negotiate commercial treaties. Like many of Jefferson's carefully made plans, this one would be upset: his stay abroad would be not for two years, but for more than five years; it would be not for a mission limited to the negotiation of trade concessions and commercial regulations, but for a wide-ranging adventure in European diplomacy and politics. Excitement seemed unlikely when he arrived in Paris the first week in August. During the first few months suitable lodging had to be found for himself and his official family. Patsy had to be properly dressed in Parisian style and then enrolled in the convent school at the Abbaye Royale de Panthémont. Jefferson's friendship with Adams and Franklin was reestablished as the trio was reunited for the first time since 1776.

Despite his obligations as householder, father, and diplomat, Jefferson found some time to behave like any tourist in a new country. His friends in America were kept informed of foreign curiosities that Jefferson felt would interest them, as well as of political events that it was his duty to report. He interrupted a report to James Madison on French politics and trade to give him a description of "Phosphoretic matches" and an Argand lamp.

> Paris Nov. 11. 1784.
>
> By having them [matches] at your bedside with a candle, the latter may be lighted at any moment of the night without getting out of bed. By keeping them on your writing table, you may seal three or four letters with one of them, or light a candle if you want to seal more which in the summer is convenient. In the woods they supply the want of steel, flint and punk. . . . There is a new lamp

invented here lately which with a very small consumption of oil (of olives) is thought to give a light equal to six or eight candles. The wick is hollow in the middle of the form of a hollow cylinder, and permits the air to pass up thro' it. It requires no snuffing. They make shade candlesticks of them at two guineas price, which are excellent for reading and are much used by studious men.

Jefferson's fascination with the latest practical advances in European technology was far more than mere interest in gadgets; it was part of his personal mission to Europe. As he explained to President Joseph Willard of Harvard, America had a special need to cultivate scientific knowledge and a special opportunity for contributing to that field.

CABINET DES ESTAMPES, BIBLIOTHÈQUE NATIONALE

The Grille de Chaillot, near Jefferson's residence in Paris, looking down the Champs-Elysées

Paris Mar. 24. 1789.

What a feild have we at our doors to signalize ourselves in! The botany of America is far from being exhausted: it's Mineralogy is untouched, and it's Natural history or Zoology totally mistaken and misrepresented. As far as I have seen there is not one single species of terrestrial birds common to Europe and America, and I question if there be a single species of quadrupeds. (Domestic animals are to be excepted.) It is for such institutions as that over which you preside so worthily, Sir, to do justice to our country, it's productions, and it's genius. It is the work to which the young men, whom you are forming, should lay their hands. We have spent the prime of our lives in procuring them the precious blessing of liberty. Let them spend theirs in shewing that it is the great parent of science and of virtue; and that a nation will be great in both always in proportion as it is free.

It was Jefferson's public mission, however, that consumed most of his time in the fall and winter of 1784. As soon as John Adams had returned from welcoming his wife and daughter in London, the three commissioners began their work.

Autobiography, 1821

Mr. Adams soon joined us at Paris, & our first employment was to prepare a general form to be proposed to such nations as were disposed to treat with us. During the negotiations for peace with the British Commissioner David Hartley, our Commissioners had proposed, on the suggestion of Doctr. Franklin, to insert an article exempt-

The Hôtel de Langeac, where he lived from 1785 to 1789, is also at far left in the picture opposite.

ing from capture by the public or private armed ships of either belligerent, when at war, all merchant vessels and their cargoes, employed merely in carrying on the commerce between nations. It was refused by England, and unwisely, in my opinion. For in the case of a war with us, their superior commerce places infinitely more at hazard on the ocean than ours; and as hawks abound in porportion to game, so our privateers would swarm in proportion to the wealth exposed to their prize, while theirs would be few for want of subjects of capture. We inserted this article in our form, with a provision against the molestation of fishermen, husbandmen, citizens unarmed and following their occupations in unfortified places, for the humane treatment of prisoners of war, the abolition of contraband of war, which exposes merchant vessels to such vexatious & ruinous detentions and abuses; and for the principle of free bottoms, free goods.

At the beginning of his mission, Jefferson was optimistic about prospects for favorable trade treaties. The Austrian Empire had reopened an old dispute with the Netherlands over the Scheldt River, and Jefferson wrote James Monroe of the advantages American diplomats might gain from a European war. He also outlined what he thought United States policy should be in dealing with the Barbary pirates.

Paris Nov. 11. 1784.

The die is thrown here and has turned up war. Doubts whether an accomodation may not yet take place are still entertained by some, but I hold it impossible.... Supposing we are not involved in a new contest with Great Britain, this war may possibly renew that disposition in the powers of Europe to treat with us on liberal principles, a disposition which blazed out with enthusiasm on the conclusion of peace, but which had subsided as far below the just level in consequence of the anarchy, and depravation of principle which the British papers have constantly held forth as having taken place among us. I think when it shall become certain that war is to take place, that those nations at least who are engaged in it will be glad to ensure our neutrality and friendly dispositions by a just treaty. Such a one, or none is our business.

[But, he warned Congressman Monroe, there was little

Engraving of David Hartley after a portrait by George Romney

chance of success in forcing commercial concessions from Britain, the commissioners' main goal, until Congress enforced the principle that "there should be no trade where there is no treaty."]

With England nothing will produce a treaty but an enforcement of the resolutions of Congress proposing that there should be no trade where there is no treaty. The infatuation of that nation seems really preternatural. If any thing will open their eyes it will be an application to the avarice of their merchants who are the very people who have opposed the treaty first meditated, and who have excited the spirit of hostility at present prevailing against us. Deaf to every principle of common sense, insensible of the feelings of man, they firmly beleive they shall be permitted by us to keep all the carrying trade and that we shall attempt no act of retaliation because they are pleased to think it our interest not to do so.... We have taken some pains to find out the sums which the nations of Europe give to the Barbary states to purchase their peace. They will not tell this; yet from some glimmerings it appears to be very considerable; and I do expect that they would tax us at one, two, or perhaps three hundred thousand dollars a year. Surely our people will not give this. Would it not be better to offer them an equal treaty. If they refuse, why not go to war with them? Spain, Portugal, Naples and Venice are now at war with them. Every part of the Mediterranean therefore would offer us friendly ports. We ought to begin a naval power, if we mean to carry on our own commerce. Can we begin it on a more honourable occasion or with a weaker foe? I am of opinion Paul Jones with half a dozen frigates would totally destroy their commerce: not by attempting bombardments as the Mediterranean states do wherein they act against the whole Barbary force brought to a point, but by constant cruising and cutting them to peices by peicemeal.

As the winter wore on, progress on trade agreements was slow, despite the threat of war. Subsequently the commissioners decided, for strategic reasons, to propose no new treaties.

Autobiography, 1821

In a conference with the Count de Vergennes [Foreign

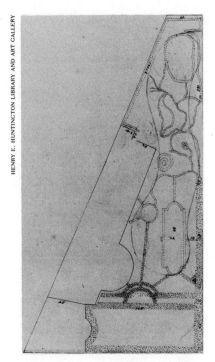

Jefferson made this drawing of the Hôtel de Langeac and its gardens.

*John Paul Jones
by Charles Willson Peale*

Minister of France], it was thought better to leave to legislative regulation on both sides such modifications of our commercial intercourse as would voluntarily flow from amicable dispositions. Without urging, we sounded the ministers of the several European nations at the court of Versailles, on their dispositions towards mutual commerce, and the expediency of encouraging it by the protection of a treaty. Old Frederic of Prussia met us cordially and without hesitation, and appointing the Baron de Thulemeyer, his minister at the Hague, to negotiate with us, we communicated to him our Project, which with little alteration by the King, was soon concluded. Denmark and Tuscany entered also into negociations with us. Other powers appearing indifferent we did not think it proper to press them. They seemed in fact to know little about us, but as rebels who had been successful in throwing off the yoke of the mother country. They were ignorant of our commerce, which had been always monopolized by England, and of the exchange of articles it might offer advantageously to both parties. They were inclined therefore to stand aloof until they could see better what relations might be usefully instituted with us. The negotiations therefore begun with Denmark & Tuscany we protracted designedly until our powers had expired; and abstained from making new propositions to others having no colonies; because our commerce being an exchange of raw for wrought materials, is a competent price for admission into the colonies of those possessing them: but were we to give it, without price, to others, all would claim it without price on the ordinary ground of gentis amicissimae [most favored nation].

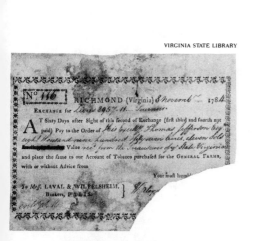

Bill of exchange made out to Jefferson for first payment on proposed statue of Washington

Gradually Jefferson's responsibilities increased. William Short, a young protégé Jefferson had invited to join him in France, arrived from Virginia at the end of November, 1784, with a letter from Governor Benjamin Harrison. Harrison asked Jefferson and Franklin to select a sculptor for a statue of Washington commissioned by the Virginia assembly. At first this seemed a simple enough matter, and Jefferson replied to Harrison after conferences with the famed Jean Antoine Houdon.

Paris Jan. 12. 1785

There could be no question raised as to the Sculptor who should be employed, the reputation of Monsr. Houdon of

Houdon's statue of Washington for
Virginia state capitol in Richmond

this city being unrivalled in Europe. He is resorted to for
the statues of most of the sovereigns in Europe. On conversing with him, Doctr. Franklin and myself became
satisfied that no statue could be executed so as to obtain
the approbation of those to whom the figure of the
original is known, but on an actual view by the artist.
Of course no statue of Genl. Washington, which might
be a true evidence of his figure to posterity could be
made from his picture. Statues are made every day from
portraits but if the person be living, they are always
condemned by those who know him for a want of resemblance, and this furnishes a conclusive presumption that
similar representations of the dead are equally unfaithful.
Monsr. Houdon whose reputation is such as to make it
his principal object, was so anxious to be the person who
should hand down the figure of the General to future
ages, that without hesitating a moment he offered to
abandon his business here, to leave the statues of kings
unfinished, and to go to America to take the true figure
by actual inspection and mensuration.

The artistic commission proved unexpectedly com-
plicated, and Jefferson would have to correspond for several years with
Harrison's successor, his old political enemy Patrick Henry. It was no wonder that the statue was not completed until 1796, for every detail was the
subject of endless discussion and debate. In 1787 Jefferson wrote Washington of the expert opinion sought concerning Washington's decision to be
represented in modern dress.

> Paris Aug. 14. 1787.
> I was happy to find by the letter of Aug. 1. 1786. which
> you did me the honour to write me, that the modern dress
> for your statue would meet your approbation. I found
> it strongly the sentiment of [Benjamin] West, [John
> Singleton] Copeley, [John] Trumbul and [Mather] Brown
> in London, after which it would be ridiculous to add that
> it was my own. I think a modern in an antique dress as
> *just* an object of ridicule as an Hercules or Marius with a
> periwig and chapeau bras.

In January another friend was reunited with Jefferson
when the Marquis de Lafayette returned to France from a triumphal American tour. Lafayette had to break the unhappy news that Jefferson's youngest

daughter, Lucy, had died at the age of two and a half of whooping cough. Jefferson ended his first winter in Paris mourning the death of the last child born to his wife. In this mood, he wrote bitterly to Monroe of new demands made by the Barbary pirates.

[Paris, February 6, 1785]

The attempts heretofore made to suppress these powers have been to exterminate them at one blow. They are too numerous and powerful by land for that. A small effort, but long continued, seems to be the only method. By suppressing their marine and trade totally and continuing this till the present race of seamen should be pretty well out of the way and the younger people betaken to husbandry for which their soil and climate is well fitted, these nests of banditti might be reformed. I am not well enough acquainted with the present dispositions of the European courts to say whether a general confederacy might be formed for suppressing these pyracies. Such as should refuse would give us a just right to turn pyrates also on their West India trade, and to require an annual tribute which might reimburse what we may be obliged to pay to obtain a safe navigation in their seas. Were we possessed even of a small naval force what a bridle would it be in the mouths of the West India powers and how respectfully would they demean themselves toward us. Be assured that the present disrespect of the nations of Europe for us will inevitably bring on insults which must involve us in war. A coward is much more exposed to quarrels than a man of spirit.

Jefferson's compilation of his salary for several years in Paris; he wrote to James Monroe that meeting his diplomatic expenses required "rigid economy bordering...on meanness."

Fortunately, the mild spring brought a fresh assignment sure to return him to his usual energy and good humor. In May the aging Franklin was granted leave to return to America; Jefferson and Adams would become America's ministers at Paris and London, respectively. Their joint commission had produced only one successful negotiation, an agreement with Prussia; but Jefferson would henceforth be free to function more independently. One of his main objects was to open up the subject of fundamental reciprocity; he immediately wrote to Adams suggesting that they negotiate a treaty granting virtually unlimited reciprocity of rights to nationals among the contracting powers. He knew that Britain would reject it, but France might go along. It was really beyond their powers, but Jefferson was willing to risk proposing it; Adams never replied.

As Adams and Franklin made arrangements to leave France, Jefferson hurried to work out necessary details for his own responsibilities. Now certain that he would be abroad for some time, he decided to bring his younger daughter Mary, or Polly, to live with him. He began a campaign to persuade the nine-year-old girl to leave her beloved Aunt Eppes through letters that blended outright bribery with stern moral lessons.

Paris Sep. 20. 1785.

I know, my dear Polly, how sorry you will be, and ought to be, to leave them and your cousins but your [sister and m]yself cannot live without you, and after a while we will carry you back again to see your friends in Virginia. In the meantime you shall be taught here to play on the harpsichord, to draw, to dance, to read and talk French and such other things as will make you more worthy of the love of your friends. But above all things, by our care and love of you, we will teach you to love us more than you will do if you stay so far from us.... when you come here you shall have as many dolls and playthings as you want for yourself....I hope you are a very good girl, that you love your uncle and aunt very much, and are very thankful to them for all their goodness to you; that you never suffer yourself to be angry with any body, that you give your playthings to those who want them, that you do whatever any body desires of you that is right, that you never tell stories, never beg for any thing, mind your book and your work when your aunt tells you, never play but when she permits you, nor go where she forbids you. Remember too as a constant charge not to go out without your bonnet because it will make you very ugly and then we should not love you so much....We shall hope to have you with us next summer....

Miniature of Martha Jefferson at age seventeen, by Joseph Boze

By June Jefferson's melancholy had disappeared. Even in reporting a fatal ballooning accident to Joseph Jones, he emphasized the scientific significance of the ascension rather than its tragic outcome.

Paris, June 19, 1785.

An accident has happened here which will probably damp the ardour with which aerial navigation has been pursued. Monsr. Pilatre de Rosiere had been attending many months at Boulogne a fair wind to cross the channel in a baloon which was compounded of one of inflammable air and another called a Montgolfier with rarefied air only. He at length thought the wind fair and with a companion ascended. After proceeding in a proper direction about two leagues the wind changed and brought them again over the French coast. Being at the height of about 6000 feet some accident, unknown, burst the balloon of inflammable air and the Montgolfier being unequal alone to sustain their weight they precipitated from that height to the earth and were crushed to atoms. Though navigation by water is attended with frequent accidents, and in it's infancy must have been attended with more, yet these are now so familiar that we think little of them, while that which has signalised the two first martyrs to the aeronautical art will probably deter very many from the experiments they would have been disposed to make.

Jefferson made these calculations on his rate of walking from the Grille de Chaillot to various spots, noting that he walked a "French mile [1¼ English miles] in 17½ minutes."

Summer also brought an artistic assignment more to Jefferson's taste than the long negotiations with Houdon.

Autobiography, 1821

I was written to in 1785 (being then in Paris) by Directors appointed to superintend the building of a Capitol in Richmond, to advise them as to a plan, and to add to it one of a prison. Thinking it a favorable opportunity of introducing into the state an example of architecture in the classic style of antiquity, and the Maison quarrée of Nismes, an antient Roman temple, being considered as the most perfect model existing of what may be called Cubic architecture, I applied to M. Clerissault, who had published drawings of the Antiquities of Nismes, to have me a model of the building made in stucco, only changing the order from Corinthian to Ionic, on account of the difficulty of the Corinthian capitals. I yielded with reluctance to the taste of Clerissault, in his preference of the

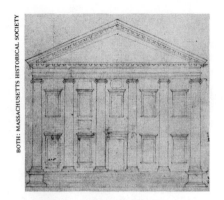

Jefferson's drawing of the front elevation of the Virginia capitol

modern capital of Scamozzi to the more noble capital of antiquity. This was executed by the artist whom Choiseul Gouffier [a Frenchman who had traveled in the Ottoman Empire] had carried with him to Constantinople, and employed while Ambassador, there, in making those beautiful models of the remains of Grecian architecture which are to be seen at Paris. To adapt the exterior to our use, I drew a plan for the interior, with the apartments necessary for legislative, executive & judiciary purposes, and accommodated in their size and distribution to the form and dimensions of the building.

As this fascinating project went forward, Jefferson received alarming news from Virginia: construction of the capitol had begun before his design was completed. He wrote indignantly to Madison.

Paris Sep. 20. 1785.

I have been much mortified with information which I received two days ago from Virginia that the first brick of the Capitol would be laid within a few days. But surely the delay of this peice of a summer would have been repaid by the savings in the plan preparing here, were we to value it's other superiorities as nothing. But how is a taste in this beautiful art to be formed in our countrymen, unless we avail ourselves of every occasion when public buildings are to be erected, of presenting to them models for their study and imitation? Pray try if you can effect the stopping of this work.... The loss will be only of the laying the bricks already laid, or a part of them.... This loss is not to be weighed against the saving of money which will arise, against the comfort of laying out the public money for something honourable, the satisfaction of seeing an object and proof of national good taste, and the regret and mortification of erecting a monument of our barbarism which will be loaded with execrations as long as it shall endure.

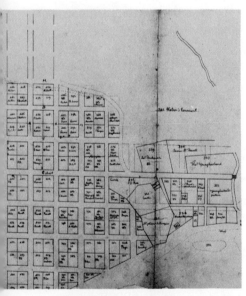

Plan Jefferson had made c. 1782–85 for extending the town of Richmond

The construction already started in Richmond was not irreversible and Jefferson continued his work on the plans. In January the drawings were ready, and he forwarded them to a friend, Dr. James Currie, with a touch of justifiable pride.

Paris Jan. 28. 1786.

I send by this conveiance designs for the Capitol. They

are not the brat of a whimsical conception never before brought to light, but copied from the most precious the most perfect model of antient architecture remaining on earth; one which has received the approbation of near 2000 years, and which is sufficiently remarkable to have been visited by all travellers.

With minor alterations, Jefferson's plans were used for the completion of the capitol, giving his state a splendid example of neoclassical architecture to symbolize the commonwealth. Even as he was collaborating with the French architectural expert Charles-Louis Clérisseau on the designs, Jefferson had begun assuming his duties as Minister to France. His position was a delicate one, due to Benjamin Franklin's overwhelming personal popularity with the French court and nation. Jefferson explained how he had successfully dealt with one aspect of this problem after Franklin's departure for the United States in July, 1785.

Philadelphia, Feb. 19. 1791

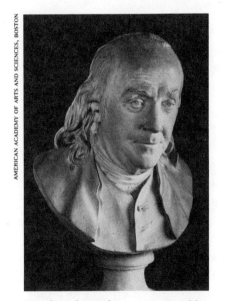

Houdon's bust of Benjamin Franklin

I can only therefore testify in general that there appeared to me more respect & veneration attached to the character of Doctor Franklin in France than to that of any other person in the same country, foreign or native....

When he left Passy, it seemed as if the village had lost it's Patriarch. On taking leave of the court, which he did by letter, the king ordered him to be handsomely complimented, & furnished him with a litter & mules of his own, the only kind of conveyance the state of his health could bear....

The succession to Dr. Franklin at the court of France, was an excellent school of humility. On being presented to any one as the Minister of America, the common-place question, used in such cases was *'c'est vous, Monsieur, qui remplace le Docteur Franklin?'* 'It is you, Sir, who replace Doctor Franklin?' I generally answered 'no one can replace him, Sir: I am only his successor.'

Jefferson never sought to rival his predecessor's popularity. Franklin had been an excellent representative for America during wartime, and he had been, in a sense, an advertisement for the new nation with his witty anecdotes and conscious role-playing. Jefferson, on the other hand, preferred to work quietly, often doggedly, behind the scenes—a method far better suited to the needs of America's diplomatic interests in the Confederation period. Jefferson's major task was to win concessions from France's powerful Minister of Foreign Affairs, the Comte de Vergennes, who, Jefferson once remarked, was guided by "devotion to the principles of pure despotism" and had no love for the American Republic. But the Count's "fear of England" made him "value us as a make weight." The elderly nobleman and the young American diplomat found each other surprisingly congenial colleagues, for they shared a dislike of intrigues.

Autobiography, 1821

The Count de Vergennes had the reputation with the diplomatic corps of being wary & slippery in his diplomatic intercourse; and so he might be with those whom he knew to be slippery and double-faced themselves. As he saw that I had no indirect views, practised no subtleties, meddled in no intrigues, pursued no concealed object, I found him as frank, as honorable, as easy of access to reason as any man with whom I had ever done business; and I must say the same for his successor Montmorin, one of the most honest and worthy of human beings.

In the summer of 1785, Jefferson had begun arranging for the personal direction of his embassy. William Short was named as his secretary, an appointment that gave Jefferson an invaluable and trusted aide during his remaining years in Paris. John Jay, in the Department for Foreign Affairs, received Jefferson's outline of his views on America's long-term commercial goals and the role of diplomacy in promoting them.

Paris Aug. 23, 1785.

We have now lands enough to employ an infinite number of people in their cultivation. Cultivators of the earth are the most valuable citizens. They are the most vigorous, the most independant, the most virtuous, and they are tied to their country and wedded to it's liberty and interests by the most lasting bands. As long therefore as they can find emploiment in this line, I would not convert them into mariners, artisans, or any thing else. But our citizens will find emploiment in this line till their numbers, and of course their productions, become too great for the demand both internal and foreign. This is not the case as yet, and probably will not be for a considerable time. As soon as it is, the surplus of hands must be turned to something else. I should then perhaps wish to turn them to the sea in preference to manufactures, because comparing the characters of the two classes I find the former the most valuable citizens. I

Secretary Jay, to whom Jefferson reported, did not support his policy of multiplying diplomatic and commercial bonds with France; he once leaked part of the Minister's dispatches to the press.

Historic Mansions, WESTCOTT

Office of Secretary for Foreign Affairs, John Jay, in Philadelphia

consider the class of artificers as the panders of vice and the instruments by which the liberties of a country are generally overturned. However we are not free to decide this question on principles of theory only. Our people are decided in the opinion that it is necessary for us to take a share in the occupation of the ocean, and their established habits induce them to require that the sea be kept open to them, and that that line of policy be pursued which will render the use of that element as great as possible to them. I think it a duty in those entrusted with the administration of their affairs to conform themselves to the decided choice of their constituents: and that therefore we should in every instance preserve an equality of right to them in the transportation of commodities, in the right of fishing, and in the other uses of the sea. But what will be the consequence? Frequent wars without a doubt. Their property will be violated on the sea, and in foreign ports, their persons will be insulted, emprisoned &c. for pretended debts, contracts, crimes, contraband &c. &c. These insults must be resented, even if we had no feelings, yet to prevent their eternal repetition. Or in other words, our commerce on the ocean and in other countries must be paid for by frequent war. The justest dispositions possible in ourselves will not secure us against it. It would be necessary that all other nations were just also. Justice indeed on our part will save us from those wars which would have been produced by a contrary disposition. But how to prevent those produced by the wrongs of other nations? By putting ourselves in a condition to punish them. Weakness provokes insult and injury, while a condition to punish it often prevents it. This reasoning leads to the necessity of some naval force, that being the only weapo[n] with which we can reach an enemy. I think it to our interest to punis[h] the first insult: because an insult unpunished is the parent of many oth[ers]. We are not at this moment in a condition to do it, but we should put ourselv[es] into it as soon as possible. If a war with England should take place it see[ms] to me that the first thing necessary would be a resolution to abandon the carrying trade because we cannot protect it. Foreign nations must in that case be invited to bring us what we want and to take our productions in their own bottoms. This alone could prevent the loss of those productions to us and the acquisition of them to our enemy. Our seamen might be emploied in depredations on their trade. But how dreadfully we shall suffer on our coasts, if we have no force on the water, former experience has taught us. Indeed I look forward with horror to the very possible case of war with an European power, and think there is no protection against them but from the possession of some force on the sea. Our vicinity to their West India possessions and to the fisheries is a bridle which a small naval force on our part would hold in the mouths of the most powerful of these countries. I hope our land office will rid us of our debts, and that our first attention then will be to the beginning a naval force of some sort. This alone can countenance our people as carriers on the water, and I suppose them to be determined to continue such.

In France, Jefferson could do little to further his proposal for developing an American navy; his own contribution to strengthening American commerce was to attempt to remove foreign restrictions on American goods and ships. He described his duties at Paris as "the receipt of our whale-oils, salted fish, and salted meats on favorable terms, the admission of our rice on equal terms with that of Piedmont, Egypt, & the Levant, a mitigation of the monopolies of our tobacco by the Farmers-general, and a free admission of our productions into their islands [the West Indies]...." His campaign began with a letter to Vergennes suggesting that the King abolish the monopoly held by the Farmers General, which had the sole right to purchase tobacco imports.

Paris August 15. 1785.

In truth no two countries are better calculated for the exchanges of commerce. France wants rice, tobacco, potash, furs, ship-timber. We want wines, brandies, oils and manufactures. There is an affection too between the two people which disposes them to favour one another. If they do not come together then to make the exchange in their own ports, it shews there is some substantial obstruction in the way. We have had the benefit of too many proofs of his majesty's friendly disposition towards the United states, and know too well his affectionate care of his own subjects, to doubt his willingness to remove these obstructions, if they can be unequivocally pointed out. It is for his wisdom to decide whether the [tobacco] monopoly which is the subject of this letter be deservedly classed with the principal of these.

Even as he cautiously introduced Vergennes to his theories of commercial reciprocity, Jefferson knew that his own nation could nullify his efforts. The American states, free to adopt individual trade restrictions, made it virtually impossible for a United States envoy in Europe to promise that a consistent American policy on trade existed. While his experiences abroad confirmed his dissatisfaction with the halting American Confederation, continued exposure to European society produced a subtle change in his reports home. As soon as he reached Europe, he had obliged friends in America with observations on politics and excited descriptions of scientific advances and the latest inventions. But Jefferson was primarily a student of the human condition; as a careful observer and conscientious reporter, he did not record his feelings on such complicated matters as the nature of the French people and their society until he was sure of his conclusions. Perhaps the best known of his analyses was contained in a 1785 letter to Carlo Bellini, William and Mary's first professor of modern languages. Jefferson had fought for Bellini's appointment at the college and he fulfilled a promise to give the Florentine savant his impressions of Europe with this famous and sometimes biting critique of the Old World.

Paris Sep. 30. 1785.

Behold me at length on the vaunted scene of Europe! It is not necessary for your information that I should enter into details concerning it. But you are perhaps curious to know how this new scene has struck a savage of the mountains of America. Not advantageously I assure you. I find the general fate of humanity here most deplorable. The truth of Voltaire's observation offers itself perpetually, that every man here must be either the hammer or the anvil. It is a true picture of that country to which they say we shall pass hereafter, and where we are to see god and his angels in splendor, and crouds of the damned trampled under their feet. While the great mass of the people are thus suffering under physical and moral oppression, I have endeavored to examine more nearly the condition of the great, to appreciate the true value of the circumstances in their situation which dazzle the bulk of the spectators, and especially to compare it with that degree of happiness which is enjoyed in America by every class of people. Intrigues of love occupy the younger, and those of ambition the more elderly part of the great. Conjugal love having no existence among them, domestic happiness, of which that is the basis, is utterly unknown. In lieu of this are substituted pursuits which nourish and invigorate all our bad passions, and which offer only moments of extasy amidst days and months

The Comte de Vergennes

*One of the calling cards
Jefferson used in France*

of restlessness and torment. Much, very much inferior this to the tranquil permanent felicity with which domestic society in America blesses most of it's inhabitants, leaving them to follow steadily those pursuits which health and reason approve, and rendering truly delicious the intervals of these pursuits. In science, the mass of people is two centuries behind ours, their literati half a dozen years before us. Books, really good, acquire just reputation in that time, and so become known to us and communicate to us all their advances in knowlege. Is not this delay compensated by our being placed out of the reach of that swarm of nonsense which issues daily from a thousand presses and perishes almost in issuing? With respect to what are termed polite manners, without sacrificing too much the sincerity of language, I would wish [my] countrymen to adopt just so much of European politeness as to be ready [to] make all those little sacrifices of self which really render European manners amiable, and relieve society from the disagreeable scenes to which rudeness often exposes it. Here it seems that a man might pass a life without encountering a single rudeness. In the pleasures of the table they are far before us, because with good taste they unite temperance. They do not terminate the most sociable meals by transforming themselves into brutes. I have never yet seen a man drunk in France, even among the lowest of the people. Were I to proceed to tell you how much I enjoy their architecture, sculpture, painting, music, I should want words. It is in these arts they shine. The last of them particularly is an enjoiment, the deprivation of which with us cannot be calculated. I am almost ready to say it is the only thing which from my heart I envy them, and which in spight of all the authority of the decalogue I do covet. — But I am running on in an estimate of things infinitely better known to you than to me, and which will only serve to convince you that I have brought with me all the prejudices of country, habit and age.

Yet Jefferson's unfavorable reactions to French society were mitigated by a sincere affection for the French people, whose inbred gentility and courtesy were so like his own. He described their congenial temperament to Elizabeth Trist.

Paris Aug. 18. 1785.

I am much pleased with the people of this country. The roughnesses of the human mind are so thoroughly rubbed off with them that it seems as if one might glide thro' a whole life among them without a justle. Perhaps too their manners may be the best calculated for happiness to a people in their situation. But I am convinced they fall far short of effecting a happiness so temperate, so uniform and so lasting as is generally enjoyed with us. The domestic bonds here are absolutely done away. And where can their compensation be found? Perhaps they may catch some moments of transport above the level of the ordinary tranquil joy we experience, but they are separated by long intervals during which all the passions are at sea without rudder or compass. Yet fallacious as these pursuits of happiness are, they seem on the whole to furnish the most effectual abstraction from a contemplation of the hardness of their government. Indeed it is difficult to conceive how so good a people, with so good a king, so well disposed rulers in general, so genial a climate, so fertile a soil, should be rendered so ineffectual for producing human happiness by one single curse, that of a bad form of government. But it is a fact. In spite of the mildness of their governors the people are ground to powder by the vices of the form of government.

Jefferson's love for the common people of France was deepened by his compassion for their plight under the monarchy. In America he had written much of the evils of tyranny, but he had seen nothing of the human suffering of the subjects of a king until he came to Europe. The reality of despotism was far worse than anything he had imagined. "Of twenty millions of people supposed to be in France," he wrote an American correspondent, "I am of opinion there are nineteen millions more wretched, more accursed in every circumstance of human existence, than the most conspicuously wretched individual of the whole United States." Jefferson recounted to Madison an incident during a visit to Fountainebleau that illustrated the hopeless conditions under which the French lived.

Fontainebleau Oct. 28. 1785.

As soon as I had got clear of the town I fell in with a poor woman walking at the same rate with myself and going the same course. Wishing to know the condition of the labouring poor I entered into conversation with her, which I began by enquiries for the path which would lead

BOTH: *Geography*, GOODRICH

The lives of French peasants such as the above aroused Jefferson's compassion; below, women washing their clothes in the Seine.

me into the mountain: and thence proceeded to enquiries into her vocation, condition and circumstance. She told me she was a day labourer, at 8. sous [about eight cents] or 4 d. sterling the day; that she had two children to maintain, and to pay a rent of 30 livres [600 sous a year] for her house (which would consume the hire of 75 days), that often she could get no emploiment, and of course was without bread. As we had walked together near a mile and she had so far served me as a guide, I gave her, on parting 24 sous. She burst into tears of a gratitude which I could perceive was unfeigned, because she was unable to utter a word. She had probably never before received so great an aid. This little attendrissement, with the solitude of my walk led me into a train of reflections on that unequal division of property which occasions the numberless instances of wretchedness which I had observed in this country and is to be observed all over Europe. The property of this country is absolutely concentered in a very few hands, having revenues of from half a million of guineas a year downwards....I asked myself what could be the reason that so many should be permitted to beg who are willing to work, and in a country where there is a very considerable proportion of uncultivated lands?... Whenever there is in any country, uncultivated lands and unemployed poor, it is clear that the laws of property have been so far extended as to violate natural right. The earth is given as a common stock for man to labour and live on.

Such experiences confirmed Jefferson's conviction that America was especially fortunate in being isolated from European influences and that those born American were blessed by Providence. He confessed his own homesickness to a Hessian friend, the Baron de Geismar, who had been a prisoner of war in Charlottesville during the Revolution.

Paris Sep. 6. 1785.

I am now of an age which does not easily accomodate itself to new manners and new modes of living: and I am savage enough to prefer the woods, the wilds, and the independance of Monticello, to all the brilliant pleasures of this gay capital. I shall therefore rejoin myself to my native country with new attachments, with exaggerated esteem for it's advantages, for tho' there is less wealth there, there is more freedom, more ease and less misery.

He disapproved of wealthy Americans who sent their sons to Europe for an education and warned friends not to endanger their children's morals by sending them abroad. He dismissed the supposed advantages of such travel in a letter to John Banister, Jr., the son of an old friend in Williamsburg.

Paris Oct. 15. 1785.

Let us view the disadvantages of sending a youth to Europe. To enumerate them all would require a volume. I will select a few. If he goes to England he learns drinking, horse-racing and boxing. These are the peculiarities of English education. The following circumstances are common to education in that and the other countries of Europe. He acquires a fondness for European luxury and dissipation and a contempt for the simplicity of his own country; he is fascinated with the privileges of the European aristocrats, and sees with abhorrence the lovely equality which the poor enjoys with the rich in his own country: he contracts a partiality for aristocracy or monarchy; he forms foreign friendships which will never be useful to him, and loses the season of life for forming in his own country those friendships which of all others are the most faithful and permanent: he is led by the strongest of all the human passions into a spirit for female intrigue destructive of his own and others happiness, or a passion for whores destructive of his health, and in both cases learns to consider fidelity to the marriage bed as an ungentlemanly practice and inconsistent with happiness: he recollects the voluptuary dress and arts of the European women and pities and despises the chaste affections and simplicity of those of his own country; he retains thro' life a fond recollection and a hankering after those places which were the scenes of his first pleasures and of his first connections; he returns to his own country, a foreigner, unacquainted with the practices of domestic œconomy necessary to preserve him from ruin; speaking and writing his native tongue as a foreigner, and therefore unqualified to obtain those distinctions which eloquence of the pen and tongue ensures in a free country.... Cast your eye over America: who are the men of most learning, of most eloquence, most beloved by their country and most trusted and promoted by them? They are those who have been educated among them, and whose manners, morals and habits are perfectly homogeneous with those of the country.

Bᴜt whatever France's faults, Jefferson could console himself on being stationed in Paris rather than London. Early reports of John Adams's experiences in the British capital convinced Jefferson that his dislike of that nation (which he had never visited) was justified. He sympathized with Abigail Adams on her residence among the Britons and offered a facetious explanation for their ungracious behavior.

Paris Sep. 25. 1785.

William Stephens Smith

I receive by Mr. Short a budget of London papers. They teem with every horror of which human nature is capable. Assassinations, suicides, thefts, robberies, and, what is worse than assassination, theft, suicide or robbery, the blackest slanders! Indeed the man must be of rock, who can stand all this; to Mr. Adams it will be but one victory the more. It would have illy suited me. I do not love difficulties. I am fond of quiet, willing to do my duty, but irritable by slander and apt to be forced by it to abandon my post. These are weaknesses from which reason and your counsels will preserve Mr. Adams. I fancy it must be the quantity of animal food eaten by the English which renders their character insusceptible of civilisation. I suspect it is in their kitchens and not in their churches that their reformation must be worked, and that Missionaries of that description from hence would avail more than those who should endeavor to tame them by precepts of religion or philosophy.

Jefferson soon had an unwelcome opportunity to become better acquainted with the British. At the end of February, he received an unexpected visit from William Stephens Smith, John Adams's secretary. Smith brought word that the Portugese minister in London was ready to negotiate a treaty, and "more Important," that Adams had met three times with the ambassador from Tripoli and begged Jefferson to "come here without loss of Time." Jefferson seized the opportunity to discuss his views on the Barbary powers with Adams and arrived in London March 11.

It was Jefferson's only extended visit to England and as a diplomatic mission, it was inconclusive. A commercial treaty was reached with the Portugese envoy, but it was eventually repudiated by the Lisbon government. As for the Tripolitan ambassador, Abdrahamar, he revealed himself as an unabashed extortionist who regaled Adams and Jefferson with a narrative of his country's piratical history and an analysis of the religious justification for enslaving Christian "sinners" encountered on their raids. Jefferson wrote William Carmichael, the chargé d'affaires in Madrid, of the sum needed to exempt American shipping from such treatment.

Paris May 5. 1786.

He asked us thirty thousand guineas for a peace with his court, and as much for Tunis for which he said he could answer. What we were authorized to offer being to this but as a drop to a bucket, our conferences were repeated only for the purpose of obtaining information. If the demands of Algiers and Marocco should be proportioned to this, according to their superior power, it is easy to foresee that the U.S. will not buy a peace with money.

Such ridiculous demands only strengthened Jefferson's determination to resist the time-honored custom of blackmail by the Barbary States. When he returned to Paris, he drew up a plan for a federation with the smaller European maritime powers to act as an international patrol of the Mediterranean. His idea was not adopted at the time, however, and the problem of the Barbary pirates would plague him and the United States for almost twenty years more. The last task Jefferson and Adams undertook together, a final attempt to reach a trade agreement with Britain, was no more successful. The British ministers ignored them, and the bad manners of George III, who turned his back on the diplomats, confirmed Jefferson's contempt for that monarch.

Autobiography, 1821

On my presentation as usual to the King and Queen at their levees, it was impossible for anything to be more ungracious than their notice of Mr. Adams & myself. I saw at once that the ulcerations in the narrow mind of that mulish being left nothing to be expected on the subject of my attendance.

Jefferson's early dislike of Britain as an enemy in wartime hardened into smoldering resentment in time of peace. As he revealed in a letter to Carmichael, Jefferson did not believe that the conflict that had led to the Revolution was really over.

Paris May 5. 1786.

I think the king, ministers, and nation are more bitterly hostile to us at present than at any period of the late war.... Our enemies (for such they are in fact) have for 12. years past followed but one uniform rule, that of doing exactly the contrary of what reason points out. Having early during our contest observed this in the British conduct, I governed myself by it in all prognostications of their measures; and I can say with truth it never failed me but in the circumstance of their making peace with us.

The only pleasant memories Jefferson carried back to France from Britain were those of English gardens he and Adams toured during his stay. Thomas Whately's *Observations on Modern Gardening* had been Jefferson's botanical bible when he laid out his own gardens at Monticello. In touring some of the famous sites described by Whately, Jefferson was delighted to find that the descriptions he had read so carefully in Virginia were "remarkable for their exactness."

"Notes of a Tour of English Gardens" [April, 1786] I always walked over the gardens with his book in my hand, examined with attention the particular spots he described, found them so justly characterised by him as to be easily recognised, and saw with wonder, that his fine imagination had never been able to seduce him from the truth. My enquiries were directed chiefly to such practical things as might enable me to estimate the expence of making and maintaining a garden in that style.

In a description of his British visit to John Page, Jefferson could, indeed, find little to commend except those gardens.

Paris May 4. 1786.
The gardening in that country is the article in which it surpasses all the earth. I mean their pleasure gardening. This indeed went far beyond my ideas. The city of London, tho' handsomer than Paris, is not so handsome as Philadelphia. Their architecture is in the most wretched stile I ever saw, not meaning to except America where it is bad, nor even Virginia where it is worse than in any other part of America, which I have seen. The mechanical arts in London are carried to a wonderful perfection.

The best part of his stay was the chance to confirm his ties with the Adamses. Jefferson wrote James Madison of his reassessment of his colleague in London.

Paris Jan. 30. 1787.
You know the opinion I formerly entertained of my friend Mr. Adams. Yourself and the governor [Edmund Randolph] were the first who shook that opinion. I

170

John Adams, 1788, by Mather Brown

afterwards saw proofs which convicted him of a degree of vanity, and of a blindness to it, of which no germ had appeared in Congress. A 7-months' intimacy with him here and as many weeks in London have given me opportunities of studying him closely. He is vain, irritable and a bad calculator of the force and probable effect of the motives which govern men. This is all the ill which can possibly be said of him. He is as disinterested as the being which made him: he is profound in his views: and accurate in his judgment except where knowledge of the world is necessary to form a judgment. He is so amiable, that I pronounce you will love him if ever you become acquainted with him.

Leaving the Adamses, a haven of American hospitality and affectionate family life, Jefferson must have journeyed to Paris a lonely man. Patsy would soon be of age to marry and leave him, and young Polly still resisted efforts to bring her to France. At forty-three Jefferson had been a widower four and a half years, devoted to the memory of his wife and the education of their daughters. When he returned to Paris, he was vulnerable to emotional attachments as he had never been since Martha's death. Since then he had formed many friendships with women, mainly with the wives of colleagues like Adams and Lafayette and with the stimulating intellectuals of the Paris salons. But there had been no hint of romance in his life. The idleness and dissipation of most of the ladies of the French upper class disgusted Jefferson, and he would hardly have been attracted by one of the glittering creatures he described to Mrs. William Bingham, a beautiful young Philadelphia matron who had visited Paris with her husband.

Paris Feb. 7. 1787.

Country Seats of the United States . . . BY WILLIAM BIRCH, 1808

Lansdowne, the country home of the William Binghams of Philadelphia

You are then engaged to tell me truly and honestly whether you do not find the tranquil pleasures of America preferable to the empty bustle of Paris. For to what does that bustle tend? At eleven o'clock it is day chez Madame. The curtains are drawn. Propped on bolsters and pillows, and her head scratched into a little order, the bulletins of the sick are read, and the billets of the well. She writes to some of her acquaintance and receives the visits of others. If the morning is not very thronged, she is able to get out and hobble round the cage of the Palais royal: but she must hobble quickly, for the Coeffeur's turn is come; and a tremendous turn it is! Happy, if he does not make her arrive when dinner is half over! The torpitude of digestion a little passed, she flutters half an hour thro' the streets by way of paying visits, and then to the Spectacles. These finished, another half hour is devoted to dodging in and out of the doors of her very sincere friends, and away to supper. After supper cards; and after cards bed, to rise at noon the next day, and to tread, like a mill-horse, the same trodden circle over again. Thus the days of life are consumed, one by one, without an object beyond the present moment. . . .

In America, on the other hand, the society of your husband, the fond cares for the children, the arrangements of the house, the improvements of the grounds fill every moment with a healthy and an useful activity. Every exertion is encouraging, because to present amusement it joins the promise of some future good. The intervals of leisure are filled by the society of real friends, whose affections are not thinned to cob-web by being spread over a thousand objects.

In the summer of 1786, Jefferson met a woman whose accomplishments went beyond those of Parisian socialites—Maria Hadfield Cosway. At twenty-seven, Mrs. Cosway had begun to earn a reputation as a miniaturist, and she shared Jefferson's musical talents. Maria was quite unlike the French aristocrats Jefferson scorned, and she was equally unlike the provincial ladies of Virginia and the serious, intellectual Abigail Adams. An Englishwoman who had spent her girlhood in Italy, Maria Cosway was cosmopolitan and charming—and an incurable flirt. When she visited Paris with her husband Richard, a fashionable painter, they were introduced to Jefferson by the American artist John Trumbull.

It was soon apparent that Jefferson found the blonde, blue-eyed Mrs. Cosway irresistible, and the summer ended with a month of clandestine meetings with Maria. Jefferson was hopelessly infatuated, and Mrs. Cosway encouraged his restrained but flattering advances. Their brief romance ended in October when she and her husband returned to England, and that sad occasion was immortalized by a letter Jefferson composed after bidding her farewell. His "dialogue between my Head and my Heart" is a touching love letter made all the more poignant because the "Head" of the Virginia philosopher and diplomat seems to emerge a victor over the "Heart" of the lonely widower.

Paris Octob. 12. 1786.

[My dear] Madam

Having performed the last sad office of handing you into your carriage at the Pavillon de St. Denis, and seen the wheel get actually into motion, I turned on my heel and walked, more dead than alive, to the opposite door, where my own was awaiting me....I was carried home. Seated by my fire side, solitary and sad, the following dialogue took place between my Head and my Heart.

HEAD.   Well, friend, you seem to be in a pretty trim.

HEART.   I am indeed the most wretched of all earthly beings. Overwhelmed with grief, every fibre of my frame distended beyond it's natural powers to bear, I would willingly meet whatever catastrophe should leave me no more to feel or to fear.

HEAD.   These are the eternal consequences of your warmth and precipitation. This is one of the scrapes into which you are ever leading us. You confess your follies indeed: but still you hug and cherish them, and no reformation can be hoped, when there is no repentance.

HEART.   Oh my friend! This is no moment to upbraid my foibles. I am rent into fragments by the force of my grief! If you have any balm, pour it into my wounds: if none, do not harrow them by new torments. Spare me in this awful moment! At any other I will attend with patience to your admonitions....

[Here the "dialogue" becomes a recollection of Jefferson's brief friendship with the Cosways, from the day they met.]

*Maria Cosway, engraving after
a drawing by Richard Cosway*

HEAD.   Thou art the most incorrigible of all the beings that ever sinned! I reminded you of the follies of the first day, intending to deduce from thence some useful lessons for you, but instead of listening to these, you kindle at the recollection, you retrace the whole series with a fondness which shews you want nothing but the opportunity to act it over again. I often told you during it's course that you were imprudently engaging your affections under circumstances that must cost you a great deal of pain: that the persons indeed were of the greatest merit, possessing good sense, good humour, honest hearts, honest manners, and eminence in a lovely art: that the lady had moreover qualities and accomplishments, belonging to her sex, which might form a chapter apart for her: such as music, modesty, beauty, and that softness of disposition which is the ornament of her sex and charm of ours. But that all these considerations would increase the pang of separation: that their stay here was to be short: that you rack our whole system when you are parted from those you love, complaining that such a separation is worse than death, inasmuch as this ends our sufferings, whereas that only begins them: and that the separation would in this instance be the more severe as you would probably never see them again.

HEART.   But they told me they would come back again the next year.

HEAD.   But in the mean time see what you suffer: and their return too depends on so many circumstances that if you had a grain of prudence you would not count upon it. Upon the whole it is improbable and therefore you should abandon the idea of ever seeing them again.

HEART.   May heaven abandon me if I do! ...

[Next Jefferson fantasized on a visit to America by the two painters: "Where could they find such objects as in America for the exercise of their enchanting art?"]

HEAD.   I did not begin this lecture my friend with a view to learn from you what America is doing. Let us return then to our point. I wished to make you sensible how imprudent it is to place your affections, without reserve, on objects you must so soon lose, and whose loss when it comes must cost you such severe pangs. Remember the last night. You knew your friends were to leave Paris to-day. This was enough to throw you into agonies. All night you tossed us from one side of the bed to the other. No sleep, no rest.... This is not a world to live at random in as you do. To avoid these eternal distresses, to which you are for ever exposing us, you must learn to look forward before you take a step which may interest our peace. Everything in this world is matter of calculation. Advance then with caution, the balance in your hand. Put into one scale the pleasures which any object may offer; but put fairly into the other the pains which are to follow, and see which preponderates. The making an acquaintance is not a matter of indifference. When a new one is proposed to you, view it all round. Consider what advan-

Both Maria Cosway and her husband were accomplished painters. Richard drew the charming portrait of Maria (opposite), possibly while they were in Paris. Maria exhibited her painting The Hours *in the Royal Academy, from which the engraving (above) was made by Bartolozzi.*

tages it presents, and to what inconveniencies it may expose you. Do not bite at the bait of pleasure till you know there is no hook beneath it. The art of life is the art of avoiding pain: and he is the best pilot who steers clearest of the rocks and shoals with which it is beset. Pleasure is always before us; but misfortune is at our side: while running after that, this arrests us. The most effectual means of being secure against pain is to retire within ourselves, and to suffice for our own happiness.... Friendship is but another name for an alliance with the follies and the misfortunes of others....

HEART.   And what more sublime delight than to mingle tears with one whom the hand of heaven hath smitten! To watch over the bed of sickness, and to beguile it's tedious and it's painful moments! To share our bread with one to whom misfortune has left none! This world abounds indeed with misery: to lighten it's burthen we must divide it with one another.... Let the gloomy Monk, sequestered from the world, seek unsocial pleasures in the bottom of his cell! Let the sublimated philosopher grasp visionary happiness while pursuing phantoms dressed in the garb of truth! Their supreme wisdom is supreme folly: and they mistake for happiness the mere absence of pain. Had they ever felt the solid pleasure of one generous spasm of the heart, they would exchange for it all the frigid speculations of their lives, which you have been vaunting in such elevated terms. Believe me then, my friend, that that is a miserable arithmetic which would estimate friendship at nothing, or at less than nothing. Respect for you has induced me to enter into this discussion, and to hear principles uttered which I detest and abjure. Respect for myself now obliges me to recall you into the proper limits of your office. When nature assigned us the same habitation, she gave us over it a divided empire. To you she allotted the field of science, to me that of morals. When the circle is to be squared, or the orbit of a comet to be traced; when the arch of greatest strength, or the solid of least resistance is to be investigated, take you the problem: it is yours: nature has given me no cognisance of it. In like manner in denying to you the feelings of sympathy, of benevolence, of gratitude, of justice, of love, of friendship, she has excluded you from their controul....Fill paper as you please with triangles and squares: try how many ways you can hang and combine them together. I shall never envy nor controul your sublime delights. But leave me to decide when and where friendships are to be contracted....

I thought this a favorable proposition whereon to rest the issue of the dialogue. So I put an end to it by calling for my nightcap. Methinks I hear you wish to heaven I had called a little sooner, and so spared you the ennui of such a tedious sermon....Present me in the most friendly terms to Mr. Cosway, and receive me into your own recollection with a partiality and a warmth, proportioned, not to my own poor merit, but to the sentiments of sincere affection and esteem with which I have the honour to be, my dear Madam, your most obedient and humble servant,

TH: JEFFERSON

Jefferson was left alone in Paris with bittersweet memories of the coquettish Maria and a painful reminder of the romantic interlude: a severely injured right wrist resulting from a mysterious accident on September 18. Jefferson himself never explained the mishap beyond a rather sheepish reply to William Stephens Smith's concerned inquiries: "How the right hand became disabled would be a long story for the left to tell. It was by one of those follies from which good cannot come, but ill may." One theory is that he injured it trying to vault a wall in an attempt to impress Maria. If so, he paid dearly for playing the energetic suitor.

Diagnosed as a dislocation, the injury caused him constant pain in the fall of 1786. The continued swelling and the amount of physical pain indicate that the wrist may actually have been broken and never properly treated. Whatever its cause and precise nature, the injury prevented him from writing, and for an eighteenth-century diplomat in a foreign post, that was a major handicap. William Short could copy many official dispatches and Jefferson tried valiantly to write with his left hand, but his personal correspondence lapsed in the autumn months, and he carefully limited the number and length of official reports.

One topic had to be reported promptly, and proudly, to Secretary Jay: the success of Jefferson's efforts to gain trade concessions from France. Lafayette had guided Jefferson in implementing the proposals given to Vergennes in the fall of 1785. Prominent French business experts, introduced to Jefferson by the Marquis, urged him to propose that the government appoint a committee to consider Franco-American trade. Lafayette undertook this delicate assignment for him, and Calonne, the French

Minister of Finance, approved the proposal and even named Lafayette to the committee. On October 23, Jefferson gave Jay an account of the outcome of the committee's sessions.

Paris Oct. 23. 1786.

...[A] Committee had been established for considering the means of promoting the general commerce with America, and the M. de la Fayette was named of that committee. His influence in obtaining that establishment was valuable, but his labors and his perseverance as a member of it became infinitely more so....we thought it expedient to bring the general subject of the American commerce before the Committee; and as the members were much unacquainted with the nature and value of our Commercial productions, the Marquis proposed that in a letter to him as a member I should give as particular details of them as I could, as a ground for the committee to proceed on. I did so....The committee were well disposed, and agreed to report not only the general measures which they thought expedient to be adopted, but the form of the letter to be written by the Minister of finance to me, for the communication of those measures. I have received his letter this morning and have now the honour to inclose it. I accompany it with the one proposed by the committee...: it furnishes a proof of the disposition of the king and his ministers to produce a more intimate intercourse between the two nations. Indeed I must say that, as far as I am able to see, the friendship of the people of this country towards us is cordial and general, and that it is a kind of security for the friendship of ministers who cannot in any country be uninfluenced by the voice of the people. To this we may add that it is their interest as well as ours to multiply the bands of friendship between us.

Houdon's bust of Lafayette

Calonne's letter endorsing the committee's propositions did not solve all of the problems of American trade with France; but it was a triumph for Jefferson and an example of his flexibility as a diplomat and advocate of his country's interests. But even this could not distract him from the continuing, nagging pain of his right arm. His disability increased his interest in an invention he had designed while in England: a portable copying machine that would eliminate much unnecessary writing. He delightedly announced its successful manufacture to Madison and promised to send his friend a duplicate.

Paris Jan. 30. 1787.

Having a great desire to have a portable copying machine, and being satisfied from some experiments that the principle of the large machine might be applied in a small one, I planned one when in England and had it made. It answers perfectly. I have since set a workman to making them here, and they are in such demand that he has his hands full. Being assured that you will be pleased to have one, when you shall have tried it's convenience, I send you one by Colo. [David] Franks. The machine costs 96 livres, the appendages 24. livres, and I send you paper and ink for 12 livres, in all 132 livres. There is a printed paper of directions: but you must expect to make many essays before you succeed perfectly.

In December Jefferson gradually resumed his personal correspondence, using his left hand. That month he learned of Shays' Rebellion, the insurrection in Massachusetts of debtors against creditors. His first reaction was a calm one as shown in these remarks to Ezra Stiles, president of Yale.

Paris Dec. 24. 1786

The commotions which have taken place in America, as far as they are yet known to me, offer nothing threatening. They are a proof that the people have liberty enough, and I would not wish them less than they have. If the happiness of the mass of the people can be secured at the expence of a little tempest now and then, or even of a little blood, it will be a precious purchase.

As Jefferson heard more about those "commotions" in Massachusetts, he took an even more sympathetic position toward the followers of Daniel Shays. He came to see insurrection as an example of the need for expressions of discontent in a free society. This view was expressed to James Madison.

Paris Jan. 30. 1787.

I hold it that a little rebellion now and then is a good thing, and as necessary in the political world as storms in the physical. Unsuccesful rebellions indeed generally establish the incroachments on the rights of the people which have produced them. An observation of this truth should render honest republican governors so mild in their punishment of rebellions, as not to discourage them too much. It is a medecine necessary for the sound health of government.

Indeed, Shays' Rebellion gave Jefferson an opportunity to articulate a theory of the relationship of public authority to the right of freedom of expression by the governed. He saw less need to punish the insurgents than for America's leaders to draw proper lessons from the incident, as he outlined to Edward Carrington, a Virginia congressman.

Paris Jan. 16. 1787.

The people are the only censors of their governors: and even their errors will tend to keep these to the true principles of their institution. To punish these errors too severely would be to suppress the only safeguard of the public liberty. The way to prevent these irregular interpositions of the people is to give them full information of their affairs thro' the channel of the public papers, and to contrive that those papers should penetrate the whole mass of the people. The basis of our governments being the opinion of the people, the very first object should be to keep that right; and were it left to me to decide whether we should have a government without newspapers, or newspapers without a government, I should not hesitate a moment to prefer the latter.... Cherish therefore the spirit of our people, and keep alive their attention. Do not be too severe upon their errors, but reclaim them by enlightening them. If once they become inattentive to the public affairs, you and I, and Congress, and Assemblies, judges and governors shall all become wolves. It seems to be the law of our general natures, in spite of individual exceptions; and experience declares that man is the only animal which devours his own kind, for I can apply no milder term to the government of Europe, and to the general prey of the rich on the poor.

John Trumbull painted this miniature in London in 1788 for Mrs. Angelica Church; it was a replica of a likeness of Jefferson he had done from life the previous year for the Declaration of Independence.

Even the opportunity to reflect on the nature of revolution could not distract Jefferson from his discomfort. By December, 1786, he had decided to follow his physicians' advice to visit the mineral springs at Aix-en-Provence in the hope the waters might help his wrist heal. Before the accident, he had made preliminary plans to visit southern France to see the famed Canal of Languedoc, and his original itinerary could easily be expanded to include Aix. By February, he had completed arrangements for the trip. His gloomy mood reflected the hardships of the last months. A few days before his departure, he witnessed the opening of the Assembly of Notables, an advisory body convened to prepare some plan to rescue France from economic collapse. Parisians' attitudes toward the Notables prompted Jefferson to write an uncharacteristically dour letter to Abigail Adams.

Voyage Pittoresque de la France
BY JEAN BENJAMIN DE LA BORDE, 1780-96

View of the city of Lyon where Jefferson ran into bad weather

Paris Feb. 22. 1787.

This occasion, more than any thing I have seen, convinces me that this nation is incapable of any serious effort but under the word of command. The people at large view every object only as it may furnish puns and bon mots; and I pronounce that a good punster would disarm the whole nation were they ever so seriously disposed to revolt. Indeed, Madam, they are gone. When a measure so capable of doing good as the calling of the Notables is treated with so much ridicule, we may conclude the nation desperate, and in charity pray that heaven may send them good kings.

Jefferson clearly needed a vacation from Paris and the duties of his office. His carriage left the city on February 28 and he journeyed down the Rhone Valley to Aix. At Lyon he grumbled: "No complaints except against the weather maker, who has pelted me with rain, hail, and snow, almost from the moment of my departure to my arrival here." But his mood improved quickly. He began to fill a notebook with observations on local agriculture, trade patterns, and social conditions, descriptions of forges and bridges, chimneys and pumps. Nearly three weeks after leaving Paris, Jefferson at last saw the Maison Carrée at Nîmes, which he had grown to love secondhand and which had inspired his designs for the Virginia capitol. He told his friend Madame de Tessé of his rapture at actually viewing the ruins of the ancient building that had so long obsessed him.

Nismes. Mar. 20. 1787.

Here I am, Madam, gazing whole hours at the Maison quarrée, like a lover at his mistress. The stocking-weavers and silk spinners around it consider me as an hypochondriac Englishman, about to write with a pistol the last chapter of his history. This is the second time I have been in love since I left Paris. The first was with a Diana at the Chateau de Laye Epinaye in the Beaujolois, a delicious morsel of sculpture, by Michael Angelo Slodtz. This, you will say, was in rule, to fall in love with a fine woman: but, with a house! It is out of all precedent! No, madam, it is not without a precedent in my own history. While at Paris, I was violently smitten with the hotel de Salm, and used to go to the Thuileries almost daily to look at it.

180

The loueuse des chaises [chair keeper], inattentive to my passion, never had the complaisance to place a chair there; so that, sitting on the parapet, and twisting my neck round to see the object of my admiration, I generally left it with a torticollis. From Lyons to Nismes I have been nourished with the remains of Roman grandeur.

Continuing south to Aix-en-Provence, Jefferson wrote William Short that he had at last escaped the cold winter weather.

Aix en Provence March. 27. 1787.
I am now in the land of corn, wine, oil, and sunshine. What more can man ask of heaven? If I should happen to die at Paris I will beg of you to send me here, and have me exposed to the sun. I am sure it will bring me to life again. It is wonderful to me that every free being who possesses cent ecus de rente, does not remove to the Southward of the Loire. It is true that money will carry to Paris most of the good things of this canton. But it cannot carry thither it's sunshine, nor procure any equivalent for it. This city is one of the cleanest and neatest I have ever seen in any country.

Two days later he added a description of the language spoken in Provence to Short.

Aix Mar. 29. 1787.
I had thought the Provençale only a dialect of the French; on the contrary the French may rather be considered as a dialect of the Provençale. That is to say, the Latin is the original. . . . it is my Italian which enables me to understand the people here, more than my French. This language, in different shades occupies all the country South of the Loire. Formerly it took precedence of the French under the name of la langue Romans. The ballads of it's Troubadours were the delight of the several courts of Europe, and it is from thence that the novels of the English are called Romances. Every letter is pronounced, the articulation is distinct, no nasal sounds disfigure it, and on the whole it stands close to the Italian and Spanish in point of beauty. I think it a general misfortune that historical circumstances gave a final prevalence to the French instead of the Provençale language.

William Short

181

Jefferson spent four days trying the baths at Aix. But the treatment of his wrist, the ostensible reason for his visit, did not hold him long. There were better things to do, as he indicated in a letter from Marseilles to Jay: "Having staid at Aix long enough to prove the inefficacy of the waters, I came on to this place for the purpose of informing myself here, as I mean to do at the other seaport towns, of whatever may be interesting to our commerce." His exuberance was apparent in a letter to a friend in Paris, written from the Mediterranean seaport where he remained a week, very much the seasoned traveler.

> Marseilles Apr. 5. 1787.
>
> 'A traveller, sais I, retired at night to his chamber in an Inn, all his effects contained in a single trunk, all his cares circumscribed by the walls of his apartment, unknown to all, unheeded, and undisturbed, writes, reads, thinks, sleeps, just in the moments when nature and the movements of his body and mind require. Charmed with the tranquillity of his little cell, he finds how few are our real wants, how cheap a thing is happiness, how expensive a one pride. He views with pity the wretched rich, whom the laws of the world have submitted to the cumbrous trappings of rank: he sees him labouring through the journey of life like an ass oppressed under ingots of gold, little of which goes to feed, to clothe, or to cover himself; the rest gobbled up by harpies of various description with which he has surrounded himself....
>
> ...I should go on, Madam, detailing to you my dreams and speculations; but that my present situation is most unfriendly to speculation. Four thousand three hundred and fifty market-women (I have counted them one by one) brawling, squabbling, and jabbering Patois, three hundred asses braying and bewailing to each other, and to the world, their cruel oppressions, four files of mule-carts passing in constant succession, with as many bells to every mule as can be hung about him, all this in the street under my window, and the weather too hot to shut it. Judge whether in such a situation it is easy to hang one's ideas together.

From Nice Jefferson wrote to Lafayette, one of the members of the Assembly of Notables then meeting at Versailles, of his "continued rapture" during his travels and urged his young friend to make a similar trip to familiarize himself with his native land and to prepare himself better for political leadership in France.

Nice, April 11, 1787.

I am constantly roving about, to see what I have never seen before and shall never see again. In the great cities, I go to see what travellers think alone worthy of being seen; but I make a job of it, and generally gulp it all down in a day. On the other hand, I am never satiated with rambling through the fields and farms, examining the culture and cultivators, with a degree of curiosity which makes some take me to be a fool, and others to be much wiser than I am. . . . I have often wished for you. I think you have not made this journey. It is a pleasure you have to come, and an improvement to be added to the many you have already made. It will be a great comfort to you to know, from your own inspection, the condition of all the provinces of your own country, and it will be interesting to them at some future day to be known to you. This is perhaps the only moment of your life in which you can acquire that knolege. And to do it most effectually you must be absolutely incognito, you must ferret the people out of their hovels as I have done, look into their kettles, eat their bread, loll on their beds under pretence of resting yourself, but in fact to find if they are soft. You will feel a sublime pleasure in the course of this investigation, and a sublimer one here-after when you shall be able to apply your knolege to the softening of their beds, or the throwing a morsel of meat into the kettle of vegetables.

On April 13 Jefferson crossed the Alpes Maritimes into Italy on a mule. His notebook swelled with notes on his dogged research into such things as the secrets of rice culture in the Piedmont, which he hoped to introduce in the American South, and the preparation of Parmesan cheese. On his return to France he made his way to Cette where he continued on the Canal of Languedoc, a link between the Mediterranean and the Atlantic built by Louis XIV in the seventeenth century. It was this canal that had first inspired him to plan the trip and the waterway met all his expectations, he wrote William Short.

On the Canal of Languedoc, approaching Toulouse.

May 21. 1787.

I have passed through the Canal from it's entrance into the mediterranean at Cette to this place, and shall be immediately at Toulouse, in the whole 200 American miles, by water; having employed in examining all it's

Voyage, DE LA BORDE

Jefferson measured the bricks at these ruins of a Roman amphitheater in Bordeaux, which he saw in May.

details nine days, one of which was spent in making a tour of 40 miles on horseback, among the Montagnes noires, to see the manner in which water has been collected to supply the canal; the other eight on the canal itself. I dismounted my carriage from it's wheels, placed it on the deck of a light bark, and was thus towed on the canal instead of the post road. That I might be perfectly master of all the delays necessary, I hired a bark to myself by the day, and have made from 20. to 35 miles a day, according to circumstances, always sleeping ashore. Of all the methods of travelling I have tried this is the pleasantest. I walk the greater part of the way along the banks of the canal, level, and lined with a double row of trees which furnish shade. When fatigued I take seat in my carriage where, as much at ease as if in my study, I read, write, or observe. My carriage being of glass all round, admits a full view of all the varying scenes thro' which I am shifted, olives, figs, mulberries, vines, corn and pasture, villages and farms. I have had some days of superb weather, enjoying two parts of the Indian's wish, cloudless skies and limpid waters. . . .

At Toulouse Jefferson left the canal and made his way on to Paris, still taking notes of vineyards and chateaus and anything else that seemed worthy of description. He arrived in the capital on June 11, rested by his trip and invigorated by the chance to observe new people and places, novel machines, and unfamiliar seaports. The first three years of his mission had been exhilarating. He had built on the foundations of Franklin's embassy with hard work and patience. Despite the limitations placed on his negotiations by the Confederation's lack of tax and commerce powers and a Secretary of Foreign Affairs who did not often share his views, Jefferson had done much to improve trade relations with France. His personal life had been full of friends, intellectual stimulation, and even a romantic affair. Ever the student, Jefferson had come to know France almost as well as his native Virginia. He expected to complete his mission secure in the confidence such knowledge gave him.

Chapter 7

A Rising Race of Republicans

After three years spent studying the French monarchy and devising ways to function with some effectiveness as an envoy of the Continental Congress, Jefferson would spend his last two years in Paris contemplating the disintegration of Bourbon power and the end of the Confederation of states that had sent him abroad. A friend to neither despotism nor inefficient government, Jefferson did not mourn the end of either regime. But he was concerned that the successors to these two discredited systems serve the interests of the French and American peoples.

The political and social changes that colored his last years abroad had already begun while Jefferson toured southern France. On May 25, as he took notes on the vineyards of Bordeaux, delegates met at Philadelphia in a convention called to revise the Articles of Confederation. That same day, Louis XVI dissolved the Assembly of Notables in Paris. Both actions reflected the failure of a political structure: Americans gathered in recognition of the need for a stronger government; the Notables' very existence was a tacit admission by the King that a financial crisis had developed which required him to consult his subjects, even a limited and privileged few, rather than impose his will upon them.

Jefferson was prevented from exerting direct influence on either developing reform movement. His residence in Europe meant that he had to rely on the effect of advice and guidance he had given earlier to friends in America. There was no time to offer immediate encouragement to delegates elected to the Federal Convention, and he could only wait in Paris to learn whether men like Madison and Wythe had been able to implement the changes he and they had advocated so long. Similarly, his position as a foreign diplomat in France meant that he could not properly intervene openly in the country's internal affairs. He was able to counsel friends like Lafayette who led the movement for liberal reforms, but that advice had to be offered discreetly and with no assurance that it would be followed. For a man of Jefferson's temperament, this was often a frustrating predicament. At a time when he would have chosen to take an active role in changing the courses of two nations he loved, he had to content himself with watching, observing, and patiently waiting for a moment when he might be of use.

He had already missed one chance to contribute to events in America. In December, 1786, he had learned that a constitutional convention would be called, but the difficulty of writing with his left hand limited his comments on that event to a brief recommendation to Madison for the separation of governmental powers. Only after his return to Paris in June, 1787, did Jefferson prepare lengthy discussions of specific reforms he thought should be implemented. By then several letters from correspondents had brought details of the election of delegates and of some of the proposals that might be advanced. Madison was chosen as one representative from Virginia and was to become the intellectual leader of the proceedings. Jefferson urged his friend to fight for an independent executive branch, but the advice did not reach Madison until the closing days of the convention.

Paris June 20. 1787.

The idea of separating the executive business of the confederacy from Congress, as the judiciary is already in some degree, is just and necessary. I had frequently pressed on the members individually, while in Congress, the doing this by a resolution of Congress for appointing an Executive committee to act during the sessions of Congress, as the Committee of the states was to act during their vacations. But the referring to this Committee all executive business as it should present itself, would require a more persevering self-denial than I supposed Congress to possess. It will be much better to make that separation by a federal act. The negative proposed to be given them on all the acts of the several legislatures is now for the first time suggested to my mind. Primâ facie I do not like it. It fails in an essential character, that the hole and the patch should be commensurate. But this proposes to mend a small hole by covering the whole garment.... Would not an appeal from the state judicatures to a federal court, in all cases where the act of Confederation controuled the question, be as effectual a remedy, and exactly commensurate to the defect.... An appeal to a federal court sets all to rights. It will be said that this court may encroach on the jurisdiction of the state courts. It may. But there will be a power, to wit Congress, to watch and restrain them. But place the same authority in Congress itself, and there will be no power above them to perform the same office.

Jefferson waited several weeks before replying to Edward Carrington who had also favored him with political news during his absence in southern France. It is clear from his reply that Jefferson expected the convention to retain the Articles of Confederation as the basic governmental framework, only adding centralization of the power to regulate commerce. He expounded the theory that the Confederation already had the powers necessary to compel the states to meet national requisitions — that such powers were clearly implied if not explicitly granted by the Articles.

Paris Aug. 4. 1787.

I confess I do not go as far in the reforms thought necessary as some of my correspondents in America; but if the Convention should adopt such propositions I shall suppose them necessary. My general plan would be to make the states one as to every thing connected with foreign nations, and several as to every thing purely domestic. But with all the imperfections of our present government, it is without comparison the best existing or that ever did exist. It's greatest defect is the imperfect manner in which matters of commerce have been provided for. It has been so often said, as to be generally believed, that Congress have no power by the confederation to enforce any thing, e.g. contributions of money. It was not necessary to give them that power expressly; they have it by the law of nature. When two nations make a compact, there results to each a power of compelling the other to execute it. Compulsion was never so easy as in our case, where a single frigate would soon levy on the commerce of any state the deficiency of it's contributions; nor more safe than in the hands of Congress which has always shewn that it would wait, as it ought to do, to the last extremities before it would execute any of it's powers which are disagreeable. — I think it very material to separate in the hands of Congress the Executive and Legislative powers, as the Judiciary already are in some degree. This I hope will be done. The want of it has been the source of more evil than we have ever experienced from any other cause. Nothing is so embarrassing nor so mischievous in a great assembly as the details of execution. The smallest trifle of that kind occupies as long as the most important act of legislation, and takes place of every thing else. Let any man recollect, or look over the files of Congress, he will observe the most important propositions hanging over from week to week and month to month, till the occasions have past them, and the thing

Thomas Rossiter's painting of the
Constitutional Convention of 1787

never done. I have ever viewed the executive details as
the greatest cause of evil to us, because they in fact
place us as if we had no federal head, by diverting the
attention of that head from great to small objects; and
should this division of power not be recommended by the
Convention, it is my opinion Congress should make it
itself by establishing an Executive committee.

Jefferson's advocacy of a mere revision of the Articles
may have been related to rumors Carrington had relayed that some in
America were ready to "go to a monarchy at once." Having witnessed the
collapse of France's economy at the hands of an inept king, Jefferson could
not conceal his impatience in commenting on such proposals to Benjamin
Hawkins, a member of Congress from North Carolina.

Paris Aug. 4. 1787.
And above all things I am astonished at some people's
considering a kingly government as a refuge. Advise such
to read the fable of the frogs who sollicited Jupiter for a
king. If that does not put them to rights, send them to
Europe to see something of the trappings of monarchy,
and I will undertake that every man shall go back thoroughly cured. If all the evils which can arise among us
from the republican form of our government from this
day to the day of judgment could be put into a scale
against what this country suffers from it's monarchical
form in a week, or England in a month, the latter would
preponderate....No race of kings has ever presented
above one man of common sense in twenty generations.

The best they can do is to leave things to their ministers, and what are their ministers but a Committee, badly chosen? If the king ever meddles it is to do harm.

Jefferson's friends in the convention, bound by an oath of secrecy concerning the proceedings, could not allay his fears by telling him of the debates that summer. There was much to divert his attention from Philadelphia, however, for Paris had broken out in an unprecedented public protest against the monarchy. Jefferson sent a vivid account to John Adams.

Paris Aug. 30. 1787.
From the separation of the Notables to the present moment has been perhaps the most interesting interval ever known in this country. The propositions of the Government, approved by the Notables, were precious to the nation and have been in an honest course of execution, some of them being carried into effect, and others preparing. Above all the establishment of the Provincial assemblies ... bid fair to be the instrument for circumscribing the power of the crown and raising the people into consideration.... In the mean time all tongues in Paris (and in France as it is said) have been let loose, and never was a license of speaking against the government exercised in London more freely or more universally. Caracatures, placards, bon mots, have been indulged in by all ranks of people, and I know of no well attested instance of a single punishment. For some time mobs of 10; 20; 30,000 people collected daily, surrounded the parliament house, huzzaed the members, even entered the doors and examined into their conduct, took the horses out of the carriages of those who did well, and drew them home. The government thought it prudent to prevent these, drew some regiments into the neighborhood, multiplied the guards, had the streets constantly patrolled by strong parties, suspended privileged places, forbad all clubs, etc. The mobs have ceased; perhaps this may be partly owing to the absence of parliament. The Count d'Artois [the King's brother], sent to hold a bed of justice in the Cour des Aides [court with jurisdiction in matters of tax revenues], was hissed and hooted without reserve by the populace; the carriage of Madame de (I forget the name) in the queen's livery was stopped by the populace under a belief that it was Madame de

A badge worn by the early revolutionaries in France

MUSÉE CARNAVALET; PHOTO BULLOZ

189

Polignac's [the royal children's governess] whom they would have insulted, the queen going to the theater at Versailles with Madame de Polignac was received with a general hiss. The king, long in the habit of drowning his cares in wine, plunges deeper and deeper; the queen cries but sins on.

It was November before Jefferson received a copy of the Constitution adopted by the Federal Convention from Adams's secretary, William Stephens Smith. Although it revealed that nothing close to a monarchy had been established, Jefferson was displeased by his first impression of the document, and he did not hesitate to describe his dissatisfaction to Adams.

> Paris Nov. 13. 1787.
>
> How do you like our new constitution? I confess there are things in it which stagger all my dispositions to subscribe to what such an assembly has proposed. The house of federal representatives will not be adequate to the management of affairs either foreign or federal. Their President seems a bad edition of a Polish king. He may be reelected from 4. years to 4. years for life. Reason and experience prove to us that a chief magistrate, so continuable, is an officer for life....Once in office, and possessing the military force of the union, without either the aid or check of a council, he would not be easily dethroned, even if the people could be induced to withdraw their votes from him. I wish that at the end of the 4. years they had made him for ever ineligible a second time. Indeed I think all the good of this new constitution might have been couched in three or four new articles to be added to the good, old, and venerable fabrick, which should have been preserved even as a religious relique.

In a letter the same day to Smith, Jefferson grumbled that the Federal Convention had apparently come to believe the "lies" of the "British ministry" concerning the "anarchy" that the Articles of Confederation had imposed on America. In particular, Jefferson believed that Shays' Rebellion had exerted an influence out of all proportion to its importance. "Our Convention," he wrote, "has been too much impressed by the insurrection of Massachusetts: and in the spur of the moment they are setting up a kite to keep the hen yard in order."

CULVER PICTURES, INC.

Shays' followers, farmers and veterans, wanted to stop court-ordered foreclosures for debts until the state legislature granted them relief. In their attack on the Springfield arsenal (above), three men were killed by the militia.

Paris Nov. 13. 1787.

God forbid we should ever be 20. years without such a rebellion. The people can not be all, and always, well informed. The part which is wrong will be discontented in proportion to the importance of the facts they misconceive. If they remain quiet under such misconceptions it is a lethargy, the forerunner of death to the public liberty. We have had 13. states independant 11. years. There has been one rebellion. That comes to one rebellion in a century and a half for each state. What country before ever existed a century and half without a rebellion? And what country can preserve it's liberties if their rulers are not warned from time to time that their people preserve the spirit of resistance? Let them take arms. The remedy is to set them right as to facts, pardon and pacify them. What signify a few lives lost in a century or two? The tree of liberty must be refreshed from time to time with the blood of patriots and tyrants. It is it's natural manure.

Jefferson saved his most serious, and lengthy, critique for Madison, who had sent him a copy of the Constitution that arrived in December, along with a letter explaining the background of some of its provisions. Tactfully, Jefferson opened his reply with a list of those provisions he liked.

Paris Dec. 20. 1787.

I like much the general idea of framing a government which should go on of itself peaceably, without needing continual recurrence to the state legislatures. I like the organization of the government into Legislative, Judiciary and Executive. I like the power given the Legislature to levy taxes; and for that reason solely approve of the greater house being chosen by the people directly. For tho' I think a house chosen by them will be very illy qualified to legislate for the Union, for foreign nations &c. yet this evil does not weigh against the good of preserving inviolate the fundamental principle that the people are not to be taxed but by representatives chosen immediately by themselves. I am captivated by the compromise of the opposite claims of the great and little states, of the latter to equal, and the former to proportional influence. I am much pleased too with the substitution of the method of voting by persons, instead of that of

191

voting by states: and I like the negative given to the Executive with a third of either house, though I should have liked it better had the Judiciary been associated for that purpose, or invested with a similar and separate power. . . .

[As the author of the Declaration of Independence, with its forthright statement of human rights, Jefferson left little doubt about what he did not like.]

I will now add what I do not like. First the omission of a bill of rights providing clearly and without the aid of sophisms for freedom of religion, freedom of the press, protection against standing armies, restriction against monopolies, the eternal and unremitting force of the habeas corpus laws, and trials by jury in all matters of fact triable by the laws of the land and not by the law of Nations. . . . Let me add that a bill of rights is what the people are entitled to against every government on earth, general or particular, and what no just government should refuse, or rest on inference. The second feature I dislike, and greatly dislike, is the abandonment in every instance of the necessity of rotation in office, and most particularly in the case of the President. Experience concurs with reason in concluding that the first magistrate will always be re-elected if the constitution permits it. He is then an officer for life. . . . If once elected, and at a second or third election outvoted by one or two votes, he will pretend false votes, foul play, hold possession of the reins of government, be supported by the states voting for him, especially if they are the central ones lying in a compact body themselves and separating their opponents: and they will be aided by one nation of Europe, while the majority are aided by another. The election of a President of America some years hence will be much more interesting to certain nations of Europe than ever the election of a king of Poland was. Reflect on all the instances in history antient and modern, of elective monarchies, and say if they do not give foundation for my fears, the Roman emperors, the popes, while they were of any importance, the German emperors till they became hereditary in practice, the kings of Poland, the Deys of the Ottoman dependancies. It may be said that if elections are to be

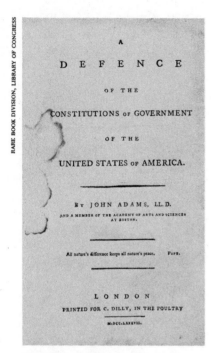

A

D E F E N C E

OF THE

CONSTITUTIONS of GOVERNMENT

OF THE

UNITED STATES of AMERICA.

By JOHN ADAMS, LL.D.

AND A MEMBER OF THE ACADEMY OF ARTS AND SCIENCES
AT BOSTON.

All nature's difference keeps all nature's peace.   POPE.

L O N D O N
PRINTED FOR C. DILLY, IN THE POULTRY
M.DCC.LXXXVII.

Title page of John Adams's three-volume treatise on government; the first volume was published in London early in 1787 and reached Philadelphia during the Convention.

THOMAS JEFFERSON

attended with these disorders, the seldomer they are renewed the better. But experience shews that the only way to prevent disorder is to render them uninteresting by frequent changes. . . .

[Jefferson admitted that he did "not pretend to decide what would be the best method" of rectifying these flaws, but he urged Madison "not to be discouraged from other trials." He closed his letter with an analysis of his own philosophy.]

I own I am not a friend to a very energetic government. It is always oppressive. . . . Nor will any degree of power in the hands of government prevent insurrections. France with all it's despotism, and two or three hundred thousand men always in arms has had three insurrections in the three years I have been here in every one of which greater numbers were engaged than in Massachusets and a great deal more blood was spilt. In Turkey, which Montesquieu supposes more despotic, insurrections are the events of every day. In England, where the hand of power is lighter than here, but heavier than with us they happen every half dozen years. Compare again the ferocious depredations of their insurgents with the order, the moderation and the almost self extinguishment of ours. — After all, it is my principle that the will of the Majority should always prevail. If they approve the proposed Convention in all it's parts, I shall concur in it chearfully, in hopes that they will amend it whenever they shall find it work wrong. I think our governments will remain virtuous for many centuries; as long as they are chiefly agricultural; and this will be as long as there shall be vacant lands in any part of America. When they get piled upon one another in large cities, as in Europe, they will become corrupt as in Europe. Above all things I hope the education of the common people will be attended to; convinced that on their good sense we may rely with the most security for the preservation of a due degree of liberty.

Soon after examining the shortcomings of the Constitution, Jefferson was given a sharp reminder of the failings of the old Confederation. Early in 1788 Adams received permission to return home.

Among the many commissions he had held was one to negotiate loans for the United States, principally in the Netherlands. As soon as Adams knew he would be released from his unpleasant duties in London, he notified the bankers in Holland and "referred them to consult with me [Jefferson] in their future difficulties." This was an unpleasant surprise for Jefferson, for America's Treasury commissioners had recently notified the bankers that the United States might have to default on interest payments on old loans because of the unsatisfactory progress of a new loan recently floated in Europe. Willink & Van Staphorst, America's principal bankers in Amsterdam, proposed a plan to meet the crisis and at the same time profit at America's expense. European speculators in America's domestic debt would take up the balance of the new loan if they were allowed to deduct from their payments one year's interest due them on the old obligations. Jefferson probably never seriously believed that this scheme of financial extortion would be approved, but he told the Treasury commissioners: "One thing I could easily determine which was that the proposition was totally out of my province." When Adams visited The Hague in March to announce his departure, Jefferson met him there and subsequently reported to the commissioners the emergency measure he had initiated.

Amsterdam Mar. 29. 1788.

... I set out immediately for that place to get him [Adams] to come on here and join in conferences with the bankers to see what could be done to set the loan in motion again. We came here and our first object was to convince them there was no power on this side the Atlantic to accede to that proposition. At length we prevailed to get them and the brokers to abandon this idea.... It was agreed to push the loan on other grounds. But this appeared not enough. Your letter looked forward to the new government as the only resource for remittance. It was evident that for that to be adopted, it's legislature assembled, system of taxation established, the collection made and remitted, neither this year nor the next would suffice; and that to place the government perfectly at it's ease till this process could be gone through, the years 1789. and 1790. should be provided for as to all our European demands.... this will require another million of florins. The bankers joined us in opinion therefore that as Mr. Adams's powers to borrow had not been revoked, he should execute bonds for another million, which should be kept up till the ratification of Congress could be received. This being done, Mr. Adams was obliged to return to England.... I have now waited twelve days since the departure of Mr.

RIJKSMUSEUM, AMSTERDAM

Jefferson stayed at this hotel, The Amsterdam Arms, during his visit.

Adams; and...both bankers and brokers from what they learn...are become well enough satisfied that the month of June will be provided for.

Jefferson was justly proud of his success in meeting this crisis, as he revealed in his *Autobiography.*

Autobiography, 1821

I had the satisfaction to reflect that by this journey, our credit was secured, the new government was placed at ease for two years to come, and that, as well as myself, relieved from the torment of incessant duns, whose just complaints could not be silenced by any means within our power.

At the end of March, Jefferson left Amsterdam and treated himself to a brief tour of a part of Europe with which he was not yet familiar. Instead of returning directly to Paris, he took a roundabout route, traveling up the Rhine and into Germany. His democratic biases were confirmed when he left Holland, with its republican regime, for imperial Germany and noted the "transition from ease and opulence to extreme poverty.... The soil and climate are the same," he remarked pointedly. "The governments alone differ." His notes on this trip showed a characteristic range, from comments on the "sublime" art gallery at Dusseldorf to observations on the hogs—"tall, gaunt, and with heavy lop ears"—that produced "the celebrated ham" of Westphalia. He confessed to William Short that one scene in particular seemed unexpectedly familiar.

Frankfort on the Maine April 9. 1788.

The neighborhood of this place is that which has been to us a second mother country. It is from the palatinate on this part of the Rhine that those swarms of Germans have gone, who, next to the descendants of the English, form the greatest body of our people. I have been continually amused by seeing here the origin of whatever is not English among us. I have fancied myself often in the upper parts of Maryland and Pennsylvania.

At Strasbourg Jefferson crossed the Rhine to continue back through France to Paris. The "awkward figure" of the moldboards on the peasants' plows inspired him to sketch a design for a more efficient plow, and the sight of women working as manual laborers in the French countryside merited an entry in his notes on the journey.

In Strasbourg Jefferson stayed at one of the city's oldest hostelries, to the left, on the Ill River.

Memorandums on a Tour from Paris to Amsterdam, Strasburg and back to Paris [April 19, 1788]

The women here, as in Germany do all sorts of work. While one considers them as useful and rational companions, one cannot forget that they are also objects of our pleasures. Nor can they ever forget it. While employed in dirt and drudgery some tag of a ribbon, some ring or bit of bracelet, earbob or necklace, or something of that kind will shew that the desire of pleasing is never suspended in them. How valuable is that state of society which allots to them internal emploiments only, and external to the men. They are formed by nature for attentions and not for hard labour. A woman never forgets one of the numerous train of little offices which belong to her; a man forgets often.

Jefferson arrived in Paris on the evening of April 23, by now an experienced traveler ready to offer advice to American visitors. In June he sent some hints for traveling abroad to John Rutledge, Jr., the son of a Charleston friend.

Gallery of Palais Royal in Paris

[Paris, June 19, 1788]

Buy beforehand the map of the country you are going into. On arriving at a town, the first thing is to buy the plan of the town, and the book noting it's curiosities. Walk round the ramparts when there are any. Go to the top of a steeple to have a view of the town and it's environs.

When you are doubting whether a thing is worth the trouble of going to see, recollect that you will never again be so near it, that you may repent the not having seen it, but can never repent having seen it. But there is an opposite extreme too. That is, the seeing too much. A judicious selection is to be aimed at, taking care that the indolence of the moment have no influence on the decision. Take care particularly not to let the porters of churches, cabinets &c. lead you thro' all the little details in their possession, which will load the memory with trifles, fatigue the attention and waste that and your time.... When one calls in the taverns for the vin du pays they give you what is natural and unadulterated and cheap: when vin etrangere is called for, it only gives a pretext for charging an extravagant price for an unwholsome stuff, very often of their own brewing. The people you will naturally see the most of will be tavern keepers, Valets de place, and postillions. These are the hackneyed rascals of every country. Of course they must never be considered when we calculate the national character.

Back in Paris, Jefferson was in a far better humor about the new Constitution. Even before he knew of its progress through the various state ratifying conventions, he confessed to Edward Carrington that its virtues had "gained" on him.

> Paris May 27. 1788.
>
> I learn with great pleasure the progress of the new Constitution. Indeed I have presumed it would gain on the public mind, as I confess it has on my own. At first, tho I saw that the great mass and groundwork was good, I disliked many appendages. Reflection and discussion have cleared off most of these.

Still, Jefferson had not been won over completely. His objections to unlimited terms for the President had faded, but his insistence on a bill of rights had not. In many states proponents of ratification argued that such provisions should be added as amendments through the process provided in the Constitution; they feared that if a new convention had to be called, the basic structure of the Constitution would be damaged and dangerous delay might result. Jefferson became reconciled to the idea of later amendments, but he demanded that they come as soon as possible. A letter from Madison explained some of the opposition to a bill of rights and contained a reference to the ineffectiveness of "parchment barriers" to tyranny. "In Virginia," Madison reminded his friend, "I have seen the bill of rights violated in every instance where it has been opposed to a popular current." Determined to convince Madison to continue the fight, Jefferson made a vigorous restatement of his views.

> Paris Mar. 15. 1789.
>
> The [Virginia] Declaration of rights is like all other human blessings alloyed with some inconveniences, and not accomplishing fully it's object. But the good in this instance vastly overweighs the evil. I cannot refrain from making short answers to the objections which your letter states to have been raised. 1. That the rights in question are reserved by the manner in which the federal powers are granted. Answer. A constitutive act may certainly be so formed as to need no declaration of rights. The act itself has the force of a declaration as

far as it goes: and if it goes to all material points nothing more is wanting. In the draught of a constitution which I had once a thought of proposing in Virginia, and printed afterwards, I endeavored to reach all the great objects of public liberty, and did not mean to add a declaration of rights. Probably the object was imperfectly executed: but the deficiencies would have been supplied by others in the course of discussion. But in a constitutive act which leaves some precious articles unnoticed, and raises implications against others, a declaration of rights becomes necessary by way of supplement. This is the case of our new federal constitution. This instrument forms us into one state as to certain objects, and gives us a legislative and executive body for these objects. It should therefore guard us against their abuses of power within the feild submitted to them. 2. A positive declaration of some essential rights could not be obtained in the requisite latitude. Answer. Half a loaf is better than no bread. If we cannot secure all our rights, let us secure what we can. 3. The limited powers of the federal government and jealousy of the subordinate governments afford a security which exists in no other instance. Answer. The first member of this seems resolvable into the 1st. objection before stated. The jealousy of the subordinate governments is a precious reliance. But observe that those governments are only agents. They must have principles furnished them whereon to found their opposition. The declaration of rights will be the text whereby they will try all the acts of the federal government. In this view it is necessary to the federal government also: as by the same text they may try the opposition of the subordinate governments. 4. Experience proves the inefficacy of a bill of rights. True. But tho it is not absolutely efficacious under all circumstances, it is of great potency always, and rarely inefficacious. A brace the more will often keep up the building which would have fallen with that brace the less. There is a remarkeable difference between the characters of the Inconveniencies which attend a Declaration of rights, and those which attend the want of it. The inconveniences of the Declaration are that it may cramp government in it's useful exertions. But the evil of this is shortlived, moderate, and reparable. The inconveniencies of the want of a Declaration are perma-

Jefferson made this tally in 1791 of the states' votes to ratify ten of twelve amendments (the Bill of Rights) Madison proposed to the First Congress in 1789.

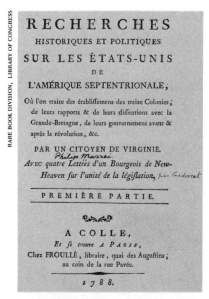

RECHERCHES
HISTORIQUES ET POLITIQUES
SUR LES ÉTATS-UNIS
DE
L'AMÉRIQUE SEPTENTRIONALE;

Où l'on traite des établiſſemens des treize Colonies;
de leurs rapports & de leurs diſſentions avec la
Grande-Bretagne, de leurs gouvernemens avant &
après la révolution, &c.

PAR UN CITOYEN DE VIRGINIE.
Philip Mazzei
Avec quatre Lettres d'un Bourgeois de New-
Heaven ſur l'unité de la légiſlation, *par Condorcet*

PREMIÈRE PARTIE.

A COLLE,
Et ſe trouve A PARIS,
Chez FROULLÉ, libraire, quai des Auguſtins;
au coin de la rue Pavée.

1 7 8 8.

Book from Jefferson's library on the history and politics of the United States, which he had helped Philip Mazzei prepare in Paris in 1786

nent, afflicting and irreparable: they are in constant progression from bad to worse. The executive in our governments is not the sole, it is scarcely the principal object of my jealousy. The tyranny of the legislatures is the most formidable dread at present, and will be for long years. That of the executive will come in it's turn, but it will be at a remote period. I know there are some among us who would now establish a monarchy. But they are inconsiderable in number and weight of character. The rising race are all republicans. We were educated in royalism: no wonder if some of us retain that idolatry still. Our young people are educated in republicanism. An apostacy from that to royalism is unprecedented and impossible. I am much pleased with the prospect that a declaration of rights will be added: and hope it will be done in that way which will not endanger the whole frame of the government, or any essential part of it.

Jefferson could be frank with Madison concerning his reservations. In a letter to David Humphreys, an aide to Washington who had written of the general's expected election as the first President, Jefferson offered his official and public position on the new government.

Paris Mar. 18. 1789.

The operations which have taken place in America lately, fill me with pleasure. In the first place they realize the confidence I had that whenever our affairs get obviously wrong, the good sense of the people will interpose and set them to rights. The example of changing a constitution by assembling the wise men of the state, instead of assembling armies, will be worth as much to the world as the former examples we had given them. The constitution too which was the result of our deliberations, is unquestionably the wisest ever yet presented to men, and some of the accomodations of interest which it has adopted are greatly pleasing to me who have before had occasions of seeing how difficult those interests were to accomodate.

David Humphreys

If Jefferson was more sanguine about America's future in the spring of 1788, he was increasingly concerned for France's fate. "On my return from Holland," he recalled, "I found Paris as I had left it, still in high fermentation." The monarchy's efforts to find new sources of revenue met stubborn resistance from the local parlements, which withheld approval for additional borrowing. Delays in implementing reforms suggested by the Notables allowed, in Jefferson's phrase, "a pressure to arise for a fixed constitution, not subject to changes at the will of the king."

Autobiography, 1821

BOTH: BRITISH MUSEUM

The Royal Gardens at Versailles were enjoyed only by the well-born.

Nor should we wonder at this pressure when we consider the monstrous abuses of power under which this people were ground to powder, when we pass in review the weight of their taxes, and inequality of their distribution; the oppressions of the tythes, of the tailles, the corvées, the gabelles [an impost on salt], the farms & barriers; the shackles on Commerce by Monopolies; on Industry by gilds & corporations; on the freedom of conscience, of thought, and of speech; on the Press by the Censure; and of person by lettres de Cachet. The cruelty of the criminal code generally, the atrocities of the Rack, the venality of judges, and their partialities to the rich; the Monopoly of Military honors by the Noblesse; the enormous expenses of the Queen, the princes & the Court; the prodigalities of pensions; & the riches, luxury, indolence & immorality of the clergy. Surely under such a mass of misrule and oppression, a people might justly press for thoro' reformation, and might even dismount their roughshod riders, & leave them to walk on their own legs.

Finally, Louis XVI responded to public pressure by calling for a session the following May of the Estates General, a legislative body of the nobles, clergy, and common people that had not met since 1614. In September Jefferson wrote Jay that the kingdom seemed tranquil, and he capped his diplomatic duties in November by drafting a paper later printed as *Observations on the Whale-Fishery* that successfully persuaded France to except American whale oil from a general prohibition on its importation. That done, he wrote Jay asking for a brief leave so that he might spend the summer of 1789 in America putting business and family matters in order. As he waited for a reply, Jefferson witnessed the hardships of the French winter of 1788-89, hardships that made the need for reform all the more obvious. He described the conditions to Madame de Bréhan, who was in America with her brother-in-law, France's Minister to the United States.

Paris Mar. 14. 1789

We have had such a winter Madam, as makes me shiver

yet whenever I think of it. All communications almost were cut off. Dinners and suppers were suppressed, and the money laid out in feeding and warming the poor, whose labours were suspended by the rigour of the season. Loaded carriages past the Seine on the ice, and it was covered with thousands of people from morning to night skaiting and sliding. Such sights were never seen before, and they continued two months.

Famine struck France as well. "In cards of invitation to dine in the richest houses," Jefferson remembered, "the guest was notified to bring his own bread." In January Jefferson wrote Dr. Richard Price, an English liberal with republican views, of his optimism with respect to a new political force, the "Patriotic party." If its power were felt in the elections for the Estates General, he thought, France might be saved.

Paris Jan. 8. 1789.

You say you are not sufficiently informed about the nature and circumstances of the present struggle here. Having been on the spot from it's first origin and watched it's movements as an uninterested spectator, with no other bias than a love of mankind I will give you my ideas of it. Tho' celebrated writers of this and other countries had already sketched good principles on the subject of government, yet the American war seems first to have awakened the thinking part of this nation in general from the sleep of despotism in which they were sunk. The officers too, who had been to America, were mostly young men, less shackled by habit and prejudice, and more ready to assent to the dictates of common sense and common right. They came back impressed with these. The press, notwithstanding it's shackles, began to disseminate them: conversation too assumed new freedoms; politics became the theme of all societies, male and female, and a very extensive and zealous party was formed, which may be called the Patriotic party, who sensible of the abusive government under which they lived, longed for occasions of reforming it. This party comprehended all the honesty of the kingdom, sufficiently at it's leisure to think: the men of letters, the easy bourgeois, the young nobility, partly from reflection partly from mode; for those sentiments became a matter of mode, and as such united most of the young women to the party.

Opening session of the Estates General at Versailles, May, 1789

The complicated system of electing members of the Estates went into operation in February. Jefferson advanced some predictions to Jay.

A mob running through the streets of Paris with lighted torches

Paris Jan. 11. 1789.

The moment of crisis will be the meeting of the States; because their first act will be to decide whether they shall vote by persons or by orders. The clergy will leave nothing unattempted to obtain the latter; for they see that the spirit of reformation will not confine itself to the political but will extend to the ecclesiastical establishment also. With respect to the Nobles, the younger members are generally for the people, and the middle aged are daily coming over to the same side: so that by the time the states meet we may hope there will be a majority of that body also in favor of the people, and consequently for voting by persons and not by orders.

In balloting for the Second Estate, the clergy, the results were far better than Jefferson had expected. Older, conservative members of the Catholic hierarchy lost much of their influence to younger, more liberal priests. Jefferson had not received leave to visit America that spring, and he probably did not regret being forced to remain, for he became a daily visitor to the meetings that convened in May. He commented of the opening session at Versailles: "Had it been enlightened with lamps and chandeliers, it would have been almost as brilliant as the opera." But the splendor of the rooms did not conceal the problems facing the Estates General. Nobles and clergy still insisted on voting by order, which would allow them to override the Third Estate or "Commons." At the end of May, the King was called on to arbitrate this dispute; Jefferson advised Lafayette, a member of the nobility who supported the Commons, to exercise moderation. Realistically, Jefferson knew that France was not ready for full, responsible democracy, and he hoped to see the kingdom move slowly but steadily toward a free society. He proposed to Lafayette a charter to be issued by the King and signed by all three estates, but the Third Estate moved too quickly. On June 17 the representatives in the Commons proclaimed themselves the National Assembly and proceeded to consider public affairs without consulting the other two estates. Jefferson did not seem displeased with this abrupt turn when he wrote to Madison the next day.

Paris June 18. 1789.

The Commons have in their chamber almost all the talents of the nation; they are firm and bold, yet moderate. There is indeed among them a number of very hot headed members; but those of most influence are cool, temperate, and sagacious. Every step of this house has been marked with caution and wisdom. The Noblesse on the contrary are absolutely out of their senses. They are so furious they can seldom debate at all.

Shortly thereafter the "talents" of the Commons seemed to triumph. Royal guards barred the National Assembly from its meeting chamber on June 20, but the members promptly found an indoor tennis court for their sessions. Here they subscribed to the Tennis Court Oath which bound the deputies to sit until, in Jefferson's words, "they had settled a constitution for their nation on a solid basis." Within a week the Assembly included a majority of the clergy as well as forty-eight nobles who had cast their lot with the subscribers to the pledge. Public discontent increased, and royal troops began to balk at enforcing the King's decrees. On June 27 Louis XVI was forced to recognize the Assembly's ascendancy, and all nobles and clergymen were ordered to meet jointly with the Commons.

The tempo of revolution continued in July. On the eleventh, Lafayette introduced a draft Declaration of the Rights of Man, a statement Jefferson had assisted him in preparing. On July 14 the Bastille fell to the Paris mob, and with it seemed to fall the last of royal tyranny. Jefferson reported to a fellow diplomat, the Count Diodati, that the way was clear for the establishment of a new regime for the French people.

à Paris ce 3me. Aout, 1789

The National assembly have now as clean a canvas to work on here as we had in America. Such has been the firmness and wisdom of their proceedings in moments of adversity as well as prosperity, that I have the highest confidence that they will use their power justly. As far as I can collect from conversation with their members, the constitution they will propose will resemble that of England in it's outlines, but not in it's defects. They will certainly leave the king possessed completely of the Executive powers, and particularly of the public force. Their legislature will consist of one order only, and not of two as in England: the representation will be equal and not abominably partial as that of England....I have so much confidence in the good sense of man, and his qualifications for self-government, that I am never afraid of the issue where reason is left free to exert her force; and I will agree to be stoned as a false prophet if all does not end well in this country. Nor will it end with this country. Here is but the first chapter of European liberty.

A 1789 cartoon of Finance Minister Jacques Necker showing Louis XVI how to trick the people of France by hiding a huge deficit from them

But it seemed that Jefferson might well be proved a false prophet. The general outlines of the constitution reported to the Assembly were approved, but the details of the new government divided the patriot party, and Jefferson was given a chance to help solve the crisis. On August 25 Lafayette sent him an urgent note: "I Beg for liberty's sake You will Breack Every Engagement to Give us a dinner to Morrow Wenesday." The pronoun "us" referred to members of the Assembly whom Lafayette hoped "to Coalize as Being the only Means to prevent a total dissolution and civil war." The plea placed Jefferson in an embarrassing position. Although he had given Lafayette encouragement and advice throughout 1789, he had avoided open alliance with the patriots, or with any other French faction. The charter he had submitted to Lafayette in June and his counsel on the Declaration of the Rights of Man had both been offered confidentially. In July, when he was asked to confer with the Assembly's committee on the constitution, Jefferson had declined the invitation to avoid compromising his position as a neutral diplomat. But the crisis of August was so grave that Jefferson disregarded the limits of diplomatic propriety. Thirty years later he recalled the outcome of that decision.

Autobiography, 1821

I assured him of their welcome. When they arrived, they were La Fayette himself, Duport, Barnave, Alexander La Meth, Blacon, Mounier, Maubourg, and Dagout. These were leading patriots, of honest but differing opinions sensible of the necessity of effecting a coaliton by mutual sacrifices, knowing each other, and not afraid therefore to unbosom themselves mutually. This last was a material principle in the selection. With this view the Marquis had invited the conference, and had fixed the time & place inadvertently as to the embarrassment under which it might place me. The cloth being removed and wine set on the table, after the American manner, the Marquis introduced the objects of the conference by summarily reminding them of the state of things in the assembly, the course which the principles of the constitution was taking, and the inevitable result, unless checked by more concord among the Patriots themselves. He observed that altho' he also had his opinion, he was ready to sacrifice it to that of his brethren of the same cause: but that a common opinion must now be formed, or the Aristocracy would carry everything, and that whatever they should now agree on, he, at the head of the National force, would maintain. The discussions began at the hour of four, and were continued till ten o'clock in the evening; during which time I was a

The Comte de Montmorin

silent witness to a coolness and candor of argument unusual in the conflicts of political opinion; to a logical reasoning, and chaste eloquence, disfigured by no gaudy tinsel of rhetoric or declamation, and truly worthy of being placed in parallel with the finest dialogues of antiquity, as handed to us by Xenophon, by Plato and Cicero. The result was an agreement that the king should have a suspensive veto on the laws, that the legislature should be composed of a single body only, & that to be chosen by the people. This Concordate decided the fate of the constitution. The Patriots all rallied to the principles thus settled, carried every question agreeably to them, and reduced the Aristocracy to insignificance and impotence. But duties of exculpation were now incumbent on me. I waited on Count Montmorin the next morning, and explained to him with truth and candor how it happened that my house had been made the scene of conferences of such a character. He told me he already knew every thing which had passed, that, so far from taking umbrage at the use made of my house on that occasion, he earnestly wished I would habitually assist at such conferences, being sure I should be useful in moderating the warmer spirits, and promoting a wholesome and practicable reformation only. I told him I knew too well the duties I owed to the king, to the nation, and to my own country to take any part in councils concerning their internal government, and that I should persevere with care in the character of a neutral and passive spectator, with wishes only and very sincere ones, that those measures might prevail which would be for the greatest good of the nation. I have no doubt indeed that this conference was previously known and approved by this honest minister, who was in confidence and communication with the patriots, and wished for a reasonable reform of the Constitution.

Jefferson may have been more willing to stretch the definition of ministerial protocol because he had learned, three days before the patriots dined at his home, that he had been granted leave to return to the United States. He would at last be able to check up on his affairs in Virginia, and Patsy, almost seventeen, and eleven-year-old Polly would have the "society & care of their friends" as they approached young womanhood. He expected to return to Paris in the spring of 1790 and resume his role as Minister to France and friend to the Revolution, as he indicated to Madison that summer.

> Paris Aug. 28. 1789
>
> I propose to sail from Havre as soon after the 1st. of October as I can get a vessel: and shall consequently leave this place a week earlier than that. As my daughters will be with me . . . I shall endeavour if possible to obtain passage for Virginia directly. Probably I shall be there by the last of November. . . . I expect to proceed to my own house directly. Staying there two months . . . and allowing for the time I am on the road, I may expect to be at New York in February, and to embark from thence, or some eastern port. — You ask me if I would accept any appointment on that side the water? You know the circumstances which led me from retirement, step by step and from one nomination to another, up to the present. My object is a return to the same retirement. Whenever therefore I quit the present, it will not be to engage in any other office, and most especially any one which would require a constant residence from home.

Jefferson's plans for a prompt departure were disrupted, however, by illness — probably one of the agonizing headaches he suffered periodically through life. As he recovered in the first week of September, he was visited by Dr. Richard Gem, an English physician who divided his time between London and Paris and between medicine and political theory. Gem was on close terms with many members of France's revolutionary groups and he gave Jefferson a series of propositions based on the premise "that one generation of men in civil society have no right to make acts to bind another. . . ." This premise went to the heart of the dilemma faced by France: the justification for dismantling an old, feudal society whose existence no longer served the needs of the people forced to live within it. Jefferson's remarks on the propositions, contained in the form of a letter to James Madison, constitute one of his most important commentaries on human society and political structure. Modern scholars have concluded that the document, drafted hastily before Jefferson left France in early October, was not really intended as advice to Madison, but was rather Jefferson's last attempt to communicate on-the-spot advice to Lafayette and his fellow reformers through Gem. This interpretation is buttressed not only by the tone of the letter, which was obviously concerned with the realities of French, not American, politics, but also by the fact that it was not even delivered to Madison until early in 1790. Jefferson's answer to the French radicals' dilemma was that "the earth belongs in usufruct to the living."

Paris September 6. 1789.

The question Whether one generation of men has a right to bind another, seems never to have been started either on this or our side of the water. Yet it is a question of such consequences as not only to merit decision, but place also, among the fundamental principles of every government. The course of reflection in which we are immersed here on the elementary principles of society has presented this question to my mind; and that no such obligation can be so transmitted I think very capable of proof.—I set out on this ground, which I suppose to be self evident, 'that the earth belongs in usufruct to the living': that the dead have neither powers nor rights over it. The portion occupied by any individual ceases to be his when himself ceases to be, and reverts to the society.... Then no man can, by *natural right,* oblige the lands he occupied, or the persons who succeed him in that occupation, to the paiment of debts contracted by him. For if he could, he might, during his own life, eat up the usufruct of the lands for several generations to come, and then the lands would belong to the dead, and not to the living, which would be the reverse of our principle....

This principle that the earth belongs to the living, and not to the dead, is of very extensive application and consequences, in every country, and most especially in France. It enters into the resolution of the questions Whether the nation may change the descent of lands holden in tail? Whether they may change the appropriation of lands given antiently to the church, to hospitals, colleges, orders of chivalry, and otherwise in perpetuity? Whether they may abolish the charges and privileges attached on lands, including the whole catalogue ecclesiastical and feudal? It goes to hereditary offices, authorities and jurisdictions; to hereditary orders, distinctions and appellations; to perpetual monopolies in commerce, the arts and sciences; with a long train of et ceteras: and it renders the question of reimbursement a question of generosity and not of right. In all these cases, the legislature of the day could authorize such appropriations and establishments for their own time, but no longer; and the present holders, even where they, or their ancestors, have purchased, are in the case of bonâ fide purchasers of what the seller had no right to convey.

Passport issued to Jefferson by the Commune of Paris and endorsed by Lafayette, the commandant of the Garde Nationale; it permitted the diplomat and his entourage to pass through customs. Jefferson also had one from Louis XVI.

Jefferson's desire to use even this last opportunity to guide his French friends was not the whim of a political philosopher who hoped to see his maxims implemented. Instead, it came from his affection for the French and his hope that the Revolution could give political and social justice to the land where he had spent five of the most happy and fulfilling years of his life. In his *Autobiography,* Jefferson closed his recollections of those years with this touching tribute to a people he had come to love only a little less than those he had left behind in Virginia.

Autobiography, 1821

And here I cannot leave this great and good country without expressing my sense of it's preeminence of character among the nations of the earth. A more benevolent people, I have never known, nor a greater warmth and devotedness in their select friendships. Their kindness and accomodation to strangers is unparalleled, and the hospitality of Paris is beyond any thing I had concieved to be practicable in a large city. Their eminence too in science, the communicative dispositions of their scientific men, the politeness of the general manners, the ease and vivacity of their conversation, give a charm to their society to be found no where else. In a comparison of this with other countries we have the proof of primacy, which was given to Themistocles after the battle of Salamis. Every general voted to himself the first reward of valor, and the second to Themistocles. So ask the travelled inhabitant of any nation, In what country on earth would you rather live?— Certainly in my own, where are all my friends, my relations, and the earliest & sweetest affections and recollections of my life. Which would be your second choice? France.

Jefferson sailed from France, his second home, in the early hours of October 8, 1789. He had come five years earlier as an eager, questioning American awed by European culture and pained by the suffering he saw among the subjects of the King at whose court he was to serve. He left behind a nation on the threshold of constitutional government, with the promise of justice and freedom for the people he had come to know so well. As the small packet ship *Anna* moved from the harbor at Le Havre just after midnight, Jefferson may have wondered if, in keeping with his own plans and desires, he would ever see France again.

Chapter 8

First Secretary of State

On November 23, 1789, Thomas Jefferson and his daughters returned to their native Virginia. They landed at Norfolk with servants and baggage, excited travelers who had come back eager to see old friends and fond relatives, impatient to share their experiences abroad and to learn the latest news of politics and family marriages and births. But they began their leisurely overland journey to Albemarle with different motives. Patsy and Polly concentrated on readjusting to life in Virginia; Jefferson worried about accumulating enough knowledge of changes in American political thought and attitudes to be able to represent the new government well when he returned to France.

He had not expected that the task of reeducation would be easy. In March, 1789, he had confided to David Humphreys: "I know only the Americans of the year 1784. They tell me this is to be much a stranger to those of 1789." But almost as soon as he disembarked, he learned that his reintroduction might be more extensive than he had planned. Friends and well-wishers rushed to congratulate him on his appointment as Secretary of State in Washington's administration.

Jefferson himself had received no official notification of the appointment, and as his carriage rolled from Norfolk to Richmond, he still hoped he could decline. In Richmond, he viewed progress on construction of the new capitol with satisfaction. If "finished with the proper ornaments belonging to it," he reported to William Short, "it will be worthy of being exhibited along side the most celebrated remains of antiquity." At Eppington, where Polly was reunited with her Aunt and Uncle Eppes, Jefferson received, at last, Washington's letter of October 13.

Autobiography, 1821

On my way home I passed some days at Eppington in Chesterfield, the residence of my friend and connection, Mr. Eppes, and, while there, I received a letter from the

President, Genl. Washington, by express, covering an appointment to be Secretary of State. I recieved it with real regret. My wish had been to return to Paris, where I had left my houshold establishment, as if there myself, and to see the end of the revolution, which, I then thought would be certainly and happily closed in less than a year. I then meant to return home, to withdraw from Political life, into which I had been impressed by the circumstances of the times, to sink into the bosom of my family and friends, and devote myself to studies more congenial to my mind. In my answer of Dec. 15. I expressed these dispositions candidly to the President, and my preference of a return to Paris; but assured him that if it was believed I could be more useful in the administration of the government, I would sacrifice my own inclinations without hesitation, and repair to that destination. This I left to his decision.

Silhouette of Martha Jefferson

After sending his reply on its way to Washington, Jefferson continued to Monticello. Patsy later recalled their arrival on December 23: "The negroes discovered the approach of the carriage as soon as it reached Shadwell, and such a scene I never witnessed in my life. They collected in crowds around it, and almost drew it up the mountain by hand. The shouting, etc., had been sufficiently obstreperous before, but the moment it arrived at the top it reached the climax. When the door of the carriage was opened, they received him in their arms and bore him to the house, crowding around and kissing his hands and feet—some blubbering and crying—others laughing. It seemed impossible to satisfy their anxiety to touch and kiss the very earth which bore him."

Jefferson's holiday reunion was marked by a visit from one of his dearest and most influential friends—James Madison. As a leader in the new House of Representatives, Madison was determined that Jefferson remain in America to aid the administration. He promptly wrote Washington of Jefferson's disinterest in the domestic concerns of the Secretary of State, for Congress had assigned the office numerous duties in internal affairs as well as responsibility for supervising foreign relations. Washington responded with a second letter to Jefferson, urging him to accept the appointment and confessing that: "I know of no person, who, in my judgement could better execute the Duties of it than yourself." On February 14, Jefferson conceded to Washington that he could "no longer hesitate to undertake the office to which you are pleased to call me."

Part of the campaign to persuade Jefferson to accept had been an address by a self-appointed committee of the citizens of Albemarle. His neighbors reminded him that they had elected him to his first public office, as a burgess from their county, and they urged him to continue in the national councils, for he had demonstrated a "strong attachment... to the rights of mankind." They concluded that "America has still occasion for your services." Jefferson had already made his decision when he delivered a heartfelt response of acceptance and rededication, which Dumas Malone has described as "one of the finest expressions of the thoughts and hopes of a philosophical statesman."

[Feb. 12. 1790]

The testimony of esteem with which you are pleased to honour my return to my native county fills me with gratitude and pleasure. While it shews that my absence has not lost me your friendly recollection, it holds out the comfortable hope that when the hour of retirement shall come, I shall again find myself amidst those with whom I have long lived, with whom I wish to live, and whose affection is the source of my purest happiness. Their favor was the door thro' which I was ushered on the stage of public life; and while I have been led on thro' it's varying scenes, I could not be unmindful of those who assigned me my first part.

Second page of an April 4, 1790, letter to Martha from her father, concerning the duties of a wife

My feeble and obscure exertions in their service, and in the holy cause of freedom, have had no other merit than that they were my best. We have all the same. We have been fellow-labourers and fellow-sufferers, and heaven has rewarded us with a happy issue from our struggles. It rests now with ourselves alone to enjoy in peace and concord the blessings of self-government, so long denied to mankind: to shew by example the sufficiency of human reason for the care of human affairs and that the will of the majority, the Natural law of every society, is the only sure guardian of the rights of man. Perhaps even this may sometimes err. But it's errors are honest, solitary and short-lived. — Let us then, my dear friends, for ever bow down to the general reason of the society. We are safe with that, even in it's deviations, for it soon returns again to the right way. These are lessons we have learnt together. We have prospered in their practice, and the liberality with which you are pleased to approve my attachment to the general rights of mankind assures me we are still together in these it's kindred sentiments.

Wherever I may be stationed, by the will of my country, it will be my delight to see, in the general tide of happiness, that yours too flows on in just place and measure. That it may flow thro' all times, gathering strength as it goes, and spreading the happy influence of reason and liberty over the face of the earth, is my fervent prayer to heaven.

There was much for Jefferson to do before he could join the administration in New York. Patsy had fallen in love with her second cousin, twenty-one-year-old Thomas Mann Randolph, Jr., the eldest son of Colonel Randolph of Tuckahoe. The courtship went quickly, and the couple was married at Monticello on February 23. Jefferson prepared to leave Virginia secure in the knowledge that his eldest daughter had chosen "a young gentleman of genius, science and honorable mind." Six days after the wedding he set out for New York, with stops in Richmond to arrange his share of payment on his father-in-law's debt and in Philadelphia to visit Benjamin Rush and the eighty-four-year-old Franklin, who was near death.

Autobiography, 1821

He was then on the bed of sickness from which he never rose. My recent return from a country in which he had left so many friends, and the perilous convulsions to which they had been exposed, revived all his anxieties to know what part they had taken, what had been their course, and what their fate. He went over all in succession, with a rapidity and animation almost too much for his strength.

On March 21 Jefferson arrived in New York City, which had been the seat of government for the last five years, and immediately faced an intimidating backlog of work. Congress was in session, Washington had been President for more than a year, and the other department heads—Alexander Hamilton in the Treasury, Henry Knox in the War Department, and Edmund Randolph, the Attorney General—had been functioning for several months. Jefferson's main concern was with the development of a foreign policy that would strengthen the nation's commercial independence and assert United States neutrality in European wars. When a Senate committee met in May to consider an appropriation bill to enable the President to employ representatives abroad, Jefferson was ill with another of his periodic headaches. But he felt it was important to speak to the committee in person. William Maclay, a senator from central Pennsylvania who was hostile to the idea of having diplomatic agents at all, recorded his impressions of the new Secretary whose "scrany Aspect" betrayed his pain.

A crude 1820 silhouette, thought to be of Jefferson, illustrating his "loose shackling Air."

Journal of William Maclay..., May 24th [1790]
Jefferson is a slender Man. Has rather the Air of Stiffness in his Manner. His cloaths seem too small for him. He sits in a lounging Manner on one hip, commonly, and with one of his shoulders elevated much above the other. His face has a scrany Aspect. His whole figure has a loose shackling Air. He had a rambling Vacant look and nothing of that firm collected deportment which I expected would dignify the presence of a Secretary or Minister. I looked for Gravity but a laxity of Manner, seemed shed about him. He spoke almost without ceasing. But even his discourse partook of his personal demeanor. It was loose and rambling and yet he scattered information wherever he went, and some even brilliant Sentiments sparkled from him. The information which he gave us respecting foreign Ministers, &ca. was all high Spiced. He has been long enough abroad to catch the tone of European folly.

The senators were persuaded by Jefferson's apt arguments in support of the bill, and he recovered from his illness at the end of May in time to help solve a legislative crisis that threatened to cripple the new government at its start. In December Alexander Hamilton had submitted to Congress his first *Report on the Public Credit.* It recommended systematic repayment of America's domestic and foreign debts through a system of funding, the conversion of existing certificates of indebtedness into new securities that would be redeemed by opening new loans. This portion of his program was comparatively noncontroversial, but the Secretary also argued that the United States should assume unpaid state debts incurred during the Revolution. Most of the opponents of assumption were from states that had already paid a large proportion of their war debts and saw no reason to be burdened with the obligations of less provident states. But they had a moral argument as well. They insisted that Hamilton's proposals would enrich wealthy speculators who had bought up the certificates from the soldiers and farmers who had originally accepted them in lieu of payment for services or produce.

The stalemate in Congress over funding and assumption had become entangled in yet another issue—the location of the national capital. Southerners, who opposed assumption, supported a temporary move to Philadelphia and the eventual construction of a new capital on the Potomac. For some, their eagerness to leave New York was not only a matter of sectional pride but a desire to remove government from the influence of the "monied" interests. Northerners blocked funding of the public debt unless assumption was included with it. Jefferson was no friend to assumption, but he was primarily concerned that the government not be threatened with disunion. He intended to keep a proper distance from the legislative branch, but some compromise was obviously needed. "My duties preventing me from mingling in these questions," he told George Mason on June 13, "I do not pretend to be very competent to their decision. In general I think it necessary to give as well as take in a government like ours." Some two years later, he jotted down the details of the part he played in working out an agreement.

[1792?]

Going to the President's one day I met Hamilton as I approached the door. His look was sombre, haggard, and dejected beyond description. Even his dress uncouth and neglected. He asked to speak with me. We stood in the street near the door. He opened the subject of the assumption of the state debts, the necessity of it in the general fiscal arrangement and it's indispensible necessity towards a preservation of the union.... That as to his own part, if he had not credit enough to carry such a measure as that, he could be of no use, and was determined to resign. He observed at the same time, that tho' our particular business laid in separate departments, yet the administration and it's success was a common concern, and that we should make common cause in supporting one another. He added his wish that I would interest my friends from the South, who were those most opposed to it. I answered that I had been so long absent from my country that I had lost a familiarity with it's affairs, and being but lately returned had not yet got into the train of them, that the fiscal system being out of my department, I had not yet undertaken to consider and understand it, that the assumption had struck me in an unfavorable light, but still not having considered it sufficiently I had not concerned in it, but that I would revolve what he had urged in my mind.... On considering the situation of things I thought the first step towards some conciliation of views would be to bring Mr. Madison and Colo. Hamilton to a friendly discussion of the subject. I immediately wrote to each to come and dine with me the next day, mentioning that we should be alone, that the object was to find some temperament for the present fever, and that I was persuaded that men of sound heads and honest views needed nothing more than explanation and mutual understanding to enable them to unite in some measures which

An original cast of Houdon's bust of Washington which Jefferson kept in the dining room at Monticello

A watercolor of the upper end of Broad Street in New York City, looking uptown to Federal Hall

GEORGE-TOWN, *October* 20.

Laſt Friday arrived here, from Mount-Vernon, the PRESIDENT of the United States, and on Saturday morning, in company with the principal Gentlemen if this town and neighbourhood, set out to view the country adjacent to the River Patowmac, in order to fix upon a proper ſituation, for the GRAND COLUMBIAN FEDERAL CITY. The PRESIDENT returned on Saturday evening, and on Sunday morning early ſet out for the Great Falls and Conogocheague.

We are informed, that ſince the arrival of the PRESIDENT in our parts, bets reſpecting the Seat of Government run high in favour of George-Town; by the return of the PRESIDENT, we hope to have it in our power to lay a circumſtantial account of this important matter before the Public.

News item from the Maryland Journal *of October 26, 1790, describing a visit by Washington to "the country adjacent to the River Patowmac" to look over the site of the Federal City*

might enable us to get along. They came. I opened the subject to them, acknoleged that my situation had not permitted me to understand it sufficiently but encouraged them to consider the thing together. They did so. It ended in Mr. Madison's acquiescence in a proposition that the question should be again brought before the house by way of amendment from the Senate, that tho' he would not vote for it, nor entirely withdraw his opposition, yet he should not be strenuous, but leave it to it's fate. It was observed, I forget by which of them, that as the pill would be a bitter one to the Southern states, something should be done to soothe them; that the removal of the seat of government to the Patowmac was a just measure, and would probably be a popular one with them, and would be a proper one to follow the assumption. It was agreed to speak to Mr. [Alexander] White and Mr. [Richard Bland] Lee, whose districts lay on the Patowmac and to refer to them to consider how far the interests of their particular districts might be a sufficient inducement to them to yield to the assumption. This was done. Lee came into it without hesitation. Mr. White had some qualms, but finally agreed. The measure came down by way of amendment from the Senate and was finally carried by the change of White's and Lee's votes. But the removal to Patowmac could not be carried unless Pennsylvania could be engaged in it. This Hamilton took on himself, and chiefly, as I understood, through the agency of Robert Morris, obtained the vote of that state, on agreeing to an intermediate residence at Philadelphia.

Jefferson's part in the bargain may not have been as central as he believed. The necessary realignment of votes was well under way before his meeting with Hamilton and Madison. But he came to consider the bargain a bad one, not merely for Virginia but for the nation as well, and he later deeply regretted the role he felt he had been "duped" into assuming. As the residence and funding bills moved through Congress, Jefferson was completing one of the most important state papers of his career, the *Report on Weights and Measures.* Two months before he arrived in New York, Congress had requested that the Secretary of State draft a plan "for establishing uniformity in the Currency, Weights and Measures of the United States." Jefferson took to the task with relish. After carefully working out a standard measure of invariable length, he recommended a decimal system of weights and measures similar to the coinage system Congress had adopted at his suggestion in 1785. He favored a thorough reform of the existing hodgepodge of bushels, barrels, firkins, crooms, wine gallons, etc., but he realistically suggested an alternative, less comprehensive plan and recommended a gradual transition.

Report on Weights and Measures [July 4, 1790]
To obtain uniformity in measures, weights and coins, it is necessary to find some measure of invariable length, with which, as a standard, they may be compared....

The motion of the earth round it's axis, tho' not absolutely uniform. and invariable, may be considered as such for every human purpose. It is measured obviously but unequally, by the departure of a given meridian from the sun, and it's return to it, constituting a solar day. Throwing together the inequalities of Solar days, a mean interval, or day, has been found, and divided by very general consent into 86,400 equal parts.

A pendulum, vibrating freely in small and equal arcs, may be so adjusted in it's length as by it's vibrations, to make this division of the earth's motion into 86,400 equal parts called seconds of mean time.

Such a pendulum then becomes itself a measure of determinate length, to which all others may be referred, as to a standard....

[There were "uncertainties," however, with that kind of pendulum, and Jefferson took up the suggestion of Robert Leslie, a Philadelphia watchmaker, of using a "uniform cylindrical rod."]

Let the Standard of measure then be an uniform cylindrical rod of iron, of such length as in lat. 45.° in the level of the ocean, and in a cellar or other place, the temperature of which does not vary thro' the year, shall perform it's vibrations, in small and equal arcs, in one second of mean time.

A standard of invariable length being thus obtained, we may proceed to identify by that the measures, weights, and coins of the U.S....

[Jefferson's alternative plan, which he described first, was to retain existing measures but render them "uniform and invariable, by bringing them to the same invariable standard." The second proposal was more thorough.]

But if it be thought that, either now, or at any future time, the citizens of the U.S. may be induced to undertake a thorough reformation of their whole system of measures, weights and coins, reducing every branch to the same decimal ratio already established in their coins, and thus bringing the calculation of the principal affairs of life within the arithmetic of every man who can multiply and divide plain numbers, greater changes will be necessary.

The Unit of measure is still that which must give law through the whole system: and from whatever unit we set out, the coincidences between the old and new ratios will be rare. All that can be done will be to chuse such an Unit as will produce the most of these....

Measures of length.

Let the Second rod then, as before described, be the Standard of measure; and let it be divided into five equal parts, each of which shall be called a *Foot:* for perhaps it may be better, generally to retain the name of the nearest present measure, where there is one tolerably near. It will be about one quarter of an inch shorter than the present foot.

Let the foot be divided into 10. inches;
The Inch into 10. lines;
The line into 10. points;
Let 10. feet made a decad;
10. decads a rood;
10. roods a furlong;
10. furlongs a mile....

[After a similar delineation of measures of capacity and weights and coins, Jefferson concluded the lengthy report.]

Measures, weights, and coins thus referred to standards, unchangeable in their nature, (as is the length of a rod vibrating seconds, and the weight of a definite mass of rain water) will themselves be unchangeable. These standards too are such as to be accessible to all persons, in all times and places. The measures and weights derived from them fall in so nearly with some of those now in use, as to facilitate their introduction; and being arranged in decimal ratio, they are within the calculation of every one who possesses the first elements of

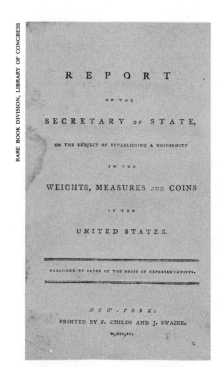

R E P O R T

of the

SECRETARY of STATE,

ON THE SUBJECT OF ESTABLISHING A UNIFORMITY

IN THE

WEIGHTS, MEASURES and COINS

OF THE

UNITED STATES.

PUBLISHED BY ORDER OF THE HOUSE OF REPRESENTATIVES.

N E W - Y O R K:
PRINTED BY F. CHILDS AND J. SWAINE.
M,DCC,XC,

*Jefferson's copy, from his library,
of* Report on Weights and Measures

arithmetic, and of easy comparison, both for foreigners and citizens, with the measures, weights, and coins of other countries.

A gradual introduction would lessen the inconveniences which might attend too sudden a substitution, even of an easier, for a more difficult system. After a given term, for instance, it might begin in the Custom houses, where the merchants would become familiarised to it. After a further term, it might be introduced into all legal proceedings, and merchants, and traders in foreign commodities, might be required to use it in their dealings with one another. After a still further term, all other descriptions of people might recieve it into common use. — Too long a postponement on the other hand, would increase the difficulties of it's reception, with the increase of our population.

To Jefferson's disappointment, Congress and the practical men of Hamiltonian persuasion did not share his farsightedness; they failed to adopt a metric system when it might have been implemented most easily in the United States. Jefferson continued throughout his life, nevertheless, to promote a simple, universal system that could be easily understood by the ordinary person in his daily transactions. The same day the Secretary sent his report to the House, he wrote Edward Rutledge of the resolution of the funding and residence controversies. Simultaneously, a jurisdictional dispute between Britain and Spain over Nootka Sound on the Pacific Coast threatened to develop into a general war and focus the administration's attention on foreign policy.

New York July 4. 1790.
Some questions have lately agitated the mind of Congress more than the friends of union on catholic principles would have wished....The question of residence you know was always a heating one. A bill has past the Senate for fixing this at Philadelphia ten years, and then at Georgetown: and it is rather probable it will pass the lower house. That question then will be put to sleep for ten years; and this and the funding business being once out of the way, I hope nothing else may be able to call up local principles. If the war between Spain and England takes place, I think France will inevitably be involved in it. In that case I hope the new world will fatten on the follies of the old. If we can but establish the principles of the armed neutrality for ourselves, we must

become the carriers for all parties as far as we can raise vessels.

In an effort to communicate America's intent to remain neutral, Jefferson wrote to a friend in London, Benjamin Vaughan, describing some of his new duties in the area of issuing patents for new inventions. Beneath all the discussion of maple sugar and prevention of worm damage to ships and wharves was a message that the United States would soon cease to be dependent on British manufactures and was already independent of Britain's West Indian sugar plantations. Vaughan grasped the meaning of the letter correctly and immediately forwarded it to the British foreign office. The letter is a typical example of Jefferson's use of private and indirect means to transmit views about public policy.

New York June 27. 1790.

Late difficulties in the sugar trade have excited attention to our sugar trees, and it seems fully believed by judicious persons, that we can not only supply our own demand, but make for exportation. I will send you a sample of it if I can find a conveyance without passing it through the expensive one of the post. What a blessing to substitute a sugar which requires only the labour of children, for that which it is said renders the slavery of the blacks necessary.

An act of Congress authorising the issuing patents for new discoveries has given a spring to invention beyond my conception. Being an instrument in granting the patents, I am acquainted with their discoveries. Many of them indeed are trifling, but there are some of great consequence which have been proved by practice, and others which if they stand the same proof will produce great effect. Yesterday, the man who built the famous bridge from Boston to Charlestown was with me, asking a patent for a pile engine of his own construction. He communicated to me another fact of which he makes no secret, and it is important. He was formerly concerned in shipbuilding, but for 30. years past, has been a bridge builder. He had early in life observed on examining worm eaten ships, that the worms never eat within the seams where the corking chissel enters, and the oil &c. He had observed that the whaling vessels would be eaten to a honeycomb except a little above and below water where the whale is brought into contact with the vessel and lies beating against it till it is cut up. A plank

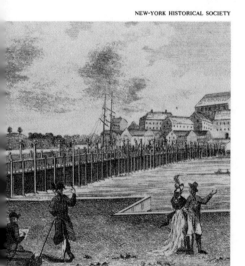

The timbers of the Charles River Bridge, which opened for public use in June, 1786, had been soaked with codfish oil to preserve them.

lying under water at a mill of his had been obliged to be renewed annually, because eaten up by the worm within the course of the year. At length a plank was accidentally put down which for some purpose had been thoroughly impregnated with oil. It remained seven years without being affected. Hence he took the idea of impregnating the timber of his bridges thoroughly with oil, by heating the timber as deeply as possibly, and doing it well in that state with the liver oil of the codfish. He has practised this for 30. years and there is no instance of the worm attacking his timbers, while those in neighboring places are immediately destroyed. . . .

We are told you are going to war. Peace and profit I hope will be our lot. A high price and sure market for our productions, and no want of carrying business will I hope enable my countrymen to pay off both their private and public debts. . . .

One of Jefferson's goals as Secretary of State was to secure the territorial boundaries of the United States, especially with respect to control of navigation on the Mississippi and access to the seas through New Orleans. This was a matter of paramount importance to the settlers in the West, a group Jefferson was anxious to tie to the Republic. He saw in the Nootka Sound controversy an opportunity for bargaining with the two principals from a position of neutrality. Jefferson conferred with Madison at the President's request and discussed the possibility that France, with whom the United States still had a treaty of amity and commerce, might be called on to aid Spain and that Britain might "attempt the conquest of Louisiana and the Floridas." On July 12 he gave Washington a succinct outline of the dangers if Britain tried to acquire Western territories, of the decisions that had to be confronted, and of the initiatives that were possible.

July 12. 1790.

The dangers to us should Great Britain possess herself of those countries.

She will possess a territory equal to half ours, beyond the Missisipi

She will seduce that half of ours which is on this side the Missisipi by her language, laws, religion, manners, government, commerce, capital.

by the possession of N. Orleans, which draws to it the dependance of all the waters of Misspi

by the markets she can offer them in the gulph of Mexico and elsewhere.

George Beckwith

She will take from the remaining part of our States the markets they now have for their produce by furnishing those markets cheaper with the same articles....

She will have then possessions double the size of ours, as good in soil and climate.

She will encircle us compleatly, by these possessions on our landboard, and her fleets on our sea-board.

Instead of two neighbors balancing each other, we shall have one, with more than the strength of both.

Would the prevention of this be worth a war?

Consider our abilities to take part in a war.

Our operations would be by land only.

How many men should we need to employ?—Their cost?

Our resources of taxation and credit equal to this....

No need to take a part in the war as yet. We may chuse our own time. Delay gives us many chances to avoid it altogether....

Delay enables us to be better prepared:

To obtain from the allies a price for our assistance.

[After making recommendations as to policy toward Spain, Jefferson confronted the question of policy toward Britain. Since the fall of 1789, Hamilton had been in close touch with an unofficial agent of the British government, George Beckwith, who had hurried down from Quebec in July to try to determine what the United States would do if a war developed. Since he was not accredited, he could speak to neither Washington nor Jefferson, but Hamilton reassured him that the United States would maintain its friendly disposition, despite the harder line Jefferson recommended.]

As to England? Say to Beckwith

'that as to a Treaty of commerce, we would prefer amicable, to adversary arrangements, tho the latter would be infallible, and in our own power:

That our ideas are that such a treaty should be founded in perfect reciprocity; and would therefore be it's own price:

That as to an Alliance, we can say nothing till it's object be shewn, and that it is not to be inconsistent with existing engagements:

That in the event of war between Gr. Brit. and Spain

we are disposed to be strictly neutral:

That however, we should view with extreme uneasiness any attempts of either power to seize the possessions of the other on our frontier, as we consider our own safety interested in a due balance between our neighbors'....

As a price for American neutrality, Jefferson hoped for concessions from both Britain and Spain. In his instructions to William Carmichael, the United States envoy in Madrid, he emphasized America's natural right to the navigation of the Mississippi, a right Spain should not contravene, he warned, except at the risk of war. He included a long outline of the American position with the letter.

New York August 2d. 1790.

The present appearances of war between our two neighbours, Spain and England, cannot but excite all our attention. The part we are to act is uncertain, and will be difficult. The unsettled state of our dispute with Spain may give a turn to it very different from what we would wish. As it is important that you should be fully apprised of our way of thinking on this subject, I have sketched, in the enclosed paper, general heads of consideration arising from present circumstances.... With this information ... you will be enabled to meet the minister in conversations on the subject of the navigation of the Mississippi to which we wish you to lead his attention immediately. Impress him thoroughly with the necessity of an early and even an immediate settlement of this matter, and of a return to the field of negociation for this purpose: and though it must be done delicately, yet he must be made to understand unequivocally that a resumption of the negociation is not desired on our part, unless he can determine, in the first opening of it, to yield the immediate and full enjoyment of that navigation.... It may be asked what need of negociation, if the navigation is to be ceded at all events? You know that the navigation cannot be practised without a port where the sea and river vessels may meet and exchange loads, and where those employed about them may be safe and unmolested. The right to use a thing comprehends a right to the means necessary to it's use, and without which it would be useless: the fixing on a proper port, and the degree of freedom it is to enjoy in it's operations, will require negociation, and be governed

Impression of official seal of the United States, used by Jefferson

by events. There is danger indeed that even the unavoidable delay of sending a negociator here, may render the mission too late for the preservation of peace: it is impossible to answer for the forbearance of our western citizens. We endeavor to quiet them with the expectation of an attainment of their rights by peaceable means, but should they, in a moment of impatience, hazard others, there is no saying how far we may be led: for neither themselves nor their rights will ever be abandoned by us.

The Secretary directed William Short in Paris to use his influence with the French government to exert pressure on Spain. Since January, 1790, Washington had used Gouverneur Morris, a private citizen from New York, as his personal agent in Britain, and Jefferson wrote to him, outlining his part in the overall strategy. Morris was to communicate to the ministry in London that American neutrality might be guaranteed by Britain's adherence to the Treaty of 1783—especially the provision requiring withdrawal from forts in the Northwest—and by her forbearance from seizing lands on the American frontiers.

New York August 12th. 1790.
You have placed their proposition of exchanging a Minister on proper ground. It must certainly come from them, and come in unequivocal form; with those who respect their own dignity so much, ours must not be counted at nought.... Besides what they are saying to you, they are talking to us through Quebec; but so informally that they may disavow it when they please.... These tamperings prove they view a war as very possible; and some symptoms indicate designs against the Spanish possessions adjoining us. The consequences of their acquiring all the country on our frontier from the St. Croix to the St. Mary's [rivers] are too obvious to you to need developement. You will readily see the dangers which would then environ us. We wish you therefore to intimate to them that we cannot be indifferent to enterprizes of this kind, that we should contemplate a change of neighbours with extreme uneasiness; and that a due balance on our borders is not less desireable to us, than a balance of power in Europe has always appeared to them. We wish to be neutral, and we will be so, *if they will execute the treaty fairly,* and *attempt no conquests adjoining us.* The first condition is just; the second imposes no hardship on them.... If the war takes

223

place, we would really wish to be quieted on these two points, offering in return an honorable neutrality; more than this they are not to expect.

The Nootka Sound affair did not develop into a war. Jefferson's instructions to Morris had no effect, but the negotiations with Spain would eventually bear fruit. As the summer ended, Congress and Cabinet scattered for the fall legislative recess. Just before leaving New York, Jefferson prepared a draft "Agenda" for Washington on the location of the seat of government, a step toward insuring that the other half of the funding bargain would be carried out.

[August 29, 1790]

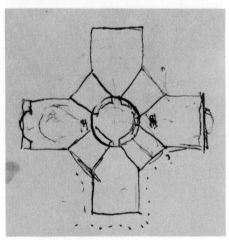

Jefferson's sketches suggesting the Pantheon in Paris as a model for the new Capitol; floor plan shows space for the Senate and House, conferences, vestibule, and rotunda.

Proceedings to be had under the Residence act.

A territory not exceeding 10. miles square (or, I presume, 100 square miles in any form) to be located by metes and bounds.

3. commissioners to be appointed.

I suppose them not entitled to any salary....

The Commissioners to purchase or accept 'such quantity of land on the E. side of the river as the President shall deem *proper for the U.S.*' viz. for the federal Capitol, the offices, the President's house and gardens, the town house, Market house, publick walks, hospital....

The expression 'such quantity of land as the President shall deem *proper for the U.S.*' is vague. It may therefore be extended to the acceptance or purchase of land enough for the town, and I have no doubt it is the wish, and perhaps expectation. In that case it will be to be laid out in lots and streets. I should propose these to be at right angles as in Philadelphia, and that no street be narrower than 100. feet, with foot-ways of 15. feet....

The Commissioners should have some taste in Architecture, because they may have to decide between different plans.

They will however be subject to the President's direction in every point.

When the President shall have made up his mind as to the spot for the town, would there be any impropriety in his saying to the neighboring landholders, 'I will fix the town here if you will join and purchase and give the lands.' They may well afford it from the increase of value

Bas-relief of James Madison modeled from life by Ceracchi in 1792, then carved in alabaster at Florence

it will give to their own circumjacent lands.

The lots to be sold out in breadths of 50. feet: their depths to extend to the diagonal of the square.

I doubt much whether the obligation to build the houses at a given distance from the street, contributes to it's beauty. It produces a disgusting monotony. All persons make this complaint against Philadelphia. The contrary practice varies the appearance, and is much more convenient to the inhabitants.

In Paris it is forbidden to build a house beyond a given height, and it is admitted to be a good restriction. It keeps down the price of ground, keeps the houses low and convenient, and the streets light and airy. Fires are much more manageable where houses are low. This however is an object of legislation.

As he left for Virginia with James Madison on September 1, Jefferson had time to reflect and to share impressions with the man who had become the principal "opposition" leader in New York City. The Secretary of State and the congressman from Virginia had begun collaborating on domestic affairs and foreign policy in the new government while Jefferson was still at Monticello, where Madison sent him a copy of Hamilton's *Report on Public Credit.* Their thoughts and conversations, as they visited acquaintances in Philadelphia and surveyed possible sites on the Potomac, must have been disquieting. There was good reason to believe that the compromise on assumption had ended only one cause of division in the Union and had not eliminated basic areas of disagreement. Jefferson's introduction to New York society and to the opinions of members of the First Congress had put him on notice that a new faction was developing, one with "monarchical" leanings. More than forty years later, he wrote of those disturbing discoveries.

Monticello Jan. 8. [18]25.

When I arrived at N. York in 1790, to take a part in the administration, being fresh from the French revolution, while in it's first and pure stage, and consequently somewhat whetted up in my own republican principles, I found a state of things, in the general society of the place, which I could not have supposed possible. Being a stranger there, I was feasted from table to table, at large set dinners, the parties generally from 20. to 30. The revolution I had left, and that we had just gone thro' in the recent change of our own government, being the common topics of conversation, I was astonished to

While home at Monticello in 1790, Jefferson made this sketch and noted specifications for a desk.

find the general prevalence of monarchical sentiments, insomuch that in maintaining those of republicanism, I had always the whole company on my hands, never scarcely finding among them a single co-advocate in that argument, unless some old member of Congress happened to be present.

The next session of Congress, beginning in December, convinced Jefferson that the "monarchical" interest he had sensed was no phantom and that the leader of that interest was Alexander Hamilton. The conflict between Jefferson and Hamilton reflected basically different views of government. Hamilton distrusted the common man as much as Jefferson venerated his intelligence and sense of responsibility. Hamilton saw America's future as best served by strengthening economic ties with Britain, whereas Jefferson thought the United States was already much too dependent on Britain commercially; he wanted to continue developing commerce with France and promoting trade with other nations. Foreign policy was closely connected to Hamilton's fiscal and domestic plans, a fact that led him to meddle freely outside the concerns of his department. His interference was facilitated by the manner in which foreign policy decisions were made: by collective deliberation in the Cabinet. Hamilton's views as to domestic policy unfolded more completely that same month when he submitted a series of reports that included a proposal for a national bank. The bank would hold the funds of the government but would be controlled by private citizens. Madison fought doggedly against the bank bill in the House after it was approved by the Senate, but it was sent to the President for signing in mid-February.

In the meantime, Jefferson had submitted to the President a report on the failure of Gouverneur Morris's mission to Great Britain. He concluded that Britain would not surrender the forts in the Northwest nor negotiate a treaty of commerce without a treaty of alliance as well. Furthermore, it was still uncertain whether an accredited minister would be sent. Washington delayed reporting dispatches to Congress until February, when, in a terse note Jefferson had drafted, he said he "thought it proper to give you this information, as it might at some time have influence on matters under your consideration."

The matters Jefferson hoped would be under consideration were proposals for discriminatory navigation laws aimed at Great Britain. Jefferson had made such recommendations in a report on the plight of the New England cod and whale fisheries he had submitted the first week in February, in response to a request from the General Court of Massachusetts. The fisheries had been in a decline, primarily as a result of British dominance of the seas and a loss of markets after the Revolution. Jefferson criticized the British

Navigation Act's regulations "for mounting their navigation on the ruin of ours." He proposed counterregulations, recommended measures for establishing new markets and relief from certain taxes, and stressed the importance of reviving the carrying trade.

Report on the Cod and Whale Fisheries
[February 1, 1791]

The representation [of the General Court of Massachusetts] sets forth that, before the late war, about 4,000 Seamen and 24,000 Tons of shipping were annually employed from that State in the Whale Fishery, the produce whereof was about £350,000 lawful money a year.

That, previous to the same period, the Cod Fishery of that State employed 4000 men and 28,000 Ton of Shipping and produced about £250,000 a year.

That these branches of business, annihilated during the war, have been in some degree recovered since: but that they labour under many and heavy embarrassments, which, if not removed, or lessened, will render the Fisheries every year less extensive and important.

That these embarrassments are, heavy duties on their produce abroad, and bounties on that of their competitors: and duties at home on several articles particularly used in the Fisheries.

And it asks that the duties be taken off, that bounties be given to the fishermen, and the national influence be used abroad for obtaining better markets for their produce.

The Cod and Whale Fisheries, carried on by different persons, from different Ports, in different vessels, in different Seas, and seeking different markets, agree in one circumstance, in being as unprofitable to the adventurer, as important to the public....

[Jefferson surveyed the history of the cod fishery and then listed the advantages under which it operated, including the proximity of the great fisheries, the cheapness of the American vessels used, and the "superiority of our mariners in skill, activity, enterprise, sobriety and order." Despite these advantages, there were numerous disadvantages.]

Of the disadvantages opposed to us, those which depend on ourselves are

Alexander Hamilton as Secretary of the Treasury (above) and Thomas Jefferson as Secretary of State (below), both by Charles W. Peale

227

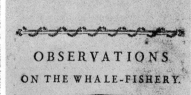

OBSERVATIONS

ON THE WHALE-FISHERY.

Whale oil enters, as a raw material, into several branches of manufacture, as of wool, leather, soap: it is used also in painting, architecture and navigation. But its great consumption is in lighting houses and cities. For this last purpose however it has a powerful competitor in the vegetable oils. These do well in warm, still weather, but they fix with cold, they extinguish easily with the wind, their crop is precarious, depending on the seasons, and to yield the same light, a larger wick must be used, and greater quantity of oil consumed. Estimating all these articles of difference together, those employed in lighting cities find their account in giving about 25 per cent. more for whale than for vegetable oils. But higher than this the whale oil, in its present form cannot rise; because it then becomes more advantageous to the city-lighters to use others. This competition then limits its price, higher than which no encouragement can raise it, and becomes, as it were, a law of its nature, but, at this low price; the whale fishery is the poorest business into which a merchant or sailor can enter. If the sailor, instead of wages, has a part of what is taken, he finds that this, one year with another, yields him less than he could have got as wages in any other business. It is attended too with great risk, singular hardships, and long absences from his family. If the voyage is made solely at the expence of the merchant, he finds that, one year with another, it does

A

Jefferson's report to Congress on the New England fisheries continued the research he had begun in Paris, which resulted in Observations on the Whale-Fishery, *printed in 1788.*

Tonnage and Naval duties on the vessels employed in the fishery.

Impost duties on Salt.
on Tea, Rum, Sugar, Molasses
hooks, Lines and Leads.
Duck, Cordage and Cables.
Iron, Hemp and Twine

} used in the fishery....

Of the disadvantages which depend on others are

1. The loss of the Mediterranean markets.
2. Exclusions from the markets of some of our neighbours.
3. High duties in those of others, and
4. Bounties to the individuals in competition with us....

[Jefferson similarly perused the history of the whale fishery, the effects of British bounties and trade restrictions, and the 50 percent decline in the number of American ships involved in the industry from 1771 to 1789. These observations led him to make certain conclusions.]

These details will enable Congress to see with what a competition we have to struggle for the continuance of this fishery, not to say it's increase. Against prohibitory duties in one country, and bounties to the adventurers in both of those which are contending with each other for the same object, ours have no auxiliaries but poverty and rigorous economy. The business, unaided, is a wretched one....

This brings us to the question what relief does the condition of this fishery require?

1. A remission of duties on the Articles used for their calling.

2. A retaliating duty on foreign oils, coming to seek a competition with them in or from our Ports.

3. Free markets abroad.

1. The remission of duties will stand on nearly the same ground with that to the Cod fishermen.

2. The only Nation whose oil is brought hither for competition with our own, makes ours pay a duty of about 82. dollars the Ton in their Ports....

The 3d. and principal object is to find markets for the

vent of oil....

England is the market for the greater part of our Spermaceti oil. They impose on all our oils a duty of £18.5. sterling the Ton, which, as to the common kind, is a prohibition as has been before observed, and as to that of the Spermaceti, gives a preference of theirs over ours to that amount, so as to leave in the end but a scanty benefit to the fisherman, And not long since, by a change of construction, without any change of the law, it was made to exclude our oils from their ports, when carried in our own vessels. On some change of circumstances it was construed back again to the reception of our oils, on paying always however the same duty of £18.5. This serves to shew that the tenure by which we hold the admission of this commodity in their markets, is as precarious as it is hard. Nor can it be announced that there is any disposition on their part to arrange this or any other commercial matter to mutual convenience. The exparte regulations which they have begun for mounting their navigation on the ruins of ours, can only be opposed by counter-regulations on our part. And the loss of seamen, the natural consequence of lost and obstructed markets for our fish and oil, calls in the first place for serious and timely attention. It will be too late when the seaman shall have changed his vocation, or gone over to another interest....

If regulations, exactly the counterpart of those established against us, would be ineffectual, from a difference of circumstances, other regulations equivalent can give no reasonable ground of complaint to any nation. Admitting their right of keeping their markets to themselves, ours cannot be denied of keeping our carrying trade to ourselves. And if there be any thing unfriendly in this, it was in the first example.

The loss of seamen, unnoticed, would be followed by other losses in a long train. If we have no seamen, our ships will be useless, consequently our Ship timber, Iron and hemp: our Ship building will be at an end, ship carpenters go over to other nations, our young men have no call to the Sea, our produce, carried in foreign bottoms, be saddled with war freight and insurance, in times of war.... It is easier, as well as better, to stop this train at it's entrance, than when it shall have ruined or banished whole classes of useful and industrious Citizens.

The fisheries report and the disclosure of the intransigent British attitude revealed in Morris's dispatches prompted a navigation bill that was reported out of a House committee headed by Madison. It was delayed by being referred to the Secretary of State with a request for a general report on the state of American commerce, but the Hamiltonians had been thrown on the defensive. Although Hamilton could not oppose the navigation bill openly, he disliked its anti-British stance; much of the Treasury's revenue depended on duties on imported British goods. The split in the national councils between those who sought a rapprochement with England, led by Hamilton, and those who wanted to lessen American commercial dependence on that country, led by Madison and Jefferson, was widening.

Jefferson was less directly involved in consideration of the national bank, but the issue of its constitutionality was troubling Washington. He asked for opinions from his Cabinet, and Jefferson—after listing his legal objections—gave his opinion that the bill was unconstitutional. He concluded with the recommendation of a veto.

Hamilton won the fight for the bank bill and the first Bank of the United States rose in Philadelphia.

Feb. 15. 1791.

I consider the foundation of the Constitution as laid on this ground that 'all powers not delegated to the U.S. by the Constitution, not prohibited by it to the states, are reserved to the states or to the people' [XIIth. Amendmt.]. To take a single step beyond the boundaries thus specially drawn around the powers of Congress, is to take possession of a boundless feild of power, no longer susceptible of any definition.

The incorporation of a bank, and other powers assumed by this bill have not, in my opinion, been delegated to the U.S. by the Constitution....

It has been much urged that a bank will give great facility, or convenience in the collection of taxes. Suppose this were true: yet the constitution allows only the means which are 'necessary,' not those which are merely 'convenient' for effecting the enumerated powers. If such a latitude of construction be allowed to this phrase as to give any non-enumerated power, it will go to every one, for there is no one which ingenuity may not torture into a *convenience, in some way or other,* to *some one* of so long a list of enumerated powers. It would swallow up all the delegated powers, and reduce the whole to one phrase as before observed. Therefore it was that the constitution restrained them to the *necessary* means, that is to say, to those means without which the grant of the power would be nugatory....

Pencil sketch, perhaps by Cornelia Jefferson Randolph, a granddaughter, of the lost bust of Jefferson by Ceracchi, modeled from life c. 1791

Can it be thought that the Constitution intended that for a shade or two of *convenience,* more or less, Congress should be authorised to break down the most antient and fundamental laws of the several states, such as those against Mortmain, the laws of alienage, the rules of descent, the acts of distribution, the laws of escheat and forfeiture, the laws of monopoly? Nothing but a necessity invincible by any other means, can justify such a prostration of laws which constitute the pillars of our whole system of jurisprudence. Will Congress be too strait-laced to carry the constitution into honest effect, unless they may pass over the foundation-laws of the state-governments for the slightest convenience to theirs?

The Negative of the President is the shield provided by the constitution to protect against the invasions of the legislature 1. the rights of the Executive 2. of the Judiciary 3. of the states and state legislatures. The present is the case of a right remaining exclusively with the states and is consequently one of those intended by the constitution to be placed under his protection.

It must be added however, that unless the President's mind on a view of every thing which is urged for and against this bill, is tolerably clear that it is unauthorised by the constitution, if the pro and the con hang so even as to balance his judgment, a just respect for the wisdom of the legislature would naturally decide the balance in favour of their opinion. It is chiefly for cases where they are clearly misled by error, ambition, or interest, that the constitution has placed a check in the negative of the President.

Washington evidently found Jefferson's legal and constitutional arguments unconvincing, and he did not respond to the thrust of the Secretary's final implication, that the bill was indeed the product of "error, ambition, and interest." Instead, the President signed it into law on February 23. That defeat made Jefferson realize that he must combat the underlying principles of Hamilton's policies as well as his programs. In April, 1791, the President left Philadelphia for a semiofficial tour of the southern states. In his absence, the Vice President and Cabinet were to "consult & act" on any "serious and important cases" that arose in his absence. The procedure gave rise to the following incident, recalled in a compilation of notes and memorandums Jefferson titled the *Anas.*

Invitation to dinner with engraved
facsimile of Jefferson's signature

Anas, [February 4, 1818]

Some occasion for consultation arising, I invited those gentlemen (and the Attorney genl. as well as I remember) to dine with me in order to confer on the subject. After the cloth was removed, and our question agreed & dismissed, conversation began on other matters and, by some circumstance, was led to the British constitution, on which Mr. Adams observed 'purge that constitution of it's corruption, and give to it's popular branch equality of representation, and it would be the most perfect constitution ever devised by the wit of man.' Hamilton paused and said, 'purge it of it's corruption, and give to it's popular branch equality of representation, & it would become an *impracticable* government: as it stands at present, with all it's supposed defects, it is the most perfect government which ever existed.' And this was assuredly the exact line which separated the political creeds of these two gentlemen. The one was for two hereditary branches and an honest elective one: the other for a hereditary King with a house of lords & commons, corrupted to his will, and standing between him and the people. Hamilton was indeed a singular character. Of acute understanding, disinterested, honest, and honorable in all private transactions, amiable in society, and duly valuing virtue in private life, yet so bewitched & perverted by the British example, as to be under thoro' conviction that corruption was essential to the government of a nation.

In an earlier account of this meeting Jefferson described another incident that revealed even more about the character of the man he was subsequently to refer to as "our Buonaparte." Hamilton had looked around the room of his home and asked whose portraits hung on the wall.

Monticello Jan. 16. [18]11.

Another incident took place on the same occasion which will further delineate Hamilton's political principles. The room being hung around with a collection of the portraits of remarkable men, among them were those of Bacon, Newton & Locke. Hamilton asked me who they were. I told him they were my trinity of the three greatest men the world had ever produced, naming them. He paused for some time: 'The greatest man, said he, that ever lived was Julius Cæsar.'

Before Jefferson could escape Philadelphia for a vacation during the legislative recess in the summer, he saw traces of the hated monarchism in a man he considered an "antient" and trusted friend, John Adams. A copy of the English edition of Tom Paine's *The Rights of Man*, a pamphlet written in praise of the French Revolution, was lent to Jefferson with the request that it be forwarded to a Philadelphia printer when the Secretary had finished studying it. Jefferson obliged and sent it to Jonathan B. Smith with a brief covering note which said, in part, that he was pleased the pamphlet was to be reprinted and "that something is at length to be publicly said against the political heresies which have sprung up among us."

This note, unfortunately, was included in the preface to the Philadelphia edition without Jefferson's prior knowledge or permission. No one needed to be told that the "political heresies" referred to were such essays as John Adams's "Discourses on Davila," which had recently been published in the *Gazette of the United States.* Jefferson wrote immediately to the President explaining the circumstances of the publication, but it was more than two months before he could bring himself to write to the Vice President.

Philadelphia July 17. 1791.

I have a dozen times taken up my pen to write to you and as often laid it down again, suspended between opposing considerations. I determine however to write from a conviction that truth, between candid minds, can never do harm....I thought so little of this note that I did not even keep a copy of it: nor ever heard a tittle more of it till, the week following, I was thunderstruck with seeing it come out at the head of the pamphlet. I hoped however it would not attract notice....Thus were our names thrown on the public stage as public antagonists. That you and I differ in our ideas of the best form of government is well known to us both: but we have differed as friends should do, respecting the purity of each other's motives, and confining our difference of opinion to private conversation. And I can declare with truth in the presence of the almighty that nothing was further from my intention or expectation than to have had either my own or your name brought before the public on this occasion. The friendship and confidence which has so long existed between us required this explanation from me, and I know you too well to fear any misconstruction of the motives of it.

THE following Extract from a note accompanying a copy of this Pamphlet for republication, is fo refpectable a teftimony of its value, that the Printer hopes the diftinguifhed writer will excufe its prefent appearance. It proceeds from a character equally eminent in the councils of America, and converfant in the affairs of France, from a long and recent refidence at the Court of Verfailles in the Diplomatic department; and, at the fame time that it does juftice to the writings of Mr. Paine, it reflects honor on the fource from which it flows, by directing the mind to a contemplation of that Republican firmnefs and Democratic fimplicity which endear their poffeffor to every friend of the " RIGHTS OF MAN."

After fome prefatory remarks, the Secretary of State obferves:

" I am extremely pleafed to find it will be re-printed here, and that " fomething is at length to be publicly faid againft the political herefies " which have fprung up among us.

" I have no doubt our citizens will *rally* a fecond time round the " *ftandard* of COMMON SENSE."

Extract of the note to Jonathan B. Smith which appeared as a printer's notice in the American edition of The Rights of Man *by Thomas Paine*

The incident embarrassed Jefferson. It not only interrupted his close friendship with the Adamses but also altered his relationship with Washington. With these regrets in mind, Jefferson set out on a "botanizing tour" of the northern states with James Madison on May 17. Their observations and studies would not be confined to botany, however, and their enemies charged then, as their critics still do, that the tour had political motives and that the pair planned their travels through upstate New York and New England with an eye to mobilizing opposition to Hamilton and his policies. The two Virginians journeyed north not so much to talk to the leaders of these areas, whose views they already knew, but to learn whether their constituents agreed with the positions the New England bloc had taken on assumption, the Bank, and commercial retaliation against Britain. Yet Jefferson's reports on the journey were scrupulously confined to nature and scenic beauty. After sailing up the Hudson to Albany and traveling to Lakes George and Champlain, he wrote his daughter Martha of the splendors he had seen.

Public Men, SULLIVAN

A view of "muddy" Lake Champlain

Lake Champlain May 31 [1791]
Lake George is without comparison the most beautiful water I ever saw: formed by a contour of mountains into a bason 35 miles long, and from 2 or 4 miles broad, finely interspersed with islands, its waters limpid as chrystal and the mountain sides covered with rich groves of Thuya, silver fir, white pine, Aspen, and paper birch down to the water edge, here and there precipices of rock to checquer the scene and save it from monotony. An abundance of speckled trout, salmon trout, bass, and other fish, with which it is stored, have added, to our other amusements the sport of taking them. Lake Champlain, tho much larger, is a far less pleasant water. It is muddy, turbulent, and yields little game. After penetrating into it about 25 miles we have been obliged by a head wind and high sea to return, having spent a day and a half in sailing on it.... Our journey hitherto has been prosperous and pleasant except as to the weather which has been as sultry hot through the whole as could be found in Carolina or Georgia.... On the whole, I find nothing any where else in point of climate which Virginia need envy to any part of the world. Here they are locked up in ice and snow for six months. Spring and autumn, which make a paradise of our country, are rigorous winter with them, and a Tropical summer breaks on them all at once.

From New York the travelers went to Vermont, which had recently been admitted to the Union, and to areas of Massachusetts and

Connecticut. The leisurely tour was cut short in mid-June when Madison fell ill. Nonetheless, their travels had made Jefferson less a stranger to public opinion in the region. Shortly after their return, Madison finally succeeded in enlisting a new ally—a New York journalist named Philip Freneau—in the fight against Hamilton. For some time, Hamiltonians had been at an advantage in exerting influence through Joseph Fenno's *Gazette of the United States*. Jefferson's main objective in encouraging another newspaper was to see that the one-sided view of European affairs, taken by Fenno from the British press, was counterbalanced with information he could supply from other European sources. Just before leaving for New York in May, Jefferson had written his son-in-law of the sad condition of the Philadelphia press where only Benjamin Franklin Bache's amateurishly produced *General Advertiser* opposed Fenno.

> Philadelphia, May 15. 1791.
>
> I inclose you Bache's as well as Fenno's papers. You will have percieved that the latter is a paper of pure Toryism, disseminating the doctrines of monarchy, aristocracy, & the exclusion of the influence of the people. We have been trying to get another *weekly or half weekly* paper set up excluding advertisements, so that it might go through the states, & furnish a whig-vehicle of intelligence. We hoped at one time to have persuaded Freneau to set up here, but failed. In the mean time Bache's paper, the principles of which were always republican, improves in it's matter. If we can persuade him to throw all his advertisements on one leaf, by tearing that off, the leaf containing intelligence may be sent without over-charging the post, & be generally taken instead of Fenno's.

Freneau, Madison's friend since college days, had declined an earlier offer of a post in the State Department but in August agreed to come to Philadelphia. He received an appointment as a department translator and also set up shop as proprietor of the new *National Gazette*, which published its first issue late in October. By the time the next session of Congress was underway that winter, this opposition press was gaining flattering recognition. Jefferson did not interfere with Freneau's paper or contribute to its columns. Even if he had felt such an inclination, his increasing official duties left little time for journalism. Britain had, at last, sent a minister, twenty-eight-year-old George Hammond, but Jefferson soon forced him to admit that he had no power to conclude a commercial treaty. Hammond conversed immediately and frequently with Hamilton, whose views toward Britain he found more sympathetic.

France, too, had sent a new minister, Jean Baptiste Ternant. In December, the President submitted reciprocal nominations to the Senate: Thomas Pinckney of South Carolina to London and Gouverneur Morris to Paris. William Short, who had hoped to succeed Jefferson as minister at the French court, would have to content himself with duties as minister at The Hague. Congress was also persuaded to confirm Short and Carmichael in a joint mission to Spain for a renewal of negotiations on the subject of the Mississippi. As a result of an initiative by Jefferson on an indemnification issue and pressure from the French, Spain was willing to negotiate. But Short was delayed from joining Carmichael in Madrid until February, 1793, and by that time the opportunity had temporarily passed.

Jefferson was determined to leave the government at the end of "our first Federal cycle," Washington's first term in office, and his determination grew during the fall session. At that time he began making regular notes of his conversations and activities; "very often ...," he wrote, "I made memorandums on loose scraps of paper, taken out of my pocket in the moment, and laid by to be copied fair at leisure, which, however, they hardly ever were." These "memorandums" were later bound in three volumes which became known as the *Anas* and are an invaluable record of these years of public service. Two notes in this series were made in 1791, but regular entries began with a description of conversations with President Washington on February 28 and 29, 1792. Washington, driven by an "irresistible passion" for retirement, confided that recent "symptoms of dissatisfaction" might become dangerous if there were "too great a change in the administration." Jefferson, alarmed by Hamilton's recent *Report on Manufactures,* permitted himself a frank statement of what he felt were the causes of those "symptoms"—the policies of the Treasury Department.

Anas [March 1, 1792]

I told him that in my opinion there was only a single source of these discontents. Tho' they had indeed appear[ed] to spread themselves over the war department also, yet I considered that as an overflowing only from their real channel which would never have taken place, if they had not first been generated in another department, to wit that of the treasury. That a system had there been contrived, for deluging the states with paper-money instead of gold and silver, for withdrawing our citizens from the pursuits of commerce, manufactures, buildings, and other branches of useful industry, to occupy themselves and their capitals in a species of gambling, destructive of morality, and which had introduced it's poison into the government itself. That it was a fact, as certainly known as that he and I were then conversing, that particular members of the legislature,

Gilbert Stuart portrait of José de Jaudenes y Nebot, Spanish diplomat who was sent by his government to negotiate the Mississippi question

while those laws were on the carpet, had feathered their nests with paper, had then voted for the laws, and constantly since lent all the energy of their talents, and instrumentality of their offices to the establishment and enlargement of this system: that they had chained it about our necks for a great length of time; and in order to keep the game in their hands had from time to time aided in making such legislative constructions of the constitution as made it a very different thing from what the people thought they had submitted to: that they had now brought forward a proposition, far beyond every one ever yet advanced, and to which the eyes of many were turned, as the decision which was to let us know whether we live under a limited or an unlimited government. He asked me to what proposition I alluded? I answered, to that in the Report on manufactures....

That winter Jefferson filled scraps of paper with reflections on Hamilton's program, past and present. On March 11 he summarized Hamilton's role in furthering British interests throughout the 1791–92 session and recounted the ploy Hamilton used to prevent him from submitting the report on American trade Congress had requested.

Anas [March 11, 1792]

Explanatory note to the Anas

It was observable that whenever at any of our consultations, anything was proposed as to Great Britain Hamilton has constantly ready something which Mr. Hammond had communicated to him, which suited the subject, and proved the intimacy of their communications; insomuch that I believe he communicated to Hammond all our views and knew from him in return the views of the British court.... At one of our consultations, about the last of December [1791], I mentioned that I wished to give in my report on commerce, in which I could not avoid recommending a commercial retaliation against Great Britain. Hamilton opposed it violently; and among other arguments observed that it was of more importance to us to have the posts [in the Northwest] than to commence a commercial war; that this, and this alone, would free us from the expence of the Indian wars; that it would therefore be the height of imprudence in us while treating for the surrender of the posts to engage in anything which would irritate them; that if we did so, they would naturally say, 'these

Example of Jefferson's personal seal with motto: "Rebellion to Tyrants is Obedience to God"

people mean war, let us therefore hold what we have in our hands.' This argument struck me forcibly, and I said, 'if there is a hope of obtaining the posts, I agree it would be imprudent to risk that hope by a commercial retaliation. I will therefore wait till Mr. Hammond gives me in his assignment of breaches, and if that gives a glimmering of hope that they mean to surrender the posts, I will not give in my report till the next session.' Now, Hammond had received my assignment of breaches on the 15th of December, and about the 22d or 23d had made me an apology for not having been able to send me his counter-assignment of breaches; but in terms which showed I might expect it in a few days. From the moment it escaped my lips in the presence of Hamilton that I would not give in my report till I should see Hammond's counter-complaint, and judge if there were a hope of the posts, Hammond never said a word to me on any occasion as to the time he should be ready.

At the end of the legislative session, some of the forward momentum of Hamilton's fiscal program had been stopped. The *Report on Manufactures,* calling for government subsidies and bounties for industrial development, had been ignored by Congress; the House had launched an embarrassing investigation of the Treasury Department; and speculators in bank stock and government securities had triggered a financial panic that confirmed all the warnings issued by Jefferson and his supporters. But after two years of Cabinet struggles, Jefferson no longer enjoyed the close confidence of the President, who often sided with the Federalist position. At sixty, Washington was determined to retire after one term. In 1792 Jefferson believed America could do without his own services, but he knew full well the nation could not survive without Washington. After the President had returned to Virginia in May, Jefferson urged him to reconsider.

Philadelphia May 23. 1792.

When you first mentioned to me your purpose of retiring from the government, tho' I felt all the magnitude of the event, I was in a considerable degree silent. I knew that, to such a mind as yours, persuasion was idle & impertinent: that before forming your decision, you had weighed all the reasons for & against the measure, had made up your mind on full view of them, & that there could be little hope of changing the result. Pursuing my reflections too I knew we were some day to try to walk alone; and if the essay should be made while you should be alive & looking on, we should derive confidence from that circumstance, & resource if it failed. The public mind too was then calm & confident, and therefore in a favorable state for making the experiment. Had no change of circumstances supervened, I should not, with any hope of success, have now ventured to propose to you a change of purpose. But the public mind is no longer so confident and serene; and that from causes in which you are no ways personally mixed.... I am perfectly aware of the oppression under which your present office lays your mind, & of the ardor with which you pant for retirement to domestic life. But there is sometimes an eminence of character on which society have such peculiar claims as to controul the predilection of the individual for a particular walk of happiness, & restrain him to that alone arising from the present & future benedictions of mankind. This seems to be your condition, & the law imposed on you by providence in forming your character, & fashioning the events on which it was to operate: and it is to motives like these, & not to personal anxieties of mine or others who have no right to call on you for sacrifices, that I appeal from your former determination & urge a revisal of it, on the ground of change in the aspect of things.

The campaign to persuade Washington to accept a second term was bipartisan: Hamilton pleaded as urgently as Jefferson and Madison did to keep the President in office. By midsummer, Washington had not yet conceded, but he had gone so far as to admit that it would be his duty to remain in office if America was in danger of disunion. The same men who urged him to a second term gave him that evidence. A bitter journalistic battle had developed. Freneau's *National Gazette* attacked government policies, Hamilton, and eventually even Washington; while Hamilton, using a pseudonym, attacked the Secretary of State in a series of letters that appeared in Fenno's *Gazette of the United States* between July and December of 1792. It was obvious to any reader that a serious conflict existed in the Cabinet. At the end of August, Washington wrote to Jefferson and Hamilton urging a conciliation so that the administration might continue. From Jefferson he demanded "liberal allowances, mutual forbearances, and temporizing yieldings on all sides." Stung by what he considered unjustified criticism, Jefferson replied from Monticello on September 9. He surveyed the development of his differences with Hamilton, especially his bitterness over being "duped" into cooperating in the bargain on assumption.

A page from Jefferson's letter to Washington of September 9, 1792

Monticello Sep. 9. 1792.

When I embarked in the government, it was with a determination to intermeddle not at all with the legislature, and as little as possible with my co-departments. The first and only instance of variance from the former part of my resolution, I was duped into by the Secretary of the treasury and made a tool for forwarding his schemes, not then sufficiently understood by me; and of all the errors of my political life this has occasioned me the deepest regret.... That I have utterly, in my private conversations, disapproved of the system of the Secretary of the treasury, I acknolege & avow: and this was not merely a speculative difference. His system flowed from principles adverse to liberty, & was calculated to undermine and demolish the republic, by creating an influence of his department over the members of the legislature.... These were no longer the votes then of the representatives of the people, but of deserters from the rights & interests of the people: & it was impossible to consider their decisions, which had nothing in view but to enrich themselves, as the measures of the fair majority, which ought always to be respected....

[Jefferson turned to the Secretary of the Treasury's meddling in foreign policy, an action that was contrary to his own views on the independence of each department.]

To say nothing of other interferences equally known, in the case of the two nations with which we have the most intimate connections, France & England, my system was to give some satisfactory distinctions to the former, of little cost to us, in return for the solid advantages yielded us by them; and to have met the English with some restrictions which might induce them to abate their severities against our commerce. I have always supposed this coincided with your sentiments. Yet the Secretary of the treasury, by his cabals with members of the legislature, & by hightoned declamation on other occasions, has forced down his own system, which was exactly the reverse. He undertook, of his own authority, the conferences with the ministers of those two nations, and was, on every consultation, provided with some report of a conversation with the one or the other of them, adapted to his views. These views, thus made to prevail, their execution fell of course to me. . . . Whose principles of administration best justify, by their purity, conscientious adherence? And which of us has, notwithstanding, stepped farthest into the controul of the department of the other?

[As to charges that Freneau was his official spokesman in the *Gazette,* Jefferson asserted that he had not taken any hand in Freneau's paper, unlike Hamilton who had contributed to Fenno's press. Jefferson reminded Washington of his intention to leave the Cabinet at the end of the first term, and he hinted that in retirement he would not feel obliged to keep silent about his differences with Hamilton.]

When I came into this office, it was with a resolution to retire from it as soon as I could with decency. It pretty early appeared to me that the proper moment would be the first of those epochs at which the constitution seems to have contemplated a periodical change or renewal of the public servants. In this I was confirmed by your resolution respecting the same period; from which however I am happy in hoping you have departed. I look to that period with the longing of a wave-worn mariner who has at length the land in view, & shall count the days & hours which still lie between me & it. . . . I will not suffer my retirement to be clouded by the slanders of a man whose history, from the moment at which history can stoop to notice him, is a tissue of machinations against the liberty of the country which has not only recieved and given him bread, but heaped it's honors on his head.

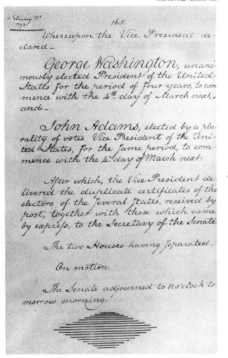

The Senate Journal's *record of the unanimous reelection of George Washington to a second term*

P ressure on Washington continued that fall. Jefferson visited the President at Mount Vernon to urge him to stay in office. Letters from other friends and advisers argued the same course, and by the end of October, Washington's colleagues knew that he would accept another term. His promised "valedictory" at the opening of Congress was not delivered, and he and Adams were easy victors in the November elections. But Jefferson would not be dissuaded from leaving. In a letter to Thomas Pinckney in London Jefferson reported an event that would make his retirement easier and that he wanted to make well known in England: Republican victories in the recent elections for the Third Congress.

Philadelphia Dec. 3. 1792.

The elections for Congress have produced a decided majority in favor of the republican interest....I think we may consider the tide of this government as now at the fullest, and that it will from the commencement of the next session of Congress retire and subside into the true principles of the Constitution.

But disturbing news from France soon shook Jefferson's determination to retire. He had always felt that America and France stood in a special relationship to each other, their wartime alliance deepened by France's turn from despotism to constitutional government. That friendship would become harder to maintain, however, in 1793. With the new year, Americans learned of the alarming train of events in France since September—a reign of terror against aristocrats and royalist sympathizers, followed by the abolition of the monarchy and the institution of a republican government under the National Convention. William Short had been disgusted by the excesses of the Jacobins, or radical French republicans, and Jefferson knew that Hamilton and his followers would be even more eager to attack that movement. His letter to Short in January reflected the defense of French policies Jefferson would soon have to offer at home.

Philadelphia Jan 3. 1793.

A French anti-Jacobin cartoon

The tone of your letters had for some time given me pain, on account of the extreme warmth with which they censured the proceedings of the Jacobins of France. I considered that sect as the same with the Republican patriots, & the Feuillants as the Monarchical patriots, well known in the early part of the revolution, & but little distant in their views, both having in object the establishment of a free constitution, & differing only on the question whether their chief Executive should be hereditary or not. The Jacobins (as since called) yeilded to the Feuillants & tried the experiment of retaining their hereditary Executive. The experiment failed completely, and would have brought on the re-establishment of despotism had it been pursued. The Jacobins saw this, and that the expunging that officer was of absolute necessity. And the Nation was with them in opinion, for however they might have been formerly for the constitution framed by the first assembly, they were come over from their hope in it, and were now generally Jacobins. In the struggle which was necessary, many guilty persons fell without the forms of

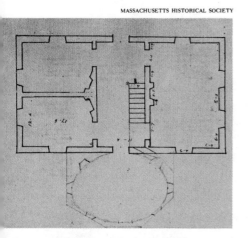

*Floor plan of the house Jefferson
rented in the summer of 1793 on
the banks of the Schuylkill River*

trial, and with them some innocent. These I deplore as much as any body, & shall deplore some of them to the day of my death. But I deplore them as I should have done had they fallen in battle. It was necessary to use the arm of the people, a machine not quite so blind as balls and bombs, but blind to a certain degree. A few of their cordial friends met at their hands the fate of enemies. But time and truth will rescue & embalm their memories, while their posterity will be enjoying that very liberty for which they would never have hesitated to offer up their lives. The liberty of the whole earth was depending on the issue of the contest, and was ever such a prize won with so little innocent blood? My own affections have been deeply wounded by some of the martyrs to this cause, but rather than it should have failed, I would have seen half the earth desolated. Were there but an Adam & an Eve left in every country, & left free, it would be better than as it now is.

France stood in even greater need of a friend in the Cabinet as the year progressed, and Jefferson notified Washington, to the President's relief, of his willingness to stay on a while longer. On January 21 Louis XVI was guillotined. Eleven days later France was at war with Britain, Holland, and Spain. Shortly after Congress adjourned, Jefferson reported to James Madison on the public reaction in Philadelphia and the response Congress might make to interference by the three powers with American trade to France.

[Philadelphia] March. [24,] 1793.
I should hope that Congress instead of a denunciation of war, would instantly exclude from our ports all the manufactures, produce, vessels & subjects of the nations committing this aggression, during the continuance of the aggression & till full satisfaction made for it. This would work well in many ways, safely in all, & introduce between nations another umpire than arms. It would relieve us too from the risks & the horrors of cutting throats. The death of the king of France has not produced as open condemnations from the Monocrats as I expected. I dined the other day in a company where the subject was discussed....It is certain that the ladies of this city, of the first circle are all open-mouthed against the murderers of a sovereign, and they generally speak those sentiments which the more cautious husband smothers.

The bloody progress of the French Revolution gave Hamilton an opportunity to press for what Jefferson perceived had long been his goal: a destruction of the Franco-American alliance of 1778. This became clear in April when official reports of the hostilities in Europe brought Washington back from Mount Vernon for emergency sessions with the Cabinet. All agreed that America should remain neutral, though Jefferson was dissatisfied with the timing and form of the Proclamation of Neutrality issued on April 22. But there was little agreement on how that neutrality could be maintained. Under the treaties of 1778, France might call on the United States to guarantee the safety of the French West Indies. Ternant the last royal minister, was due to be succeeded by Edmond Charles Genêt, the first republican envoy, and the Cabinet was asked to consider the implications of his mission: would the United States be bound by the treaty with Louis XVI to aid the republican government that had executed him? Could Genêt be given an unqualified reception without an implicit recognition of the treaty obligations? Hamilton answered both questions in the negative. In an opinion submitted April 28, Jefferson answered firmly in favor of fulfilling the treaty obligations (if France demanded it) and in favor of granting Genêt a full and cordial reception.

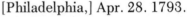

[Philadelphia,] Apr. 28. 1793.

I consider the people who constitute a society or nation as the source of all authority in that nation, as free to transact their common concerns by any agents they think proper, to change these agents individually, or the organisation of them in form or function whenever they please: that all the acts done by those agents under the authority of the nation, are the acts of the nation, are obligatory on them, & enure to their use, & can in no wise be annulled or affected by any change in the form of the government, or of the persons administering it. Consequently the Treaties between the U.S. and France, were not treaties between the U S & Louis Capet, but between the two nations of America & France, and the nations remaining in existence, tho' both of them have since changed their forms of government, the treaties are not annulled by these changes. . . .

Badge of the French Revolution

Washington, quite sensibly, left the question of treaty obligations in abeyance. He decided, also, to receive Genêt with appropriate dignity and warmth. When the young French diplomat arrived in Philadelphia on May 16, local citizens greeted him enthusiastically. Jefferson's enthusiasm faded quickly, however. The ambitious, irresponsible young "Citizen" had violated American neutrality by commissioning privateers for the

French service at Charleston, South Carolina, and other towns before he even arrived in Philadelphia. As the privateers brought their prizes into American ports, the Cabinet was overwhelmed by the protests of the British minister. Jefferson's comment to Monroe of June 28 was a carefully modulated understatement: "I do not augur well of the mode of conduct of the new French minister; I fear he will enlarge the circle of those disaffected to his country." Genêt ignored the protests of the Cabinet and continued to use coastal towns as bases for French naval raids on the British. In July matters came to a head. The *Little Sarah,* captured by the French and renamed the *Petit Democrat*, was fitted out as a privateer in Philadelphia. The ship was at anchor near Mud Island in the Delaware River when Jefferson met with Genêt on Sunday, July 7, to investigate reports that the brig would be sent to sea before Washington could return to the capital. The next day, the three Cabinet members still in Philadelphia —Jefferson, Hamilton, and Knox—met to consider Pennsylvania Governor Thomas Mifflin's request for advice. The minutes of their conference carried an account of Jefferson's position.

[Cabinet meeting, Philadelphia, July 8, 1793]
...that a conversation has been had between the Secretary of State and the Minister Plenipotentiary of France, in which conversation the Minister refused to give any explicit assurance that the brigantine would continue until the arrival of the President, and his decision in the case, but made declarations respecting her not being ready to sail within the time of the expected return of the President, from which the Secretary of State infers with confidence, that she will not sail till the President will have an opportunity of considering and determining the case; that in the course of the conversation, the Minister declared that the additional guns which had been taken in by the Little Sarah were French property, but the Governor of Pennsylvania declared that he has good ground to believe that two of her cannon were purchased here of citizens of Philadelphia....

Governor Thomas Mifflin

The Secretary of the Treasury and the Secretary of War are of opinion, that it is expedient that immediate measures should be taken provisionally for establishing a battery on Mud Island, under cover of a party of militia, with direction that if the brig Sarah should attempt to depart before the pleasure of the President shall be known concerning her, military coercion be employed to arrest and prevent her progress.

The Secretary of State dissents from this opinion.

245

Before Washington arrived on the morning of July 11, the *Petit Democrat* had moved downriver out of reach of any guns that might be set on Mud Island. Despite the President's explicit orders to keep the privateer in the Delaware, Genêt then sent it out to sea. This action damaged the French cause, Jefferson reported sadly to Monroe.

> Philadelphia July 14. 1793.
> I fear the disgust of France is inevitable. We shall be to blame in part. But the new minister much more so. His conduct is indefensible by the most furious Jacobin. I only wish our countrymen may distinguish between him & his nation, and if the case should ever be laid before them, may not suffer their affection to the nation to be diminished. H[amilton] sensible of the advantage they have got, is urging a full appeal by the Government to the people. Such an explosion would manifestly endanger a dissolution of the friendship between the two nations, & ought therefore to be deprecated by every friend to our liberty.

His assessment of the damage to the Republican cause and to friendship with France was not exaggerated. By his actions, Genêt had discredited himself and played into Federalist hands. Hamilton successfully proposed a system of enforcement of the Proclamation of Neutrality by customs officers of the Treasury Department and Jefferson suffered another foreign policy defeat. By the end of July, he was again convinced that he should leave the proximity of a "circle which I know to bear me peculiar hatred." He submitted a letter of resignation to the President that revealed his discouragement.

> Philadelphia, July 31, 1793.
> When you did me the honor of appointing me to the office I now hold, I engaged in it without a view of continuing any length of time, & I pretty early concluded on the close of the first four years of our republic as a proper period for withdrawing; which I had the honor of communicating to you. When the period however arrived, circumstances had arisen, which, in the opinion of some of my friends, rendered it proper to postpone my purpose for awhile. These circumstances have now ceased in such a degree as to leave me free to think again of a day on which I may withdraw, without it's exciting disadvantageous opinions or conjectures of any kind. The close of the present quarter seems to be a convenient period.... At the close, therefore, of the ensuing month

of September, I shall beg leave to retire to scenes of greater tranquility, from those which I am every day more & more convinced that neither my talents, tone of mind, nor time of life fit me. I have thought it my duty to mention the matter thus early, that there may be time for the arrival of a successor, from any part of the union, from which you may think proper to call one. That you may find one more able to lighten the burthen of your labors, I most sincerely wish; for no man living more sincerely wishes that your administration could be rendered as pleasant to yourself, as it is useful & necessary to our country, nor feels for you a more rational or cordial attachment & respect than, Dear Sir, your most obedient & most humble servant.

At Washington's request, Jefferson consented to remain in office until the end of the year, a continuation that allowed him to finish one item at the heart of his program: the report on American trade Congress had requested almost three years earlier. This document, which bore the imposing title of *Report on the Privileges and Restrictions on the Commerce of the United States in Foreign Countries,* was submitted on December 16. It has been unfairly neglected in the history of great state papers of the Federal period, although it brilliantly outlined the continuing thread of Jefferson's policies: retaliation by a navigation act against Great Britain and full reciprocity with any nation ready to engage in amicable commercial relations. Opening with detailed tables of American tonnage, imports, and exports, Jefferson proceeded to ask, concerning restrictions on American ships and goods in foreign ports, "in what way they may best be removed, modified or counteracted." He conceded that the "most eligible" method was "by friendly arrangements with the several nations with whom these restrictions exist" but pointed out that this would not always be possible. America's problems lay not with nations willing to negotiate equitable trade treaties, but with the powers that continued to bar free commerce.

Report on Commerce
[Philadelphia, December 16, 1793]

But should any nation, contrary to our wishes, suppose it may better find it's advantage by continuing it's system of prohibitions, duties and regulations, it behoves us to protect our citizens, their commerce and navigation, by counter prohibitions, duties and regulations, also. Free commerce and navigation are not to be given in exchange for restrictions and vexations; nor are they likely to produce a relaxation of them.

Our navigation involves still higher considerations. As a branch of industry, it is valuable, but as a resource of defence essential.

It's value, as a branch of industry, is enhanced by the dependence of so many other branches on it. In times of general peace it multiplies competitors for employment in transportation, and so keeps that at it's proper level; and in times of war, that is to say, when those nations who may be our principal carriers, shall be at war with each other, if we have not within ourselves the means of transportation, our produce must be exported in belligerent vessels, at the increased expence of war-freight and insurance, and the articles which will not bear that must perish on our hands.

But it is as a resource for defence that our navigation will admit neither negligence nor forbearance. The position and circumstances of the United States leave them nothing to fear on their land-board, and nothing to desire beyond their present rights. But on their sea-board, they are open to injury, and they have there, too, a commerce which must be protected. This can only be done by possessing a respectable body of citizen-seamen, and of artists and establishments in readiness for ship-building.

Were the Ocean, which is the common property of all, open to the industry of all, so that every person and vessel should be free to take employment wherever it could be found, the United States would certainly not set the example of appropriating to themselves, exclusively, any portion of the common stock of occupation....But if particular nations grasp at undue shares, and, more especially, if they seize on the means of the United States, to convert them into aliment for their own strength, and withdraw them entirely from the support of those to whom they belong, defensive and protecting measures become necessary on the part of the nation whose marine resources are thus invaded....

[Jefferson outlined several plans for commercial retaliation against those who hesitated to open their ports to American vessels and goods. He conceded that schedules of discriminatory duties and other measures might produce "some inconvenience," but that would be nothing compared to eventual benefits for the United States.]

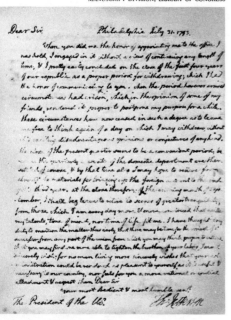

Jefferson's letter of July 31
asking to be relieved of office

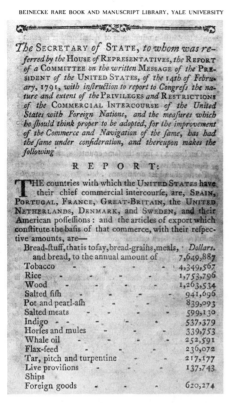

First page of Report on Commerce

It is true we must expect some inconvenience in practice from the establishment of discriminating duties. But in this, as in so many other cases, we are left to chuse between two evils. These inconveniences are nothing, when weighed against the loss of wealth and loss of force, which will follow our perseverance in the plan of indiscrimination. When once it shall be perceived that we are either in the system or in the habit of giving equal advantages to those who extinguish our commerce and navigation by duties and prohibitions, as to those who treat both with liberality and justice, liberality and justice will be converted by all into duties and prohibitions. It is not to the moderation and justice of others we are to trust for fair and equal access to market with our productions, or for our due share in the transportation of them; but to our own means of independence, and the firm will to use them.... In our case one distinction alone will suffice: that is to say, between nations who favor our productions and navigation, and those who do not favor them. One set of moderate duties, say the present duties, for the first, and a fixed advance on these as to some articles and prohibitions as to others, for the last.

Like so many of the reports Jefferson had drafted as Secretary of State, this one, too, was virtually ignored and once again his attempts to promote a foreign policy based on commercial reciprocity were thwarted. As he prepared to leave Philadelphia in January, 1794, Jefferson was justifiably disheartened by his four years in the Cabinet. On all major aspects of his official policies, both domestic and foreign, the Hamiltonian forces had triumphed. Only the negotiations with Spain were successful, resulting in Pinckney's Treaty of 1795 guaranteeing free navigation of the Mississippi. The battles had been bitter and Jefferson felt that he was powerless to reverse the drift away from republican principles.

Beyond the sense of frustration and repudiation he felt, however, were some grounds for optimism: Hamilton's influence was waning; a cloud of distrust hung over the Treasury Department; and Jefferson's estimation in the eyes of the people had risen as his stock in the administration declined. A man of integrity, honor, and devotion to the public interest would not long be allowed the diversions and pleasures of retirement.

Chapter 9

Retirement and Recall

When Jefferson returned to Monticello on January 16, 1794, he viewed his withdrawal from national politics as a much-needed chance to enjoy family life, to catch up with his reading, and to superintend his land and home which he had long been forced to neglect. He immediately plunged into the life of a Piedmont farmer, and during the next three years he never ventured more than seven miles from his mountaintop. Two weeks after his arrival home, Jefferson received an invitation to visit General Horatio Gates at Rose Hill, but he declined, preferring to give full attention to his domestic pursuits.

> Monticello Feb. 3. 1794.
> [T]he length of my tether is now fixed ... from Monticello to Richmond. My private business can never call me elsewhere, and certainly politics will not, which I have ever hated both in theory & practice. I thought myself conscientiously called from those studies which were my delight by the political crisis of my country.... In storms like those all hands must be aloft. But calm is now restored, & I leave the bark with joy to those who love the sea. I am but a landsman, forced from my element by accident, regaining it with transport, and wishing to recollect nothing of what I have seen, but my friendships.

Nevertheless, Jefferson seems to have experienced a brief period of irksome readjustment during his first months at Monticello. Occasionally he seemed to vacillate between reveling in his freedom from official duties and chafing at his isolation from the outside world. The first mood is apparent from a remark in a letter to Edmund Randolph on February 3: "I think it is Montaigne who has said that ignorance is the softest pillow on which a man can rest his head. I am sure it is true as to every thing political, and shall endeavor to estrange myself to every thing of that character." But twelve days later, he confessed concern to Madison for Virginia's ignorance of current political events.

Notes Jefferson made in 1791 on sugar maples and a variety of fruit trees to be planted at Monticello

Monticello, Feb. 15, 1794.

We are here in a state of great quiet, having no public news to agitate us. I have never seen a Philadelphia paper since I left that place, nor learnt anything of later date except some successes of the French the account of which seemed to have come by our vessel from Havre....I could not have supposed, when at Philadelphia, that so little of what was passing there could be known even at Kentuckey, as is the case here. Judging from this of the rest of the Union, it is evident to me that the people are not in a condition either to approve or disapprove of their government, nor consequently to influence it.

By mid-March, when he wrote to James Monroe, Jefferson betrayed distinct irritation with the dearth of news in Albemarle County, due in part to a smallpox epidemic.

Monticello Mar. 11, 1794.

The small pox at Richmond has cut off the communication by post to or through that place. I should have thought it [the postmaster's] duty to have removed his office a little way out of town, that the communication might not have been interrupted. Instead of that it is said the inhabitants of the country are to be prosecuted because they thought it better to refuse a passage to his postriders than take the smallpox from them. Straggling travellers who have ventured into Richmd. now and then leave a newspaper with Colo. Bell....I have never received a letter from Philadelphia since I left it except a line or two once from E[dmund] R[andolph].

In April, the post office in Richmond reopened and Jefferson could at last keep abreast of maneuvers in Congress. Madison's navigation bill, benefiting from public reaction to renewed British interference with American shipping, had come close to passage. Madison had delayed pressing the matter in April, he wrote Jefferson, because even harsher anti-British resolutions were on the floor. But Federalists managed to counteract cries for retaliation against Britain by proposing a special envoy to negotiate Anglo-American differences in London. Rumors that Hamilton himself might be given the appointment appalled Jefferson; the whole scheme was evidence of the control the Treasury Secretary had asserted over foreign policy since Jefferson's resignation. On April 24 he wrote Monroe, one of Virginia's two senators, describing the anti-British sentiment he had found in the state and offering his personal opinion of the proposed mission.

HENRY E. HUNTINGTON LIBRARY AND ART GALLERY

Jefferson's survey of his fields at Shadwell shows ground set aside for tobacco, a crop he did not like but depended on for cash income.

Monticello Apr. 24. [17]94

The spirit of war has grown much stronger, in this part of the country, as I can judge of myself, and in other parts along the mountains from N.E. to S.W. as I have had opportunities of learning by enquiry. Some few very quiet people, not suffering themselves to be inflamed as others are by the kicks & cuffs Gr. Britain has been giving us, express a wish to remain in peace. But the mass of thinking men seem to be of opinion that we have borne so much as to invite eternal insults in future should not a very spirited conduct be now assumed. For myself, I wish for peace, if it can be preserved, salva fide et honore. I learn...that a special mission to England is meditated, & H. the missionary. A more degrading measure could not have been proposed: and why is Pinckney to be recalled? For it is impossible he should remain there after such a testimony that he is not confided in. I suppose they think him not thorough paced enough: I suspect too the mission, besides the object of placing the aristocracy of this country under the patronage of that government, has in view that of withdrawing H. from the disgrace & the public execrations which sooner or later must fall on the man who...has alienated for ever all our ordinary & easy resources, & will oblige us hereafter to extraordinary ones for every little contingency out of the common line....

With the resumption of the mail and the reopening of communications to the world outside Albemarle County, Jefferson seemed more content as a farmer; he could regulate the degree of his solitude at Monticello. As the spring planting season began, he initiated his plans for scientific crop rotation on his acres. John Adams wrote congratulating him "on the charming opening of the Spring" and added that he heartily wished

"I was enjoying of it as you are upon a Plantation, out of the hearing of the Din of Politicks." Jefferson responded that his ardor as a farmer had made him neglect even the love of study that had hitherto marked his life.

> Monticello Apr. 25. 1794.
>
> The difference of my present and past situation is such as to leave me nothing to regret but that my retirement has been postponed four years too long. The principles on which I calculate the value of life are entirely in favor of my present course. I return to farming with an ardour which I scarcely knew in my youth, and which has got the better entirely of my love of study. Instead of writing 10. or 12. letters a day, which I have been in the habit of doing as a thing of course, I put off answering my letters now, farmer-like, till a rainy day, & then find it sometimes postponed by other necessary occupations.

The next month brought a letter from the President. Washington commiserated with Jefferson on their mutual problems as farm-owners, then revealed that foreign policy was continuing along the same lines that had led to Jefferson to resign. "We are going on in the old way 'Slow'," he wrote. "I hope events will justify me in adding 'and sure' that the proverb may be fulfilled—'Slow and Sure'." As he remarked to John Adams that spring, Jefferson had "seen enough of one war never to wish to see another." But he had seen enough, too, of subservience to Britain. His reply to Washington opened with an enthusiastic explanation of his plans to restore his fields and closed with a reaffirmation of the political opinions he had held from the beginning.

> Monticello May 14. 1794.
>
> I find on a more minute examination of my lands, than the short visits heretofore made to them permitted, that a 10. years abandonment of them to the unprincipled ravages of overseers, has brought on a degree of degradation far beyond what I had expected. As this obliges me to adopt a milder course of cropping, so I find that they have enabled me to do it by having opened a great deal of lands during my absence. I have therefore determined on a division of my farms into 6. fields to be put under this rotation: 1st. year, wheat; 2d. corn, potatoes, peas; 3d. rye or wheat, according to circumstances; 4th. & 5th. clover where the fields will bring it, & buckwheat dressings where they will not; 6th. folding, and buckwheat dressings. But it will take me

from 3. to 6. years to get this plan underway.... Time, patience & perseverance must be the remedy; and the maxim of your letter 'slow & sure' is not less a good one in agriculture than in politics. I sincerely wish it may extricate us from the event of a war, if this can be done saving our faith and our rights. My opinion of the British government is that nothing will force them to do justice but the loud voice of their people, & that this can never be excited but by distressing their commerce.

Jefferson's attitude toward his political enemies during his early retirement was probably similar to his feelings about the "invading tyrants" who threatened the French republic: "I am still warm whenever I think of these scoundrels, tho I do it as seldom as I can." After Congress recessed in the summer, Jefferson lived contentedly without bulletins from his friends of affairs at Philadelphia. At the end of the summer, he received a request from Edmund Randolph, his successor in the State Department, to go to Spain as a special envoy. Negotiations over navigation of the Mississippi had broken down, and Washington was alarmed by talk of secession in the West. Jefferson firmly declined the appointment.

Monticello Sep. 7. [17]94.
No circumstances my dear Sir will ever more tempt me to engage in any thing public. I thought myself perfectly fixed in this determination when I left Philadelphia, but every day & hour since has added to it's inflexibility.

The curtness of Jefferson's answer was prompted partly by the fact that the offer had been channeled through Randolph, like any routine matter, rather than coming from the President. This discourtesy was compounded by an enclosure asking Jefferson to forward a duplicate invitation to Washington's second choice—Jefferson's time-honored enemy, Patrick Henry. Jefferson sent the note to Henry, who also turned down the mission, and then resumed his domestic duties, more certain than ever that he had chosen well in returning to Monticello.

With Jefferson no longer providing an antidote to Hamilton's policies, the administration veered farther from the neutral, above-politics course Washington had originally charted. Fresh evidence of this drift came in the President's reaction to the Whisky Rebellion in the late summer and fall of 1794. Small farmers in the backcountry of western Pennsylvania protested Hamilton's excise tax on their only cash product. Having sent an expedition accompanied by Hamilton to quell the "rebels," Washington, in his annual address to Congress, blamed the rebellion on the influence of "certain self-created societies." This was a reference to the new pro-French, Republican-dominated Democratic Societies which had sprung up in various states. Jefferson vented his private indignation at the speech's unfounded charges in a letter to Madison.

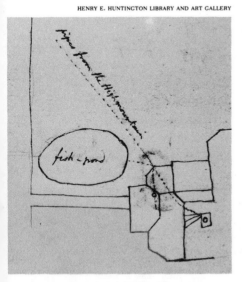

Jefferson's sketch for a fish pond and water supply at Monticello

An exciseman, lured by his "evil genius," carries off two kegs of whiskey in detail from a cartoon about the Whisky Rebellion.

Monticello Dec. 28. [17]94.

The denunciation of the democratic societies is one of the extraordinary acts of boldness of which we have seen so many from the faction of Monocrats. It is wonderful indeed that the President should have permitted himself to be the organ of such an attack on the freedom of discussion, the freedom of writing, printing & publishing. It must be a matter of rare curiosity to get at the modifications of these rights proposed by them, and to see what line their ingenuity would draw between democratical societies, whose avowed object is the nourishment of the republican principles of our constitution, and the society of the Cincinnati [the organization of Revolutionary War officers of which Hamilton was a member], *a self-created* one, carving out for itself hereditary distinctions, lowering over our constitution eternally, meeting together in all parts of the Union periodically, with closed doors ... corresponding secretly & regularly, & of which society the very persons denouncing the democrats are themselves the fathers, founders or high officers.

[Washington's justification of the expedition against the perpetrators of the Whisky Rebellion also inspired Jefferson's acid sarcasm.]

I expected to have seen some justification of arming one part of the society against another, of declaring a civil war the moment before the meeting of that body which has the sole right of declaring war, of being so patient of the kicks & scoffs of our enemies, & rising at a feather against our friends, of adding a million to the public debt & deriding us with recommendations to pay it if we can &c., &c. But the part of the speech which was to be taken as a justification of the armament reminded me of parson Saunders' demonstration why minus into minus make plus. After a parcel of shreds of stuff from Aesop's fables, & Tom Thumb, he jumps all at once into his Ergo, minus multiplied into minus makes

James Madison married the widow Dolley Payne Todd on September 15, 1794; this miniature of her was made from a 1789 drawing.

plus. Just so the 15,000 men enter after the fables in the speech. . . .

[Jefferson closed by encouraging Madison in his fight for Republican measures.]

The changes in your house I see are going on for the better, and even the Augean herd over your heads are slowly purging off their impurities. Hold on then, my dear friend, that we may not ship-wreck in the mean while. I do not see in the minds of those with whom I converse a greater affliction than the fear of your retirement; but this must not be, unless to a more splendid & a more efficacious post. There I should rejoice to see you: I hope I may say, I shall rejoice to see you. I have long had much in my mind to say to you on that subject. But double delicacies have kept me silent.

Throughout the winter, Jefferson expanded on the "more splendid" post Madison should seek—that of Washington's successor. Jefferson himself was content to remain at home, delighting in his lively grandchildren, four-year-old Anne and three-year-old Thomas Jefferson Randolph. When their parents left the toddlers at Monticello that winter, while they prepared their Varina plantation for occupancy, Jefferson sent his daughter reports on the children's antics.

Monticello Jan. 22. [17]95

TH. J. TO HIS DEAR M. J.

. . . Jefferson is very robust. His hands are constantly like lumps of ice, yet he will not warm them. He has not worn his shoes an hour this winter. If put on him, he takes them off immediately & uses one to carry his nuts &c. in. Within these two days we have put both him & Anne into mockaseens, which being made of soft leather, fitting well & lacing up, they have never been able to take them off. So that I believe we may consider that as the only effectual shoe which can be made for them. They are inseparable in their sports. Anne's temper begins to develope itself advantageously. His tempests give her opportunities of shewing & exercising a placid disposition: and there is no doubt but that a little time will abate of his impatience as it has done hers. I called her in to ask what I should write for her to yourself & her papa. She says I must tell you that she loves you, & that you must come home. In both these sentiments we all join her.

With the end of that bitter winter ("so much the better for our wheat, and for the destruction of the weavil," Jefferson remarked) came the spring planting. As the master of plantations and uncleared lands scattered across central and western Virginia, Jefferson presided over more than ten thousand acres worked by two hundred slaves. He wrote William Branch Giles, the stalwart Republican congressman, of his new pursuits.

Monticello Apr. 27. 1795.

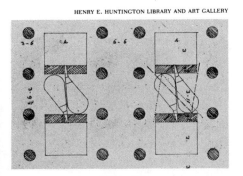

If you visit me as a farmer, it must be as a condisciple: for I am but a learner; an eager one indeed but yet desperate, being too old now to learn a new art. However I am as much delighted & occupied with it as if I was the greatest adept. I shall talk with you about it from morning till night, and put you on very short allowance as to political aliment. Now and then a pious ejaculation for the French & Dutch republicans, returning with due dispatch to clover, potatoes, wheat, &c.

It should not be imagined that Jefferson approached the management of Monticello and his other lands as a "gentleman farmer." His family's income came from these acres, and agriculture was, quite simply, the source of his livelihood. His years of public service had forced him to leave his business in the hands of overseers who had farmed out the soil. A careful program of crop rotation could eventually restore the land, but he seized every opportunity to gain additional income until the soil was once again completely productive. In the spring of 1795 he wrote optimistically to Jean Nicolas Demeunier, a French scholar, of a new enterprise on his plantation.

Monticello. Virginia Apr. 29. [17]95

...I found my farms so much deranged, that I saw evidently they would be a burthen to me instead of a support till I could regenerate them; and consequently that it was necessary for me to find some other resource in the mean time. I thought for a while of taking up the manufacture of pot-ash, which requires but small advances of money. I concluded at length however to begin a manufacture of nails, which needs little or no capital, & I now employ a dozen little boys from 10. to 16. years of age, overlooking all the details of their business myself and drawing from it a profit on which I can get along

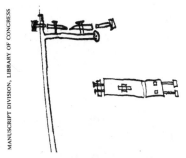

Jefferson's plan for a nailery (top), which he built in 1794, and the design of a nail-cutting machine used at Monticello (above)

till I can put my farms into a course of yielding profit. My new trade of nailmaking is to me in this country what an additional title of nobility, or the ensigns of a new order are in Europe.

Theories Jefferson had sketched out years before were put to practical application. A request from the American Philosophical Society, the group of scientists and promoters of useful knowledge organized by Benjamin Franklin, evoked a modest description from Jefferson of his design for a moldboard plow "of least resistance," which he had conceived during his travels abroad.

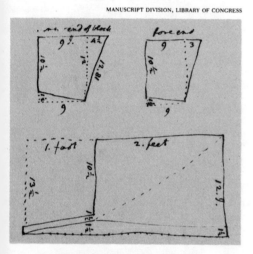

Sketches reproduced in the American Philosophical Society's Transactions *of Jefferson's design for moldboard*

Monticello July 3. 1796.

You wish me to present to the Philosophical society the result of my philosophical researches since my retirement. But my good Sir I have made researches into nothing but what is connected with agriculture. In this way I have a little matter to communicate, and will do it ere long. It is the form of a Mouldboard *of least resistance.* I had some years ago concieved the principles of it, and I explained them to Mr. [David] Rittenhouse [the president of the society]. I have since reduced the thing to practice and have reason to believe the theory fully confirmed. I only wish for one of those instruments used in England for measuring the force exerted in the draughts of different ploughs &c. that I might compare the resistance of my mould board with that of others. But these instruments are not to be had here.

It was perhaps the happiest of the three summers of his retirement. Jefferson's slave Isaac remembered the master as a "straight up man" who was always to be heard "singing when ridin or walking. Hardly see him anywhar out doors but what he was a-singing," Isaac recounted. Jefferson enjoyed the company of his daughters and grandchildren; his nail manufacturing seemed promising and his plans to remodel his home were almost ready for execution. He was indeed, for those few months, a content and ardent farmer.

The summer ended on a less pleasant note. John Jay, who had been appointed the special envoy to London, returned with a treaty that triggered a national crisis when its terms were made public. Although the treaty had been concluded in London in November, 1794, it did not reach America until Congress had adjourned in the spring of 1795. The President called the Senate back into special session in June, and despite some provisions that alarmed even the Federalists, the treaty scraped through to ratification at the end of the month. Public opposition was so great that Washington hesitated to sign it, and Jefferson viewed the outcome of Jay's negotiations with undisguised disgust. He described the agreement's apparent sacrifice of American rights and prerogatives to Monroe, who had become the United States Minister to France.

A Federalist cartoon, c. 1795, of Washington repelling an invasion by French "cannibals" and Jefferson, at far right, trying to "Stop de wheels of de gouvernement"

Monticello. Sep. 6, [17]95.

Mr. Jay's treaty has at length been made public. So general a burst of dissatisfaction never before appeared against any transaction. Those who understand the particular articles of it, condemn these articles. Those who do not understand them minutely, condemn it generally as wearing a hostile face to France. This last is the most numerous class, comprehending the whole body of the people, who have taken a greater interest in this transaction than they were ever known to do in any other. It has in my opinion completely demolished the monarchial party here....*Adams* holds his tongue with an address above his character. We do not know whether the President has signed it or not. If he has it is much believed the H. of representatives will oppose it as constitutionally void, and thus bring on an embarrassing & critical state in our government.

The matter was not settled even when the President signed the treaty—after considerable pressure from Hamilton. Trying to rally public support, Hamilton had begun publishing in July a series of essays signed "Camillus" in the New York press. Near the end of September Jefferson urged Madison, the only Republican he felt could effectively oppose Hamilton, to reply.

Monticello Sep. 21. [17]95.

Hamilton is really a colossus to the antirepublican party. Without numbers, he is an host within himself. They have got themselves into a defile, where they might be finished; but too much security on the Republican part, will give time to his talents & indefatigableness to extricate them. We have had only midling performances to oppose to him. In truth, when he comes forward, there is nobody but yourself who can meet him. His adversaries having begun the attack, he has the advantage of answering them, & remains unanswered himself.... For god's sake take up your pen, and give a fundamental reply to Curtius & Camillus.

Many of the treaty's provisions required expenditures, and the Republican opposition, led by Madison, continued in the House which had sole power to originate appropriations. Madison hardly needed Jefferson's reminder on strategy in November.

[Monticello,] Nov. 26. [17]95.
...as the articles which stipulate what requires the consent of the three branches of the legislature, must be referred to the H. of R. for their concurrence, so they, being free agents, may approve or reject them, either by a vote declaring that, or by refusing to pass acts. I should think the former mode the most safe and honorable. The people in this part of the country continue very firmly disposed against the treaty....I observe an expression in Randolph's printed secret [a pamphlet published by Edmund Randolph] intimating that the President, tho' an honest man himself, may be circumvented by snares and artifices, and is in fact surrounded by men who wish to clothe the Executive with more than constitutional powers. This when public, will make great impression. It is not only a truth, but a truth levelled to every capacity and will justify to themselves the most zealous votaries, for ceasing to repose the unlimited confidence they have done in the measures which have been pursued.

A page dated January 1, 1796, in Jefferson's notebook of plans for remodeling Monticello calculates amounts of stone and brick needed.

A few days later Jefferson wrote in a similar vein to Edward Rutledge of South Carolina, who was active in his state's politics. The letters show Jefferson's desire to continue his enjoyment of retirement and his simultaneous encouragement of friends to remain active in politics. The President, searching for men who would accept the vacant posts of Secretary of State, Secretary of War, and Attorney General, was in dire need of competent advisers.

Monticello Nov. 30. [17]95.
He [Rutledge's son] found me in a retirement I doat on, living like an Antediluvian patriarch among my children & grand children, and tilling my soil....You hope I have not abandoned entirely the service of our country. After a five & twenty years continual employment in it, I trust it will be thought I have fulfilled my tour, like a punctual soldier, and may claim my discharge. But I am glad of the sentiment from you my friend, because it gives a hope you will practice what you preach, and come forward in aid of the public vessel. I will not admit your

old excuse, that you are in public service tho' at home. The campaigns which are fought in a man's own house are not to be counted. The present situation of the President, unable to get the offices filled, really calls with uncommon obligation on those whom nature has fitted for them.

Jefferson's support of others who were serving the nation was a consistent thread in his correspondence that winter while he added another item to his own program of busy rustication: the remodeling of Monticello. The modest but handsome house, which had seemed appropriate for a Virginia planter in the 1770s, would not do for the sophisticated traveler who returned to Albemarle in 1794. As early as 1792, Jefferson had decided to incorporate the original structure into a larger mansion that would show to advantage his European furniture and art and would accommodate his growing library and constant train of guests. Throughout 1794 and 1795 bricks and stone were collected on the mountaintop, but actual demolition of the old wings and construction of the new did not begin until 1796. In March Jefferson jovially invited William Branch Giles to visit.

> Monticello Mar. 19. 1796.
> I have begun the demolitions of my house, and hope to get through it's re-edification in the course of this summer. But do not let this discourage you from calling on us if you wander this way in the summer. We shall have the eye of a brick-kiln to poke you into, or an Octagon to air you in.

The Duke de La Rochefoucauld-Liancourt, who visited Monticello later that year, described the progress of reconstruction.

> Travels through the United States
> of North America, 1799
> The house stands on the summit of the mountain, and the taste and arts of Europe have been consulted in the formation of its plan. Mr. Jefferson had commenced its construction before the American revolution; since that epocha his life has been constantly engaged in public affairs, and he has not been able to complete the execution of the whole extent of the project which it seems he had at first conceived.... Mr. Jefferson ... is now employed in repairing the damage occasioned by this interruption, and still more by his absence; he continues his original plan, and even improves on it, by giving to

Duke de La Rochefoucauld-Liancourt

261

According to his slave Isaac, Jefferson spent forty years at work on Monticello; the 1803 rendering above by Robert Mills is the west elevation of the final version.

his buildings more elevation and extent. He intends that they should consist only of one story, crowned with balustrades; and a dome is to be constructed in the center of the structure. The apartments will be large and convenient; the decoration, both outside and inside, simple, yet regular and elegant. Monticello, according to its first plan, was infinitely superior to all other houses in America, in point of taste and convenience; but at that time Mr. Jefferson had studied taste and the fine arts in books only. His travels in Europe have supplied him with models; he has appropriated them to his design; and his new plan, the execution of which is already much advanced, will be accomplished before the end of next year, and then his house will certainly deserve to be ranked with the most pleasant mansions in France and England.

From the top of the "little mountain," Jefferson's perspective on what he called the balance in American government among the "three branches of the legislature" was a dim one that winter. The Senate was firmly in Federalist hands; the House, despite Republican gains in 1794, was still largely unsympathetic to Jefferson and Madison's goals; and the President, the "third branch," continued to depart from his earlier nonpartisan course. Jefferson still admired Washington but remarked that he "errs as other men do, but errs with integrity." Perhaps encouraged by Vice President Adams's uncharacteristic silence in the Jay Treaty controversy, Jefferson sent his old friend this exhortation to keep America free of the corrupting influence of the British example of government.

Monticello Feb. 28. [17]96.

This I hope will be the age of experiments in government, and that their basis will be founded on principles of honesty, not of mere force. We have seen no instance of this since the days of the Roman republic, nor do we read of any before that. Either force or corruption has been the principle of every modern government, unless the Dutch perhaps be excepted, & I am not well enough informed to except them absolutely. If ever the morals of a people could be made the basis of their own government, it is our case; and he who could propose to govern such a people by the corruption of their legislature, before he could have one night of quiet sleep, must convince himself that the human soul as well as body is mortal. . . . I am sure, from the honesty of your heart, you join me in detestation of the corruption of the English government, and that no man on earth is more incapable than yourself of seeing that copied among us, willingly. I have been among those who have feared the design to introduce it here, & it has been a strong reason with me for wishing there was an ocean of fire between that island and us.

Oceans of fire, alas, would not spring up at Jefferson's bidding, and he relied on James Madison to protect America from British domination by persuading the House to withhold appropriations for the Jay Treaty. Madison's chances of success seemed good, and Jefferson reminded him at the end of March that his Virginia constituents looked on him as "their last hope" in breaking the chain of conspiracy between the Hamiltonians and Britain.

[Monticello,] Mar. 27. [17]96.

If you decide in favor of your right to refuse cooperation in any case of treaty, I should wonder on what occasion it is to be used, if not on one where the rights, the interest, the honor & faith of our nation are so grossly sacrificed, where a faction has entered into a conspiracy with the enemies of their country to chain down the legislature at the feet of both; where the whole mass of your constituents have condemned this work in the most unequivocal manner, and are looking to you as their last hope to save them from the effects of the avarice & corruption of the first agent, the revolutionary machinations of others, and the incomprehensible acquiescence of the only honest man who has assented to it. I wish that his honesty and his political errors may not furnish a second occasion to exclaim, 'curse on his virtues, the've undone his country.'

In March, it was not known how much longer that "honest man"—Washington—would continue in office. It seemed unlikely that he would accept a third term, but no other candidates could be announced until the President gave his decision to retire. Jefferson continued to urge Madison to seek the Presidency. His slight, bookish friend had developed into a brilliant leader in the rough world of congressional politics, and Jefferson had every reason to believe Madison would be best suited to lead their fledgling Republican party in the executive branch. The President's errors, honest though they might be, were becoming more dangerous, and his successor would have to be able to deal with the corruption Jefferson saw in American politics. In this mood he wrote to Philip Mazzei, a former neighbor in Virginia, who had returned to Italy.

Monticello Apr. 24. 1796.

The aspect of our politics has wonderfully changed since you left us. In place of that noble love of liberty & republican government which carried us triumphantly thro' the war, an Anglican, monarchical & aristocratical party has sprung up, whose avowed object is to draw over us the substance, as they have already done the forms, of the British government. The main body of our citizens however remain true to their republican principles. The whole landed interest is republican; and so is a great mass of talents. Against us are the Executive, the Judiciary, two out of three branches of the legislature, all the officers of the government, all who want to be officers, all timid men who prefer the calm of despotism to the boisterous sea of liberty, British merchants, & Americans trading on British capitals, speculators & holders in the banks & public funds, a contrivance invented for the purposes of corruption, & for assimilating us, in all things, to the rotten as well as the sound parts of the British model. It would give you a fever were I to name to you the Apostates who have gone over to these heresies; men who were Samsons in the field and Solomons in the council, but who have had their heads shorn by the harlot England. In short, we are likely to preserve the liberty we have obtained only by unremitting labors & perils.

Philip Mazzei, a Florentine who had settled near Monticello in 1773 and cultivated vineyards

More than a year later, the Mazzei letter would be published in the American press and Federalists would denounce Jefferson, based on his reference to "Samsons and Solomons," as an enemy of Washington. Jefferson certainly felt that Washington had been led astray, but the allusion was to members of the Cincinnati, he later declared. Although its language was not intended for publication, the letter stated the same opinions Jefferson had communicated to Washington in September, 1792.

Jefferson soon had more reason to despair of the President's ability to face the "unremitting labors and perils" America now demanded from her patriots. Republicans failed to win the fight against the treaty when Federalists raised the phantom fear of war with Great Britain if the provisions were not funded. Some Republicans argued as strongly that implementation would mean a rupture with France, but Washington seemed unable to accept the sincerity of the opposition. At the same time, the President confided that he would not accept another term. His decision was not public knowledge, but political leaders, Federalist and Republican alike, spent May and June fashioning "tickets" for the 1796 election.

Jefferson's name, of course, was prominently mentioned in his own party, and his possible candidacy must have been known to Washington. In this strained atmosphere, Jefferson saw a copy of the Philadelphia *Aurora* that contained thirteen queries the President had presented to the Cabinet in April, 1793, concerning America's policy of neutrality in the war between France and Great Britain. Jefferson discerned the fine hand of the former Treasury Secretary trying to implicate him in the leak and hastened to assure Washington that he had not been responsible for its publication.

Monticello, June 19, 1796.

I cannot be satisfied as to my own part till I relieve my mind by declaring, and I attest everything sacred & honorable to the declaration, that it has got there neither thro' me nor the paper confided to me. This has never been from under my own lock & key, or out of my own hands. No mortal ever knew from me that these questions had been proposed. Perhaps I ought to except one person who possesses all my confidence as he has possessed yours. I do not remember indeed that I communicated it even to him. But as I was in the habit of unlimited trust & counsel with him, it is possible I may have read it to him. No more: for the quire of which it makes a part was never in any hand but my own, nor was a word ever copied or taken down from it, by any body. I take on myself, without fear, any divulgation on his part. We both know him incapable of it. From myself then or my paper this publication has never been derived. I have formerly mentioned to you that, from a very early period of my life, I had laid it down as a rule of conduct never to write a word for the public papers. From this I have never departed in a single instance: & on a late occasion when all the world seemed to be writing, besides a rigid adherence to my own rule, I can say with truth that not a line for the press was ever communicated to me by any other....

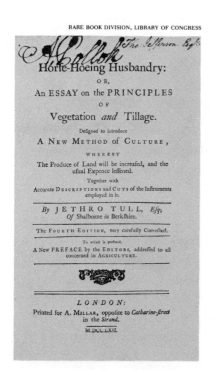

Horse-Hoeing Husbandry:
OR,
An ESSAY on the PRINCIPLES
OF
Vegetation *and* Tillage.

Designed to introduce
A NEW METHOD OF CULTURE,
WHEREBY
The Produce of Land will be increased, and the usual Expence lessened.

Together with
Accurate DESCRIPTIONS and CUTS of the Instruments employed in it.

By JETHRO TULL, *Esq;*
Of Shalborne in Berkshire.

The FOURTH EDITION, very carefully Corrected.

To which is prefixed,
A New PREFACE by the EDITORS, addressed to all concerned in AGRICULTURE.

LONDON:
Printed for A. MILLAR, opposite to *Catharine-street* in the *Strand.*
M.DCC.LXII.

Jefferson's library included a book that revolutionized English agriculture, Jethro Tull's famous Horse-Hoeing Husbandry.

[Jefferson categorized the imputation as typical of attacks on his loyalty by such men as Henry Lee of Virginia.]

I learn that this last [Lee] has thought it worth his while to try to sow tares between you & me, by representing me as still engaged in the bustle of politics, & in turbulence & intrigue against the government. I never believed for a moment that this could make any impression on you, or that your knolege of me would not overweigh the slander of an intriguer, dirtily employed in sifting the conversations of my table, where alone he could hear of me, and seeking to atone for his sins against you by sins against another who had never done him any other injury than that of declining his confidences. Political conversations I really dislike, & therefore avoid where I can without affectation. But when urged by others, I have never concieved that having been in public life requires me to bely my sentiments, nor even to conceal them. When I am led by conversation to express them, I do it with the same independance here which I have practised everywhere, and which is inseparable from my nature....

I put away this disgusting dish of old fragments, & talk to you of my peas & clover.

Washington, in reply, assured Jefferson that he had not suspected him of the leak, but he conceded that he had heard reports that Jefferson and his followers had described him as "a person under a dangerous influence." "My answer invariably has been," Washington wrote, "that I had never discovered any thing in the conduct of Mr. Jefferson to raise suspicions, in my mind, of his insincerity...." After this statement, however, Washington angrily turned to the subject of the Republican press. He implied that if Jefferson had not connived at or inspired the scurrilous attacks on his character, he had at least not exercised his influence to condemn them, something Jefferson would not have done given his previously stated views on the role of a free press.

Jefferson found the tone of the letter and the implication of character assassination so wounding that he made a tacit decision to end their twenty-year correspondence. Since there was nothing in Washington's letter that demanded an immediate reply, Jefferson simply did not answer it, thus closing an association that had begun in the Virginia House of Burgesses in 1769. In later years, Jefferson was generous in praising the Washington he had known and respected in the first two decades of their friendship. His sketch of the President's personality, given in response to a request for information in 1814, is a classic and perceptive study.

Monticello Jan. 2. [18]14.

His mind was great and powerful, without being of the very first order; his penetration strong, tho' not so acute as that of a Newton, Bacon or Locke; and as far as he saw, no judgment was ever sounder. It was slow in operation, being little aided by invention or imagination, but sure in conclusion.... He was incapable of fear, meeting personal dangers with the calmest unconcern. Perhaps the strongest feature in his character was prudence, never acting until every circumstance, every consideration was maturely weighed; refraining if he saw a doubt, but, when once decided, going through with his purpose, whatever obstacles opposed. His integrity was most pure, his justice the most inflexible I have ever known, no motives of interest or consanguinity, of friendship or hatred, being able to bias his decision. He was indeed, in every sense of the words, a wise, a good, & a great man. His temper was naturally irritable and high toned; but reflection & resolution had obtained a firm and habitual ascendancy over it. If ever however it broke it's bonds he was most tremendous in his wrath.... His heart was not warm in it's affections; but he exactly calculated every man's value, and gave him a solid esteem proportioned to it....

...I am satisfied the great body of republicans thinks of him as I do. We were indeed dissatisfied with him on his ratification of the British treaty. But this was short lived. We knew his honesty, the wiles with which he was encompassed, and that age had already begun to relax the firmness of his purposes: and I am convinced he is more deeply seated in the love and gratitude of the republicans, than in the Pharisaical homage of the Federal monarchists. For he was no monarchist from preference of his judgment. The soundness of that gave him correct views of the rights of man, and his severe justice devoted him to them. He has often declared to me that he considered our new constitution as an experiment on the practicability of republican government, and with what dose of liberty man could be trusted for his own good: that he was determined the experiment should have a fair trial, and would lose the last drop of his blood in support of it.

Portrait of Washington as Patriæ Pater *by Rembrandt Peale*

Although Jefferson himself would never have phrased the matter so harshly, Washington had outlived his usefulness to the Republic. An old man, in failing health, the President was surrounded by a

Cabinet of second-rate men who were unable to advise him well. The publication of Washington's Farewell Address in early September finally made it possible for other candidates to declare themselves. John Adams became the Federalist choice; Jefferson had hoped that Madison would be the Republican candidate, but he had just married and would not even stand for re-election to the House. Madison, with a shrewder sense of practical politics, knew that Jefferson would lend far more prestige to their party's ticket, but he had all he could do to keep Jefferson from discouraging his would-be supporters. At the end of September, Madison confided to Monroe: "I have not seen Jefferson and have thought it best to present him no opportunity of protesting to his friends against being embarked in the contest."

An unwilling candidate, Jefferson waited patiently to learn his fate after the November elections. The cumbersome system of voting meant that the victor would not be definitely known for several weeks, but by early December, Jefferson had accurately analyzed the polls. He told Madison of the strategy to be followed should a tie vote in the Electoral College threaten Adams's majority in the popular vote.

> Monticello Dec. 17. [17]96.
>
> It begins to appear possible that there may be an equal division where I had supposed the republican vote would have been considerably minor. It seems also possible that the Representatives [who would decide the issue if the electoral votes were tied] may be divided. This is a difficulty from which the constitution has provided no issue. It is both my duty & inclination therefore to relieve the embarrasment should it happen: and in that case I pray you and authorize you fully to sollicit on my behalf that Mr. Adams may be preferred. He has always been my senior from the commencement of our public life, and the expression of the public will being equal, this circumstance ought to give him the preference.... Let those come to the helm who think they can steer clear of the difficulties. I have no confidence in myself for the undertaking.

Knowing Adams well, Jefferson was aware that it was not enough simply to inform his fellow Republicans of his willingness to accept second place, which would make him Vice President. Three days after Christmas, he drafted a letter to Adams.

> Monticello Dec. 28. 1796
>
> The public & the public papers have been much occupied lately in placing us in a point of opposition to each other. I trust with confidence that less of it has been felt by

First page of the Farewell Address

ourselves personally. In the retired canton where I am, I learn little of what is passing. Pamphlets I see never; papers but a few; and the fewer the happier. Our latest intelligence from Philadelphia at present is of the 16th. inst. But tho' at that date your election to the first magistracy seems not to have been known as a fact, yet with me it has never been doubted.... I have never one single moment expected a different issue; tho' I know I shall not be believed, yet it is not the less true that I have never wished it. My neighbors, as my compurgators, could aver that fact, because they see my occupations & my attachment to them. Indeed it is possible that you may be cheated of your succession by a trick worthy the subtlety of your arch-friend [Hamilton, who had supported the Federalist vice-presidential candidate, Thomas Pinckney, against Adams] of New York, who has been able to make of your real friends tools to defeat their & your just wishes. Most probably he will be disappointed as to you; & my inclinations place me out of his reach. I leave to others the sublime delights of riding in the storm, better pleased with sound sleep & a warm birth below, with the society of neighbors, friends & fellow laborers of the earth, than of spies & sycophants. No one then will congratulate you with purer disinterestedness than myself.

Even as he completed the letter, Jefferson had doubts about its propriety. Instead of sending it directly to Adams, he enclosed it with a covering note to Madison, asking him to read it and to return it "if anything should render the delivery of it ineligible in your opinion." He assured Madison that neither his ambitions nor his vanity had been disappointed by the outcome of the elections, in which he had received 68 electoral votes to Adams's 71 and Pinckney's 59.

[Monticello,] Jan. 1. [17]97.
I know the difficulty of obtaining belief to one's declarations of a disinclination to honors, and that it is greatest with those who still remain in the world. But no arguments were wanting to reconcile me to a relinquishment of the first office or acquiescence under the second. As to the first it was impossible that a more solid unwillingness settled on full calculation, could have existed in any man's mind, short of the degree of absolute refusal.... As to the second, it is the only office in the

world about which I am unable to decide in my own mind whether I had rather have it or not have it. Pride does not enter into the estimate; for I think with the Romans that the General of to-day should be a soldier tomorrow if necessary. I can particularly have no feelings which would revolt at a secondary position to mr. Adams. I am his junior in life, was his junior in Congress, his junior in the diplomatic line, his junior lately in the civil government.

Madison prudently chose to return the enclosure to its author at Monticello, fearing it might be misinterpreted. "You know the temper of Mr. A. better than I do," he tactfully told Jefferson, "but I have always conceived it to be rather a ticklish one." Even before Jefferson learned of Madison's decision, he heard news that made personal assurances of loyalty to the President-elect seem unnecessary. He wrote happily to Madison in Philadelphia on January 22.

[Monticello,] Jan. 22. [17]97.
My letters inform me that Mr. A speaks of me with great friendship, and with satisfaction in the prospect of administering the government in concurrence with me. I am glad of the first information, because tho' I saw that our antient friendship was affected by a little leaven produced partly by his constitution, partly by the contrivance of others, yet I never felt a diminution of confidence in his integrity, and retained a solid affection for him. His principles of government I knew to be changed, but conscientiously changed.

To be sure Adams did not mistake his intentions, Jefferson wrote several New Englanders of his pleasure in serving as Vice President under his old colleague. He had done all that he could to reassure the President-elect that he would have a faithful and cooperative aide in the administration. The need for a new regime became more obvious daily. French reaction to Jay's Treaty had been as bitter as the most "Jacobin" of American Republicans had predicted, and Washington clearly could not meet the crisis. On January 4, Jefferson wrote his friend Archibald Stuart that it would be futile to petition the President concerning the danger of war with France.

Monticello, Jan 4, 1797.
Such is the popularity of the President that the people will support him in whatever he will do, or will not do,

John Adams, in an engraving by Amos Doolittle which appeared in The Connecticut Magazine

without appealing to their own reason or to anything but their feelings toward him. His mind has been so long used to unlimited applause that it could not brook contradiction, or even advice offered unasked. To advice, when asked, he is very open. I have long thought therefore it was best for the republican interest to soothe him by flattery where they could approve his measures, & to be silent where they disapprove, that they may not render him desperate as to their affections, & entirely indifferent to their wishes; in short to lie on their oars while he remains at the helm, and let the bark drift as his will and a superintending providence shall direct.... It seems he is earnest that the war should be avoided, & to have the credit of leaving us in full peace. I think then it is best to leave him to his own movements, & not to risk the ruffling them by what he might deem an improper interference with the constituted authorities.... As to the President elect, there is reason to believe that he (Mr. Adams I mean) is detached from Hamilton, & there is a possibility he may swerve from his politics in a greater or less degree. Should the British faction attempt to urge him to the war by addresses of support with life & fortune, as may happen, it would then be adviseable to counteract their endeavors by dissuasive addresses.

Jefferson returned to public life because the electorate compelled it, but he was reassured in doing so by the independence of mind that characterized the President he would serve. Adams was his own man, not a tool of Hamilton, and whatever the New Englander's peculiarities of temperament and pro-British leanings, Jefferson pointed out to Edward Rutledge that "he is perhaps the only sure barrier against Hamilton's getting in." The nature of the office he would hold also appealed to Jefferson. He believed that the Vice Presidency was solely a legislative position, confined to presiding over the Senate, and that it should be conducted within the strict limits laid down by the Constitution. He had warned Madison in his letter of January 22 to expect nothing more of him.

[Monticello,] Jan. 22. [17]97.
As to my participating in the administration, if by that he [Adams] meant the executive cabinet, both duty & inclination will shut that door to me. I cannot have a wish to see the scenes of 93. revived as to myself, & to descend daily into the arena like a gladiator to suffer

martyrdom in every conflict. As to duty, the constitution will know me only as the member of a legislative body: and it's principle is that of a separation of legislative executive & judiciary functions.

Indeed, although Jefferson was flattered and pleased by the Republican showing in the polls, he seemed relieved that they had not won. He had informed Edward Rutledge in December that he had no illusions about the glories of the Presidency.

Monticello Dec. 27. 1796.

I know well that no man will ever bring out of that office the reputation which carries him into it. The honey moon would be as short in that case as in any other, & it's moments of extasy would be ransomed by years of torment & hatred. I shall highly value indeed the share which I may have had in the late vote, as an evidence of the share I hold in the esteem of my countrymen. But in this point of view a few votes more or less will be little sensible, and in every other the minor will be preferred by me to the major vote.

Silhouette of Jefferson distributed at Peale's Museum, Philadelphia

The office of Vice President seemed ideal for Jefferson. He looked forward to attending meetings of the American Philosophical Society in Philadelphia but expected to spend much of his time at home. He commented to Benjamin Rush in late January, "I have no wish to meddle again in public affairs....If I am to act however, a more tranquil & unoffending station could not have been found for me....It will give me philosophical evenings in the winter, & rural days in the summer."

And so, on February 20, Jefferson left Monticello for Philadelphia to take his oath of office. He would miss the spring planting, but as he rode north to give his personal support to Adams, he was convinced that the sacrifice would be minor and temporary. He left his peaceful little mountain, with its unfinished mansion and his growing brood of grandchildren, planning to be away only a few weeks of the year for the next four years. "I would not have wished to leave it at all," Jefferson confessed. "However, if I am to be called from it, the shortest absences and most tranquil station suit me best." The absences, however, would not be short, nor would the station be tranquil.

Chapter **10**

Second Vice President

When Jefferson left Monticello to serve as Vice President to John Adams, he regarded his comrade from Massachusetts as a man who might reunite the nation, now divided between British and French partisans, and liberate politics and the economy from the legacy of Hamilton's influence. If Jefferson, by his mere presence in the administration, could persuade Southerners and Westerners of the merits of Adams's regime, he would feel that he had played as active and useful a role as any Vice President should properly assume. But this modest goal for his Vice Presidency was to fail, not from any lack of sincerity on his part but because others refused to accept him at his word. On his arrival in Philadelphia, most Federalists and even some Republicans considered him a party leader, a role he had not yet consciously adopted. If anyone deserved the title in 1797 it was James Madison who had marshaled the Republican interest in the House since 1789 and turned it into a disciplined legislative force while courting support among state officeholders and coordinating propaganda programs to broaden the party's support. Jefferson, however, had long been the symbol of Republican strength, and with Madison's retirement he was to become the dominant Republican.

Before leaving Monticello, Jefferson wrote to George Wythe, under whose tutelage he had made a thorough study of English parliamentary history and law, asking for any notes the scholar still had pertaining to rules of order the Vice President would be enforcing in the Senate. Although Wythe was unable to help him, Jefferson eventually compiled a manual of parliamentary procedure which was long used by both houses of Congress.

> Monticello Jan. 22. [17]97
>
> It seems probable that I shall be called on to preside in a legislative chamber. It is now so long since I have acted in the legislative line that I am entirely rusty in the Parliamentary rules of procedure. I know they

have been more studied and are better known by you than by any man in America, perhaps by any man living. I am in hopes that while enquiring into the subject you made notes on it. If any such remain in your hands, however informal, in books or in scraps of paper, and you will be so good as to trust me with them a little while, they shall be most faithfully returned.

Even the timing of his trip to Philadelphia reflected Jefferson's desire to become a modest, secondary member of the new administration. He told Madison he did not think it was necessary for him to go that far to take the oath of office, but he had decided that "respect to the public" demanded the inconvenience.

LIBRARY OF CONGRESS

Congress Hall (with cupola), where Jefferson presided over the Senate

[Monticello,] Jan. 30. [17]97.

I have turned to the constitution & laws, and find nothing to warrant the opinion that I might not have been qualified here or wherever else I could meet with a Senator, every member of that body being authorised to administer the oath, without being confined to time or place, & consequently to make a record of it, and to deposit it with the records of the Senate. However, I shall come on on the principle which had first determined me, respect to the public. I hope I shall be made a part of no ceremony whatever. I shall escape into the city as covertly as possible.

Jefferson's arrival in Philadelphia was not quite as "covert" as he had hoped: an artillery salute and a banner proclaiming "Jefferson the Friend of the People" greeted him as he alighted from the stagecoach. But his inaugural address to the Senate maintained the modest tone he felt was in keeping with the nature of the office. The message opened with an apology for any errors of procedure he might commit and closed with a tribute to the man he succeeded.

[March 4, 1797]

Entering on the duties of the office to which I am called, I feel it incumbent on me to apologize to this honorable House for the insufficient manner in which I fear they may be discharged. At an earlier period of my life, and through some considerable portion of it, I have been a member of legislative bodies, and not altogether inattentive to the forms of their proceedings; but much time has elapsed since that; other duties have occupied my

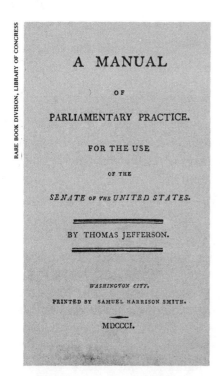

A MANUAL

OF

PARLIAMENTARY PRACTICE.

FOR THE USE

OF THE

SENATE OF THE UNITED STATES.

BY THOMAS JEFFERSON.

WASHINGTON CITY.

PRINTED BY SAMUEL HARRISON SMITH.

MDCCCI.

Jefferson's personal copy of his Manual of Parliamentary Practice, *which he completed in 1800; it was printed in Washington in 1801.*

mind, and in a great degree it has lost its familiarity with this subject. I fear that the House will have but too frequent occasion to perceive the truth of this acknowledgment. If a diligent attention, however, will enable me to fulfil the functions now assigned me, I may promise that diligence and attention shall be sedulously employed....

I might here proceed, and with the greatest truth, to declare my zealous attachment to the constitution of the United States, that I consider the union of these States as the first of blessings, and as the first of duties, the preservation of that constitution which secures it; but I suppose these declarations not pertinent to the occasion of entering into an office whose primary business is merely to preside over the forms of this House, and no one more sincerely prays that no accident may call me to the higher and more important functions which the constitution eventually devolves on this office. These have been justly confided to the eminent character which has preceded me here, whose talents and integrity have been known and revered by me through a long course of years, have been the foundation of a cordial and uninterrupted friendship between us, and I devoutly pray he may be long preserved for the government, the happiness, and prosperity of our common country.

Jefferson and the senators then adjourned to the House chamber where that "eminent character" took the presidential oath resplendent in sash and sword. Jefferson recorded no reaction to the new President's remarkable costume; he may have concentrated more on Adams's speech, which was conciliatory, reaffirming his faith in the Constitution and in republican institutions. Adams even spoke of his personal esteem for the French, who were then governed by the three-man Directory. Before leaving Virginia, Jefferson had learned that Charles C. Pinckney, Monroe's successor as minister in Paris, had been denied an official reception. The pro-British policies that dominated Washington's second term had brought their inevitable result. As he remarked to Madison, Jefferson expected Adams to be saddled with the diplomatic errors of his predecessor.

[Monticello,] Jan. 8. [17]97.

The President [Washington] is fortunate to get off just as the bubble is bursting, leaving others to hold the bag. Yet, as his departure will mark the moment when the difficulties begin to work, you will see, that they will

275

be ascribed to the new administration, and that he will have his usual good fortune of reaping credit from the good acts of others, and leaving to them that of his errors.

As soon as Jefferson arrived in Philadelphia, he had been approached by Adams with a plan to establish a rapprochement with France: the creation of a special bipartisan commission, drawing its members from different regions, to be sent to Paris to negotiate French grievances. He recorded the progress of the plan before and after Inauguration Day.

Anas

Mar. 2. 1797. I arrived at Phila. to qualify as V. P., and called instantly on Mr. Adams who lodged at Francis's in 4th. street. The next morning he returned my visit at Mr. Madison's, where I lodged. He found me alone in my room, and, shutting the door himself, he said he was glad to find me alone for that he wished a free conversation with me. He entered immediately on an explanation of the situation of our affairs with France, & the danger of rupture with that nation, a rupture which would convulse the attachments of this country. That he was impressed with the necessity of an immediate mission to the Directory; that it would have been the first wish of his heart to have got me to go there, but that he supposed it was out of the question, as it did not seem justifiable for him to send away the person destined to take his place in case of accident to himself, nor decent to remove from competition one who was a rival in the public favor. That he had therefore concluded to send a mission which by it's dignity should satisfy France, & by it's selection from the three great divisions of the Continent should satisfy all parts of the US. In short that he had determind to join [Elbridge] Gerry and Madison to Pinckney, and he wished me to consult Mr. Madison for him. I told him that as to myself I concurred in the opinion of the impropriety of my leaving the post assigned me, and that my inclinations moreover would never permit me to cross the Atlantic again: that I would as he desired consult Mr. Madison, but I feared it was desperate.... He said that if Mr. Madison should refuse, he would still appoint him, and leave the responsibility on him.— I consulted Mr. Madison who declined as I expected. I think it was on Monday the 6th. of March, Mr. Adams

These contemporary views by William Birch of Market Street from the County Market (above) and Second Street from the corner of Second and Market (opposite) were not far from Adams's and Jefferson's usual lodgings at Francis's Hotel.

and myself met at dinner at General Washington's, and we happened in the evening to rise from table and come away together. As soon as we got into the street I told him the event of my negociation with Mr. Madison. He immediately said that on consultation some objections to that nomination had been raised which he had not contemplated, and was going on with excuses which evidently embarrassed him, when we came to 5th. street where our road separated, his being down Market street, mine off along 5th. and we took leave.... The opinion I formed at the time on this transaction was that Mr. A. in the first moments of the enthusiasm of the occasion (his inauguration,) forgot party sentiments, and as he never acted on any system, but was always governed by the feeling of the moment, he thought for a moment to steer impartially between the parties; that Monday the 6th. of Mar. being the first time he had met his cabinet, on expressing ideas of this kind he had been at once diverted from them, and returned to his former party views.

Adams's puzzling about-face on Madison's appointment could be traced to his Cabinet—all holdovers from Washington's second-rate council who were still strongly influenced by Hamilton. In this case the former Secretary of the Treasury urged that Madison be included on the commission for the sake of national unity, but Jefferson guessed correctly that the Cabinet had advised Adams against it. Adams's conciliatory attitude and his differences of opinion with some of his fellow party members presaged the split between moderate and High Federalists that would develop during his term.

A few days after the inauguration, Jefferson and Adams left Philadelphia for their homes in Virginia and Massachusetts. They returned in May for a special session of Congress called to consider the international situation. By then, Jefferson was less sanguine about the possibility of harmonious relations with the President. Two days before the Senate met, he wrote of his concern to Elbridge Gerry, the moderate Massachusetts Republican who was being considered for the mission to France.

Philadelphia May 13. 1797.

You express apprehensions that stratagems will be used to produce a misunderstanding between the President and myself. Tho' not a word having this tendency has ever been hazarded to me by any one, yet I consider as a certainty that nothing will be left untried

Elbridge Gerry

to alienate him from me. These machinations will proceed from the Hamiltonians by whom he is surrounded, and who are only a little less hostile to him than to me. It cannot but damp the pleasure of cordiality when we suspect that it is suspected. I cannot help fearing that it is impossible for Mr. Adams to believe that the state of my mind is what it really is; that he may think I view him as an obstacle in my way. I have no supernatural power to impress truth on the mind of another, nor he any to discover that the estimate which he may form on a just view of the human mind as generally constituted, may not be just in it's application to a special constitution. This may be a source of private uneasiness to us. I honestly confess that it is so to me at this time. But neither of us are capable of letting it have effect on our public duties. Those who may endeavor to separate us, are probably excited by the fear that I might have influence on the executive councils. But when they shall know that I consider my office as constitutionally confined to legislative functions, and that I could not take any part whatever in executive consultations, even were it proposed, their fears may perhaps subside, & their object be found not worth a machination.

During the special legislative session, Jefferson took no part in executive policy conferences spurred by the French rejection of Charles C. Pinckney. The discussion of the commission to France in March was the last time Adams "ever consulted me as to any measures of government," Jefferson later noted. The Federalists in Congress seemed driven by a war fever, which he described to Thomas Pinckney.

Philadelphia May 29. 1797.
When I contemplate the spirit which is driving us on here, & that beyond the water which will view us but as a mouthful the more, I have little hope of peace. I anticipate the burning of our seaports, havoc of our frontiers, household insurgency, with a long train of et ceteras, which it is enough for a man to have met once in his life. . . . War is not the best engine for us to resort to. Nature has given us one in our *commerce* which, if properly managed, will be a better instrument for obliging the interested nations of Europe to treat us with justice. If the commercial regulations had been adopted which

our legislature were at one time proposing, we should at this moment have been standing on such an eminence of safety & respect as ages can never recover.

Adams's program of increased military preparedness at home and a joint commission to Paris was adopted in May and June. Jefferson considered the plan for defense needlessly expensive, and he hardly approved of the Virginian named to the commission instead of Madison — young John Marshall, his Federalist kinsman. But Elbridge Gerry, who was sympathetic to France, would be the New England representative, and Jefferson sent him a warm letter of congratulations, urging him to seize the chance to fight for both interest and honor.

Philadelphia June 21. [17]97.

Peace is undoubtedly at present the first object of our nation. Interest & honor are also national considerations. But interest, duly weighed, is in favor of peace even at the expence of spoliations past & future; & honor cannot now be an object. The insults & injuries committed on us by both the belligerent parties from the beginning of 1793. to this day, & still continuing by both, cannot now be wiped off by engaging in war with one of them. As there is great reason to expect this is the last campaign in Europe, it would certainly be better for us to rub thro this year as we have done through the four preceding ones, and hope that on the restoration of peace we may be able to establish some plan for our foreign connections more likely to secure our peace, interest & honor in future. Our countrymen have divided themselves by such strong affections to the French & the English, that nothing will secure us internally but a divorce from both nations. And this must be the object of every real American, and it's attainment is practicable without much self-denial. But for this, peace is necessary. Be assured of this, my dear Sir, that if we engage in a war during our present passions & our present weakness in some quarters, that our union runs the greatest risk of not coming out of that war in the shape in which it enters it.

Silhouette of John Marshall as an older man, by William H. Brown

Political factionalism reached new heights that summer in Philadelphia. Jefferson described the atmosphere to Edward Rutledge, a colleague in the old Continental Congress.

Philadelphia June 24. [17]97.
You & I have formerly seen warm debates and high political passions. But gentlemen of different politics would then speak to each other, & separate the business of the senate from that of society. It is not so now. Men who have been intimate all their lives cross the streets to avoid meeting, & turn their heads another way, lest they should be obliged to touch their hat.

In a letter more than six months later, Jefferson explained to John Wise of Virginia what he thought were the differences between the first two major political parties to develop in America.

Philadelphia February 12. 1798.
It is now well understood that two political Sects have arisen within the U.S. the one believing that the executive is the branch of our government which the most needs support; the other that like the analogous branch in the English Government, it is already too strong for the republican parts of the constitution; and therefore in equivocal cases they incline to the legislative powers: the former of these are called federalists, sometimes aristocrats or monocrats, and sometimes tories, after the corresponding sect in the English Government of exactly the same definition: the latter are stiled republicans, whigs, jacobins, anarchists, disorganizers &c. these terms are in familiar use with most persons... both parties claim to be federalists and republicans, and I believe with truth as to the great mass of them....

John Wayles Eppes by St. Mémin

As June drew to a close, Jefferson waited impatiently for the Senate adjournment that would allow him to "exchange the roar & tumult of bulls & bears, for the prattle of my grand-children & senile rest." Family life at Monticello was becoming even more idyllic, for young Mary had fallen in love with her cousin, John Wayles Eppes. Jefferson wrote lightheartedly of the engagement to his older daughter, Martha Randolph.

Philadelphia June 8. 1797.
I now see our fireside formed into a groupe, no one member of which has a fibre in their composition which can ever produce any jarring or jealousies among us. No irregular passions, no dangerous bias, which may render problematical the future fortunes and happiness of our descendants.

Even at Monticello, Jefferson could not escape reminders of the political animosities he had left behind. His enemies skillfully used and misused his own words to hound him. A garbled version of his letter to Philip Mazzei, with its reference to the "Samsons" and "Solomons" who had succumbed to British influence, had been published in a New York newspaper. Federalists labeled the letter an attack on Washington. That implication was a distortion, but, as Jefferson explained to Madison in August, there seemed no way to defend himself without making the situation even worse.

Monticello, Aug 3, [17]97.

I first met with it [the published Mazzei letter] at Bladensburgh, and for a moment concieved I must take the field of the public papers. I could not disavow it wholly, because the greatest part was mine in substance tho' not in form. I could not avow it as it stood because the form was not mine, and in one place the substance very materially falsified. This then would render explanations necessary. Nay, it would render proofs of the whole necessary, & draw me at length into a publication of all (even the secret) transactions of the administration while I was of it; and embroil me personally with every member of the Executive, with the Judiciary, and with others still. I soon decided in my own mind to be entirely silent.... Now it would be impossible for me to explain this publicly without bringing on a personal difference between Genl. Washington & myself, which nothing before the publication of this letter has ever done. It would embroil me also with all those with whom his character is still popular, that is to say, nine tenths of the people of the U S. And what good would be obtained by my avowing the letter with the necessary explanations? Very little indeed in my opinion to counterbalance a good deal of harm.

In a Federalist cartoon entitled "The Providential Detection," an American eagle prevents Jefferson, with the letter to Mazzei in his hand, from burning the Constitution on an "Altar to Gallic Despotism."

When Jefferson left Monticello in December for the second session of the Fifth Congress, he did so with none of the optimism he had felt on his journey to the inauguration. Adams seemed to be under the control of his High Federalist advisors, and Jefferson was increasingly forced to assume the leadership of the opposition. Isolated, almost ostracized by Federalists in and out of Congress that winter, Jefferson's evenings were almost entirely "philosophical," his social life confined to close friends and political associates and members of the American Philosophical Society of which he was then president. He went out of his way to avoid social occasions that might be politically embarrassing, and in Federalist Philadelphia, that meant such polite evasions as "attention to Health" in declining an invitation to a ball.

A membership certificate in the American Philosophical Society signed by Jefferson, as president, for architect Benjamin Latrobe

[Philadelphia,] Feb. 23. [17]98.

Th: Jefferson presents his respects to Mr. [Thomas] Willing, and other gentlemen managers of the ball of this evening. He hopes his non-attendance will not be misconstrued. He has not been at a ball these twenty years, nor for a long time permitted himself to go to any entertainments of the evening, from motives of attention to health. On these grounds he excused to Genl. Washington then living in the city his not going to his birthnight; to Mrs. Washington her evenings; to Mr. Adams his soirées; and to all and sundry who have been so good as to invite him to tea and card parties. Tho desirous to go to them it is an indulgence which his age and habits will he hopes obtain and continue to him. He has always testified his homage to the occasion by his subscription to it.

Adams's coolness was becoming even more marked. Another of Jefferson's letters to a friend, its criticism of the administration misquoted and exaggerated, had been reported to the President in the fall. "It will be a motive," Adams commented to his informant, "in addition to many others, for me to be upon my guard. It is evidence of a mind, soured, yet seeking for popularity, and eaten to a honeycomb with ambition, yet weak, confused, uninformed, and ignorant." Thus Adams dismissed the integrity and intelligence of a man he had known and trusted for more than twenty years. Franklin had once said that Adams was "always an honest man, often a wise one, but sometimes and in some things absolutely out of his senses." And so he must have seemed to Jefferson, who filled the *Anas* that winter with notes on the President's remarks. Jefferson recorded Adams's blunt comments on popular government after a dinner conversation in February, 1798.

Anas

Feb. 15. 98. . . . That as to trusting to a popular assembly for the preservn of our liberties it was the merest chimœra imaginable. They never had any rule of decision but their own will. That he would as lieve be again in the hands of our old committees of safety who made the law & executed it at the same time. That it had been observed by some writer (I forget whom he named) that anarchy did more mischief in one night than tyranny in a age.... The point in which he views our Senate, as the Colossus of the constitution serves as a key to the politics of the Senate, who are two thirds of them in his sentiments, and accounts for the bold line of conduct they pursue.

Barred from Cabinet conferences, Jefferson was not privy to all the information that influenced Adams's conduct of foreign policy. In March, news arrived that required no inside knowledge for evaluation: France planned to seize neutral ships carrying British goods, and Gerry, Pinckney, and Marshall had been denied recognition. Instead, Talleyrand, the Minister of Foreign Affairs, had referred the diplomats to three agents, designated in their dispatches as X, Y, and Z. The commissioners were told, diplomatically but clearly that they might win recognition and hope to begin negotiations with the Directory if America provided a sizable bribe for the Directory and a large loan to France, the terms of repayment to be almost indefinite. Just as clearly, if less diplomatically, the commissioners had replied: "No; no; not a sixpence." Jefferson indicated to Edmund Pendleton that the only possible Republican response that spring was to try to buy time.

Philadelphia Apr. 2. [17]98.

Talleyrand

The only source of anxiety therefore is to avoid war for the present moment. If we can defeat the measures leading to that during this session, so as to gain this summer, time will be given as well for the tide of the public mind to make itself felt, as for the operations of France to have their effect in England as well as here. If on the contrary war is forced on, the tory interest continues dominant, and to them alone must be left, as they alone desire to ride on the whirlwind & direct the storm. The present period therefore of two or three weeks is the most eventful ever known since that of 1775. and will decide whether the principles established by that contest are to prevail or give way to those they subverted.

Jefferson anticipated, correctly, that time was on the Republicans' side. Writing in May, he foresaw that the expense of internal defence would be an important "sedative" for the war fever.

Philadelphia, May 9, [17]98.

At this moment all the passions are boiling over, and one who keeps himself cool and clear of the contagion, is so far below the point of ordinary conversation, that he finds himself insulated in every society. However, the fever will not last. War, land tax & stamp act, are sedatives which must clam it's ardor. They will bring on reflection, and that, with information, is all which our countrymen need, to bring themselves and their affairs to rights. They are essentially republican. They retain unadulterated the principles of 75. and those who are conscious of no change in themselves, have nothing to fear in the long run.

The Adams administration reached its height of popularity that spring and summer, but Federalists did not succeed in forcing America into war or even press for particularly effective defense measures. Rather, they provided for a makeshift army of "provisional" troops, to be commanded by George Washington from his retreat at Mount Vernon. While settling for a quasi war with France, they launched a full-scale campaign against Republicans at home with a series of statutes known as the Alien and Sedition Acts. When Jefferson first heard of the bills, he believed that the mass of the people would not be swayed by them. In discussing them with Madison, he still expected taxes to be the Republicans' best issue.

Philadelphia, April 26, 1798.

One of the war party, in a fit of unguarded passion, declared some time ago they would pass a citizen bill, an alien bill, & a sedition bill. Accordingly, some days ago, [Joshua] Coit laid a motion on the table of the H. of R. for modifying the citizen law.... Yesterday mr. [James] Hillhouse laid on the table of the Senate a motion for giving power to send away suspected aliens.... There is now only wanting, to accomplish the whole declaration beforementioned, a sedition bill which we shall certainly soon see proposed. The object of that is the suppression of the whig presses.... The popular movement in the eastern states is checked as we expected: and war addresses are showering in from New Jersey & the great trading towns. However, we still trust that a nearer view of war & a land tax will oblige the great mass of the people to attend.

An Act

To suspend the commercial intercourse between the United States and France, and the dependencies thereof.

BE it enacted by the Senate and House of Representatives of the United States of America in Congress assembled, That no ship or vessel, owned, hired, or employed, wholly or in part, by any person resident within the United States, and which shall depart therefrom after the first day of July next, shall be allowed to proceed directly, or from any intermediate port or place, to any port or place within the territory of the French Republic, or the dependencies thereof, or to any place in the West-Indies, or elsewhere, under the acknowledged government of France, or shall be employed in any traffic or commerce with or for any person resident within the jurisdiction, or under the authority of the French Republic. And if any ship or vessel, in any voyage thereafter commencing, and before her return within the United States, shall be voluntarily carried, or suffered to proceed to any French port or place as aforesaid, or shall be employed as aforesaid, contrary to the intent hereof, every such ship or vessel together with her cargo shall be forfeited, and shall accrue, the one half to the use of the United States, and the other half to the use of any person or persons, citizens of the United States, who shall inform and prosecute for the same; and shall be liable to be seized, prosecuted and condemned in any circuit or district court of the United States which shall be holden within or for the district where the seizure shall be made,

Detail from printed act of Congress to suspend commercial intercourse with France after July 1, 1798

The temper of Congress at the end of the session had gone from immoderate to hysterical. Jefferson prayed for an adjournment. "To separate Congress now," he wrote Madison on June 21, "will be withdrawing the fire from under a boiling pot." Congress did not "separate" until July, several weeks after Jefferson left Philadelphia, but he was familiar with the contents of the acts that had been passed. The Alien Enemies Act was the least offensive: it provided for the deportation of aliens from a country with which the United States was at war. The Naturalization Act extended the residence requirements for naturalization. The Alien Friends Act was especially disturbing: it granted almost unlimited power to the President to imprison or deport aliens he deemed dangerous. But the Sedition Act, which became law on July 4, ten days after Jefferson's return to Monticello, was even worse and, because it affected the rights of American citizens, was of much greater value as a political issue. This statute provided fines and imprisonment for those who conspired to prevent the execution of federal laws and for those who published "any false, scandalous and malicious writing" that criticized the President, Congress, or government.

At Monticello, away from the madness of Philadelphia for the summer, Jefferson calmly considered what the Republican reaction should be. He was confident that the essentially republican spirit of the people would reassert itself, but he was worried by rumors of disunion and even threats of secession that were circulating. On June 4, Jefferson wrote firmly to John Taylor of Caroline County, Virginia, who had suggested that the time had come for his state and North Carolina to consider withdrawing from the Union in order to escape the domination of New England Federaalists. It was not personal or party interests but patriotism that prompted Jefferson to draft an outspoken repudiation of such a move.

> Philadelphia June 4 [17]98
>
> ...in every free and deliberating society, there must from the nature of man be opposite parties, and violent dissensions and discords; and one of these for the most part must prevail over the other for a longer or shorter time. Perhaps this party division is necessary to induce each to watch and debate to the people the proceedings of the other. But if on a temporary superiority of the one party, the other is to resort to a scission of the union, no federal government can ever exist. If to rid ourselves of the present rule of Massachusets and Connecticut, we break the union, will the evil stop there? Suppose the N. England States alone cut off, will our natures be changed? Are we not men still to the South of that, and with all the passions of men? Immediately, we shall see a Pennsylvania and a Virginia party arise in the residuary confederacy, and the public mind will be distracted with the same party spirit.... If we reduce our Union to Virginia and N. Carolina, immediately the conflict will be established between the representatives

285

of these two states, and they will end by breaking into their simple units. Seeing therefore that an association of men who will not quarrel with one another is a thing which never yet existed, from the greatest confederacy of nations down to a town meeting or a vestry, seeing that we must have somebody to quarrel with, I had rather keep our New England associates for that purpose, than to see our bickerings transferred to others....A little patience, and we shall see the reign of witches pass over, their spells dissolve, and the people recovering their true sight, restore their government to it's true principles. It is true that in the meantime we are suffering deeply in spirit, and incurring the horrors of a war, and long oppressions of enormous public debt. But who can say what would be the evils of a scission and when and where they would end?...If the game runs sometimes against us at home, we must have patience, till luck turns, and then we shall have an opportunity of winning back the *principles* we have lost. For this is a game where principles are the stake.

The passage of the Alien and Sedition Acts gave secessionists even better arguments than the war preparations had: not only were New England merchants ready to force the rest of the nation into a ruinous war to defend their economic interests but the Federalists had used the issue of national security to muffle dissent. The Adams administration seemed to be the enemy of the commercial and diplomatic interests of the South and West and the enemy of the civil liberties of any who differed with its policy as well. In an August letter to Samuel Smith, a Maryland Republican leader, Jefferson weighed his desire to publicize his own sentiments and his lifelong determination "never to put a sentence into any newspaper."

Monticello Aug. 22. [17]98.

I know my own principles to be pure, & therefore am not ashamed of them. On the contrary I wish them known, & therefore willingly express them to every one. They are the same I have acted on from the year 75. to this day, and are the same, I am sure, with those of the great body of the American people. I only wish the real principles of those who censure mine were also known. But, warring against those of the people, the delusion of the people is necessary to the dominant party....

...At a very early period of my life, I determined

Wilson Cary Nicholas

never to put a sentence into any newspaper. I have religiously adhered to the resolution through my life, and have great reason to be contented with it. Were I to undertake to answer the calumnies of the newspapers, it would be more than all my own time, & that of 20. aids could effect. For while I should be answering one, twenty new ones would be invented. I have thought it better to trust to the justice of my countrymen, that they would judge me by what they *see* of my conduct on the stage where they have placed me, & what they knew of me *before* the epoch since which a particular party has supposed it might answer some view of theirs to vilify me in the public eye.

Even had Jefferson been willing to take up his pen, as the Vice President he could submit nothing over his own name. The alternative action he chose was the preparation of resolutions to be introduced in a state legislature. Resolves were drafted sometime in September and then dispatched to Wilson Cary Nicholas, a Virginia Republican, who persuaded Jefferson they would gain a sympathetic hearing in Kentucky. Nicholas passed the draft on to John Breckinridge, a former Albemarle County resident who was on his way to Kentucky, after Jefferson had received "a solemn assurance, which I strictly required, that it should not be known from what quarter they came."

This promise was the more necessary because of the tone of the resolutions and the controversial concept of state and federal relations they espoused. In an effort to save the Union, Jefferson outlined a philosophical argument that would later be used by the very secessionists he hoped to quiet: the doctrine that states might nullify federal laws they deemed unconstitutional. The resolutions opened with Jefferson's contention (stated in his opinion on the Bank in 1791) that the implied powers of the federal government could not include any of the powers reserved to the "states respectively, or to the people" and that the Federalist statutes of June and July, 1798, clearly infringed on those rights. They closed with a proposal for a committee of correspondence that would communicate these views to other state legislatures with certain assurances.

[November, 1798]

... to assure them that this commonwealth continues in the same esteem of their friendship and union which it has manifested from that moment at which a common danger first suggested a common union: that it considers union ... to be friendly to the peace, happiness, and prosperity of all the states: that faithful to that com-

Resolutions, in Jefferson's hand,
on the Alien and Sedition Acts

pact, according to the plain intent and meaning in which it was understood and acceded to by the several parties, it is sincerely anxious for it's preservation: that it does also believe, that to take from the States all the powers of self-government and transfer them to a general and consolidated government, without regard to the special delegations and reservations solemnly agreed to in that compact, is not for the peace, happiness, or prosperity of these States; and that therefore this commonwealth is determined . . . to submit to undelegated, and consequently unlimited powers in no man, or body of men on earth: that in cases of an abuse of the delegated powers, the members of the general government, being chosen by the people, a change by the people would be the constitutional remedy; but, where powers are assumed which have not been delegated, a nullification of the act is the rightful remedy: that every State has a natural right in cases not within the compact . . . to nullify of their own authority all assumptions of power by others within their limits. . . .

[It was with "its co-States" alone that the legislature should properly communicate, since the states were "solely authorized to judge" the constitutionality of federal acts, "congress being not a party, but merely the creature of the compact." Then Jefferson pointed out the consequences of allowing the statutes in question to stand unchallenged.]

. . . that the General government may place any act they think proper on the list of crimes, and punish it themselves whether enumerated or not enumerated by the constitution as cognisable by them; that they may transfer it's cognisance to the President, or any other person, who may himself be the accuser, counsel, judge and jury, whose *suspicions* may be the evidence, his *order* the sentence, his officer the executioner, and his breast the sole record of the transaction: that a very numerous and valuable description of the inhabitants of these states being, by this precedent, reduced, as Outlaws, to the absolute dominion of one man, and the barrier of the constitution thus swept away for us all, no rampart now remains against the passions and the powers of a majority in Congress, to protect from a like exportation, or other more grievous punishment the minority of the same body...who may venture to reclaim the constitutional rights and liberties of the States and people, or who for other causes, good or bad, may be obnoxious to the views, or marked by the suspicions of the President, or be thought dangerous to his or their elections, or other interests public or personal: that the friendless alien has indeed been selected as the safest subject of a first experiment; but the citizen will soon follow, or rather, has already followed; for already has a Sedition act marked him as it's prey....

["Unless arrested," the Federalist program would drive America "into revolution and blood," and democracy would suffer throughout the world.]

It would be a dangerous delusion were a confidence in the men of our choice to silence our fears for the safety of our rights: that confidence is everywhere the parent of despotism—free government is founded in jealousy, and not in confidence; it is jealousy and not confidence which prescribes limited constitutions, to bind down those whom we are obliged to trust with power: that our Constitution has accordingly fixed the limits to which, and no further, our confidence may go; and let the honest advocate of confidence read the Alien and Sedition acts, and say if the Constitution has not been wise in fixing limits to the government it created, and whether we should be wise in destroying those limits. Let him say what the government is, if it be not a tyranny, which the men of our choice have conferred on our President, and the President of our choice has assented to....In questions of power, then, let no more be heard of confidence in man, but bind him down from mischief by the chains of the Constitution.

Jefferson's response had been prompted by his conviction that the Alien and Sedition Acts were part of a concerted plan to change the form of American government. A few weeks after dispatching the resolutions to Nicholas, he predicted a "federalist reign of terror" to Senator Stevens Thomson Mason of Virginia.

Monticello Oct. 11. [17]98.

For my own part I consider those laws as merely an experiment on the American mind to see how far it will bear an avowed violation of the constitution. If this goes down, we shall immediately see attempted another act of Congress, declaring that the President shall continue in office during life, reserving to another occasion the transfer of the succession to his heirs, and the establishment of the Senate for life.... That these things are in contemplation, I have no doubt, nor can I be confident of their failure, after the dupery of which our countrymen have shewn themselves susceptible.

The Kentucky Resolutions of 1798 were adopted by that state's legislature in November with the mention of nullification deleted. Together with the more moderate resolves Madison drafted and steered through the Virginia legislature in December, they went far toward curing Americans of their "dupery." On returning to Philadelphia in December, Jefferson found other promising signs that the climate of public opinion and the tide of political events were becoming more favorable to the Republicans. Letters from Europe indicated that the Directory sincerely wished to negotiate. In mid-January, Jefferson sent Madison that news and suggested that the time was ripe for him to publish his personal notes of the debates in the Federal Convention of 1787.

> Philadelphia, Jan. 16. [17] 99.
> In a society of members between whom & yourself is great mutual esteem & respect, a most anxious desire is expressed that you would publish your debates of the Convention. That these measures of the army, navy & direct tax will bring about a revulsion of public sentiment is thought certain, & that the constitution will then recieve a different explanation. Could those debates be ready to appear critically, their effect would be decisive. I beg of you to turn this subject in your mind. The arguments against it will be personal; those in favor of it moral; and something is required from you as a set-off against the sin of your retirement.... I pray you always to examine the seals of mine to you, & the strength of the impression. The suspicions against the government on this subject are strong.

Jefferson's admonition to Madison to examine the seals of his letters for signs of tampering betrayed the tense mood during the brief congressional session. In reopening his correspondence with Elbridge

Gerry, Jefferson was even more cautious. He concluded the letter with instructions that Gerry destroy "at least the 2d & 3d leaves." Written to a man who was politically loyal to Adams but unsympathetic to the principles of the High Federalists, Jefferson's statement of Republican policy was almost a party platform.

Philada. Jan. 26. 1799.

I do then with sincere zeal wish an inviolable preservation of our present federal constitution, according to the true sense in which it was adopted by the states, that in which it was advocated by it's friends, & not that which it's enemies apprehended, who therefore became it's enemies: and I am opposed to the monarchising it's features by the forms of it's administration, with a view to conciliate a first transition to a President & Senate for life, & from that to a hereditary tenure of these offices, & thus to worm out the elective principle. I am for preserving to the states the powers not yielded by them to the Union, & to the legislature of the Union it's constitutional share in the division of powers: and I am not for transferring all the powers of the states to the general government, & all those of that government to the Executive Branch. I am for a government rigorously frugal & simple, applying all the possible savings of the public revenue to the discharge of the national debt: and not for a multiplication of officers & salaries merely to make partizans, & for increasing, by every device, the public debt, on the principle of it's being a public blessing. I am for relying, for internal defence, on our militia solely till actual invasion, and for such a naval force only as may protect our coasts and harbours from such depredations as we have experienced: and not for a standing army in time of peace which may overawe the public sentiment; nor for a navy which by it's own expences and the eternal wars in which it will implicate us, will grind us with public burthens, & sink us under them. I am for free commerce with all nations, political connection with none, & little or no diplomatic establishment: and I am not for linking ourselves by new treaties with the quarrels of Europe; entering that field of slaughter to preserve their balance, or joining in the confederacy of kings to war against the principles of liberty. I am for freedom of religion, & against all maneuvres to bring about a legal ascendancy of one sect over another: for freedom of the press, & against

Engraving after a lost portrait by the Polish patriot Thaddeus Kosciusko, who depicted the Vice President with a crown of laurel

Engraving from Century *magazine of chair, bench, and table Jefferson put together for more comfortable letter-writing as he grew older*

all violations of the constitution to silence by force & not by reason the complaints or criticisms, just or unjust, of our citizens against the conduct of their agents. And I am for encouraging the progress of science in all it's branches; and not for raising a hue and cry against the sacred name of philosophy, for awing the human mind by stories of rawhead & bloody bones, to a distrust of its own vision & to repose implicitly on that of others; to go backwards instead of forwards to look for improvement, to believe that government, religion, morality, & every other science were in the highest perfection in ages of the darkest ignorance, and that nothing can ever be devised more perfect than what was established by our forefathers. To these I will add, that I was a sincere wellwisher to the success of the French revolution, and still wish it may end in the establishment of a free & wellordered republic: but I have not been insensible under the atrocious depredations they have committed on our commerce. The first object of my heart is my own country. In that is embarked my family, my fortune, & my own existence. I have not one farthing of interest, nor one fibre of attachment out of it, nor a single motive of preference of any one nation to another, but in proportion as they are more or less friendly to us.

Gerry did not acknowledge this letter, but if Jefferson was indeed seeking recruits for the Republicans, he found many others that winter and spring. Adams, surprising Federalists and Republicans alike, had abruptly announced that he would resume negotiations with the French as soon as the United States received assurances that new envoys would be received courteously. After returning to Monticello in March, Jefferson prepared an optimistic political summary for Thomas Lomax, a Tidewater Virginian.

Monticello Mar. 12. 1799.
The spirit of 1776. is not dead. It has only been slumbering. The body of the American people is substantially republican. But their virtuous feelings have been played on by some fact with more fiction. They have been the dupes of artful maneuvres, & made for a moment to be willing instruments in forging chains for themselves. But time & truth have dissipated the delusion, & opened their eyes. They see now that France has sincerely wished peace, & their seducers have wished

war, as well for the loaves & fishes which arise out of war expences, as for the chance of changing the constitution, while the people should have time to contemplate nothing but the levies of men and money. Pennsylvania, Jersey & N York are coming majestically round to the true principles.... Those three States will be solidly embodied in sentiment with the six Southern & Western ones.

While awaiting French assurances of good faith, Jefferson outlined to Madison a Republican program for developing public discussion during the summer. Because of his position and his own love of privacy, Jefferson was unwilling to become a public spokesman, but he encouraged others to write for the newspapers.

[Philadelphia,] Feb. 5. [17]99.

The public sentiment being now on the creen [careen], and many heavy circumstances about to fall into the republican scale, we are sensible that this summer is the season for systematic energies & sacrifices. The engine is the press. Every man must lay his purse & his pen under contribution. As to the former it is possible I may be obliged to assume something for you. As to the latter, let me pray & beseech you to set apart a certain portion of every post-day to write what may be proper for the public. Send it to me while here, & when I go away I will let you know to whom you may send so that your name shall be sacredly secret.

After March 1 Jefferson spent most of the year at Monticello, and as the spring and summer wore on, he carefully refrained from making any contributions of his own to the political war he had initiated. But he was always ready to act as host or to arrange meetings for Republicans who might wish to confer on public affairs. In August he wrote Wilson Cary Nicholas of the agenda he had planned for him and Madison with the Kentucky and Virginia legislatures.

Monticello, Aug. 26, [17]99.

I am deeply impressed with the importance of Virginia & Kentuckey pursuing the same track at the ensuing sessions of their legislatures. Your going thither furnishes a valuable opportunity of effecting it, and as mr. Madison will be at our assembly as well as yourself, I thought it important to procure a meeting between you. I therefore wrote to propose to him to ride to this place on Saturday or Sunday next supposing that both he and yourself might perhaps have some matter of business at our court which might render it less inconvenient for you to be here together on Sunday. I...hope and strongly urge your favoring us with a visit at the time proposed. Mrs. Madison, who was the bearer of my letter, assured me I might count on mr. M.'s being here. Not that I mentioned to her the object of my request, or that I should propose the same to you; because I presume the less said of such a meeting the better. I shall take care that Monroe shall dine with us.

Jefferson's role as party leader and coordinator of strategy was recognized by his enemies as well as his friends. He had planned to visit Madison at his home in Orange County en route to Philadelphia for the congressional session. Sadly, he wrote Madison that James Monroe had persuaded him such a meeting would be unwise.

Monticello Nov. 22. [17] 99.
Colo. Monroe dined with us yesterday, and on my asking his commands for you, he entered into the subject of the visit and dissuaded it entirely, founding the motives on the espionage of the little wretch in Charlottesville [the postmaster] who would make it a subject of some political slander, and perhaps of some political injury. I have yeilded to his representations, and therefore shall not have the pleasure of seeing you till my return from Philadelphia. I regret it sincerely, not only on motives of affection but of affairs. Some late circumstances change considerably the aspect of our situation and must affect the line of conduct to be observed. I regret it the more too, because from the commencement of the ensuing session, I shall trust the post offices with nothing confidential, persuaded that during the ensuing twelve-month they will lend their inquisitorial aid to furnish matter for new slanders. I shall send you as usual printed communications, without saying anything confidential on them. You will of course understand the cause.

George Washington BY WOODROW WILSON, 1897

James Madison's home, Montpelier

The "ensuing twelve-month" would be a critical period, since 1800 was an election year. The Federalists had begun quarreling among themselves and would never regain their strength of the year before. Jefferson clearly would be the Republican candidate. His fears of interference with his mail, however, meant that he had more leisure than usual that winter in Philadelphia. Madison did not receive the usual detailed, time-consuming descriptions of congressional politics, and Jefferson had time to consider such nonpolitical projects as the creation of a "broad & liberal & modern" university for Virginia. In that endeavor he sought the expert advice of Joseph Priestley, the British Unitarian clergyman-scientist who had emigrated to Pennsylvania.

Philadelphia Jan. 18. 1800.

We have in that state a college (Wm. & Mary) just well enough endowed to draw out the miserable existence to which a miserable constitution has doomed it. It is moreover eccentric in it's position, exposed to bilious diseases as all the lower country is, & therefore abandoned by the public care, as that part of the country itself is in a considerable degree by it's inhabitants. We wish to establish in the upper & healthier country, & more centrally for the state an University on a plan so broad & liberal & *modern,* as to be worth patronising with the public support, and be a temptation to the youth of other states to come, and drink of the cup of knolege & fraternize with us. The first step is to obtain a good plan; that is a judicious selection of the sciences, & a practicable grouping of some of them together, & ramifying of others, so as to adapt the professorships to our uses, & our means. In an institution meant chiefly for use, some branches of science, formerly esteemed, may be now omitted, so may others now valued in Europe, but useless to us for ages to come.... Now there is no one to whom this subject is so familiar as yourself.... To you therefore we address our sollicitations. And to lessen to you as much as possible the ambiguities of our object, I will venture even to sketch the sciences which seem useful & practicable for us, as they occur to me while holding my pen. Botany. Chemistry. Zoology. Anatomy. Surgery. Medecine. Natl. Philosophy. Agriculture. Mathematics. Astronomy. Geology. Geography. Politics. Commerce. History. Ethics. Law. Arts. Fine arts. This list is imperfect because I make it hastily, and because I am unequal to the subject. It is evident that some of these articles are too much for one professor & must therefore be ramified; others may be ascribed in groups to a single professor. This is the difficult part of

Joseph Priestley by Ellen Sharples

the work, & requires a head perfectly knowing the extent of each branch, & the limits within which it may be circumscribed; so as to bring the whole within the powers of the fewest professors possible, & consequently within the degree of expence practicable for us.

On the rare occasions when a confidential means of communication was available, Jefferson did what he could to supervise the campaign, or what passed for a campaign in 1800. Learning that two trusted friends planned to ride to Virginia, Jefferson wrote Governor James Monroe of Republican prospects in other regions as described to him by Aaron Burr ("113" in his code). The brilliant and flamboyant New York congressman had reported on the Federalist-Republican balance in that state's bicameral legislature. New York was one of several states in which the legislature appointed presidential electors.

[Philadelphia,] Jan. 12. 1800.
I have had today a conversation with 113, who has taken a flying trip here from N. Y. He says, they have really now a majority in the H. of R. but for want of some skilful person to rally around, they are disjointed, & will lose every question. In the Senate there is a majority of 8. or 9. against us. But in the new election which is to come on in April, three or 4. in the Senate will be changed in our favor; & in the H. of R. the county elections will still be better than the last: but still all will depend on the City election, which is of 12. members. At present there would be no doubt of our carrying our ticket there; nor does there seem to be time for any events arising to change that disposition. There is therefore the best prospect possible of a great & decided majority on a joint vote of the two houses. They are so confident of this that the Republican party there will not consent to elect either by districts or a general ticket. They chuse to do it by their legislature. I am told the Republicans of N. J. are equally confident, & equally anxious against an election either by districts or a general ticket.... Perhaps it will be thought I ought in delicacy to be silent on this subject. But you, who know me, know that my private gratifications would be most indulged by that issue which should leave me most at home. If anything supersedes this propensity, it is merely the desire to see this government brought back to it's republican principles.

At the end of the Senate session in May Jefferson was free to communicate in person with his trusted lieutenants in Virginia, and he carried news that made the outcome of the fall elections almost a foregone conclusion. Aaron Burr had done his work well in New York City where the April polls gave Republicans control of the state legislature. New York's support would probably insure a Republican victory in November. In a later letter to Benjamin Rush, Jefferson recalled a painful meeting with John Adams shortly after word of those results reached Philadelphia.

Monticello Jan. 16. 1811.

Aaron Burr by Gilbert Stuart, 1794

On the day on which we learned in Philadelphia the vote of the city of New York, which it was well known would decide the vote of the state, and that again the vote of the Union, I called on Mr. Adams on some official business. He was very sensibly affected, and accosted me with these words: 'Well, I understand that you are to beat me in this contest, and I will only say that I will be as faithful a subject as any you will have.' 'Mr. Adams, said I, this is no personal contest between you & me. Two systems of principles on the subject of government divide our fellow-citizens into two parties. With one of these you concur, and I with the other. As we have been longer on the public stage than most of those now living, our names happen to be more generally known. One of these parties therefore has put your name at it's head, the other mine. Were we both to die to-day, tomorrow two other names would be in the place of ours, without any change in the motion of the machine. It's motion is from its principle, not from you or myself.' 'I believe you are right, said he, that we are but passive instruments, and should not suffer this matter to affect our personal dispositions.'

In large part as a reward for his role in winning New York, Burr was chosen as Jefferson's running mate at a caucus of congressional Republicans. Perhaps because Adams's partisans knew they had little chance of victory, they launched an extremely vicious campaign in the press. The President's decision to send envoys to France at the end of 1799 had destroyed any war issue the Federalists might have hoped to use and had infuriated Alexander Hamilton, the Inspector General of the provisional troops which were now disbanded. Hamilton had mobilized strong opposition to Adams within his own party, and Federalist journalists had little to offer on their own behalf but slanders on Jefferson. That year he was accused of every sin from Jacobinism to atheism. He ignored most of these calumnies but could not resist replying to one Uriah McGregory of Connecticut, who had inquired concerning reports that Jefferson had defrauded a poverty-stricken widow and her children. Although Jefferson cautioned the unknown McGregory to keep his reply secret, he must have expected and hoped that it would be publicized.

Monticello Aug. 13. 1800.

From the moment that a portion of my fellow citizens looked towards me with a view to one of their highest offices, the floodgates of calumny have been opened upon me; not where I am personally known, where their slanders would be instantly judged and suppressed from a general sense of their falsehood; but in the remote parts of the union, where the means of detection are not at hand, and the trouble of an enquiry is greater than would suit the hearers to undertake. I know that I might have filled the courts of the United States with actions for these slanders, & have ruined perhaps many persons who are not innocent. But this would be no equivalent to the loss of character. I leave them therefore to the reproof of their own consciences. If these do not condemn them, there will yet come a day when the false witness will meet a judge who has not slept over his slanders.

With trusted personal friends, Jefferson could be more frank about his anger at attacks on his character. Sermons preached from some pulpits concerning his religious views prompted Jefferson to send Benjamin Rush a personal defense that evolved into a stirring statement of his views on freedom of conscience versus religious bigotry.

Monticello Sep. 23. 1800.

I promised you a letter on Christianity, which I have not forgotten. On the contrary it is because I have reflected on it, that I find much more time necessary for it than I can at present dispose of. I have a view of the subject which ought to displease neither the rational Christian or Deist; & would reconcile many to a character they have too hastily rejected. I do not know however that it would reconcile the genus irritabile vatum, who are all in arms against me. Their hostility is on too interesting ground to be softened. The delusions into which the XYZ plot shewed it possible to push the people, the successful experiment made under the prevalence of that delusion, on the clause of the constitution which while it secured the freedom of the press, covered also the freedom of religion, had given to the clergy a very favorite hope of obtaining an establishment of a particular form of Christianity, thro' the US. And as every sect believes it's own form the true one, every one perhaps hoped for it's own: but especially the Episcopalians & Congregationalists. The returning good sense of our country threatens abortion to their hopes, & they believe that any portion of power confided to me will be exerted in opposition to their schemes. And they believe truly. For I have sworn upon the altar of god eternal hostility against every form of tyranny over the mind of man.

At the end of November, Jefferson left Monticello for the last time as Vice President. He would await final news of the election at Washington, the new capital city on the Potomac. By mid-December, his and Burr's victory in the state votes for electors was confirmed. But Federalists in Congress were not ready to admit defeat. Under the cumbersome system for choosing a President each elector was granted two votes, but the Constitution did not stipulate that these could be cast separately for President and Vice President. If each Republican elector cast votes for Jefferson and Burr, the two would be tied and the final decision would rest in a vote by the House of Representatives. To allow for this, the Republicans planned to withhold a few votes from Burr. Jefferson presented the problem to the vice-presidential candidate, tactfully combining a discussion of a possible tie vote with a gracious compliment to Burr's abilities.

Public Men, SULLIVAN

The city of Washington in 1800

Aaron Burr's daughter, Theodosia, was engaged to Joseph Alston of South Carolina who supported his prospective father-in-law against Jefferson in the House vote.

Washington Dec. 15. 1800.

Although we have not official information of the votes for President & Vice President...yet the state of the votes is given on such evidence, as satisfies both parties that the two Republican candidates stand highest....we know enough to be certain that what it is surmised will be withheld will still leave you 4. or 5. votes at least above Mr. A. However it was badly managed not to have arranged with certainty what seems to have been left to hazard. It was the more material because I understand several of the highflying federalists have expressed their hope that the two republican tickets may be equal, & their determination in that case to prevent a choice by the H. of R. (which they are strong enough to do) and let the government devolve on a President of the Senate. Decency required that I should be so entirely passive during the late contest that I never once asked whether arrangements had been made to prevent so many from dropping votes intentionally as might frustrate half the republican wish; nor did I doubt till lately that such had been made.

While I must congratulate you, my dear Sir, on the issue of this contest, because it is more honourable and doubtless more grateful to you than any station within the competence of the chief magistrate, yet for myself, and for the substantial service of the public, I feel most sensibly the loss we sustain of your aid in our new administration. It leaves a chasm in my arrangements, which cannot be adequately filled up.

The tie Jefferson had feared occurred in the Electoral College: Jefferson and Burr received 73 votes each; Adams and Thomas Pinckney were given 65 and 64 votes, respectively. High Federalists then tried to play the Republican victors against one another in the House vote, which was to be by state delegations, each having only one vote. Luckily for the Republicans, Alexander Hamilton was an even more bitter foe of Burr than of Jefferson, and he urged friends in Congress to accept Jefferson. Senator Gouverneur Morris of New York led a move to gain some preliminary promises from Jefferson as a price for Federalist support. In the midst of this bitter scene—the balloting stretched over a period of six days—Jefferson consulted with Adams. In retelling the incident a dozen years later in the letter to Rush, he recaptured his surprise and pain at the President's reaction.

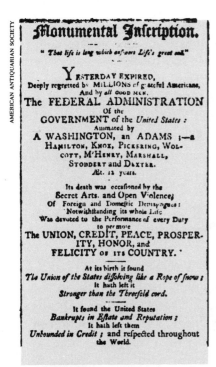

The Columbian Centinel *of Boston lamented Jefferson's election and the expiration of an "animated" government under the Federalists.*

Monticello Jan. 16. 1811.

When the election between Burr and myself was kept in suspence by the federalists, and they were meditating to place the President of the Senate at the head of the government, I called on Mr. Adams with a view to have this desperate measure prevented by his negative. He grew warm in an instant, and said with a vehemence he had not used towards me before, 'Sir, the event of the election is within your own power. You have only to say you will do justice to the public creditors, maintain the navy, and not disturb those holding offices, and the government will instantly be put into your hands. We know it is the wish of the people it should be so.' — 'Mr. Adams, said I, I know not what part of my conduct, in either public or private life, can have authorised a doubt of my fidelity to the public engagements. I say however I will not come into the government by capitulation. I will not enter on it but in perfect freedom to follow the dictates of my own judgment'.... 'Then, said he, things must take their course.' I turned the conversation to something else, and soon took my leave.

Jefferson held firm. He made no promises to the Federalists, and at last, on the thirty-sixth ballot, the House gave him a majority; Federalists in Vermont and Maryland abstained from voting, throwing their states' two votes to Jefferson. The President-elect described the situation to Madison, closing his report on the House vote with a hopeful prediction.

Washington Feb. 18. 1801.

The minority in the H. of R. after seeing the impossibility of electing B. the certainty that a legislative usurpation would be resisted by arms, and a recourse to a Convention to reorganise and amend the government, held a consultation on this dilemma, whether it would be better for them to come over in a body and go with the tide of the times, or by a negative conduct suffer the election to be made by a bare majority, keeping their body entire & unbroken, to act in phalanx on such ground of opposition as circumstances shall offer? We knew their determination on this question only by their vote of yesterday.... There were 10. states for one candidate, 4. for another, & 2. blanks. We consider this therefore as a declaration of war, on the part of this band. But their conduct appears to have brought over to us the whole body of the Federalists, who being alarmed with the danger of a dissolution of the government, had been made most anxiously to wish the very administration they had opposed. . . . They see too their quondam leaders separated fairly from them & themselves aggregated under other banners. . . . This circumstance, with the unbounded confidence which will attach to the new ministry as soon as known, will start us on high ground.

On this optimistic note Jefferson ended his term as Vice President. On February 25, eight days after the deadlock was broken, he sent a message to Thomas Lomax.

> Washington Feb. 25. 1801.
> The suspension of public opinion from the 11th. to the 17th. the alarm into which it threw all the patriotic part of the federalists, the danger of the dissolution of our union, and unknown consequences of that, brought over the great body of them to wish with anxiety & sollicitude for a choice to which they had before been strenuously opposed. In this state of mind they separated from their Congressional leaders, and came over to us; and the manner in which the last ballot was given, has drawn a fixed line of separation between them and their leaders. . . . I am persuaded that week of ill-judged conduct here, has strengthened us more than years of prudent and conciliatory administration could have done. If we can once more get social intercourse restored to it's pristine harmony, I shall believe we have not lived in vain. And that it may, by rallying them to true republican principles, which few of them had thrown off, I sanguinely hope.

As Jefferson contemplated his duties as Chief Executive, he offered few of the plaintive requests that he be left in domestic retirement with which he had met earlier moves to keep him in public life. He could no longer aim to secure "true republican principles" by urging others to fight tyranny while he withdrew to Monticello. As Madison had recognized in 1796 when he had been urged to seek the Presidency, only Jefferson himself could command the broad public support necessary to counter the policies established during the Federalist era. In 1801 Jefferson accepted that verdict as well.

A Picture Portfolio

Foremost Republican

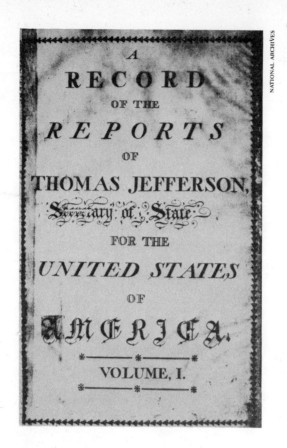

A RECORD OF THE REPORTS OF THOMAS JEFFERSON, Secretary of State FOR THE UNITED STATES OF AMERICA.

VOLUME, I.

FIRST SECRETARY OF STATE

In 1789 Jefferson returned home from France for what he expected to be a short leave; instead, he found that George Washington, the nation's first President, had named him to the top-ranking position in his Cabinet—Secretary of State. Although reluctant to quit his post in Paris, Jefferson deferred to Washington's desire: "You are to marshal us as may best be for the public good.... My chief comfort will be to work under your eye." He first met Alexander Hamilton, the brilliant thirty-three-year-old Secretary of the Treasury and his next in rank, at a dinner at the President's House in New York City shortly after he reported for duty in March, 1790. Although the mural at right, painted at a later date by Constantino Brumidi for the Capitol, shows Washington in peaceful consultation with Jefferson and Hamilton, from the outset the two Secretaries were, in Jefferson's words, "pitted like cocks." Jefferson, a republican, a realist, and a nationalist, considered Hamilton an elitist with monarchical leanings, a romantic, and a sectionalist. They often joined in bitter battles, and a torn Washington wrote to Jefferson: "I regret, deeply regret, the difference in opinions which have arisen and divided you and another principal officer of the Government...I have a great, a sincere esteem for you both." As head of the infant Department of State, Jefferson was concerned with matters that ranged from granting patents and devising a uniform system of weights and measures to securing markets for American goods and establishing an untrammeled right of access to the sea via the Mississippi River. He kept a careful record, in handsome folios, of all his reports to Congress; the title page of the first volume is reproduced above.

POLITICAL PROGRESSION

The seat of government was moved to Philadelphia in 1790. The Department of State occupied the building at far left, shown with the house in which Jefferson had drafted the Declaration of Independence. In 1793 he rented a charming house on the Schuylkill River (above), but retired at the end of that year. Three years later he became Vice President under his once good friend John Adams (above, right), and in 1800 the tables turned as the victory flag (right) proclaimed: "T. Jefferson President . . . John Adams no more."

307

"FOR JEFFERSON AND LIBERTY"

Jefferson's narrow election was seen by him later as a second American Revolution —"as real a revolution in the principles of government as that of 1776 was in form." He appointed a strong Cabinet, chief among them his close friend James Madison (below, left) as Secretary of State, and declared at the end of his term that he would select the same men if he had to choose again. Madison and his wife Dolley (below, right) lived with Jefferson in the President's House, seen in the center distance in an 1800 view of Washington (above), until they could find their own lodgings. The new President (right in an 1805 portrait by Rembrandt Peale) was honored with a patriotic song: "Rejoice! Columbia's Sons, rejoice! To Tyrants never bend your knee, but join with Heart and Soul and Voice for Jefferson and Liberty."

of kings to govern him? ... history — answer this question.

Let us then with courage and confidence pursue our principles of federal republicanism or republican federalism, kindly separated by nature & a wide ocean from the exterminating havoc of one quarter of the globe; too high minded to endure the degradations of the others; possessing a chosen country, with room enough for our descendants to the thousandth generation, enjoying the most favorable temperatures of climate, entertaining a due sense of our equal right to the use of our own faculties, to the acquisitions of our own industry, to honour & confidence from our fellow-citizens resulting not from birth but from our own good actions, enlightened by a benign religion, professed indeed and practised in various forms, yet all of them inculcating honesty, truth, temperance, gratitude & the love of man, acknoleging & adoring an overruling providence which, by all it's dispensations proves that it delights in the happiness of man here, and his greater happiness hereafter; with all these blessings what more is necessary to make us a happy & a prosperous people? still one thing more, fellow citizens, a wise & frugal government, which shall restrain men from injuring one another, shall leave them otherwise free to regulate their own pursuits of industry and improvement, and shall not take from the mouth of labour the bread it has earned. this is the sum of good government, and this is necessary to close the circle of our felicities.

About to enter, fellow citizens, on the exercise of duties which comprehend every thing dear & valuable to you, it is proper you should understand what I deem the essential principles of our government, and consequently those which are to shape it's administration. I will compress them within the shortest compass they will bear, stating only the general principle, without it's limitations.

equal and exact justice to all men of whatever state or persuasion, religious or political.

peace, commerce, and honest friendship with all nations, alliance with none.

the support of the state governments in their constitutional rights, as the most competent administrations for our domestic concerns, and our surest bulwarks against antirepublican tendencies.

the preservation of the general government in it's whole constitutional vigour, as the sheet anchor of our peace at home, and safety abroad.

free & frequent elections by the people in person & the more frequent within the limits of their convenience, and the more extensive the right of suffrage, the more perfectly within the definition of a genuine republic:

absolute acquiescence in the decisions of the majority, the vital principle of republics, from which is no appeal but to force, the vital principle and the parent of despotism.

economy in public expence, that labour may enjoy it's earnings:

a well disciplined militia, our best reliance in peace, & for the first moments of war, till regulars may relieve them:

the honest paiment of debts:

encouragement of agriculture, and of commerce as it's handmaid:

the diffusion of information, & arraignment of all abuses at the bar of the public reason:

freedom of religion: freedom of the press:

freedom of person, under the never ceasing protection of the Hab. corp.

and trial by juries impartially selected.

MANUSCRIPT DIVISION, LIBRARY OF CONGRESS

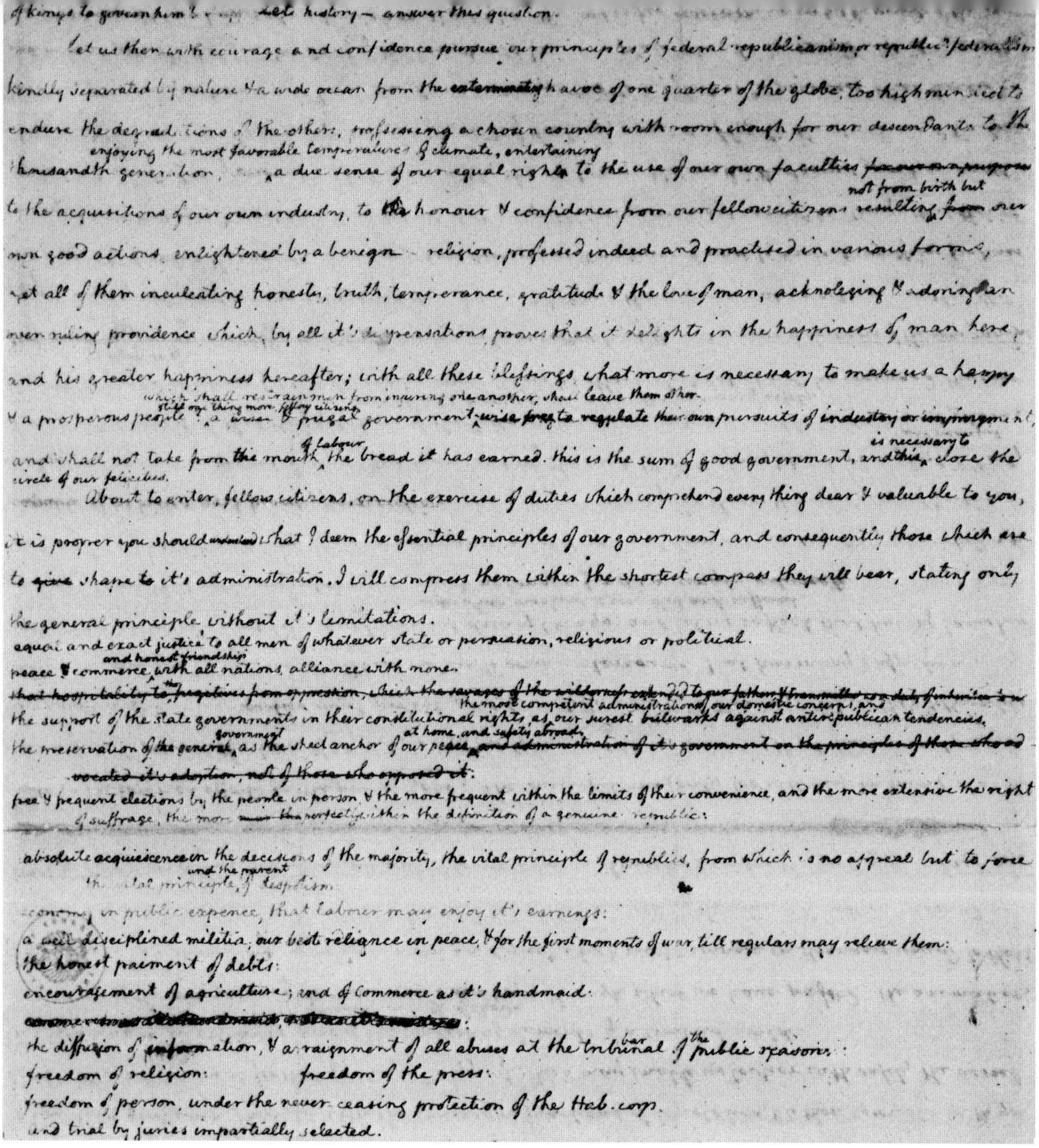

FORMIDABLE OPPONENTS

Jefferson was sworn in with Vice President Aaron Burr (right) by the Federalist Chief Justice John Marshall (right, above). In different ways these two men were to plague his Presidency. Jefferson's inaugural speech (part of which appears above) sought to bind up wounds from the bitter campaign: "We are all republicans: we are all federalists." He was incensed, however, to discover that John Adams had worked feverishly the night before appointing to the judiciary men who were his "most ardent political enemies." One of these "midnight judges," William Marbury, deprived of his commission by the new administration, brought his case to the Supreme Court. Marshall backed away from a direct confrontation with the executive in the *Marbury* v. *Madison* decision (reported in the *Aurora,* far right), but he established the right of the federal courts to annul an act of Congress. Marshall was pitted against Jefferson again in 1807 when Burr was charged with treason for attempting to raise troops to separate the West from the Union. Although Jefferson sought a conviction, Marshall presided over a trial that ended in acquittal.

SURGO UT PROSIM.

PHILADELPHIA:

FRIDAY, FEBRUARY 4, 1803.

FROM WASHINGTON.
JANUARY, 31, 1803.

" This day a debate took place of about
four hours, in the senate, upon an application made by Mr. *Marbury* of this
place, one of the *midnight appointments* of
Mr. Adams, as justice of the peace, for
a copy of such part of the executive record of the senate, as related to his nomination and approval by that body. In
this debate all the orators on both sides
spoke : we have not time to give the detailed debate, but the question was lost
13 to 15.

This business is connected with the
celebrated *Mondamus* affair of last year ;
Marbury being the person *used* by the
tories to blow up this bubble.

The petition of the *dislocated* judges
which was lately before the house of representatives, has been also before the
senate. A committee consisting of all
on one side was appointed to gratify
them, e. g. *James Ross, Gouverneur Morris* and *Jonathan Dayton* :—it will be readily conceived that they have made a
thundering report, and that it is up to the
hub, and calculated to rescue the people
from their worst enemies ! it is the order
of the day for Wednesday next ; and the
report goes that the New-York *Gouverneur*
and our would be *Gouverneur* Ross and
the would-be governor and clerk in chancery of Jersey, Ogden, are all to make
a *great noise* on that day—they mean to
shew themselves before the 4th of March
and as the thief said at Tyburn, to die
hard—die all, die nobly, die like demi gods.

The house of representatives sat with
closed doors this day, on what business is
not to be ascertained. It was reported
that it was on a motion intended to go to
the expulsion of *Rutledge* ; this is not
however, so certain as that the public
mind is much irritated at the length of
time he has been suffered to sit in the
house after the proofs have been brought
so completely home to him. There are
other circumstances concerning this man's
arts of a similar nature that have been
brought to light within a few days, and
which shall be published very speedily if
no steps are taken by the house of representatives to purify congress. Some of
the members have shewn a very honorable sense of their own dignity, a very
large number of the members declared
their determination not to remain in the
house should he be called to the chair in
committee. This has had its due effect
so far. There are others who do not appear to feel the same respect for themselves nor for the character of the government of the country which the forge-
ries were intended to dishonor."

TRIPOLITAN SHAKEDOWN

Jefferson had long been disturbed by the humiliating practice of paying a yearly, and sizable, tribute to the Barbary States for safe passage of ships in the Mediterranean. In 1801, when the Pasha of Tripoli tried to raise the ante, the President responded in characteristic fashion by sending a squadron to blockade the Tripoli coast. The *Philadelphia,* built in 1799 (right), was captured; but Lt. Stephen Decatur and seventeen volunteers slipped into the harbor at night and set fire to her (far right). During an attack on Tripoli in 1804 (opposite, above), he led his crew aboard a Tripolitan gunboat (above) and shot the captain.

312

BY BRUMIDI; ARCHITECT OF THE CAPITOL, WASHINGTON, D.C.

MUSIC DIVISION, LIBRARY OF CONGRESS

THE LOUISIANA PURCHASE

Even before Jefferson had brought the Tripolitan War to a successful conclusion in 1805, he scored one of the greatest diplomatic victories in American history. Since 1763 Spain had owned the Louisiana Territory, 828,000 square miles of virgin land west of the Mississippi, including the strategic port of New Orleans. In the spring of 1802, Jefferson discovered that Spain had secretly ceded the vast expanse to a powerful France under the ambitious Napoleon Bonaparte. Immediately he wrote the American minister in France, Robert R. Livingston: "There is on the globe one single spot, the possessor of which is our natural and habitual enemy. It is New Orleans." He dispatched able James Monroe to bolster Livingston in negotiations (above) with François de Barbé-Marbois, the French Finance Minister, to buy New Orleans and West Florida. Unexpectedly, Napoleon offered them not only New Orleans but the entire Louisiana Territory. Astonished, they accepted and for less than three cents an acre doubled the size of the United States. Jefferson was wildly acclaimed as the American flag was raised over New Orleans on December 20, 1803 (pictured in a later painting at right). In 1809 a national song (left) was published in honor of the event.

PATHFINDERS FOR AMERICA

Jefferson had long been intrigued by the uncharted lands to the west. He had urged Congress to finance a mission "even to the Western Ocean," and one was preparing to depart as the momentous news arrived from Paris of the Louisiana Purchase. Meriwether Lewis and William Clark led the expedition to map the Missouri River and are seen above after they had reached its headwaters and were proceeding west on horseback. They sent Jefferson the painted buffalo hide (right, above) depicting a Mandan Indian attack. On November 7, 1805, their diary records: "Ocian in View! O! the joy!" A detail from Clark's remarkable map (right) delineates Cape Disappointment on the estuary of the Columbia River.

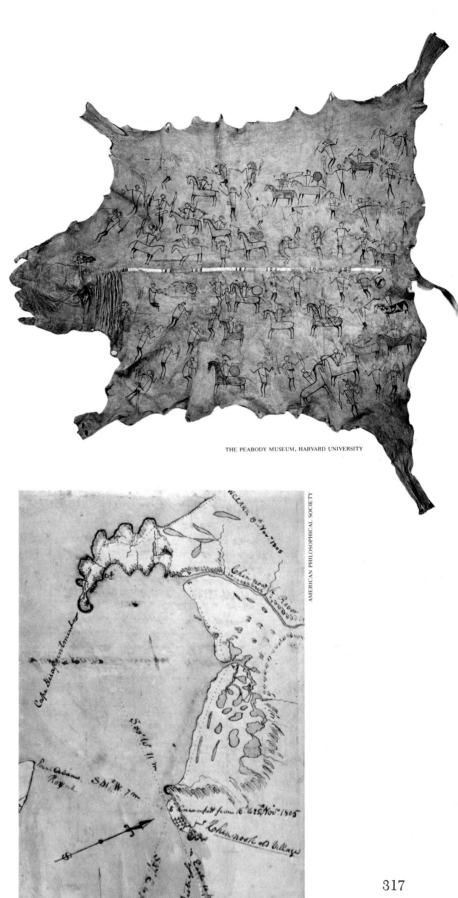

317

In response to hostile acts of Britain, Congress passed the Embargo Act in 1807. This

cartoon shows Jefferson trying to calm the opposition, especially from New England.

THE GLORIOUS FOURTH

As President, the author of the Declaration of Independence
characteristically discouraged suggestions to celebrate his
own birthday in favor of that of his country—the Fourth of
July. He must have approved the 1819 Philadelphia celebration (above), for he had held similar galas on the White House
lawn. When asked in 1826 to help mark the fiftieth anniversary
of the Declaration of Independence, he was mortally ill. But
his carefully drafted letter of June 24 expressing his regrets
(right) was a masterpiece containing the unmistakable sentiments that had shaped his life. Fittingly, he breathed his last
on that very "Glorious Fourth."

320

Respected Sir   Monticello June 24. 26

   The kind invitation I recieve from you on the part of the citizens of the city of Washington, to be present with them at their celebration of the 50th anniversary of American independance; as one of the surviving signers of an instrument, pregnant with our own, and the fate of the world, is most flattering to myself, and heightened by the honorable accompaniment proposed for the comfort of such a journey. it adds sensibly to the sufferings of sickness, to be deprived by it of a personal participation in the rejoicings of that day. but acquiescence is a duty, under circumstances not placed among those we are permitted to controul. I should indeed, with peculiar delight, have met and exchanged there, congratulations personally, with the small band, the remnant of that host of worthies, who joined with us, on that day, in the bold and doubtful election we were to make, for our country, between submission, or the sword; and to have enjoyed with them the consolatory fact that our fellow citizens, after half a century of experience and prosperity, continue to approve the choice we made. may it be to the world what I believe it will be, (to some parts sooner, to others later, but finally to all,) the Signal of arrousing men to burst the chains, under which monkish ignorance and superstition had persuaded them to bind themselves, and to assume the blessings & security of self government. the form which we have substituted restores the free right to the unbounded exercise of reason and freedom of opinion. all eyes are opened, or opening to the rights of man. the general spread of the light of science has already laid open to every view the palpable truth that the mass of mankind has not been born, with saddles on their backs, nor a favored few booted and spurred, ready to ride them legitimately, by the grace of god. these are grounds of hope for others. for selves let the annual return of this day, for ever refresh our recollections of these n and an undiminished devotion to them.

Chapter 11

Third President

A just and solid republican government maintained here," Jefferson wrote shortly after his inauguration in 1801, "will be a standing monument and example for the aim and imitation of the people of other countries; . . . they will see from our example that a free government is of all others the most energetic." This was the credo of his first administration, a belief that he could and must vindicate republican principles in practice as vigorously as he had presented them in theory during the years of Federalist rule.

Many of his theories already seemed to have been borne out in fact. For years he had disagreed with the European philosophers' argument that a republic could survive "only in a small territory." Pointing out the support he and his party had received from the expanding West, Jefferson re- marked, "The reverse is the truth. Had our territory been even a third only of what it is, we were gone. But while frenzy & delusion like an epidimic, gained certain parts, the residue remained sound & untouched, and held on till their brethren could recover from the temporary delusion." Similarly, the refusal of Federalist congressmen to heed their leaders and rob him of his election after the tie in the Electoral College confirmed his faith in the sense of justice of men in all parties. "The order and good sense displayed . . . in the momentous crisis which lately arose," he wrote Joseph Priestley, "really bespeak a strength of character in our nation which augers well for the duration of our republic, and I am much better satisfied now of it's stability than I was before it was tried."

Jefferson's views on the methods of insuring that stability were well known. Americans expected modifications of the Hamiltonian system of finance; economies in government, including a reduction of military forces; and a more balanced consideration of the interests of the South and West against the demands of the Northeast. They knew, too, that there would be a different tone and style in government and that Jefferson would not tolerate any "monarchical" trappings. But beyond this, there was much concern over just what a Jeffersonian government might mean. To disprove his Federalist critics and to win over congressmen and restless voters, Jefferson had to persuade his fellow citizens that they were truly one people with a potential for greatness. The Union, torn by the bitter debates of "Jacobins" and "Anglomen," Federalists and Republicans, must be restored. This theme of reunification was at the heart of Jefferson's inaugural message on March 4.

March 4. 1801

Let us then, fellow citizens, unite with one heart & one mind; let us restore to social intercourse that harmony & affection, without which Liberty, & even Life itself, are but dreary things.

And let us reflect that having banished from our land that religious intolerance under which mankind so long bled & suffered, we have yet gained little if we countenance a political intolerance, as despotic, as wicked & capable of as bitter & bloody persecution. . . .

But every difference of opinion, is not a difference of principle. We have called, by different names, brethren of the same principle. We are all republicans: we are all federalists. . . .

[Jefferson next answered his critics' charge that a republican government "cannot be strong" by citing America's natural resources and traditions of liberty, which he said could make the country the "strongest government on earth." He then listed the principles on which his republican administration would be based.]

With all these blessings, what more is necessary to make us a happy and a prosperous people? Still one thing more, fellow citizens a wise & frugal government, which shall restrain men from injuring one another, shall leave them otherwise free to regulate their own pursuits of industry & improvement, and shall not take from the mouth of labour the bread it has earned.

This is the sum of good government, & this is necessary to close the circle of our felicities.

About to enter, fellow citizens, on the exercise of duties which comprehend everything dear & valuable to you, it is proper that you should understand what I deem the essential principles of our government and consequently those which ought to shape it's administration. . . .

Equal & exact justice to all men, of whatever state

Jefferson presidential medal, 1801

of persuasion, religious or political:

Peace, commerce, & honest friendship with all nations, entangling alliances with none:

The support of the State governments in all their rights, as the most competent administrations for our domestic concerns, and the surest bulwarks against anti republican tendencies:

The preservation of the general government, in it's whole constitutional vigor, as the sheet anchor of our peace at home, & safety abroad.

A jealous care of the right of election by the people, a mild and safe corrective of abuses, which are lopped by the sword of revolution, where peaceable remedies are unprovided.

Absolute acquiescence in the decisions of the Majority the vital principle of republics, from which is no appeal but to force, the vital principle & immediate parent of despotism.

A well disciplined militia, our best reliance in peace, & for the first moments of war, till regulars may relieve them: The Supremacy of the Civil over the Military authority:

Economy in public expense, that labor may be lightly burdened:

The honest paiment of our debts and sacred preservation of the public faith:

Encouragement of Agriculture, & of Commerce as it's handmaid:

The diffusion of information, & arraignment of all abuses at the bar of the public reason:

Freedom of Religion, freedom of the press, & freedom of Person under the protection of the Habeas corpus: And trial by juries, impartially selected.

MAD TOM in A RAGE

This 1801 cartoon illustrates the Federalist fear that Jefferson and friends such as "Mad Tom" Paine would pull down the government.

Jefferson saw his election as an opportunity to continue the Revolution, to reaffirm its goals, and to return America to the course envisioned by himself and other revolutionaries in 1776. One of the most touching letters of his Presidency went to Samuel Adams, the Boston leader who was spending his old age in obscurity, a victim of Federalist abuse. Jefferson wrote that his inaugural address was a tribute to Adams and to all like him who had seen the Revolution distorted by Federalist administrations.

Washington Mar. 29. 1801.

I addressed a letter to you, my very dear and antient

Public Men, SULLIVAN

Samuel Adams of Massachusetts

friend, on the 4th of March: not indeed to you by name, but through the medium of some of my fellow citizens, whom occasion called on me to address.

In meditating the matter of that address, I often asked myself, is this exactly in the spirit of the patriarch of liberty, Samuel Adams? Is it as he would express it? Will he approve of it? I have felt a great deal for our country in the times we have seen: but individually for no one so much as yourself. When I have been told that you were avoided, insulated, frowned on, I could but ejaculate, 'Father, forgive them, for they know not what they do.' I confess I felt an indignation for you, which for myself I have been able under every trial to keep entirely passive. However, the storm is over, and we are in port. The ship was not rigged for the service she was put on. We will show the smoothness of her motions on her republican tack.

Jefferson was eager to begin setting the government on its new tack, but he was hampered in the months immediately after his inauguration by a Federalist-dominated Congress. The Seventh Congress, elected in the Republican sweep of 1800, would not meet until the following December. Before the Senate adjourned in March, however, Jefferson's first Cabinet appointments were approved: Madison for the State Department and two Massachusetts Republicans, Levi Lincoln and Henry Dearborn, as Attorney General and Secretary of War. Jefferson's Secretary of the Treasury would be Albert Gallatin, the brilliant Swiss immigrant who had succeeded Madison as Republican House leader; but Gallatin's nomination was withheld until the recess so that it would be considered by a more sympathetic Senate. The office of Secretary of the Navy, hardly a prize since Jefferson was known to favor radical reductions in that department, remained vacant until Robert Smith of Baltimore finally accepted in July.

Jefferson's immediate concern, however, was not so much to fill vacancies as to create them. John Adams had spent his last days in office appointing his followers to every unfilled post. A dozen years later, Jefferson recalled his bitterness at this ploy: "The last day of his political power, the last hours, and even beyond the midnight, were employed in filling all offices, & especially permanent ones, with the bitterest federalists, and providing for me the alternative, either to execute the government by my enemies, whose study it would be to thwart & defeat all my measures, or to incur the odium of such numerous removals from office as might bear me down." Jefferson chose the course of removal; he had confided this decision to James Monroe three days after the inauguration.

Washington March 7. 1801.

I have firmly refused to follow the counsels of those who have advised the giving offices to some of their leaders, in order to reconcile. I have given and will give only to republicans, under existing circumstances. But I believe with others that deprivations of office, if made on the ground of political principle alone, would revolt our new converts, and give a body to leaders who now stand alone. Some I know must be made. They must be as few as possible, done gradually, and bottomed on some malversation or inherent disqualification.

In practice this meant that Jefferson would remove few officeholders solely because of their politics, but those few places, and others that became vacant because of resignations or deaths, would be given only to Republicans. Jefferson decided, however, that he could remove immediately any obviously incompetent and corrupt officials and all those Adams had appointed since December. The occasion for presenting his policies publicly came in June when he received a formal remonstrance from Federalists in New Haven. At the urging of local Republicans, he had replaced the recent Adams appointment as collector of customs there with a member of his own party. Jefferson replied to the remonstrance with an indictment of Federalist appointment policies, measures that he said forced him to take steps to give Republicans their "just share."

Washington July 12. 1801

Declarations by myself in favor of *political tolerance*, exhortations to *harmony* and affection in social intercourse, and to respect for the *equal rights* of the minority, have on certain occasions been quoted and misconstrued into assurances that the tenure of offices was to be undisturbed. But could candor apply such a construction? . . . When it is considered that during the late administration

Jefferson's draft form for telling some of Adams's recent appointees that they should regard their appointments "as if never made"

REMOVALS AND APPOINTMENTS.

The subsequent LIST contains the Names of the FEDERAL RE-PUBLICANS *who have been dismissed from office, by the Pre-sident of the United States, on account of their political opin-ions; together with the names of the Persons who have been ap-pointed in their places, since the 4th of March, 1801.*

1. John Wilkes Kittera, Attorney for the Eastern District of Pennsylvania, *dismissed;* Alexander James Dallas appointed in his room.

2. John Hall, Marshal of the same District, *dismissed;* John Smith appointed in his room.

3. Samuel Hodgdon, Superintendant of Public Stores at Phi-ladelphia, *dismissed;* William Irvine appointed in his room.

4. John Harris, Store-keeper at the same place, *dismissed;* Robert Jones, appointed in his room.

5. Henry Miller, Supervisor of the Revenue of the District of Pennsylvania, *dismissed;* Peter Muhlenberg appointed in his room.

6. J. M. Lingan, Attorney for the District of Columbia, *dis-missed;* Daniel Carrol Brent appointed in his room.

7. Thomas Swann, Attorney, *dismissed;* John Thompson Ma-son appointed in his room.

8. John Pierce, Commissioner of Loans for the State of New-Hampshire, *dismissed;* William Gardner appointed in his room.

9. Thomas Martin, Collector of the District of Portsmouth, in the same State, *dismissed;* Joseph Whipple appointed in his room.

10. Jacob Sheaffe, Navy Agent at Portsmouth, New-Hamp-shire, *dismissed;* Woodbury Langdon appointed in his room.

List appended to the New Haven remonstrance of those who had allegedly been removed from office "on account of their political opinions"

those who were not of a particular sect of politics were excluded from all office; when, by a steady pursuit of this measure nearly the whole offices of the US. were monopolized by that sect; when the public sentiment at length declared itself and burst open the doors of honor and confidence to those whose opinions they more ap-proved, was it to be imagined that this monopoly of office was still to be continued in the hands of the minority? Does it violate their *equal rights* to assert some rights in the majority also? Is it *political intolerance* to claim a proportionate share in the direction of the public affairs? Can they not *harmonize* in society unless they have every thing in their own hands? ...

...It would have been to me a circumstance of great relief had I found a moderate participation of office in the hands of the majority. I would gladly have left to time and accident to raise them to their just share. But their total exclusion calls for prompter correctives. I shall correct the procedure: but, that done, return with joy to that state of things, when the only questions con-cerning a candidate shall be, is he honest, is he capable, is he faithful to the constitution?

After a brief stay at Monticello in April, Jefferson moved into the barren President's House in the new capital, urging his Cabinet members to return to Washington as soon as possible. May brought the first major policy consideration in foreign affairs when reports arrived of new troubles in the Mediterranean. The pirates of Tripoli had resumed raids on American shipping and the Algerians grumbled menacingly at delays in the delivery of bribes promised by the Adams administration. The Cabinet met and lent its advice, and Jefferson reached a frugal but firm decision: cruisers no longer needed to harass the French in the Caribbean would sail to the Mediterranean to guard shipping from the Tripolitans and to deliver part of the overdue "tribute." He summarized this program for Wil-son Cary Nicholas, a senator from Virginia.

Washington June 11. 1801.

In March, finding we might with propriety call in our cruisers from the W. Indies, this was done; and as 6. were to be kept armed, it was thought best... that we should send 3. with a tender into the Mediterranean to protect our commerce against Tripoli. But as this might lead to war, I wished to have the approbation of the new ad-ministration.... It was the 15th. of May before Mr.

Jefferson was the first President to respond to the Barbary pirates with force; Tripoli declared war and was bombarded in August, 1804.

Gallatin's arrival enabled us to decide definitively. It was then decided unanimously...on the 1st. of June they sailed. With respect to Algiers they are in extreme ill humour. We find 3. years arrears of tribute due to them....We have however sent them 30,000. D[ollars] by our frigates as one year's tribute, and have a vessel ready to sail with the stores for another year....We have taken these steps towards supplying the deficiencies of our predecessors merely in obedience to the law; being convinced it is money thrown away, & that there is no end to the demands of these powers, nor any security in their promises. The real alternative before us is whether to abandon the Mediterranean, or to keep up a cruize in it, perhaps in rotation with other powers who would join us as soon as there is peace. But this, Congress must decide.

Jefferson's procedure in dealing with the demands of the Barbary pirates established the routine he would follow during his entire administration. As the Cabinet members reassembled in the fall for the legislative session, Jefferson circulated a letter to them outlining his views on the "mode & degrees of communication" between the President and the heads of departments. Although he couched this directive in tactful phrases, Jefferson made his position clear: the Attorney General and Secretaries would follow the procedures of close consultation instituted by Washington, not the haphazard measures followed by Adams.

Washington Nov. 6, 1801.

Having been a member of the first administration under Gen. Washington, I can state with exactness what our course then was. Letters of business came addressed, sometimes to the President, but most frequently to the

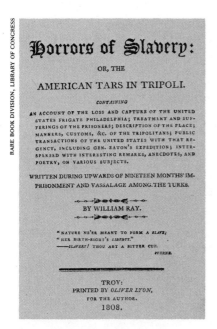

Title page of Horrors of Slavery, *a book in Jefferson's library by a man who had been imprisoned for nineteen months by the Tripolitans*

heads of departments. If addressed to himself, he referred them to the proper department to be acted on: if to one of the Secretaries, the letter, if it required no answer, was communicated to the President simply for his information. If an answer was requisite, the Secretary of the department communicated the letter & his proposed answer to the President. Generally they were simply sent back, after perusal, which signified his approbation. Sometimes he returned them with an informal note, suggesting an alteration or a query. If a doubt of any importance arose, he reserved it for conference. By this means, he was always in accurate possession of all facts and proceedings in every part of the Union, and to whatsoever department they related; he formed a central point for the different branches; preserved an unity of object and action among them, exercised that participation in the gestion of affairs which his office made incumbent on him, and met himself the due responsibility for whatever was done. During Mr. Adams's administration, his long and habitual absences from the seat of government rendered this kind of communication impracticable, removed him from any share in the transaction of affairs, and parcelled out the government in fact among four independent heads, drawing sometimes in opposite directions. That the former is preferable to the latter course cannot be doubted....

By the fall, Jefferson had already demonstrated his implementation of republican principles. The Cabinet would be an active group of councilors to the President, not merely a collection of administrators responsible only for their own departments. Incompetent officials would not be tolerated on any level. And frugality would be the new order, not merely because Jefferson abhorred waste but because he saw no room for expensive bureaucracy in a republic. The specific economies Jefferson proposed usually served more than one purpose. The Navy, for instance, had been reduced because he disapproved of large military establishments. The diplomatic service would be cut, he explained to William Short, not so much to save money as to insure America's freedom from European political interests.

Washington Oct. 3. 1801.

If we can delay but for a few years the necessity of vindicating the laws of nature on the ocean, we shall be the more sure of doing it with effect. The day is within my time as well as yours when we may say by what laws other nations shall treat us on the sea. And we will say it. In the meantime we wish to let every treaty we have drop off, without renewal. We call in our diplomatic missions, barely keeping up those to the most important nations. There is a strong disposition in our countrymen to discontinue even these; and very possibly it may be done. Consuls will be continued as usual. The interest which European nations feel as well as ourselves in the mutual patronage of commercial intercourse, is a sufficient stimulus on both sides to ensure that patronage.

In November, Jefferson received news that seemed to insure peace for those "few years." Napoleon, France's First Consul, had agreed to the Convention of 1800 setting aside the old Franco-American alliance and France and Great Britain had ended their war. European issues need no longer divide American political loyalties. Jefferson would henceforth have a free hand to pursue the program of financial retrenchment and reallocation of national resources that he presented to Congress in his first annual message.

Dec. 8. 1801.

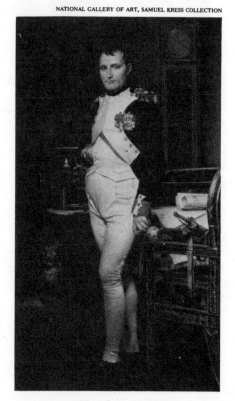

When we consider that this government is charged with the external and mutual relations only of these states that the states themselves have principal care of our persons, our property, and our reputation, constituting the great field of human concerns, we may well doubt whether our organisation is not too complicated, too expensive; whether offices or officers have not been multiplied unnecessarily, and sometimes injuriously to the service they were meant to promote. I will cause to be laid before you an essay towards a statement of those who, under public employment of various kinds, draw money from the treasury or from our citizens. Time has not permitted a perfect enumeration, the ramifications of office being too multipled and remote to be completely traced in a first trial. Among those who are dependant on Executive discretion, I have begun the reduction of what was deemed unnecessary.... Considering the general tendency to multiply offices and dependancies, and to increase expence to the ultimate term of burthen which the citizen can bear, it behoves us to avail ourselves of every occasion which presents itself for taking off the surcharge; that it never may be seen here that, after

Napoleon by David

leaving to labour the smallest portion of it's earnings on which it can subsist, government shall itself consume the whole residue of what it was instituted to guard.

[In presenting his economic policy, Jefferson did not advocate breaking faith with financial commitments made in the past, but in two other areas—the Judiciary Act passed early in 1801 and the Naturalization Act— he wanted to undo some of the damage from laws passed during the Adams administration.]

The Judiciary system of the United States, and especially that portion of it recently erected, will of course present itself to the contemplation of Congress. And that they may be able to judge of the proportion which the institution bears to the business it has to perform, I have caused to be procured from the several states, and now lay before Congress, an exact statement of all the causes decided since the first establishment of the courts, and of those which were depending when additional courts and judges were brought in to their aid. . . .

I cannot omit recommending a revisal of the laws on the subject of naturalisation. Considering the ordinary chances of human life, a denial of citizenship under a residence of fourteen years, is a denial to a great proportion of those who ask it: and controuls a policy pursued, from their first settlement, by many of these states, and still believed of consequence to their prosperity. And shall we refuse, to the unhappy fugitives from distress, that hospitality which the savages of the wilderness extended to our fathers arriving in this land? Shall oppressed humanity find no asylum on this globe?

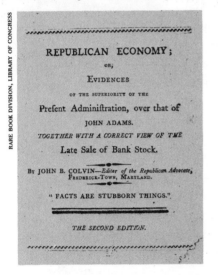

Albert Gallatin, above; below, Jefferson's copy of a book that extolled "Republican Economy"

Congress responded enthusiastically to the major portions of Jefferson's program. Federalists found their best issue in his request for repeal of the Judiciary Act—a statute that had expanded federal court jurisdiction and established an expensive judicial bureaucracy. Even this battle was won, despite some embarrassing occasions on which Vice President Burr used his tie-breaking vote to aid the Federalists. Congress restored the naturalization law of 1795—the Sedition Act had already expired—and also abolished the tangled system of internal taxes begun by Hamilton. Once this was done, Treasury Secretary Gallatin was free to present proposals for his own program. His first report was a call for reforms of the sinking fund, the fund set aside for repayment of the national debt. Jefferson congratulated him on the plans to simplify the fund's operation and suggested other modifications in Treasury policy that would make the department more republican and more economical.

Washington Apr. 1. 1802.

I have read and considered your report on the operations of the Sinking fund and entirely approve of it, as the best plan on which we can set out. I think it an object of great importance, to be kept in view, and to be undertaken at a fit season, to simplify our system of finance, and bring it within the comprehension of every member of Congress. Hamilton set out on a different plan. In order that he might have the entire government of his machine, he determined so to complicate it as that neither the President or Congress should be able to understand it, or to controul him. He succeeded in doing this, not only beyond their reach, but so that he at length could not unravel it himself. He gave to the debt, in the first instance, in funding it, the most artificial and mysterious form he could devise. He then moulded up his appropriations of a number of scraps & remnants many of which were nothing at all, and applied them to different objects in reversion and remainder until the whole system was involved in impenetrable fog, and while he was giving himself the airs of providing for the paiment of the debt, he left himself free to add to it continually as he did in fact instead of paying it. . . .

[Jefferson suggested the administration aim at a simple measure for the future reduction or increase of taxes.]

That is, to form into one consolidated mass all the monies recieved into the treasury, and to marshal the several expenditures, giving them a preference of paiment according to the order in which they should be arranged. As for example. 1. the interest of the public debt, 2. such portions of principal as are exigible. 3. the expences of government. 4. such other portions of principal, as . . . we are still free to pay when we please. The last object might be made to take up the residuum of money remaining in the treasury at the end of every year . . . and would be the barometer whereby to test the economy of the administration. It would furnish a simple measure by which every one could mete their merit, and by which every one could decide when taxes were deficient or superabundant. If to this can be added a simplification of the form of accounts in the treasury department, and in the organisation of it's officers, so as to bring every thing to a single center, we might hope to see the finances of the Union as clear and intelligible as a merchant's books, so that every member of Congress, and every man of any mind in the Union should be able to comprehend them, to investigate abuses, and consequently to controul them. . . .

[Repeal of internal taxes would allow certain economies within the department as well.]

We shall now get rid of the Commissioner of the internal revenue, and Superintendant of stamps. It remains to amalgamate the Comptroller and Auditor into one, and reduce the register to a clerk of accounts. . . . This constellation of great men in the treasury department was of a piece with the rest of Hamilton's plans. He took his own stand as a Lieutenant General, surrounded by his Major Generals, and stationing his brigadiers and Colonels under the name of Supervisors, Inspectors &c. in the different states. Let us deserve well of our country by making their interests the end of all our plans, and not our own pomp, patronage and irresponsibility.

Robert R. Livingston by Vanderlyn

A month before Congress adjourned in the spring news of events in Europe cast a pall over the optimistic economic program. Six months earlier, when Robert R. Livingston sailed to France as the new American minister, the government had heard rumors of a secret treaty under which Spain had surrendered the enormous Louisiana Territory to France. In April the rumors were confirmed. Although Madison had given Livingston firm instructions before he left, Jefferson felt the situation warranted a sharp reminder of American policy. He sent Livingston an outline of the threats and favors he might offer to save American rights to trade at New Orleans, a privilege that had finally been established by Pinckney's Treaty in 1795. Without New Orleans, American use of the Mississippi was a fiction. If the ambitious Napoleon gained control of the trans-Mississippi West, America's own territory would be in danger.

Washington, April 18, 1802.

The cession of Louisiana and the Floridas by Spain to France works most sorely on the U.S. . . . It compleatly re-

*A British map of the Mississippi,
drawn in 1763 from French surveys*

verses all the political relations of the U. S. and will form a new epoch in our political course. Of all nations of any consideration France is the one which hitherto has offered the fewest points on which we could have any conflict of right, and the most points of a communion of interests. From these causes we have ever looked to her as our *natural friend,* as one with which we never could have an occasion of difference. Her growth therefore we viewed as our own, her misfortunes ours. There is on the globe one single spot, the possessor of which is our natural and habitual enemy. It is New Orleans, through which the produce of three-eighths of our territory must pass to market...France placing herself in that door assumes to us the attitude of defiance. Spain might have retained it quietly for years. Her pacific dispositions, her feeble state, would induce her to increase our facilities there, so that her possession of the place would be hardly felt by us, and it would not perhaps be very long before some circumstance might arise which might make the cession of it to us the price of something of more worth to her. Not so can it ever be in the hands of France. The impetuosity of her temper, the energy and restlessness of her character, placed in a point of eternal friction with us, and our character, which though quiet, and loving peace and the pursuit of wealth, is high-minded, despising wealth in competition with insult or injury, enterprizing and energetic as any nation on earth, these circumstances render it impossible that France and the U. S. can continue long friends when they meet in so irritable a position. They as well as we must be blind if they do not see this; and we must be very improvident if we do not begin to make arrangements on that hypothesis. The day that France takes possession of N. Orleans fixes the sentence which is to restrain her forever within her low water mark. It seals the union of two nations who in conjunction can maintain exclusive possession of the ocean. From that moment we must marry ourselves to the British fleet and nation. We must turn all our attentions to a maritime force, for which our resources place us on very high ground: and having formed and cemented together a power which may render reinforcement of her settlements here impossible to France, make the first cannon which shall be fired in Europe the signal for tearing up any settlement she may have made, and for holding the two continents of America in sequestration for the common purposes of the United British and American nations. This is not a state of things we seek or desire. It is one which this measure, if adopted by France, forces on us. . . .

If France considers Louisiana however as indispensable for her views she might perhaps be willing to look about for arrangements which might reconcile it to our interests. If anything could do this it would be the ceding to us the island of New Orleans and the Floridas. . . .

Every eye in the U. S. is now fixed on this affair of Louisiana. Perhaps nothing since the revolutionary war has produced more uneasy sensations through the body of the nation. Notwithstanding temporary bickerings have taken place with France, she has still a strong hold on the affections of our citizens generally. I have thought it not amiss, by way of supplement to the letters of the Secretary of State, to write you this private one to impress you with the importance we affix to this transaction.

Pierre Samuel Du Pont de Nemours

To supplement Livingston's efforts, Jefferson enlisted Pierre Samuel Du Pont de Nemours, a French economist who was returning to the Continent on personal and business matters. Jefferson sent Du Pont a letter and enclosed his instructions to Livingston for Du Pont to read before delivering them. The letter repeated Jefferson's determination to keep Louisiana from Napoleon. The Frenchman's role would be to impress the Consulate with the gravity of the situation.

Washington, Apr. 25. 1802.

I am thus open with you because I trust that you will have it in your power to impress on that government considerations, in the scale against which the possession of Louisiana is nothing. In Europe nothing but Europe is seen, or supposed to have any weight in the affairs of nations. But this little event, of France possessing herself of Louisiana, which is thrown in as nothing, as a mere make-weight in the general settlement of accounts, this speck which now appears as an almost invisible point in the horizon, is the embryo of a tornado which will burst on the countries on both shores of the Atlantic and involve in it's effects their highest destinies. . . . if you can be the means of informing the wisdom of Buonaparte of all it's consequences, you will have deserved well of both countries. Peace and abstinence from European alliances

335

are our objects, and so will continue while the present order of things in America remains uninterrupted.

Although versions of the secret Franco-Spanish treaty on Louisiana had been published in America before the end of the congressional session, Jefferson did not present the problem to the legislature until Livingston or Du Pont could report on their conversations with Napoleon's ministers. It was equally prudent to keep the matter out of politics that summer because congressional elections were approaching. Jefferson could take some wry pride in the nature of the Federalist press campaign, which tried to discredit Republicans by attacking the President. Opposition editors could find little to attack in his record; instead they bombarded him with the most vicious personal slanders he suffered in his long career. The most malicious charge was made in a Richmond newspaper by James Callender, a turncoat Republican journalist whom Jefferson had once befriended. Callender recounted a tale that Jefferson kept a slave, Sally Hemings, as his concubine at Monticello and that she had borne him several children. Sally was the illegitimate offspring of Jefferson's father-in-law and a mulatto slave and thus his dead wife's half sister. Some Jefferson biographers, and Jefferson's Randolph and Eppes descendants, have claimed that Sally's white children were fathered by one of his nephews. For a man who was always reticent about his family life, the situation was most painful. He never commented publicly on this charge, but his bitterness toward the 1802 campaign was plain in a letter to Robert R. Livingston.

Washington Oct. 10. 1802.

You will have seen by our newspapers that with the aid of a lying renegade from republicanism, the federalists have opened all their sluices of calumny. They say we lied them out of power, and openly avow they will do the same by us. But it was not lies or arguments on our part which dethroned them, but their own foolish acts, sedition laws, alien laws, taxes, extravagances and heresies. Porcupine their friend [Philadelphia's *Porcupine's Gazette,* published by William Cobbett] wrote them down. Callendar, their new recruit, will do the same. Every decent man among them revolts at his filth; and there cannot be a doubt that were a presidential election to come on this day, they would have but three New England states and about half a dozen votes from Maryland and North Carolina, these two states electing by districts. Were all the states to elect by a general ticket, they would have but 3. out of 16. states. And these 3. are coming up slowly.

Jefferson kept careful records of the clothing given to the slaves at Monticello. Sally Hemings was listed among those receiving Irish linen, calamanco, and flannel.

The Republicans gained more ground in the elections for the Eighth Congress, which would convene in 1803; but in the meantime Jefferson and Madison still had no news, good or bad, from Livingston's halting negotiations. In November word came from the West that the Spanish Intendant had closed the port of New Orleans to American shipping, in violation of treaty promises. Pressure for an immediate solution to the question of possession of the trans-Mississippi West rose in Congress. There was some indication, however, that the Intendant had acted without his government's knowledge. Jefferson investigated the closing through diplomatic channels and on January 11 nominated James Monroe to join Livingston. The next day the House approved a committee report drafted by Madison, calling for an appropriation of two million dollars "to defray any expenses which may be incurred in relation to the intercourse between the United States and foreign nations." The "expenses," as the House knew from secret sessions, were to finance Monroe and Livingston's joint mission: the purchase of New Orleans and the Floridas. This accomplished, Jefferson wrote Monroe urging him to accept the appointment.

> Washington Jan. 13. 1803.
>
> The agitation of the public mind on occasion of the late suspension of our right of deposit at N. Orleans is extreme. In the Western country it is natural and grounded on honest motives. In the seaports it proceeds from a desire for war which increases the mercantile lottery; in the federalists generally and especially those of Congress the object is to force us into war if possible, in order to derange our finances, or if this cannot be done, to attach the Western country to them, as their best friends, and thus get again into power. Remonstrances, memorials &c. are now circulating thro' the whole of the Western country and signing by the body of the people. The measures we have been pursuing being invisible, do not satisfy their minds. Something sensible therefore was become necessary; and indeed our object of purchasing N. Orleans and the Floridas is a measure liable to assume so many shapes, that no instructions could be squared to fit them. It was essential then to send a Minister extraordinary, to be joined with the ordinary one, with discretionary powers, first however well impressed with all our views and therefore qualified to meet and modify to these every form of proposition which could come from the other party. This could be done only in full and frequent oral communications. Having determined on this, there could not be two opinions among the republicans as to the person. You possessed the unlimited con-

The port of New Orleans

fidence of the administration and of the Western people; and generally of the republicans every where; and were you to refuse to go, no other man can be found who does this. The measure has already silenced the feds here. Congress will no longer be agitated by them: and the country will become calm as fast as the information extends over it. All eyes, all hopes are now fixed on you; and were you to decline, the chagrin would be universal, and would shake under your feet the high ground on which you stand with the public. Indeed I know nothing which would produce such a shock. For on the event of this mission depends the future destinies of this republic.

Officially, the administration's goals were limited to the purchase of territories on the Gulf, but the ministers' instructions empowered them to sign a treaty "concerning the enlargement and more effective security of the rights and interests of the United States in the River Mississippi and in the territories eastward thereof." If they could purchase more than Florida and New Orleans with the $9,375,000 the President was willing to spend, he would not be disappointed. Jefferson's interest in the eventual possession of Louisiana was apparent in a message he sent Congress advocating a timely expedition to the West.

January 18, 1803.

MISSOURI HISTORICAL SOCIETY

An intelligent officer, with ten or twelve chosen men, fit for the enterprise, and willing to undertake it, taken from our posts, where they may be spared without inconvenience, might explore the whole line, even to the Western ocean, have conferences with the natives on the subject of commercial intercourse, get admission among them for our traders, as others are admitted, agree on convenient deposits for an interchange of articles, and return with the information acquired, in the course of two summers. Their arms and accoutrements, some instruments of observation, and light and cheap presents for the Indians, would be all the apparatus they could carry, and with an expectation of a soldier's portion of land on their return, would constitute the whole expence. Their pay would be going on, whether here or there. While other civilised nations have encountered great expence to enlarge the boundaries of knowledge, by undertaking voyages of discovery, and for other literary purposes, in various parts and directions, our nation seems to owe to the same object, as well as to its own

Drawing of a salmon trout by Clark from his journal for March, 1806

338

Charles Willson Peale painted companion portraits of William Clark (opposite) and Meriwether Lewis (above) shortly after their return from the Pacific late in 1806.

interests, to explore this, the only line of easy communication across the continent, and so directly traversing our own part of it. The interests of commerce place the principal object within the constitutional powers and care of Congress, and that it should incidentally advance the geographical knowledge of our own continent, cannot be but an additional gratification. The nation claiming the territory, regarding this as a literary pursuit, which [it] is in the habit of permitting within it's dominions, would not be disposed to view it with jealousy, even if the expiring state of it's interests there did not render it a matter of indifference. The appropriation of two thousand five hundred dollars, 'for the purpose of extending the external commerce of the United States,' while understood and considered by the Executive as giving the legislative sanction, would cover the undertaking from notice.

Congress agreed to the project and the President named his private secretary, Meriwether Lewis, to head the expedition. Once Lewis persuaded his friend and fellow Virginian William Clark to join him, preparations began for one of America's most historic missions of exploration.

The Seventh Congress, elected with Jefferson in 1800, had served the President well in financial policy and diplomatic affairs. The Republicans would dominate the Eighth Congress completely, with an increased House majority and a preponderance of two to one in the Senate. As their party's power ebbed away, Federalists' bitterness increased. Jefferson's selective removal of incumbent officials was almost complete, and the only remaining concentration of opposition power was in the judiciary. Many Federalist judges used their positions to expound political theory. When Justice Samuel Chase of the Supreme Court delivered a highly partisan charge to a grand jury in Baltimore, Jefferson suggested to Maryland Congressman Joseph Nicholson that he initiate impeachment proceedings. Chase was eventually impeached and acquitted.

Washington May 13. 1803.
You must have heard of the extraordinary charge of Chase to the grand jury at Baltimore. Ought this seditious and official attack on the principles of our constitution, and on the proceedings of a state, to go unpunished? And to whom so pointedly as yourself will the public look for the necessary measures? I ask these questions for your consideration. For myself, it is better that I should not interfere.

The symbol for Jefferson of Federalist power in the judiciary was Chief Justice John Marshall. Jefferson's first serious clash with Marshall came over the issue of Adams's "midnight" appointments. William Marbury had been appointed a justice of the peace by Adams on March 2, 1801, but Jefferson had ordered Madison to withhold his signed and sealed commission, which had not been delivered. Citing the Judiciary Act of 1789, Marbury had then petitioned the Supreme Court for a writ of mandamus granting the commission. Marshall dismissed the suit in February, 1803, saying the court lacked jurisdiction and thus avoiding an open confrontation with the executive branch. Yet his decision marked the first occasion on which an act of Congress—the section of the Judiciary Act of 1789 empowering the court to issue such a writ—was held unconstitutional.

On the eve of the Fourth of July came fitting news for the celebration of America's independence: Monroe and Livingston had negotiated a treaty with France that would give America not merely a foothold at New Orleans but possession of the entire province of Louisiana, a tract stretching from the Mississippi to the Rockies. Some High Federalists grumbled at the purchase price, and others objected to buttressing the interests of the West at the expense of the East Coast. But Gouverneur Morris expressed a more general opinion: "I am content to pay my share of fifteen millions, to deprive foreigners of all pretext for entering our interior country." Jefferson wrote proudly to John Dickinson of the accomplishment.

> Monticello Aug. 9. 1803.
>
> The acquisition of New Orleans would of itself have been a great thing, as it would have ensured to our Western brethren the means of exporting their produce: but that of Louisiana is inappreciable, because, giving us the sole dominion of the Missisipi, it excludes those bickerings with foreign powers, which we know of a certainty would have put us at war with France immediately: and it secures to us the course of a peaceable nation.

Jefferson conceded in a letter to Joseph Priestley that he had not expected the treaty so soon. Napoleon had yielded the territory because of his plans for a new war against Britain. The Louisiana cession would cut France's military expenditures and the purchase price would contribute to her war chest.

> Washington, January 29, 1804.
>
> I did not expect he would yield till a war took place between France and England, and my hope was to palliate and endure...until that event. I believed the event not very distant, but acknolege it came on sooner than I had expected. Whether, however, the good sense

of Bonaparte might not see the course predicted to be necessary & unavoidable, even before a war should be imminent, was a chance which we thought it our duty to try; but the immediate prospect of rupture brought the case to immediate decision. The *dénoument* has been happy; and I confess I look to this duplication of area for the extending a government so free and economical as ours, as a great achievement to the mass of happiness which is to ensue.

In October Jefferson called an early session of Congress to ratify the treaty, appropriate money for the purchase, and work out the details of government for the territory. He gave the two houses some details of the negotiations and submitted the matter to their wisdom. Acquisition of Louisiana would, he pointed out modestly, "promise, in due season, important aids to our treasury, an ample provision for our posterity, and a wide spread for the blessings of freedom and equal laws." But he did not ignore the circumstances that had made the promise possible—the reopening of war between Britain and France—and he suggested guidelines for maintaining American neutrality in the new dispute.

Oct. 17. 1803.

CULVER PICTURES, INC.

Sculptured group of Monroe and Livingston with the French Minister of Finance, François de Barbé-Marbois, at the signing ceremony

We have seen with sincere concern the flames of war lighted up again in Europe, and nations with which we have the most friendly and useful relations, engaged in mutual destruction. While we regret the miseries in which we see others involved, let us bow with gratitude to that kind providence, which, inspiring with wisdom and moderation our late legislative councils...guarded us from hastily entering into the sanguinary contest, and left us only to look on, and to pity it's ravages. These will be heaviest on those immediately engaged. Yet the nations pursuing peace will not be exempt from all evil. In the course of this conflict, let it be our endeavor, as it is our interest and desire, to cultivate the friendship of the belligerent nations by every act of justice, and of innocent kindness...but to administer the means of annoyance to none; to establish in our harbours such a police as may maintain law and order; to restrain our citizens from embarking individually in a war in which their country takes no part; to punish severely those persons, citizen or alien, who shall usurp the cover of our flag...; to exact from every nation the observance towards our vessels and citizens, of those principles and

341

practices which all civilized people acknowledge; to merit the character of a just nation, and maintain that of an independant one, preferring every consequence to insult and habitual wrong. Congress will consider whether the existing laws enable us efficaciously to maintain this course.... We should be most unwise indeed, were we to cast away the singular blessings of the position in which nature has placed us, the opportunity she has endowed us with of pursuing at a distance from foreign contentions, the paths of industry, peace, and happiness....

While Congress attended to the purchase, Jefferson became embroiled in one of the more lighthearted diplomatic crises of his career. If he was ever proud of causing a minor breach in foreign relations, he would have boasted of this one, for he annoyed the new British minister in Washington, Anthony Merry, by his steadfast adherence to republican principles. Although he appreciated European .graces and saw that the President's House offered its guests dishes prepared by a French chef, Jefferson himself proclaimed that "there is no 'court of the U.S.,' since the 4th of Mar. 1801. That day buried levees, birthdays, royal parades, and the arrogance of precedence in society." On being presented to Jefferson early one November morning at the President's House, Merry was shocked to find him "not merely in undress, but actually standing in slippers down at the heels, and both pantaloons, coat and underclothes indicative of an indifference to appearance."

A month later, the Merrys were invited to a dinner with the President. To Jefferson the evening was a congenial gathering of Cabinet officers and members of the diplomatic corps and their wives. The Merrys, however, obviously expected the dinner to be in their honor and conducted along lines of strict etiquette. When the meal was announced, Jefferson gave his arm to Dolley Madison, his unofficial hostess. Mrs. Merry, whose ideas of diplomatic prerogative were even more rigid than her husband's, was infuriated. Merry wrote indignantly to his government, asking further instructions in dealing with this affront. Jefferson and Madison tried vainly to placate him. Secretly amused by the whole affair, Jefferson wrote Monroe, who had become the American minister in Britain.

Washington Jan. 8. 1804.
We have told him that the principle of society, as well as of government, with us, is the equality of the individuals composing it. That no man here would come to a dinner, where he was to be marked with inferiority to any other. That we might as well attempt to force our

*Portrait of Jefferson as President
by Charles Fevret de Saint-Mémin*

principle of equality at St. James's, as he his principle of precedence here. I had been in the habit, when I invited female company (having no lady in my family) to ask one of the ladies of the 4. secretaries to come and take care of my company; and as she was to do the honors of the table I handed her to dinner myself. That Mr. Merry might not construe this as giving them a precedence over Mrs. Merry, I have discontinued it; and here as well as in private houses, the pele-mele [pell-mell] practice, is adhered to.... With respect to Merry, he appears so reasonable and good a man, that I should be sorry to lose him as long as there remains a possibility of reclaiming him to the exercise of his own dispositions. If his wife perseveres, she must eat her soup at home, and we shall endeavor to draw him into society as if she did not exist.

The Merry incident was one of the last occasions for wry humor Jefferson found in the election year of 1804. As it began, he followed his established practice of ignoring the political process by which he was to be renominated; but his hopes of completely turning his back on the race were complicated by problems with the Vice President. Burr had lost the support of New York Republicans, when he sought Federalist support in the gubernatorial elections, and had alienated party members in Congress by actions such as voting against the repeal of the Judiciary Act. Jefferson found that close association with Burr confirmed Hamilton's claims of his arrogance and ambition, and the President had quietly encouraged Governor George Clinton to remain in office in New York to foil Burr's hopes. Burr was unaware of this, but he did realize that his chances for state or federal elective office were slim and he was becoming desperate. On January 26 he visited Jefferson by appointment, and the President made notes as the Vice President opened with an oversimplified version of his political career and motives.

Anas

Jan. 26. [1804]... he had come to N. Y. a stranger, some years ago; that he found the country in possession of two rich families (the Livingstons and Clintons); that his pursuits were not political, and he meddled not. When the crisis, however, of 1800 came on, they found their influence worn out, and sollicited his aid with the people. He lent it without any views of promotion. That his being named as a candidate for V.P. was unexpected by him. He acceded to it with a view to promote my fame and advancement, and from a desire to be with me, whose company and conversation had always been fascinating to him. . . . That his attachment to me had been sincere, and was still unchanged . . . he asked if any change had taken place in mine towards him. . . . He reminded me of a letter written to him about the time of counting the votes, (say Feb. 1801) mentioning that his election had left a chasm in my arrangements; that I had lost him from my list in the admn. &c. He observed, he believed it would be for the interest of the republican cause for him to retire; that a disadvantageous schism would otherwise take place; but that were he to retire, it would be said he shrunk from the public sentence, which he never would do; that his enemies were using my name to destroy him, and something was necessary from me to prevent and deprive them of that weapon, some mark of favor from me, which would declare to the world that he retired with my confidence.

I answered by recapitulating to him what had been my conduct previous to the election of 1800. That I never had interfered directly or indirectly with my friends or any others, to influence the election either for him or myself; that I considered it as my duty to be merely passive. . . . That in the election now coming on, I was observing the same conduct. . . .

[Jefferson quickly corrected Burr's version of his letter, which actually dated to December, 1800. He had written Burr only to confirm the precedent set by Washington and Adams of confining the Vice President to domestic duties because of his role as potential successor to the President.]

I should here notice, that Colo. Burr must have thought that I could swallow strong things in my own favor, when he founded his acquiescence in the nomination as Vice-President, to his desire of promoting my honor, the being with me, whose company and conversation had always been fascinating with him, &c. I had never seen Colo. Burr till he came as a member of Senate. His conduct very soon inspired me with distrust. I habitually cautioned Mr. Madison against trusting him too much. I saw afterwards, that under General Washington's and Mr. Adams' administrations, whenever a great military appointment or a diplomatic one was to be made, he came post to Philadelphia to show himself, and in fact that he was always at market, if they had wanted him.

A month later, the Republican caucus in Congress unanimously renominated Jefferson. George Clinton was chosen as the vice-presidential candidate; Aaron Burr received not a single vote. Political wrangles were soon displaced in Jefferson's attention, however, by personal tragedy. In February Mary Jefferson Eppes, often called Polly or Maria, gave birth to her fourth child, only the second to live. The pregnancy had been difficult, and her recovery was slow. On Jefferson's return to Monticello in April, he took personal charge of her treatment and reported the results to James Madison.

> Monticello Apr. 9. 1804.
>
> I found my daughter Eppes at Monticello, whither she had been brought on a litter by hand; so weak as barely to be able to stand, her stomach so disordered as to reject almost every thing she took into it, a constant small fever, and an imposthume [abscess] rising in her breast. The indulgence of her friends had permitted her to be uninformed of the importance of strict attention to the necessity of food, and it's quality. I have been able to regulate this, and for some days she has taken food enough to support her, and of the kind only which her stomach bears without rejection. Her first imposthume has broken, but there is some fear of a second: if this latter cause does not more than countervail the effect of her present regimen, I am not without hopes of raising her again, as I should expect that restoring her strength by wine and digestible food, her fever would wear off. Her spirits and confidence are favourably affected by my being with her, and aid the effects of regimen.

Republican placard of 1804 urging election of Jefferson and Clinton

Eight days later, not yet twenty-six years old, Mary died. Her elder sister Martha, a tall, forthright woman, had always been closer to their father than pretty, quiet Polly. But Polly probably bore a stronger physical resemblance to the girls' mother, and her death was a dreadful blow to Jefferson. He had not only lost a daughter but her last illness seemed a repetition of her mother's passing and brought back all the torment he had known at Monticello in the summer of 1782. He shared his wracking grief with his old friend John Page, now Governor of Virginia.

Washington June 25. [18]04.

Others may lose of their abundance; but, I, of my want, have lost, even the half of all I had. My evening prospects now hang on the slender thread of a single life. Perhaps I may be destined to see even this last cord of parental affection broken! The hope with which I had looked forward to the moment when, resigning public cares to younger hands, I was to retire to that domestic comfort from which the last great step is to be taken, is fearfully blighted. When you and I look back on the country over which we have passed, what a field of slaughter does it exhibit. Where are all the friends who entered it with us under all the inspiring energies of health and hope? As if pursued by the havoc of war, they are strowed by the way, some earlier, some later, and scarce a few straglers remain to count the numbers fallen, and to mark yet by their own fall the last footsteps of their party. Is it a desireable thing to bear up thro' the heat of the action, to witness the death of all our companions, and merely be the last victim? I doubt it. We have however the traveller's consolation. Every step shortens the distance we have to go; the end of our journey is in sight, the bed wherein we are to rest, and to rise in the midst of the friends we have lost.

John Page by Charles W. Peale

For a time, it seemed that Jefferson might be consoled for Polly's loss by the renewal of a friendship with a family who had also loved her well, the Adamses. Without her husband's knowledge, Abigail Adams sent Jefferson a letter of condolence, recalling her first meeting with Polly when the child had stopped in London on her way to rejoin her father and sister in Paris in 1787. At first, Jefferson hoped he could reestablish old ties, but the ensuing correspondence with Abigail degenerated into charges and countercharges of political favoritism and personal spite, especially concerning Adams's midnight appointments. Mrs. Adams closed the brief exchange on October 25.

If Jefferson did not regain a friend that summer, he lost a bitter enemy when Alexander Hamilton was slain in a duel with Aaron Burr in July. With Hamilton gone and Burr's career ruined by the scandal, old political alignments and rivalries faded more quickly. In the presidential and congressional elections Jefferson and Clinton carried every state except Connecticut and Delaware. Shortly after returns from Massachusetts were announced, Jefferson wrote joyfully to William Heath, a Continental Army veteran who had fought long for Republican measures in the Bay State.

Washington Dec. 13. [18]04

I sincerely join you in congratulations on the return of Massachusets into the fold of the Union. This is truly the case wherein we may say 'this our brother was dead, and is alive again: and was lost, and is found.' It is but too true that our union could not be pronounced entirely sound while so respectable a member as Massachusets was under morbid affection. All will now come to rights. Connecticut encouraged by her elder sister will rally to catholic principles, will dismount her oligarchy, and fraternize with the great federated family. The new century opened itself by committing us on a boisterous ocean. But all is now subsiding, peace is smoothing our paths at home and abroad, and if we are not wanting in the practice of justice and moderation, our tranquility and prosperity may be preserved, until increasing numbers shall leave us nothing to fear from without.... Should we be able to preserve this state of public happiness and to see our citizens whom we found so divided, rally to their genuine principles, I [shall] hope yet to enjoy the comfort of that general good will which has been so unfeelingly wrested from me, and to sing at the close of my term the nunc demittas Domine with a satisfaction leaving nothing to desire but the last great audit.

Engraving of Hamilton-Burr duel from Lamb's History of New York

For all his letters of congratulations to New England Republicans, Jefferson did not end his first term in a state of unrealistic euphoria. The war in Europe had spread, and the nation again had to reaffirm and defend its neutral status and trade. In January Jefferson sent timely suggestions to Congressman Joseph Nicholson. With his usual thrift, he had decided to ignore the costly and grandiose plans for coastal fortifications adopted by the Adams administration, which he pointed out there was neither time nor money to erect. Instead, he outlined two methods of preventing foreign vessels from threatening towns that lined the harbors.

Washington Jan. 29. [18]05.

If we cannot hinder vessels from entering our harbours, we should turn our attention to the putting it out of their power to lie, or come to, before a town to injure it. Two means of doing this may be adopted in aid of each other. 1. Heavy cannon on travelling carriages, which may be moved to any point on the bank or beach most convenient for dislodging the vessel. A sufficient number of these should be lent to each sea port town, and their militia trained to them. The executive is authorised to do this; it has been done in a small degree, and will now be done more competently.

2. Heavy cannon on floating batteries or boats, which may be so stationed as to prevent a vessel entering the harbor, or force her after entering to depart. There are about 15. harbors in the U.S. which ought to be in a state of substantial defence. The whole of these would require, according to the best opinions 240. gunboats...the whole cost one million of Dollars. But we should allow ourselves 10. years to compleat it unless circumstances should force it sooner....We now possess 10. built and building. It is the opinion of those consulted that 15. more would enable us to put every harbour under our view into a respectable condition: and that this should limit the views of the present year. This would require an appropriation of 60,000. D. and I suppose *that* the best way of limiting it, without declaring the number, as perhaps that sum would build more. I should think it best not to give a detailed report, which exposes our policy too much.

Napoleon entering Notre-Dame to be crowned emperor in December, 1804, as Jefferson's first term ended

Ominously, Jefferson's first administration of frugality and peace ended with a call for gunboats and cannon. With freedom from the worst effects of European wars, he had been able to put republican principles into effective practice; Gallatin's financial program of reduced expenditures and tax reduction had gone smoothly as wartime trade increased America's customs' receipts; and the West had been secured and extended. But much of Jefferson's success was due to good fortune, which he used skillfully, even brilliantly. He had been given time to lay the foundations for republican government by the accidents of Continental wars and the conflicting needs of kings and emperors. No one could expect that good fortune to continue indefinitely, and Jefferson knew that his administration and the national unity he had won might soon have to prove themselves in a time of trial.

Chapter 12

From Promise to Performance

When Jefferson began his second term in 1805, he had a clear mandate to continue Republican policies. Unlike his election in 1800, his victory in 1804 was not indebted to reaction to the opposition's mistakes. His triumph was a vote of approval for his first administration and a tribute to his ability to implement the policies he had proposed as an alternative to Federalism. But the political winds during his second term would be much less favorable. The "few years" he had thought necessary to consolidate domestic affairs before America could defend her rights abroad would be all too few. The conflict between France and Great Britain developed into the War of the Third Coalition against Napoleon in 1805. British warships had already begun to patrol the American coast in search of deserters from the Royal Navy, and those squadrons were mere harbingers of further harassment of American trade to come.

The pressures of time overshadowed Jefferson's second administration—time to build gunboats for harbor defense, time to receive diplomatic dispatches from abroad, time to rally public opinion or to quiet public outrage, and time to prepare for a challenge to American rights. If it came too soon for effective retaliation, such a challenge would damage the national honor and prestige and impair the commercial privileges that had brought prosperity to merchants and farmers and financial stability to the government. Jefferson confided to his colleagues that he was working under a personal time limit as well. Even before taking his oath of office for the second time, he had decided against accepting a third term, as he explained to John Taylor of Caroline.

> Washington Jan. 6. 1805
> My opinion originally was that the President of the U. S. should have been elected for 7. years, and forever ineligible afterwards. I have since become sensible that 7. years is too long to be irremoveable, and that there should

Jefferson asked for and received authorization from Congress to purchase or construct 257 gunboats; five types can be seen above.

be a peaceable way of withdrawing a man in midway who is doing wrong. The service for 8. years with a power to remove at the end of the first four, comes nearly to my principle as corrected by experience: and it is in adherence to that, that I determine to withdraw at the end of my second term. . . . Genl. Washington set the example of voluntary retirement after 8. years. I shall follow it. And a few more precedents will oppose the obstacle of habit to any one after a while who shall endeavor to extend his term. Perhaps it may beget a disposition to establish it by an amendment of the constitution. I believe I am doing right therefore in pursuing my principle. I had determined to declare my intention but I have consented to be silent on the opinion of friends, who think it best not to put a continuance out of my power in defiance of all circumstances.

Jefferson knew he could rely on wide popular support during his second term. In notes for his second inaugural address, he defined the contrast between that message and the one he had delivered to Congress four years earlier.

[before March 4, 1805]

The former one was an exposition of the principles on which I thought it my duty to administer the government. The second then should naturally be a Compte rendu, or a statement of facts, shewing that I have conformed to those principles. The former was *promise:* this is *performance.*

The performance had been superb. In his inaugural address Jefferson had only to list his accomplishments to prove that point. He also floated a new proposition: that surplus revenues in the national treasury be put to regular use, in peacetime as a fund for education and internal improvements such as rivers, canals, and roads and in war as an easily tapped source for defense.

[March 4, 1805]

In the transaction of your foreign affairs we have endeavored to cultivate the friendship of all nations, & especially of those with which we have the most important relations. We have done them justice on all occasions; favor, where favor was lawful, cherished mutual interests & intercourse on fair & equal terms. . . .

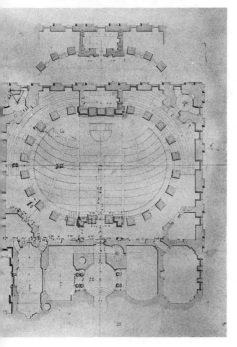

Jefferson made Benjamin H. Latrobe the Surveyor of Public Buildings in 1803; top priority was completion of the south wing of the Capitol. Latrobe's sketch of the ground-floor plan, c. 1804, is below; south elevation, 1810, above.

At home, fellow-citizens, you best know whether we have done well or ill. The suppression of unnecessary offices, of useless establishments and expences, enabled us to discontinue our internal taxes. These, covering our land with officers, & opening our doors to their intrusions, had already begun that process of domiciliary vexation, which, once entered, is scarcely to be restrained from reaching successively every article of property & produce....

The remaining revenue, on the consumption of foreign articles, is paid chiefly by those who can afford to add foreign luxuries to domestic comforts. Being collected on our sea-board and frontiers only, & incorporated with the transactions of our mercantile citizens, it may be the pleasure and the pride of an American to ask What farmer, what mechanic, what labourer ever sees a tax-gatherer of the US? These contributions enable us to support the current expences of the government, to fulfill contracts with foreign nations, to extinguish the native right of soil within our limits, to extend those limits, & to apply such a surplus to our public debts, as places at a short day their final redemption. And that redemption once effected, the revenue thereby liberated may, by a just repartition of it among the states, & a corresponding amendment of the constitution, be applied, *in time of peace,* to rivers, canals, roads, arts, manufactures, education, & other great objects within each state. *In time of war,* if injustice by ourselves or others must sometimes produce war, increased as the same revenue will be by increased population & consumption, & aided by other resources reserved for that crisis, it may meet within the year all the expenses of the year without encroaching on the rights of future generations by burthening them with the debts of the past. War will then be but a suspension of useful works; & a return to a state of peace a return to the progress of improvement.

But Jefferson knew that the Republicans' success in uniting the nation had not ended dissension but only modified it. His own party showed the strains of political victory. In opposition, Republicans could not afford the luxury of bickering among themselves; in power, they seemed determined to make up for years of suppressing conflicts of personality and philosophy by publicizing their differences. In the spring of 1805,

Jefferson was particularly concerned by factions in Pennsylvania and New York, key states in Republican control of the Middle States. But, as he explained to Senator George Logan of Pennsylvania, he would wisely choose neutrality for himself in intraparty squabbles as he had for the nation in European conflicts.

Washington May 11. [18]05.

I see with infinite pain the bloody schism which has taken place among our friends in Pensylvania & New York, & will probably take place in other states. The main body of both sections mean well, but their good intentions will produce great public evil. The minority, whichever section shall be the minority, will end in coalition with the federalists, and some compromise of principle; because these will not sell their aid for nothing. Republicanism will thus lose, & royalism gain some portion of that ground which we thought we had rescued to good government. I do not express my sense of our misfortunes from any idea that they are remediable. I know that the passions of men will take their course, that they are not to be controuled but by despotism, & that this melancholy truth is the pretext for despotism. The duty of an upright administration is to pursue it's course steadily, to know nothing of these family dissensions, and to cherish the good principles of both parties.

George Logan

The second term got off to a good start when a treaty was signed in June ending the Tripolitan War. The treaty's terms were favorable to the United States and were the culmination of Jefferson's long resistance to the pirates' depradations on shipping and demands for tribute, although some payments would continue until 1816. A month later, Jefferson's policy of using American neutrality to gain concessions from European powers was severely tested. The challenge came not from the great rivals, France and Great Britain, but from Spain. In the autumn of 1804, James Monroe had gone to Madrid to join Thomas Pinckney in negotiating several disputed matters: the western boundary of Louisiana, possession of the Floridas, and indemnification for American shipping seized by Spain or brought into Spanish ports during the last European war. The American demands were rejected and Monroe returned to London to become the new American minister there, stopping briefly at Paris, where Napoleon supported his ally. By July, Jefferson had received news of the failure. Spurred by Spanish intransigence, the President proposed an overture to Great Britain as a countermeasure to French support of Spain. Madison was surprised by the proposal, and Jefferson wrote to explain his arguments.

*Late in 1805, Jefferson received
Suliman Mellimelli, an envoy from
Tunis who brought presents, which
were refused, and demanded tribute,
which the President would not pay.*

Monticello Aug. 27 [18]05.

I have no idea of committing ourselves immediately, or independantly of our further will, to the war. The treaty should be provisional only, to come into force on the event of our being engaged in war with either France or Spain, during the present war in Europe. In that event we should make common cause, & England should stipulate not to make peace without our obtaining the objects for which we go to war, to wit, the acknolegement by Spain of the rightful boundaries of Louisiana (which we should reduce to our minimum by a secret article) and 2. indemnification for spoliations for which purpose we should be allowed to make reprisal on the Floridas & *retain them* as an indemnification. Our cooperation in the war (if we should actually enter into it) would be sufficient consideration for Great Britain to engage for it's object: and it being generally known to France & Spain that we had entered into treaty with England would probably ensure us a peaceable & immediate settlement of both points.

By the time Jefferson returned to Washington in October, however, an alliance with Great Britain seemed much less feasible. The European war then looked as if it would be a long one, and Jefferson decided to press negotiations again, this time in Paris by the new United States Minister to France, John Armstrong. Jefferson outlined his revised policy to the Secretary of State.

Washington Oct. 23. [18]05.

The probability of an extensive war on the continent of Europe strengthening every day for some time past, is now almost certain. This gives us our great desideratum, time. In truth it places us quite at our ease. We are certain of one year of campaigning at least, and one other year of negociation for their peace arrangements. Should we be now forced into war, it is become much more questionable than it was, whether we should not pursue it unembarrassed by any alliance & free to retire from it whenever we can obtain our separate terms. It gives us time too to make another effort for peaceable settlement. Where shall this be done? Not at Madrid certainly. At Paris: through Armstrong, or Armstrong & Monroe as negociators, France as the Mediator, the price of the Floridas as the means. We need not care who gets that:

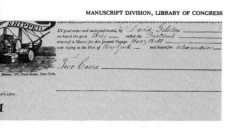

*An 1805 bill of lading for two
cases of wine ordered by Madison,
Jefferson, and a third gentleman*

353

Cartoon of Jefferson, stung by Napoleon, coughing up two million dollars for East and West Florida

and an enlargement of the sum we had thought of may be the bait to France, while the Guadaloupe as the Western boundary may be the soother of Spain providing for our spoliated citizens in some effectual way. We may announce to France that determined not to ask justice of Spain again, yet desirous of making one other effort to preserve peace, we are willing to see whether her interposition can obtain it on terms which we think just; that no delay however can be admitted, & that in the mean time should Spain attempt to change the status quo, we shall repel force by force, without undertaking other active hostilities till we see what may be the issue of her interference.

In November the Cabinet agreed on the terms to be offered by the negotiators in Paris: purchase of the Floridas and part of Texas, with the assumption of Spanish payments for depredations on American shipping as a large portion of the price. That same month Jefferson received word from Armstrong that Talleyrand was willing to force Spain to negotiate. In a confidential message to Congress, Jefferson broadly outlined the policy to be pursued.

Cartoon of Jefferson encouraging congressional dogs, including son-in-law John Eppes, to fight the bull Spain and take West Florida

[December 6, 1805]

The conduct of France, and the part she may take in the misunderstandings between the US. and Spain, are too important to be unconsidered.... Whatever direction she might mean to give to these differences, it does not appear that she has contemplated their proceeding to actual rupture, or that, at the date of our last advices from Paris, her government had any suspicion of the hostile attitude Spain had taken here. On the contrary we have reason to believe that she was disposed to effect a settlement on a plan analogous to what our ministers had proposed, and so comprehensive as to remove as far as possible the grounds of future collision & controversy on the Eastern as well as Western side of the Missisipi.

The present crises in Europe is favorable for pressing such a settlement; and not a moment should be lost in availing ourselves of it. Should it pass unimproved, our situation would become much more difficult. Formal war is not necessary. It is not probable it will follow. But the protection of our citizens, the spirit and honor of our country, require that force should be interposed to a certain degree. It will probably contribute to advance the object of peace.

But the course to be pursued will require the command of means which it belongs to Congress exclusively to yield or to deny. To them I communicate every fact material for their information, & the documents necessary to enable them to judge for themselves. To their wisdom then I look for the course I am to take, and will pursue with sincere zeal that which they shall approve.

What Jefferson really wanted from Congress was authorization for an appropriation of two million dollars to purchase the Floridas, a sum he intended to make known through the House Republican leadership and a committee headed by John Randolph of Roanoke. Randolph balked, however, at what he said was extortion, a payment through France to force cessions from Spain. Not until mid-February were resolutions finally passed for "extraordinary" but unspecified diplomatic expenses.

That was the beginning of Randolph's falling out with the executive branch, a schism among Republicans that damaged the party's prestige and the sense of invincibility that had marked Jefferson's first five years in office. A related matter drew more of Randolph's wrath in January; Jefferson sent another confidential message to Congress concerning the continuing British raids on American shipping and the impressment of American sailors.

Jan. 17. 1806.

The right of a Neutral to carry on commercial intercourse with every part of the dominions of a belligerent, permitted by the municipal laws of the country (with the exception of blockaded ports & Contraband of war), was believed to have been decided between Great Britain & the US. by the sentence of the Commissioners mutually appointed to decide on that & other questions of difference between the two nations; and by the actual paiment of damages awarded by them against Great Britain for the infractions of that right. When therefore it was percieved that the same principle was revived, with others more novel, & extending the injury, instructions were given to the Minister Plenipotentiary of the US. at the court of London, and remonstrances duly made by him on this subject, as will appear by documents transmitted herewith. These were followed by a partial & temporary suspension only, without any disavowal of the principle. He has therefore been instructed to urge this subject anew, to bring it more fully to the bar of

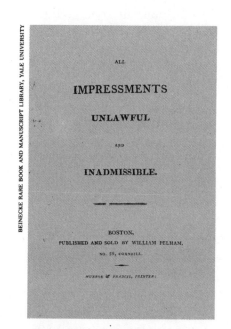

ALL

IMPRESSMENTS

UNLAWFUL

AND

INADMISSIBLE.

BOSTON,
PUBLISHED AND SOLD BY WILLIAM PELHAM,
NO. 59, CORNHILL.

MUNROE & FRANCIS, PRINTERS.

Title page of a book published in Boston in 1804 on impressment

reason, & to insist on rights too evident, and too important to be surrendered. In the mean time the evil is proceeding under adjudications founded on the principle which is denied. Under these circumstances the subject presents itself for the consideration of Congress.

On the impressment of our Seamen, our remonstrances have never been intermitted. A hope existed, at one moment, of an arrangement which might have been submitted to. But it soon passed away, & the practice, tho' relaxed at times in the distant seas, has been constantly pursued in those in our neighborhood.

Following this message, Randolph broke completely with the administration. He ridiculed the attempt to protect the interests of eastern merchants and their shipping after declining to use force in the West. "After shrinking from the Spanish jackal," he asked in debate, "do you presume to bully the British lion?" When a program of nonimportation of selected British goods passed the House over Randolph's opposition, his leadership had ended.

Although Jefferson and Madison had not let congressional leaders know precisely what measures they wanted, it was clear that they intended some effective program of commercial retaliation. But they received more than they bargained for. The commercial restrictions were not to go into effect until November, and, in the meantime, they were directed to send a special mission to London to negotiate the dispute with Britain. In theory, the British would be willing to make concessions over the summer rather than face restrictions on their trade with America the following fall and winter. Jefferson chose William Pinkney of Maryland as Monroe's colleague for this assignment. He described the circumstances leading to the mission to Monroe, whose position was especially delicate because Randolph's followers were championing him over Madison as the next Republican leader.

Washington May 4. [18]06.

His course [Randolph's] has excited considerable alarm. Timid men consider it as a proof of the weakness of our government, & that it is to be rent into pieces by demagogues & to end in anarchy. I survey the scene with a different eye, and draw a different augury from it. In a house of Representatives of a great mass of good sense, Mr. R.'s popular eloquence gave him such advantages as to place him unrivalled as the leader of the house: and, altho' not conciliatory to those whom he led, principles of duty & patriotism induced many of them to swallow humiliations he subjected them to, and to vote as was

*Late nineteenth-century engraving of
an American seaman being impressed*

Prime Minister Charles James Fox

right, as long as he kept the path of right himself. The sudden defection of such a man, could not but produce a momentary astonishment & even dismay. But for a moment only. The good sense of the house rallied around it's principles, & without any leader, pursued steadily the business of the session, did it well, & by a strength of vote which has never before been seen.... The augury I draw from this is, that there is a steady, good sense in the legislature and in the body of the nation, joined with good intentions, which will lead them to discern & to pursue the public good under all circumstances which can arise, and that no ignis fatuus will be able to lead them long astray. In the present case, the public sentiment, as far as declarations of it have yet come in, is, without a single exception, in firm adherence to the administration.... The great body of your friends are among the firmest adherents to the administration. And in their support of you will suffer Mr. R. to have no communications with them.... it is unfortunate for you to be embarrassed with such a soi-disant friend. You must not commit yourself to him.

[Jefferson saw advantages for the Monroe-Pinkney mission in the death of William Pitt and the succession of Charles James Fox as Prime Minister.]

The late change in the ministry I consider as ensuring us a just settlement of our differences, and we ask no more. In Mr. Fox personally I have more confidence than in any man in England, and it is founded in what, through unquestionable channels, I have had opportunities of knowing of his honesty & his good sense. While he shall be in the administration, my reliance on that government will be solid. We had committed ourselves in a line of proceedings adapted to meet Mr. Pitt's policy & hostility before we heard of his death, which self-respect did not permit us to abandon afterwards.... It ought not to be viewed by the ministry as looking towards them at all, but merely the consequences of the measures of their predecessors, which their nation has called on them to correct. I hope, therefore, they will come to just arrangements. No two countries upon earth have so many points of common interest and friendship: and their rulers must be great bunglers indeed if with such dispositions, they break them asunder. The only rivalry that can arise is on the ocean. England may by petty larceny thwartings, check us on that element a little, but nothing she can do will retard us there one year's growth.... We ask for peace & justice from all nations, & we will remain uprightly neutral in fact, tho' leaning in belief to the opinion that an English ascendancy on the ocean is safer for us than that of France.

Over the summer of 1806, Jefferson and Madison waited for reports from the two negotiating teams in London and Paris. It was, of course, an election year, and Jefferson wrote to Barnabas Bidwell, a freshman congressman from Massachusetts who had aided the administration against Randolph, encouraging him to seek reelection. Jefferson felt that if Bidwell did not run, the loss of his seat could upset the delicate balance between loyal Republicans and Randolph's followers, the Quids. He may also have hoped that Bidwell would become the leader the executive needed to assure that its measures were not simply abandoned in Congress, even though Randolph described the role as that of a "backstairs counsellor."

Washington July 5. 1806.

I read with extreme regret the expressions of an inclination on your part to retire from Congress. I will not say that this time, more than all others, calls for the service of every man. But I will say there never was a time when the services of those who possess talents, integrity, firmness, & sound judgment were more wanted in Congress. Some one of that description is particularly wanted to take the lead in the H. of R. to consider the business of the nation a[s] his own business, to take it up as if he were singly charged with it and carry it through. I do not mean that any gentleman relinquishing his own judgment should implicitly support all the measures of the administration; but that, where he does not disapprove of them, he should not suffer them to go off in sleep, but bring them to the attention of the house, and give them a fair chance. Where he disapproves, he will of course leave them to be brought forward by those who concur in the sentiment.... When a gentleman, through zeal for the public service, undertakes to do the public business, we know that we shall hear the cant of backstairs' counsellors. But we never heard this while the declaimer [Randolph] was himself, a backstairs' man

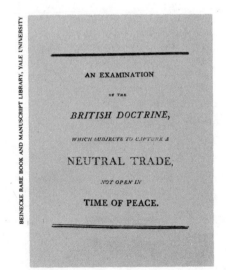

Title page of an 1806 pamphlet by Secretary of State James Madison examining the British attitude toward the neutral carrying trade

A front view of the President's House; the engraving is after a drawing by George Catlin.

as he calls it, but in the confidence & views of the administration, as may more properly & respectfully be said. But if the members are to know nothing but what is important enough to be put into a public message, & indifferent enough to be made known to all the world, if the Executive is to keep all other information to himself, & the House to plunge on in the dark, it becomes a government of chance & not of design.... The last session of Congress was indeed an uneasy one for a time: but as soon as the members penetrated into the views of those who were taking a new course, they rallied in as solid a phalanx as I have ever seen act together.... They want only a man of business and in whom they can confide, to conduct things in the house; and they are as much disposed to support him as can be wished. It is only speaking a truth to say that all eyes look to you.... Perhaps I am not entitled to speak with so much frankness; but it proceeds from no motive which has not a right to your forgiveness. Opportunities of candid explanation are so seldom afforded me, that I must not lose them when they occur.

Rumors of Republican disunion were the Federalists' best weapons in an election year, and Randolph had played into their hands. By October, when Jefferson returned to Washington to begin preparing for the congressional session, the opposition press had extended their time-honored campaign to his Cabinet. Wearily the President wrote to Gallatin of reports that there was disagreement between them. His assurances were unnecessary, for the Treasury Secretary never doubted the President's support, but Jefferson welcomed any opportunity to affirm faith in his colleagues that fall when there was reason to distrust so many Republicans.

Washington Oct. 12. [18]06.

You witnessed in the earlier part of the administration the malignant & long continued efforts which the federalists exerted, in their newspapers, to produce misunderstanding between Mr. Madison & myself. These failed compleatly. A like attempt was afterwards made through other channels to effect a similar purpose between Genl. Dearborn & myself, but with no more success. The machinations of the last session to put you at cross questions with us all were so obvious as to be seen at the first glance of every eye. In order to destroy one member of the administration, the whole were to be set

Blennerhassett's Island, in the Ohio River, was the staging area for Burr's ill-fated expedition.

to loggerheads to destroy one another. I observe in the papers lately new attempts to revive this stale artifice, & that they squint more directly towards you & myself. I cannot therefore be satisfied till I declare to you explicitly, that my affections and confidence in you are nothing impaired, & that they cannot be impaired by means so unworthy the notice of candid & honorable minds. I make the declaration that no doubts or jealousies, which often beget the facts they fear, may find a moment's harbor in either of our minds.... Our administration now drawing towards a close, I have a sublime pleasure in believing it will be distinguished as much by having placed itself above all the passions which could disturb it's harmony, as by the great operations by which it will have advanced the well-being of the nation.

More alarming than any Federalist tales of defections in the Cabinet were the well-confirmed reports of treasonous activities by Jefferson's former Vice President, Aaron Burr. An ambitious politician denied office by his state and nation, Burr had turned to fantastic schemes in the West. Rumors of his plans, which included recruiting an expedition against Spanish territory in the Southwest and Mexico, had come to Jefferson's attention earlier in the year, but there was little that could be done against Burr until he took concrete, provable action. General James Wilkinson, a co-conspirator in the early stages of the intrigues, offered the proof. Whether Wilkinson experienced an attack of conscience or a sudden realization that the expedition was doomed, he became Burr's chief attacker. The General's dispatch to Jefferson, detailing Burr's plans to lead his expedition down the Ohio and Mississippi and possibly seize New Orleans, reached Washington at the end of November. After conferring with the Cabinet, Jefferson issued a proclamation against the expedition, calling for the support of government officials and private citizens in quelling the grandiose scheme. Neither in the proclamation nor in his message to Congress five days later did he mention Burr's name. But the fact of Burr's involvement was no secret, and in private Jefferson wrote bitterly of his former Vice President to John Langdon, a New Hampshire Republican.

Washington Dec. 22. [18]06.
Our prospects are great if we can preserve external & internal peace. With England I firmly expect a friendly arrangement. With Spain we shall possibly have blows; but they will hasten, instead of preventing a peaceable settlement. The most instant pressure is now from among ourselves. Our Cataline is at the head of an

armed body (we know not it's strength) and his object is to siese N. Orleans, from thence attack Mexico, place himself on the throne of Montezuma, add Louisiana to his empire, & the Western states from the Alleganey if he can. I do not believe he will attain the crown; but neither am I certain the halter will get it's due. A few days will let us see whether the Western states suppress themselves this insurrectionary enterprize, or we shall be obliged to make a great national armament for it. In the end, I am satisfied it will exhibit to the world another proof that the people of the US. are qualified for self government. Our friends, the federalists, chuckle at all this: but in justice I must add we have found some faithful among those in the West.

Congress buzzed over Burr's expedition and seemed to have little time for other matters. Jefferson and Madison may have been relieved at the legislators' lack of curiosity in the progress of negotiations abroad: Armstrong and James Bowdoin had failed to reach any understanding with the Spanish in Madrid, and the Monroe-Pinkney mission had been jeopardized by the death of Charles James Fox in September. But the President was not pleased by congressional indifference to his pleas for military preparedness in the event of diplomatic failure. His annual message covered such diverse matters as the progress of the Lewis and Clark expedition and the approach of the year 1808 when Congress could end the slave trade. It closed with a request for a firm but typically republican program.

Dec. 2. [18]06.

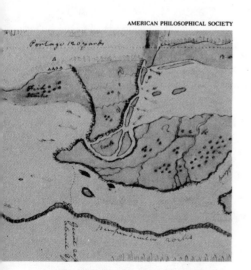

Detail of a map drawn by William Clark showing portages around the "Great Falls" of the Columbia River

The expedition of Messrs. Lewis & Clarke, for exploring the river Missouri, and the best communication from that to the Pacific ocean, has had all the success which could have been expected. They have traced the Missouri nearly to it's source, descended the Columbia to the Pacific ocean, ascertained with accuracy the geography of that interesting communication across our continent, learnt the character of the country, of it's commerce and inhabitants, and it is but justice to say that Messrs. Lewis & Clarke, and their brave companions, have, by this arduous service, deserved well of their country....

I congratulate you, fellow-citizens, on the approach of the period at which you may interpose your authority constitutionally, to withdraw the citizens of the United states from all further participation in those violations of human rights, which have been so long continued on the unoffending inhabitants of Africa, & which the morality, the reputation & the best interests of our country have long been eager to proscribe. Although no law you may pass can take prohibitory effect till the first day of the year 1808. yet the intervening period is not too long to prevent by timely notice, expeditions which cannot be compleated before that day....

...such is the situation of the nations of Europe, & such too the predicament in which we stand with some of them, that we cannot rely with certainty on the present aspect of our affairs. That may change from moment to moment, during the course of your session, or after you shall have separated. Our duty is therefore to act upon things as they are, & to make a reasonable provision for whatever they may be. Were armies to be raised whenever a speck of war is visible in our horizon, we never should have been without them. Our resources would have been exhausted on dangers which have never happened, instead of being reserved for what is really to take place. A steady, perhaps a quickened pace, in preparations for the defense of our Sea-port towns & waters, an early settlement of the most exposed and vulnerable parts of our country, a militia so organised that it's effective portions can be called to any point in the Union, or Volunteers, instead of them, to serve a sufficient time, are means which may always be ready, yet never preying on our resources until actually called into use. They will maintain the public interests, while a more permanent force shall be in a course of preparation. But much will depend on the promptitude with which these means can be brought into activity. If war be forced upon us in spite of our long & vain appeals to the justice of nations, rapid & vigorous movements in it's outset, will go far towards securing us in it's course & issue, and towards throwing it's burthens on those who render necessary the resort from reason to force.

William Pinkney

Jefferson's hopes for a peaceful settlement with Great Britain were dealt a blow in early February, 1807, when Madison received a report from Monroe indicating that he and Pinkney had agreed to omit any articles on impressment from the treaty. Jefferson hurriedly summoned the Cabinet, which decided not to notify the Senate and sent Monroe and Pinkney explicit instructions not to abandon the impressment issue. But the instructions were several weeks too late. Later in February, Madison received Monroe and Pinkney's announcement that they had signed a treaty on December 31 that would be "satisfactory." On March 3 a copy of the treaty itself arrived: not only was impressment relegated to a nonbinding note that said Britain would exercise caution, but Britain made no concessions on the seizure of neutral shipping and reserved a right to expand her policing of such trade.

That evening, the last of the session, a congressional delegation visited Jefferson to ask if there were any matters he wished to submit before adjournment. Suffering again from "periodical headache" Jefferson replied "Certainly not" to a pointed question as to whether the Monroe-Pinkney treaty might be ready for consideration. Congress adjourned, and Jefferson was left to recover from his illness and try to make peace with James Monroe, a proud man who would not look kindly on the inevitable rejection of the treaty he had signed.

Washington Mar. 21. 1807.

...I percieve uncommon efforts, and with uncommon wickedness are making by the Federal papers to produce mischief between myself personally and our negociators and also to irritate the British government, by putting a thousand speeches in my mouth, not one word of which I ever uttered. I have therefore thought it safe to guard you by stating the view which we have given out on the subject of the treaty, in conversation and otherwise; for ours, as you know, is a government which will not tolerate the being kept entirely in the dark, and especially on a subject so interesting as this treaty....depend on it, my dear Sir, that it will be considered as a hard treaty when it is known. The British commissioners appear to have screwed every article as far as it would bear, to have taken every thing, and yielded nothing....If the treaty cannot be put into an acceptable form, then the next best thing is to back out of the negociation as well as we can, letting that die away insensibly, but in the meantime agreeing informally that both parties shall act on the principles of the treaty, so as to preserve that friendly understanding which we so sincerely desire, until the one or the other may be disposed to yield the points which divide us. This will leave you to follow your desire of coming home as soon as you see that the amendment of the treaty is desperate. The power of continuing the negociations will pass over to Mr. Pinkney who, by procrastinations, can let it die away, and give us time, the most precious of all things to us.

Arrest of Burr in February, 1807, just before he tried to flee across the boundary into West Florida

The failure of the Monroe-Pinkney mission, and the political use the Federalists would make of it if the two diplomats did not revise the agreement over the summer, was but one of the threats to Republicanism that spring. Aaron Burr, arrested just above the border of Spanish Florida, had been brought to Richmond for trial on treason charges. The fact that Burr had laid the groundwork for the last stages of his buccaneering enterprise on an island within Virginia jurisdiction determined the site of the court proceedings. A trial in Richmond meant that John Marshall, Adams's appointee as Chief Justice, would preside on circuit duty. When Jefferson learned that Marshall had ordered proceedings to begin before the government could prepare its case, and had released Burr on ten-thousand-dollar bail, he lashed out against Burr, Marshall, and their Federalist adherents in a letter to William Branch Giles.

Monticello Apr. 20. [18]07.

That there should be anxiety & doubt in the public mind in the present defective state of the proof is not wonderful; and this has been sedulously encouraged by the tricks of the judges to force trials before it is possible to collect the evidence dispersed through a line of 2000. miles from Maine to Orleans. The federalists too give all their aid, making Burr's cause their own, mortified only that he did not separate the union or overturn the government, & proving that had he had a little dawn of success they would have joined him to introduce his object, their favorite monarchy, as they would any other enemy, foreign or domestic, who could rid them of this hateful republic, for any other government in exchange. ...We have set on foot an enquiry through the whole of the country which has been the scene of these transactions, to be able to prove to the courts, if they will give time, or to the public by way of communication to Congress, what the real facts have been. For obtaining this we are obliged to appeal to the patriotism of particular persons in different places, of whom we have requested to make the enquiry in their neighborhood, and on such information as shall be voluntarily offered. Aided by no process or facilities from the *federal* courts, but frowned on by their new born zeal for the liberty of those whom we would not permit to overthrow the liberties of their country, we can expect no revealments from the accomplices of the chief offender. Of treasonable intentions the judges have been obliged to confess there is probable appearance. What loophole they will find in it when it comes to trial, we cannot foresee....

Chief Justice John Marshall

If there ever had been an instance in this or the preceding administrations of federal judges, so applying principles of law as to condemn a federal, or acquit a republican offender, I should have judged them in the present case with more charity. All this however will work well. The nation will judge both offender, & judges for themselves. If a member of the Executive or Legislature does wrong, the day is never far distant when the people will remove him. They will see then and amend the error in our constitution which makes any branch independant of the nation, they will see that one of the great co-ordinate branches of the government, setting itself in opposition to the other two, and to the common sense of the nation, proclaims impunity to that class of offenders which endeavors to overturn the constitution, and are themselves protected in it by the constitution itself: for impeachment is a farce which will not be tried again. If their protection of Burr produces this amendment, it will do more good than his condemnation could have done.

Detail from contemporary cartoon shows the British Leopard *firing on the* Chesapeake, *June 22, 1807.*

Burr was acquitted by the jury in Richmond, after Marshall issued an opinion strictly construing the treason law; but the former Vice President was forced to flee the country to avoid further prosecution and the wrath of the public. The twisted logic by which some Federalists made "Burr's cause their own" was of less concern to Jefferson than the continuing Federalist domination of the bench. "This insurrection," he wrote, "will probably shew that the fault in our constitution is not that the Executive has too little power, but that the Judiciary either has too much, or holds it under too little responsibility." Indignant as he was at Federalist attempts to capitalize on Burr's case, Jefferson's real work after the close of the congressional session was to insure that negotiations in London took "a little nap" while the British government found reasons to conciliate America.

That hope was gone by July. On June 22 the British ship *Leopard*, one of a squadron off Hampton Roads, Virginia, had demanded that the American warship *Chesapeake* stop to be searched for British deserters among her crew. When the *Chesapeake*'s captain refused, the *Leopard* opened fire, killing three American sailors before the captain finally surrendered. After removing four supposed deserters, the *Leopard* allowed the *Chesapeake* to put in to shore. On June 25 members of the Cabinet were ordered to meet "without a moment's avoidable delay," and Jefferson prepared for their approval a proclamation calling for national unity and banning British ships from American waters. The *Anas* recorded subsequent meetings.

July the 2nd [1807]. Present all the Heads of Department and Attorney General. The Proclamation of this day unanimously agreed to.

A copy of the proclamation to be enclosed to the Governors.

Recall all our vessels from the Mediterranean, by a vessel to be sent express.

Send the Revenge to England, with despatches to our Minister, demanding satisfaction for the attack on the Chesapeake, in which must be included. 1. A disavowal of the Act and of the principle of searching a public armed vessel. 2. A restoration of the men taken. 3. A recall of Admiral Barclay [George Berkeley, the commander of the British fleet off the coast who had ordered the attack].... The vessels recalled from the Mediterranean are to come to Boston. When may be further orders.

July the 4th. Present the same. Agreed that a call of Congress shall issue the fourth Monday of August (24th) to meet the fourth Monday in October (26th) unless new occurrences should render an earlier call necessary. Mr. Smith wished an earlier call.

July the 5th. Present the same. It was agreed to call on the Governors of the States to have their quotas of 100,000 militia in readiness. The object is to have the portions on the sea-coast ready for any emergency, and for those in the North we may look to a winter expedition against Canada.

July the 7th. Present the Secretaries of State and Navy and Attorney General. Agreed to desire Governor of Virginia to order such portion of Militia into actual service as may be necessary for defense of Norfolk, and of the gunboats at Hampton and in Matthews County.

BY THOMAS JEFFERSON,

PRESIDENT OF THE U. STATES OF AMERICA,

A Proclamation.

During the wars which, for some time, have unhappily prevailed among the powers of Europe, the United States of America, firm in their principles of peace, have endeavored by justice, by a regular discharge of all their national and social duties, and by every friendly office their situation has admitted, to maintain, with all the belligerents, their accustomed relations of friendship, hospitality, and commercial intercourse.— Taking no part in the questions which animate these powers against each other, nor permitting themselves to entertain a wish but for the restoration of general peace, they have observed with good faith the neutrality they assumed, and they believe that no instance of a departure from its duties can be justly imputed to them by any nation. A free use of their harbors and waters, the means of refitting and of refreshment, of succour to their sick and suffering, have, at all times, and on equal principles, been extended to all, and this too amidst a constant recurrence of acts of insubordination to the laws, of violence to the persons, and of trespasses on the property of our citizens, committed by officers of one of the belligerent parties received among us. In truth these abuses of the laws of hospitality have, with few exceptions, become habitual to the commanders of the British armed vessels hovering on our coasts, and frequenting our harbors. They have been the subject of repeated representations to their government. Assurances have been given that proper orders should restrain them within the limit of the rights and of the respect due to a friendly nation: but those orders and assurances have been without effect; no instance of punishment for past wrongs has taken place.

Part of the President's July 8, 1807, proclamation following the British firing on the Chesapeake

Again Jefferson's strategy was to try to buy time and to refrain from committing the nation to war. On July 11 he outlined the three principles on which he and the Cabinet had acted to Barnabas Bidwell.

Washington July 11. [18]07.

You have long ago learnt the atrocious acts committed by the British armed vessels in the Chesapeake & it's neighborhood. They cannot be easily accomodated, altho' it is believed that they cannot be justified by orders from their government. We have acted on these principles. 1. to give that government an opportunity to disavow & make reparations. 2. to give ourselves time to get in the vessels, property and seamen now spread over the ocean. 3. to do no act which might compromit Congress in their choice between war, non-intercourse or any other measure. We shall probably call them some time in October, having regard to the return of the healthy season, and to the reciept of an answer from Great Britain, before which they could only act in the dark. In the mean time we shall make all the preparations which time will permit, so as to be ready for any alternative.

The *Chesapeake-Leopard* affair had provoked a mood of unqualified national indignation, but Jefferson was aware that public opinion and alignments within his party could change at any moment. In triumph, Republicanism had absorbed the rivalries and potential for division formerly expressed in two-party battles. Jefferson described this phenomenon to Thomas Cooper, a friend of Joseph Priestley's.

Washington July 9. [18]07.

I had always expected that when the republicans should have put down all things under their feet, they would schismatise among themselves. I always expected too that whatever names the parties might bear, the real division would be into moderate and ardent republicanism. In this division there is no great evil, not even if the minority obtain the ascendancy by the accession of federal votes to their candidate: because this gives us one shade only, instead of another, of republicanism. It is to be considered as apostacy only when they purchase the votes of federalists with a participation in honor and power. The gross insult lately recieved from the English has forced the latter into a momentary coalition with the mass of republicans. But the moment we begin to act, in the very line they have joined in approving, all will be wrong, and every act the reverse of what it should have been: still it is better to admit their coalescence, & leave to themselves their shortlived existence.

Even after his return to Monticello in August, Jefferson kept in touch with Cabinet officers and governors concerned with planning the fortification of key harbors and enforcing the ban on British ships. By October, when Congress met in special session, no word had come of British reaction to the *Chesapeake* incident. The day before presenting his annual message, Jefferson wrote confidentially to his son-in-law, Thomas Mann Randolph, of the calm mood that had succeeded the cries for war of the preceding summer.

> Washington Oct. 26. [18]07.
> At present we have nothing from Europe. The two houses have assembled earlier than usual. There was a quorum of the H. of R. here on Saturday.... The members, as far as I can judge are extremely disposed for peace: and as there is no doubt Gr. Br. will disavow the act of the Leopard, I am inclined to believe they will be more disposed to combat her practice of impressment by a non-importation law than by arms. I am at the same time not without all hope she may relinquish the pretension to impressment on our agreeing not to employ her seamen, which it is our interest to agree to. If we resort to non-importation, it will end in war and give her the choice of the moment of declaring it. Altho' I think it well that our constituents should know what is probable, yet I must not be quoted. You will be free however to mention these as your own opinions or as what you collect from your correspondence.

French cartoon of the Berlin Decree showing pace Britain could expect to receive goods from its colonies during the blockade by France

MUSÉE CARNAVALET

By mid-December, Jefferson and Madison had unofficial but reliable texts of the newest commercial restrictions on American shipping. Britain, although willing to disavow the *Leopard's* attack on the *Chesapeake*, would not abandon impressment. And, by orders in council of November 11, the Tory government had barred any vessels from the Continent that had not first paid customs duties in British ports and obtained clearance papers. To balance this, Napoleon had withdrawn his statement that American ships would be exempt from his Berlin Decree of 1806, a decree placing the British Isles under blockade and authorizing the seizure of any ships that defied the blockade. If American ships bound for Europe did not stop at British ports, they would be seized by the Royal Navy; if they did put in at British ports, they would be subject to capture by Napoleon. In the preliminary draft of a message to Congress, Jefferson indignantly summarized the situation.

> [before December 17, 1807]
> The sum of these mutual enterprizes on our national rights is that.... The whole world is thus laid under interdict by these two nations, and our vessels, their car-

goes & crews, are to be taken by the one or the other, for whatever place they may be destined, out of our own limits. If therefore on leaving our harbors we are certainly to lose them, is it not better, as to vessels, cargoes & seamen, to keep them at home? This is submitted to the wisdom of Congress, who alone are competent to provide a remedy.

Instead of submitting the original version, Jefferson sent a brief message that left no doubt of what he wanted from the two houses: a complete embargo on trade from American ports.

Dec. 17. 1807

The communications now made, showing the great and increasing dangers with which our vessels, our seamen, and merchandize, are threatened on the high seas & elsewhere, from the belligerent powers of Europe, and it being of the greatest importance to keep in safety these essential resources, I deem it my duty to recommend the subject to the consideration of Congress, who will doubtless perceive all the advantages which may be expected from an inhibition of the departure of our vessels from the ports of the United States.

Neither Randolph's Quids nor New England Federalists could block the request; the Embargo Act became law four days later. No American ships could sail to foreign ports; those engaged in the coastal trade were required to post bond to insure that they would not venture into international trade under the guise of interstate commerce. Although foreign ships were not barred from the United States, it was obvious that few would risk the voyage since they would be forbidden to carry any cargoes back across the Atlantic. Jefferson had played his last card in the game of keeping America at peace: a demand that her citizens sacrifice convenience, and even their livelihoods, in the national interest. It would be his final opportunity to win the dangerous contest. In December, in response to addresses from the state legislatures urging him to another term, he had made public the decision he had reached three years earlier.

[Washington,] Dec. 10. [18]07.

That I should lay down my charge at a proper period is as much a duty as to have borne it faithfully. If some termination to the services of the Chief magistrate be not fixed by the constitution, or supplied by practice, his office, nominally for years, will, in fact, become for life;

and history shews how easily that degenerates into an inheritance. Believing that a representative government, responsible at short periods of election, is that which produces the greatest sum of happiness to mankind, I feel it a duty to do no act which shall essentially impair that principle; and I should unwillingly be the person who, disregarding the sound precedent set by an illustrious predecessor, should furnish the first example of prolongation beyond the second term of office.

Truth also requires me to add that I am sensible of that decline which advancing years bring on; and feeling their Physical, I ought not to doubt their Mental effect. Happy if I am the first to percieve and to obey this admonition of nature, and to sollicit a retreat from cares too great for the wearied faculties of age.

The knowledge that this would be his last year in office increased Jefferson's desire to prove the energy of republican government, but his task was even more difficult because it was an election year. The unity Jefferson had hoped to create within the nation seemed to disappear within his own party. On January 23 the Republican caucus in Congress nominated Madison for President and George Clinton for Vice President, but it was well known that supporters of Monroe and Clinton would contest Madison's right to the candidacy. Almost a month later Jefferson wrote sadly to Monroe, bemoaning his rivalry with Madison and warning his old friend of the bitter nature of national political contests.

Washington, Feb. 18. [18]08.
I see with infinite grief a contest arising between yourself and another who have been very dear to each other, and equally so to me. I sincerely pray that these dispositions may not be affected between you: with me I confidently trust they will not. For independantly of the dictates of public duty which prescribe neutrality to me, my sincere friendship for you both will ensure it's sacred observance. I suffer no one to converse with me on the subject. I already percieve my *old* friend Clinton estranging himself from me. No doubt lies are carried to him, as they will be to the other two candidates. . . . The object of the contest is a fair & honorable one, equally open to you all; and I have no doubt the personal conduct of each will be so chaste as to offer no ground of dissatisfaction with each other. But your friends will not be as delicate. I know too well from experience the progress of political

Two halves of an 1807 Federalist cartoon: Washington (left) is characterized by books labeled order, law, and religion; Jefferson by sophisms, the Notes on Virginia, Tom Paine, Condorcet, *and* Voltaire

controversy, and the exacerbation of spirit into which it degenerates, not to fear for the continuance of your mutual esteem. One piquing thing said draws on another, that a third, and always with increasing acrimony, until all restraint is thrown off, and it becomes difficult for yourselves to keep clear of the toils in which your friends will endeavor to interlace you. . . . With respect to myself, I hope they will spare me. My longings for retirement are so strong that I with difficulty encounter the daily drudgeries of my duty. But my wish for retirement itself is not stronger than that of carrying into it the affections of all my friends. I have ever viewed Mr. Madison and yourself as two principal pillars of my happiness. Were either to be withdrawn, I should consider it as among the greatest calamities which could assail my future peace of mind. I have great confidence that the candor & high understanding of both will guard me against this misfortune, the bare possibility of which has so far weighed on my mind, that I could not be easy without unburthening it.

Monroe would not be dissuaded. His bitterness at the rejection of his treaty had been carefully nurtured by the Quids since his return, and he saw his candidacy as a matter of personal vindication. Despite his personal preference for Madison, Jefferson did not interfere in the race. His own contest was with the enforcement of the embargo. In mid-March he presented the Secretary of State with his views on the value of that weapon as a temporary policy.

[Washington,] Mar. 11. 1808.

I take it to be an universal opinion that war will become preferable to a continuance of the embargo after a certain time. Should we not then avail ourselves of the intervening period to procure a retraction of the obnoxious decrees peaceably if possible? An opening is given us by both parties sufficient to form a basis for such a proposition. I wish you to consider, therefore, the following course of proceeding, to wit.

To instruct our ministers at Paris & London, by the next packet, to propose immediately to both those powers a declaration on both sides that these decrees & orders shall no longer be extended to vessels of the US. in which case we shall remain faithfully neutral: but, without assuming the air of menace, to let them both percieve that if they do not withdraw these orders &

decrees, there will arrive a time when our interests will render war preferable to a continuance of the embargo: that when that time arrives, if one has withdrawn & the other not, we must declare war against that other; if neither shall have withdrawn, we must take our choice of enemies between them. This it will certainly be our duty to have ascertained by the time Congress shall meet in the fall or beginning of winter, so that taking off the embargo they may decide whether war must be declared & against whom.

As demonstrated by this letter, Jefferson realized that the embargo could not continue beyond the next congressional session. By then its merits in diplomatic negotiations would be known and continuation would be pointless. He soon found that an effective embargo, at least in some parts of the Union, might not last even that long. Opposition to enforcement was particularly strong in Massachusetts despite its Republican governor, James Sullivan; messages like this one to the Secretary of the Navy, Robert Smith, were common in the summer of 1808.

Monticello, Aug. 9. [18]08.

I have some apprehension the tories of Boston &c. with so poor a head of a governor may attempt to give us trouble. I have requested Genl. Dearborn to be on the alert, and fly to the spot where any open & forcible opposition shall be commenced and to crush it in embryo. I am not afraid but that there is sound matter enough in Massachusets to prevent an opposition to the laws by force.

Jefferson confided to Albert Gallatin, "This embargo law is certainly the most embarrassing one we have ever had to execute. I did not expect a crop of so sudden and rank growth of fraud and open opposition by force could have grown up in the United States." Opposition was most marked in New England but sprang up as well in northern New York, where the Great Lakes and the St. Lawrence River offered avenues for illicit trade. Jefferson wrote firmly to New York Governor Daniel Tompkins.

Monticello Aug. 15. [18]08.

The case of opposition to the embargo laws on the Canada line, I take to be that of distinct combinations of a number of individuals to oppose by force and arms the execution of those laws, for which purpose they go armed, fire upon the public guards, in one instance at least have wounded one dangerously, and rescue property held under these laws. This may not be an insurrection in the popular sense of the word, but being arrayed in war-like manner, actually committing acts of war, and persevering systematically in defiance of the public authority, brings it so fully within the legal definition of an insurrection, that I should not hesitate to issue a proclamation were I not restrained by motives of which Y[our] E[xcellency] seems to be apprised. But as by the laws of New York an insurrection can be acted on without a previous proclamation I should concieve it perfectly correct to act on it as such, and I cannot doubt it would be approved by every good citizen. Should you think proper to do so, I will undertake that the necessary detachments of militia called out in support of the laws, shall be considered as in the service of the US. and at their expence. And as it has been intimated to me that you would probably take the trouble of going to the spot yourself, I will refer to your own discretion the measures to be taken, & the numbers to be cal[led] out at different places....I think it so important in example to crush these audacious proceedings, and to make the offenders feel the consequences of individuals daring to oppose a law by force, that no effort should be spared to compass this object.

Detail of an 1808 caricature showing the supposed influence of Napoleon on Jefferson; the drawing is by an unknown cartoonist who always signed his name as "Peter Pencil."

CULVER PICTURES, INC.

Such defiance of the embargo could render it useless. Radical Federalists in the Northeast seemed to have adopted that course from the beginning, Jefferson wrote Dr. Michael Leib.

Washington June 23. [18]08.
They are endeavoring to convince England that we suffer more by the embargo than they do, & that if they will but hold out a while, we must abandon it. It is true the time will come when we must abandon it. But if this is before the repeal of the orders of council, we must abandon it only for a state of war. The day is not distant, when that will be preferable to a longer continuance of the embargo. But we can never remove that, & let our vessels go out & be taken under these orders, without making reprisal. Yet this is the very state of things which these Federal monarchists are endeavoring to bring about; and in this it is but too possible they may succeed. But the fact is that if we have war with England it will be solely produced by their maneuvres.

In truth, the embargo was having a greater effect at home that summer than it was abroad. Britain suffered little; France, whose navy was weak, had already lost much of her trade with America before the Embargo Act. In his last annual message on November 8, Jefferson outlined the situation to Congress but offered no recommendations for further action. He was reluctant to press his own views, for he knew he would be "but a spectator" to any programs enacted. He explained his position to Levi Lincoln, his former Attorney General.

Washington Nov. 13. [18]08.
The congressional campaign is just opening: three alternatives alone are to be chosen from. 1. embargo. 2. war. 3. submission & tribute. And, wonderful to tell, the last will not want advocates. The real question however will lie between the two first, on which there is considerable division. As yet the first seems most to prevail; but opinions are by no means yet settled down. Perhaps the advocates of the 2d. may, to a formal declaration of war, prefer *general* letters of mark & reprisal, because on a repeal of their edicts by the belligerent, a revocation of the letters of mark restores peace without the delay, difficulties & ceremonies of a treaty. On this occasion I think it is fair to leave to those who are to act on them, the decisions they prefer, being to be myself but a spectator. I should [not] feel justified in directing measures which those who are to execute them would disapprove. Our situation is truly difficult. We have been pressed by the belligerents to the very wall, & all further retreat impracticable.

Public Men, SULLIVAN

Levi Lincoln

Jefferson, quite properly, did not feel he should direct the setting of policies, but Madison, now the President-elect, found it difficult to do so from the Cabinet. Congress floundered without effective leadership for the next two months. At the end of January, Jefferson wrote to Monroe of what the eventual legislative action might be.

Washington Jan. 28. [18]09.
The course the Legislature means to pursue may be inferred from the act now passed for a meeting in May, & a proposition before them for repealing the embargo in June & then resuming & maintaining by force our right of navigation....Final propositions will therefore be soon despatched to both the belligerents through the resident ministers, so that their answers will be recieved before the meeting in May, & will decide what is to be

A cartoon depicting Madison and Jefferson dragging American ship into port on Napoleon's orders

done. This last trial for peace is not thought desperate. If, as is expected, Bonaparte should be successful in Spain, . . . it may induce both powers to be more accommodating with us. . . . Otherwise we must again take the tented field as we did in 1776. under more inauspicious circumstances. There never has been a situation of the world before, in which such endeavors as we have made would not have secured our peace. It is probable there never will be such another. If we go to war now, I fear we may renounce for ever the hope of seeing an end of our national debt. If we can keep at peace 8. years longer, our income, liberated from death, will be adequate to any war, without new taxes or loans, and our position & increasing strength will put us hors d'insulte from any nation. I am now so near the moment of retiring, that I take no part in affairs beyond the expression of an opinion. I think it fair that my successor should now originate those measures of which he will be charged with the execution & responsibility, and that it is my duty to clothe them with the forms of authority. Five weeks more will relieve me from a drudgery to which I am no longer equal, and restore me to a scene of tranquility, amidst my family & friends, more congenial to my age and natural inclinations.

But Jefferson's inference was drawn too early. New England Federalists mobilized opposition to the continuation of the embargo beyond the winter congressional session. In Connecticut the governor issued a declaration echoing the Kentucky Resolutions of 1798, a hint that the northern states might also consider nullifying distasteful federal statutes. The Essex Junto, a group of New Englanders who had explored secession as a solution to sectional grievances in 1804, were willing to take that course again in 1809 and led the anti-embargo forces in Congress. In a later letter to William Branch Giles, Jefferson recalled a meeting with Congressman John Quincy Adams of Massachusetts during that bitter session. Adams was reluctant to intrude on Jefferson's time, knowing the strained relations between his parents and the President, but the matter he had to communicate was too important to be concealed.

Monticello Dec. 25. [18]25.
He made some apologies for the call on the ground of our not being then in the habit of confidential communications, but that that which he had then to make involved too seriously the interest of our country not to

overrule all other considerations with him, and make it his duty to reveal it to myself particularly. I assured him there was no occasion for any apology for his visit.... He spoke then of the dissatisfaction of the Eastern portion of our confederacy with the restraints of the embargo then existing and their restlessness under it. That there was nothing which might not be attempted, to rid themselves of it. That he had information of the most unquestionable certainty that certain citizens of the Eastern states (I think he named Massachusets particularly) were in negotiation with Agents of the British government, the object of which was an agreement that the New England states should take no further part in the war then going on; that without formally declaring their separation from the union of the States, they should withdraw from all aid and obedience to them; that their navigation and commerce should be free from restraint and interruption by the British; that they should be considered and treated by them as Neutrals and as such might conduct themselves towards both parties; and, at the close of the war, be at liberty to rejoin the Confederacy. He assured me that there was eminent danger that the Convention would take place; that the temptations were such as might debauch many from their fidelity to the union; and that, to enable it's friends to make head against it, the repeal of the embargo was absolutely necessary. I expressed a just sense of the merit of this information, and of the importance of the disclosure to the safety & even the salvation of our country. And, however reluctant I was to abandon the measure, (a measure which, persevered in a little longer, we had subsequent and satisfactory assurance would have effected it's object completely) from that moment, and influenced by that information, I saw the necessity of abandoning it, and instead of effecting our purpose by this peaceful weapon, we must fight it out or break the Union. I then recommended to my friends to yield to the necessity of a repeal of the embargo, and to endeavor to supply it's place by the best substitute in which they could procure a general concurrence.

Two cartoons by Peter Pencil made in 1809: "Non Intercourse or Dignified Retirement" (right) shows Jefferson in ragged clothing, "stript... rather than submit to London or Parisian Fashions!"; in "Intercourse or Impartial Dealings" (above), George III wields a club while Napoleon steals his purse.

A nd thus Jefferson abandoned the embargo. Republicans in Congress were released from any ties of party discipline so that they might vote as they wished in the matter. With repeal certain Madison tried, too late, to exert influence in Congress. He managed to persuade the legislature to enact a Nonintercourse Act that would take effect when the embargo ended and reopen trade with all nations except France and Britain. But the Secretary of State failed to win a system of "letters of marque and reprisal" allowing merchant ships to arm in defense of their rights. The President-elect was given only weak support for the continuing battle ahead.

As Jefferson ended his Presidency, he saw his dreams of winning recognition of commercial rights through peaceful measures destroyed. The embargo had "Federalized" New England and had brought no concessions from Britain. On February 28 the President wrote his son-in-law of the substitution of nonintercourse for the embargo and remarked on the plans to hold meetings in his honor along the road to Monticello the next month.

Washington Feb. 28. [18]09.

By yesterday's mail I learn that it would be the desire of many of the good citizens of our county to meet me on the road on my return home, as a manifestation of their good will. But it is quite impossible for me to ascertain the day on which I shall leave this. The accumulated business at the close of a session will prevent my making any preparation for my departure till after the 4th. of March. After that, the arrangement of papers and business to be delivered over to my successor, the winding up my own affairs & clearing out from this place will employ me for several days, (I cannot conjecture even how many,) so as to render the commencement, and consequently the termination of my journey, altogether uncertain. But it is a sufficient happiness to me to know that my fellow citizens of the county generally entertain for me the kind sentiments which have prompted this proposition, without giving to so many the trouble of leaving their homes to meet a single individual. I shall have opportunities of taking them individually by the hand at our courthouse & other public places & of exchanging assurances of mutual esteem. Certainly it is the greatest consolation to me to know that in returning to the bosom of my native country, I shall be again in the midst of their kind affections: and I can say with truth that my return to them will make me happier than I have been since I left them.

In his letter to Randolph, Jefferson only hinted at his weariness and desire to escape the demands of his office. He was more frank in writing to Samuel Du Pont de Nemours four days later.

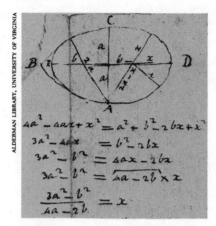

Jefferson's formula for drawing an ellipse, another example of his continuous interest in "the tranquil pursuits of science"

Washington Mar. 2. [18]09.

Within a few days I retire to my family, my books, & farms & having gained the harbor myself, I shall look on my friends still buffeting the storm, with anxiety indeed, but not with envy. Never did prisoner, released from his chains, feel such relief as I shall on shaking off the shackles of power. Nature intended me for the tranquil pursuits of science, by rendering them my supreme delight. But the enormities of the times in which I have lived have forced me to take a part in resisting them, and to commit myself on the boisterous ocean of political passions. I thank god for the opportunity of retiring from them without censure, and carrying with me the most consoling proofs of public approbation.

Like many another American President, Jefferson had lost his fight for the goal he had voiced in 1805: "at the end of a second term, [to] carry into retirement all the favor which the first has acquired." The achievements of his first term would not be erased, but the effort to purchase time in the second administration had failed, and each month he bought came at the cost of some sectional interest or political allegiance. In later years Jefferson emphasized that the embargo had not been given a fair trial, that the trade ban would have succeeded had it continued longer. By early 1809 the British had begun to feel the effects of the loss of American commerce and public opinion had at last begun to work on their government. But Jefferson himself had envisioned the policy as only a temporary measure. Unfortunately, its effects were felt slowly in Europe, but immediately in America.

Jefferson was nevertheless hopeful of his friend Madison's chances. "I leave everything in the hands of men so able to take care of them," he wrote shortly before leaving Washington that spring, "that if we are destined to meet misfortunes it will be because no human wisdom could avert them." The Treasury was sound; the federal bureaucracy was reformed; the rich, expanding West was unchallenged by foreign kings or emperors. Thanks to Jefferson's eight years in office, no Republican President would ever again have to prove that his party and its principles could govern America justly and energetically.

Chapter 13

Thomas Jefferson Survives

Shortly after returning to Monticello in March, 1809, Jefferson outlined his expectations for retirement in an address to his neighbors in Albemarle. He longed for "the enjoyment of an affectionate intercourse" with "neighbors and friends, and the endearments of family love," and looked forward to "repose and safety under the watchful cares, the labors and perplexities of younger and abler minds." He had sacrificed family and friends to help build the nation; he had neglected his own lands and crops to help build a republican system of government. No one better deserved years of peaceful retirement, but this, too, was denied him. Jefferson's last seventeen years were to be as full of challenge, hard work, and frustrating disappointments as any period in his life. Jefferson left the capital confident that Madison would preserve his public policies. One guest at the new President's inaugural ball remarked on Jefferson's pride in his younger friend. "I do believe," she wrote, "father never loved son more than he loves Mr. Madison." She also commented on Jefferson's obvious physical exhaustion, "looking as if he could scarcely stand." His weariness owed much to the strain of the last two years in office. He returned to Virginia at age sixty-five, suffering from rheumatism and headaches and weakened by an infected tooth. The Presidency had proved financially demanding as well, and he was burdened with substantial debts.

In the first winter of his retirement, Jefferson told his grandson, Thomas Jefferson Randolph, that he was busier in some ways than he had been when President. He found ample time, nevertheless, to reply to Thaddeus Kosciusko, the Polish patriot who had aided the American cause in Virginia during the Revolution. On hearing from his old comrade for the first time in decades, Jefferson answered with a long summary of American politics and closed with "a word as to myself," a portrait of daily life at Monticello.

Monticello Feb. 26. [18]10.

...in the bosom of my family, and surrounded by

my books, I enjoy a repose to which I have been long a stranger. My mornings are devoted to correspondence. From breakfast to dinner, I am in my shops, my garden, or on horseback among my farms; from dinner to dark I give to society and recreation with my neighbors and friends; and from candlelight to early bed-time I read. My health is perfect; and my strength considerably reinforced by the activity of the course I pursue; perhaps it is as great as usually falls to the lot of near 67. years of age. I talk of ploughs and harrows, seeding and harvesting, with my neighbors, and of politics too, if they chuse, with as little reserve as the rest of my fellow citizens, and feel at length the blessing of being free to say and do what I please, without being responsible for it to any mortal. A part of my occupation, and by no means the least pleasing, is the direction of the studies of such young men as ask it. They place themselves in the neighboring

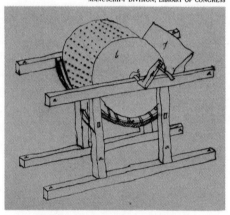

Jefferson's sketch of corn sheller he ordered for Monticello; it was designed by Paul Pillsbury in 1803.

The ex-President's response, on April 3, 1809, to an address of welcome from Albemarle residents

village, and have the use of my library and counsel, and make a part of my society. In advising the course of their reading, I endeavor to keep their attention fixed on the main objects of all science, the freedom and happiness of man. So that coming to bear a share in the councils and government of their country, they will keep ever in view the sole objects of all legitimate government.

Jefferson's early years of retirement were a period of personal happiness. His public career had taken him away from his own daughters during their childhood, and he seemed determined to make up for that loss by giving every minute he could to his grandsons and grand-daughters—one Eppes and, by 1818, eleven Randolphs. Virginia Randolph Trist later recalled those happy days after her grandfather retired.

St. Servan, France, May 26th, 1839. When he walked in the garden and would call the children to go with him, we raced after and before him, and we were made perfectly happy by this permission to accompany him. Not one of us, in our wildest moods, ever placed a foot on one of the garden-beds, for that would violate one of his rules, and yet I never heard him utter a harsh word to one of us, or speak in a raised tone of voice, or use a threat. He simply said, "Do," or "Do not"....

One of our earliest amusements was in running races on the terrace, or around the lawn. He placed us according to our ages, giving the youngest and smallest the start of all the others by some yards, and so on; and then he raised his arm high, with his white handkerchief in his hand, on which our eager eyes were fixed, and slowly counted three, at which number he dropped the handkerchief, and we started off to finish the race by returning to the starting-place and receiving our reward of dried fruit—three figs, prunes, or dates to the victor, two to the second, and one to the lagger who came in last.

Two of the Randolphs' eleven children who lived with their grandfather at Monticello were Thomas Jefferson and Cornelia.

BOTH: THOMAS JEFFERSON MEMORIAL FOUNDATION

Another source of personal happiness came as the result of intervention by Dr. Benjamin Rush. The Philadelphia physician-politician had maintained close ties with both Jefferson and John Adams and was determined that the two resume their friendship. Jefferson explained to Rush that his public differences with Adams were no barrier to their private friendship but that he believed Adams had been privy to the letters he had exchanged with Abigail Adams in 1804 and had endorsed her bitter criticism of his administration. The misunderstanding seemed insuperable until the summer of 1811 when Edward Coles, Madison's secretary, and his brother John Coles visited Quincy. Some months later reports of their conversations reached Jefferson and confirmed Mrs. Adams's contention that Adams had had no part in his wife's political remarks. From his estate at Poplar Forest, Jefferson wrote Rush that henceforth the doctor might feel free to play peacemaker, as he had tried to do previously by encouraging Jefferson to write to Adams.

Dr. Benjamin Rush by St. Mémin

Poplar Forest Dec. 5. [18]11.

Two of the Mr. Coles, my neighbors and friends...took a tour to the Northward during the last summer. In Boston they fell into company with Mr. Adams, & by his invitation passed a day with him at Braintree. He spoke out to them every thing which came uppermost, & as it occurred to his mind, without any reserve, and seemed most disposed to dwell on those things which happened during his own administration....Among many other topics, he adverted to the unprincipled licentiousness of the press against myself, adding, 'I always loved Jefferson, and still love him'—This is enough for me. I only needed this knolege to revive towards him all the affections of the most cordial moments of our lives....I wish therefore but for an apposite occasion to express to Mr. Adams my unchanged affections for him. There is an awkwardness which hangs over the resuming a correspondence so long discontinued, unless something could arise which should call for a letter. Time and chance may perhaps generate such an occasion, of which I shall not be wanting in promptitude to avail myself.

Rush went to work quickly. He wrote Adams, quoting Jefferson's letter, but Adams was not fooled. "I perceive plainly enough," he told Rush, "that you have been teasing Jefferson to write to me, as you did me some time ago to write to him." He left the doctor in suspense, merely conceding that "time and chance...or possibly design, may produce ere long a letter between us." Adams did not wait for time or chance, and on New Year's Day, 1812, he dispatched a short message to Monticello, ostensibly covering "a Packett containing two Pieces of Homespun lately produced in this quarter" by one who "was honoured in his youth with some of your Attention and much of your kindness." Although the homespun did not arrive with the letter, Jefferson sat down immediately to reply, opening with a description of the progress of textile manufactures in Virginia and moving on to the resumption of their friendship.

Monticello Jan. 21. 1812.

A letter from you calls up recollections very dear to my mind. It carries me back to the times when, beset with difficulties & dangers, we were fellow laborers in the same cause, struggling for what is most valuable to man, his right of self-government. Laboring always at the same oar, with some wave ever ahead threatening to overwhelm us & yet passing harmless under our bark, we knew not how, we rode through the storm with heart & hand, and made a happy port. Still we did not expect to be without rubs and difficulties; and we have had them....

But whither is senile garrulity leading me? Into politics, of which I have taken final leave. I think little of them & say less. I have given up newspapers in exchange for Tacitus & Thucydides, for Newton & Euclid; & I find myself much the happier. Sometimes indeed I look back to former occurrences, in remembrance of our old friends and fellow laborers, who have fallen before us. Of the signers of the Declaration of Independance I see now living not more than half a dozen on your side of the Potomak, and, on this side, myself alone. You & I have been wonderfully spared, and myself with remarkable health, & a considerable activity of body & mind....I have heard with pleasure that you also retain good health, and a greater power of exercise in walking than I do. But I would rather have heard this from yourself, & that, writing a letter, like mine, full of egotisms, & of details of your health, your habits, occupations & enjoiments, I should have the pleasure of knowing that, in the race of life, you do not keep, in it's physical decline, the same distance ahead of me which you have done in political honors & atchievements. No circumstances have lessened the interest I feel in these particulars respecting yourself; none have suspended for one moment my sincere esteem for you; and I now salute you with unchanged affections and respect.

Abigail Adams (top), after retiring with her husband to their handsome home at Braintree, renamed Quincy

The messenger who took Jefferson's letter to the post office returned with the "homespun" sent by Adams: a two-volume set of

John Quincy Adams's *Lectures on Rhetoric and Oratory.* Delighted by the joke, Jefferson congratulated his friend on his son's work and added: "A little more sagacity of conjecture in me...would have saved you the trouble of reading a long dissertation on the state of real homespun in our quarter." Jefferson and Adams assured each other that they were tired of politics, and their correspondence scrupulously avoided any topics that might reopen old wounds, including an approaching war with Great Britain. British intransigence on impressment and interference with neutral shipping had continued during Madison's first three years, and despite all his efforts to avoid it, he asked Congress to declare war in June, 1812. At first, this struggle for a second "weaning from British principles," as Jefferson described it, went well for his family. Wartime demand for foodstuffs gave him encouraging profits the first year, but a British blockade in the spring of 1813 left Jefferson with hundreds of barrels of unsold flour in Richmond warehouses. He had corresponded with Madison frequently since his retirement, offering advice on problems with Great Britain, occasional suggestions for appointments, and news of agricultural matters of interest to both planters. He used their close friendship in 1813 to plead almost desperately for a military effort to disrupt the British blockade, which was proving disastrous to Virginia's economy.

Monticello May 21. [18]13.

We have never seen so unpromising a crop of wheat as that now growing. The winter killed an unusual proportion of it, and the fly is destroying the remainder. We may estimate the latter loss at one-third at present, and fast increasing from the effect of the extraordinary drought. With such a prospect before us, the blockade is acting severely on our past labors. It caught nearly the whole wheat of the middle and upper country in the hands of the farmers and millers, whose interior situation had prevented their getting it to an earlier market. From this neighborhood very little had been sold. When we cast our eyes on the map, and see the extent of country from New York to North Carolina inclusive whose produce is raised on the waters of the Chesapeak... and consider it's productiveness in comparison with the rest of the Atlantic States, probably a full half, and that all this can be shut up by two or three ships of the line, lying at the mouth of the bay, we see that an injury so vast to ourselves and so cheap to our enemy must for ever be resorted to by them, and constantly maintained. To defend all the shores of those waters in detail, is impossible. But is there not a single point where they may be all defended by means to which the magnitude of the

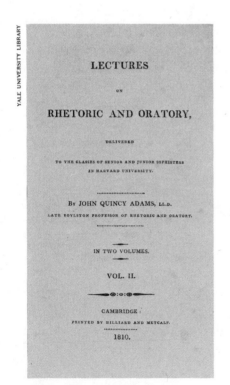

LECTURES

ON

RHETORIC AND ORATORY,

DELIVERED

TO THE CLASSES OF SENIOR AND JUNIOR SOPHISTERS
IN HARVARD UNIVERSITY.

By JOHN QUINCY ADAMS, LL.D.

LATE BOYLSTON PROFESSOR OF RHETORIC AND ORATORY.

IN TWO VOLUMES.

VOL. II.

CAMBRIDGE :

PRINTED BY HILLIARD AND METCALF.

1810.

Title page of the second volume of John Quincy Adams's Lectures on Rhetoric and Oratory, *1810*

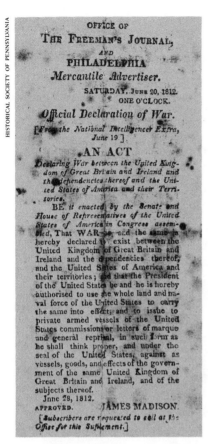

OFFICE OF
THE FREEMAN'S JOURNAL,
AND
PHILADELPHIA
Mercantile Advertiser.
SATURDAY, JUNE 20, 1812.
ONE O'CLOCK.

Official Declaration of War.
[From the National Intelligencer Extra,
June 19].

AN ACT

Declaring War between the United Kingdom of Great Britain and Ireland and the dependencies thereof and the United States of America and their Territories.

BE it enacted by the Senate and House of Representatives of the United States of America in Congress assembled, That WAR be and the same is hereby declared to exist between the United Kingdom of Great Britain and Ireland and the dependencies thereof, and the United States of America and their territories; and that the President of the United States be and he is hereby authorised to use the whole land and naval force of the United States to carry the same into effect, and to issue to private armed vessels of the United States commissions or letters of marque and general reprisal, in such form as he shall think proper, and under the seal of the United States, against as vessels, goods, and effects of the government of the same United Kingdom of Great Britain and Ireland, and of the subjects thereof.

June 28, 1812.
APPROVED. JAMES MADISON.
[Subscribers are requested to call at this Office for this Supplement.]

Broadside of declaration of war

object gives a title? I mean at the mouth of the Chesapeak. Not by ships of the line, or frigates; for I know that with our present enemy we cannot contend in that way. But would not a sufficient number of gunboats, of *small* draught, stationed in Lynhaven river, render it unsafe for ships of war either to ascend the Chesapeak or to lie at it's mouth? . . .

. . . The importance of keeping open a water which covers, wholly or considerably, five of the most productive States, containing threefifths of the population of the Atlantic portion of our union, and of preserving their resources for the support of the war, as far as the state of war, and the means of the Confederacy will admit; and especially if it can be done for less than is contributed by the union for more than one single city, will justify our anxieties to have it effected. And should my views of the subject be even wrong, I am sure they will find their apology with you in the purity of the motives of personal & public regard which induce a suggestion of them. In all cases I am satisfied you are doing what is for the best as far as the means put into your hands will enable you; and this thought quiets me under every occurrence and under every occurrence I am sincerely, affectionately & respectfully your's.

Madison did not share Jefferson's faith in gunboats, and frigates from the small navy could not be spared; the war continued to take its toll. In this context of conflict, the forbidden topic of politics became unavoidable between Monticello and Braintree. In May, 1813, Adams saw a copy of the *Memoirs of the Late Reverend Theophilus Lindsay,* an acquaintance of his London years, which contained outspoken letters Jefferson had written Joseph Priestley after the bitterly contested electoral battle of 1801. Adams demanded an explanation of remarks in the letters that seemed directed at him. The time had come for mutual explanation.

Monticello June 27. [18]13.
The same political parties which now agitate the U.S. have existed thro' all time. Whether the power of the people, or that of the aristoi should prevail, were questions which kept the states of Greece and Rome in eternal convulsions; as they now schismatize every people whose minds and mouths are not shut up by the gag of a despot. . . . To come to our own country, and to the times when you and I became first acquainted, we

An 1814 cartoon depicts John Bull
offering terms of capitulation
to some weak-kneed Americans.

well remember the violent parties which agitated the old Congress, and their bitter contests. There you & I were together, and the Jays, and the Dickinsons, and other anti-independants were arrayed against us.... When our present government was in the mew, passing from Confederation to Union, how bitter was the schism between the Feds and Antis. Here you and I were together again.... But as soon as it was put into motion, the line of division was again drawn; we broke into two parties, each wishing to give a different direction to the government; the one to strengthen the most popular branch, the other the more permanent branches, and to extend their permanence. Here you & I separated for the first time: and as we had been longer than most others on the public theatre, and our names therefore were more familiar to our countrymen, the party which considered you as thinking with them, placed your name at their head; the other, for the same reason, selected mine. But neither decency nor inclination permitted us to become the advocates of ourselves, or to take part personally in the violent contests which followed. We suffered ourselves, as you so well expressed it, to be the passive subjects of public discussion. And these discussions, whether relating to men, measures, or opinions, were conducted by the parties with an animosity, a bitterness, and an indecency, which had never been exceeded.... Shall we, at our age, become the Athletae of party, and exhibit ourselves, as gladiators, in the Arena of the newspapers? Nothing in the universe could induce me to it. My mind has been long fixed to bow to the judgment of the world, who will judge me by my acts, and will never take counsel from me as to what that judgment shall be. If your objects and opinions have been misunderstood, if the measures and principles of others have been wrongfully imputed to you, as I believe they have been, that you should leave an explanation of them, would be an act of justice to yourself.

The friendship not only survived the introduction of politics but was strengthened. Jefferson accepted the challenge of mutual self-explanation so enthusiastically that he told Adams of a subject he had concealed even from his family. He sent Adams his "Syllabus" of the teachings of Christ, a digest of basic Christian tenets compared with the beliefs of others, such as the ancients and the Jews, which he had prepared many years before. In discussing the Syllabus, Jefferson demonstrated that he was not an unbeliever but an opponent of organized religions and the priests and theologians who made a mystery of basic morality.

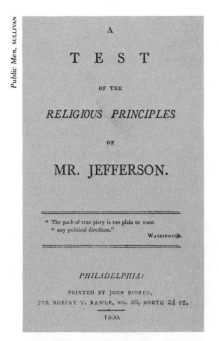

A

T E S T

OF THE

RELIGIOUS PRINCIPLES

OF

MR. JEFFERSON.

" The path of true piety is too plain to want
" any political direction."
WASHINGTON.

PHILADELPHIA:

PRINTED BY JOHN BIOREN,
FOR ROBERT T. RAWLE, NO. 50, NORTH 2d ST.
1800.

One of the many pamphlets that had attacked Jefferson's religious views in the campaign of 1800

Monticello Oct. 12. [18]13.
It was the reformation of this 'wretched depravity' of morals which Jesus undertook. In extracting the pure principles which he taught, we should have to strip off the artificial vestments in which they have been muffled by priests, who have travestied them into various forms, as instruments of riches and power to them.... We must reduce our volume to the simple evangelists, select, even from them, the very words only of Jesus, paring off the Amphibologisms into which they have been led by forgetting often, or not understanding, what had fallen from him, by giving their own misconceptions as his dicta, and expressing unintelligibly for others what they had not understood themselves. There will be found remaining the most sublime and benevolent code of morals which has ever been offered to man. I have performed this operation for my own use, by cutting verse by verse out of the printed book, and arranging, the matter which is evidently his, and which is as easily distinguishable as diamonds in a dunghill. The result is an 8vo. [octavo] of 46. pages of pure and unsophisticated doctrines, such as were professed & acted on by the *unlettered* apostles, the Apostolic fathers, and the Christians of the 1st. century.

The war dragged on, but by the summer of 1814, Jefferson was spending much of his time on a project that was to demand his attention for the rest of his life. Earlier in the year his nephew, Peter Carr, and other citizens of Albemarle County had begun to organize a private secondary school in the Charlottesville neighborhood. When Jefferson was named to the academy's board, he set to work using the scheme as the basis for his dream of giving Virginia a comprehensive system of education. On September 7 he sent Carr a plan he had drafted at the request of the other trustees "adapted, in the first instance to our slender funds, but susceptible of being enlarged." The new institution was to be considered in terms of the general needs of the state, not as an isolated preparatory school for young gentlemen.

Monticello Sept. 7. [18]14.
In the first place, we must ascertain with precision the

object of our institution, by taking a survey of the general field of science, and marking out the portion we mean to occupy at first, and the ultimate extension of our views beyond that, should we be enabled to render it, in the end, as comprehensive as we would wish.

I. Elementary Schools.

... The mass of our citizens may be divided into two classes, the laboring & the learned. The laboring will need the first grade of education to qualify them for their pursuits and duties: the learned will need it as a foundation for further acquirements....

II. General Schools.

At the discharge of the pupils from the elementary schools, the two classes separate: & those destined for labor will engage in the business of agriculture, or enter into apprenticeships...; their companions, destined to the pursuits of science, will proceed to the College, which will consist of 1st. General schools and, 2d. of Professional schools. The General schools will constitute the second grade of education.

The learned class may still be subdivided into two sections. 1. Those who are destined for learned professions as means of livelihood; and. 2. the Wealthy, who possessing independant fortunes may aspire to share in conducting the affairs of the nation, or to live with usefulness & respect in the private ranks of life.... All the branches, then, of useful science, ought to be taught in the general schools, to a competent degree....

III. Professional Schools.

At the close of this course the Students separate, the wealthy retiring with a sufficient stock of knolege to improve themselves to any degree to which their views may lead them, and the Professional section to the Professional Schools constituting the IIId. Grade of education, and teaching the particular sciences which the individuals of this section mean to pursue.... In these Professional schools each science is to be taught in the highest degree it has yet attained. They are to be in the

Ist. Department, the Fine arts....

IId. Department, Architecture, military and naval; Projectiles, Rural economy..., technical philosophy, the Practice of Medecine, Materia Medica, Pharmacy and

The burning of Washington, 1814

Surgery. In the

IIId. Department, Theology & Ecclesiastical history; Law municipal and foreign....

On this survey of the field of science, I recur to the question, what portion of it we mark out for the occupation of our Institution? With the 1st. grade of education we shall have nothing to do. The sciences of the 2d. grade are our first object....

To implement his plans, Jefferson drafted a bill for the incorporation of the planned academy as Central College, but the Virginia legislature ignored the measure that winter. In wartime, the state's lawmakers had little time for public education, and in September, 1814, the return of peace and prosperity seemed more distant than ever. In late August, British troops had landed on American soil and marched on the capital. Washington was occupied and its public buildings burned. In a typical gesture, Jefferson offered the government his most precious possession to soften a national loss: his own library to restock the Library of Congress. On September 21 he wrote to Samuel Harrison Smith, who was the chairman of the library committee for the Library of Congress, to arrange for the sale of his books.

Monticello, September 21, 1814.

I learn from the newspapers that the vandalism of our enemy has triumphed at Washington over science as well as the arts, by the destruction of the public library....

I presume it will be among the early objects of Congress to re-commence their collection. This will be difficult while the war continues, and intercourse with Europe is attended with so much risk. You know my collection, its condition and extent. I have been fifty years making it, and have spared no pains, opportunity or expense, to make it what it is.... I had standing orders during the whole time I was in Europe, on its principal book-marts... for such works relating to America as could not be found in Paris. So that in that department particularly, such a collection was made as probably can never again be effected.... During the same period, and after my return to America, I was led to procure, also, whatever related to the duties of those in the high concerns of the nation. So that the collection, which I suppose is of between nine and ten thousand volumes, while it includes what is chiefly valuable in science and literature generally, extends more particularly to whatever belongs to the American statesman. In the diplomatic and parliamentary branches, it is particularly full. It is long since I have been sensible it ought not to continue private property, and had provided that at my death, Congress should have the refusal of it at their own price. But the loss they have now incurred, makes the present the proper moment for their accommodation, without regard to the small remnant of time and the barren use of my enjoying it.

Congress authorized almost twenty-four thousand dollars for the purchase in December, and the income, though far less than the books were worth, was welcome and timely for Jefferson. That same month the Treaty of Ghent was signed, ending the war. It came just in time to quell secessionist threats in New England, but the peace left America in a severe economic depression that pressed heavily on farmers of the South and West. Jefferson pushed overseers and servants to harvest crops that might help him recover from the debts burdening his acres. But he was over seventy, increasingly troubled by rheumatism and other ills of old age, and in 1815 his eldest grandson, Thomas Jefferson Randolph, assumed responsibility for much of the estate. America's finances were no better, and the creation of banks as a prescription for all economic ills had new popularity. In his annual message of December, 1815, James Madison recommended "consideration" of a "national bank." As Congress debated provisions of the Second Bank of the United States, Jefferson wrote to fellow Virginian, Colonel Charles Yancey.

Monticello Jan. 6. [18]16

Like a dropsical man calling out for water, water, our deluded citizens are clamoring for more banks, more banks. The American mind is now in that state of fever which the world has so often seen in the history of other nations. We are under the bank-bubble, as England was under the South sea bubble, France under the Misisipi bubble, and as every nation is liable to be, under whatever bubble design or delusion may puff up in moments when off their guard. We are now taught to believe that legerdemain tricks upon paper can produce as solid wealth as hard labor in the earth. It is vain for common sense to urge that *nothing* can produce but *nothing:* that it is an idle dream to believe in a philosopher's stone which is to turn every thing into gold, and to redeem man from the original sentence of his maker, 'in the sweat of his brow shall he eat his bread'....I am willing to swim or sink with my fellow citizens.... But my exhortation would rather be 'not to give up the ship.'

The Second Bank of the United States became a reality, nevertheless, adding its branches to scores of state-chartered banks which had grown up over the nation. Instead of peaceful, prosperous retirement, Jefferson was engaged in a fight to recover from losses incurred during years of naval war. In 1816 he and Adams debated the question whether they would choose to live their lives over again. In his first comments on this query, Jefferson seemed ready to answer in the affirmative. "I think with you," he wrote Adams, "that it is a good world on the whole, that it has been framed on a principle of benevolence, and more pleasure than pain dealt out to us." But on reconsidering the matter a few months later, he qualified the statement.

Monticello Aug. 1. [18]16.

... Would I agree to live my 73. years over again for ever? I hesitate to say ... from 25. to 60. I would say Yes; and might go further back, but not come lower down. For, at the latter period, with most of us, the powers of life are sensibly on the wane, sight becomes dim, hearing dull, memory constantly enlarging it's frightful blank and parting with all we have ever seen or known, spirits evaporate, bodily debility creeps on palsying every limb, and so faculty after faculty quits us, and where then is life? ... There is a ripeness of time for death, regarding others as well as ourselves, when it is reasonable we should drop off, and make room for another growth.... I enjoy good health; I am happy in what is around me. Yet I assure you I am ripe for leaving all, this year, this day, this hour.

Gilbert Stuart's striking portrait of John Adams the year before he died

Duties as planter and head of a family were not the only ones Jefferson bore in those years. Adams's estimate of the number of books he read each year filled Jefferson with envy. He wrote his friend of the drain on his precious time caused by the innumerable and unsolicited letters he answered each day.

Monticello Jan. 11. [18]17.

Forty three volumes read in one year, and 12. of them quartos! Dear Sir, how I envy you! Half a dozen 8vos. in that space of time are as much as I am allowed. I can read by candlelight only, and stealing long hours from my rest; nor would that time be indulged to me, could I, by that light, see to write. From sun-rise to one or two aclock, and often from dinner to dark, I am drudging at the writing table. And all this to answer letters into which neither interest nor inclination on my part enters; and often for persons whose names I have never before heard. Yet, writing civilly, it is hard to refuse them civil answers. This is the burthen of my life, a very grievous one indeed, and one which I must get rid of.

The next year brought a more pleasant "burthen." In February, 1816, the legislature had agreed to Jefferson's bill to incorporate the academy at Charlottesville as Central College. The charter was a broad one, even if funds for expanding the academy were small. Fortunately the Board of Visitors was more distinguished than the endowment; Jefferson could look forward to the aid of his friends Monroe and Madison. James Monroe had become Madison's Secretary of State in 1810 and had won the 1816 presidential election handsomely. In May Jefferson cheerfully described to Adams the academic work facing the new President and the retiring executive.

Album of Virginia BY ED. BEYER 1858

Plans for the University of Virginia were agreed upon at Rockfish Gap.

Monticello. May 5. [18]17.

I do not entertain your apprehensions for the happiness of our brother Madison in a state of retirement. Such a mind as his, fraught with information, and with matter for reflection, can never know ennui. Besides, there will always be work enough cut out for him to continue his active usefulness to his country. For example, he and Monroe (the president) are now here on the work of a collegiate institution to be established in our neighborhood, of which they and myself are three of six Visitors. This, if it succeeds, will raise up children for Mr. Madison to employ his attentions thro' life. I say, if it succeeds; for we have two very essential wants in our way 1. means to compass our views & 2dly. men qualified to fulfill them. And these you will agree are essential wants indeed.

Land had been purchased west of Charlottesville for the college, and even before the first cornerstone was laid, Jefferson planned to turn it into a state university. When the legislature incorporated Central College, it had directed the trustees of the Literary Fund, an agency responsible for distributing funds to charity schools, to prepare a statewide educational plan. On September 9 Jefferson sent Joseph Cabell, his ally in the legislature, a scheme for local tax support of elementary schools that would free the Literary Fund for higher education. He included the suggestion that Central College's Visitors surrender their institution "for use as the University of Virginia, which shall be established on the said lands."

Cabell was not able to gain everything he and Jefferson sought, but he did win the state's commitment to the creation of the University of Virginia. There would be an income of only fifteen thousand dollars for the school, not the entire Literary Fund, and the legislature had not selected a site. But Jefferson was named to the commission to select the location, and at meetings at Rockfish Gap early in August, 1818, he skillfully persuaded his colleagues to recommend the Central College campus. That winter Cabell shepherded the proposal for a Charlottesville campus through the legislature. Inadequately financed, the state university would be the only part of Jefferson's educational plan, his "bantling of forty years," to become a reality in his lifetime. But its location at Charlottesville meant that he could supervise its development, and he became the first Rector of the state university.

There had always been an element of local pride in Jefferson's wish to see a coherent system of education in Virginia; he had envisioned it as a model for other states and for all Americans. Events in 1819 and 1820 provided additional justification for his plan. First the financial panic of 1819, with stock market failures and bank closings, bore out his warnings of the results of the "bank-bubble" and catering to mercantile interests. The panic was a personal disaster as well, for he had countersigned loans amounting to twenty thousand dollars for Wilson Cary Nicholas at the Bank of the United States. Nicholas's bankruptcy left Jefferson responsible for the debt, a financial burden he was never able to discharge. Jefferson's distrust of the North increased, and he saw the university as a way to insulate young Southerners from the influences of that region. This feeling was confirmed in 1820 when he saw northern "consolidation," his term for the amalgamation of federal power at the expense of states' rights, triumph in the Missouri Compromise. Under this agreement, Maine and Missouri were admitted to the Union simultaneously to preserve the balance of slave and free states, and Congress banned slavery from the Louisiana Territory north of the line 36°30'. Jefferson attacked the compromise in a letter to John Holmes, a member of the Massachusetts Senate, because it imposed the morality of one section on another and infringed on the rights of individual citizens.

Monticello Apr. 22. [18]20.

I had for a long time ceased to read newspapers or pay any attention to public affairs, confident they were in good hands, and content to be a passenger in our bark to the shore from which I am not distant. But this momentous question, like a fire bell in the night, awakened and filled me with terror. I considered it at once as the

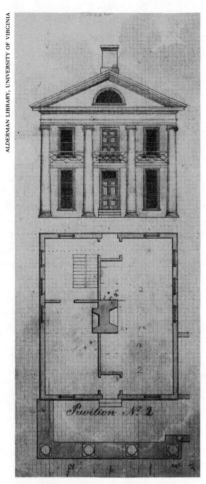

One of the pavilions Jefferson designed as residences for professors at the university

knell of the Union. It is hushed, indeed, for the moment. But this is a reprieve only, not a final sentence. A geographical line, coinciding with a marked principle, moral and political, once concieved and held up to the angry passions of men, will never be obliterated; and every new irritation will mark it deeper and deeper. I can say with conscious truth that there is not a man on earth who would sacrifice more than I would, to relieve us from this heavy reproach, in any *practicable* way. The cession of that kind of property, for so it is misnamed, is a bagatelle which would not cost me a second thought, if, in that way, a general emancipation and *expatriation* could be effected: and, gradually, and with due sacrifices, I think it might be. But, as it is we have the wolf by the ear, and we can neither hold him, nor safely let him go. Justice is in one scale, and self-preservation in the other.... An abstinence too from this act of power, would remove the jealousy excited by the undertaking of Congress, to regulate the condition of the different descriptions of men composing a state. This certainly is the exclusive right of every state, which nothing in the constitution has taken from them and given to the general government....

I regret that I am now to die in the belief that the useless sacrifice of themselves, by the generation of '76. to acquire self government and happiness to their country, is to be thrown away by the unwise and unworthy passions of their sons, and that my only consolation is to be that I live not to weep over it.

The chance for the creation of a great southern university to compete with the colleges of the North nearly died in the winter of 1820–21. The legislature allowed the Visitors to borrow sixty thousand dollars from the Literary Fund, but that was only enough for completion of housing for students and professors. Another loan was needed to begin construction of the library. Jefferson wrote another Visitor, James Breckinridge, of his "deep affliction" at news the university might be denied new funds.

Monticello Feb. 15. [18]21.
The reflections that the boys of this age are to be the men of the next; that they should be prepared to recieve the holy charge which we are cherishing to deliver over to them; that in establishing an institution of wis-

Jefferson in 1821 by Thomas Sully

dom for them we secure it to all our future generations . . . ; these are considerations which will occur to all; but all, I fear, do not see the speck in our horizon which is to burst on us as a tornado, sooner or later. The line of division lately marked out between different portions of our confederacy, is such as will never, I fear, be obliterated, and we are now trusting to those who are against us in position and principle, to fashion to their own form the minds & affections of our youth. If, as has been estimated, we send 300,000. D. a year to the Northern seminaries, for the instruction of our own sons, then we must have there at all times 500. of our sons imbibing opinions and principles in discord with those of their own country. This canker is eating on the vitals of our existence, and if not arrested at once will be beyond remedy. We are now certainly furnishing recruits to their school.

Jefferson's friends in the legislature won again; the Visitors were allowed to borrow another sixty thousand dollars. Slowly, tantalizingly, the campus at Charlottesville took shape. Jefferson brooded over the carvings on marble columns, canvassed the states for prospective faculty members, and accepted the fact that he had but a few years in which to see his dream realized. In January, 1821, he turned to a long neglected task: recording the facts of his life. He began his *Autobiography* with this explanation: "At the age of 77, I begin to make some memoranda and state some recollections of dates & facts concerning myself, for my own more ready reference & for the inform[atio]n of my family." He knew that the number who could share his memories of those dates and facts was shrinking, and in June, 1822, Jefferson wrote Adams of the sad cycle of senility and death in their revolutionary circle.

Monticello June 1. [18]22.

The papers tell us that Genl. Starke is off at the age of 93. Charles Thomson [Secretary of the Continental Congress] still lives at about the same age, chearful, slender as a grasshopper, and so much without memory that he scarcely recognises the members of his household. An intimate friend of his called on him not long since: it was difficult to make him recollect who he was, and sitting one hour, he told him the same story 4. times over. Is this life? . . . It is at most but the life of a cabbage, surely not worth a wish. When all our faculties have left, or are leaving us, one by one, sight, hearing, memory,

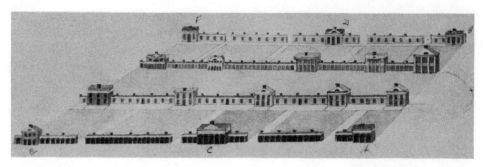

A bird's-eye view, which may have been drawn by Cornelia Randolph, of the university's lawns and ranges, pavilions, "hotels" for "dieting the students" and connecting dorms

every avenue of pleasing sensation is closed, and athumy, debility and mal-aise left in their places, when the friends of our youth are all gone, and a generation is risen around us whom we know not, is death an evil?

Adams replied in an unusually lighthearted vein. Jefferson's letter, he wrote, was "the best letter that ever was written by an Octogenearian." He told of his own failing eyesight but boasted that he teased others to read to him "most unmercifully and tyrannically, against their consent." Adams's letter dispelled Jefferson's uncharacteristically gloomy mood, and he offered to break his lifelong rule of keeping his personal correspondence confidential. If Adams would consent to publish their recent exchange of letters, the public might take pity on them both.

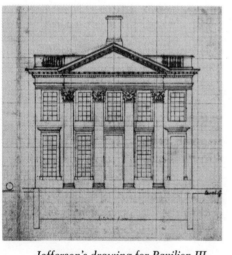

Jefferson's drawing for Pavilion III using the Corinthian order

Monticello June 27. [18]22.

I do not know how far you may suffer as I do, under the persecution of letters, of which every mail brings a fresh load....I happened to turn to my letter-list some time ago, and a curiosity was excited to count those recieved in a single year....I found the number to be 1267. many of them requiring answers of elaborate research, and all to be answered with due attention and consideration. Take an average of this number for a week or a day, and I will repeat the question suggested by other considerations in mine of the 1st. Is this life?...It occurs then that my condition of existence, truly stated in that letter, if better known, might check the kind indiscretions which are so heavily oppressing the departing hours of life. Such a relief would to me be an ineffable blessing. But yours of the 11th. equally interesting and affecting, should accompany that to which it is an answer. The two taken together would excite a joint interest, and place before our fellow-citizens the present condition of two antient servants, who having faithfully performed their

40. or 50. campaigns, stipendiis omnibus expletis [after all their military duty had been completed], have a reasonable claim to repose from all disturbance in the Sanctuary of Invalids and Superannuates.

Construction was complete for all the university buildings except the library by the fall of 1822, and to build it, the Visitors sought another loan. To allow hiring of professors and payment of operating expenses, they asked that the legislature convert earlier loans to outright grants so that repayment of interest and principal would not be a drain on yearly income. Once again, Joseph Cabell did battle in the state legislature. He did not share Jefferson's belief that all the Visitors' demands would be met and asked the Rector to state his priorities. Jefferson's continuing ill health, aggravated by a fall in which he broke his left arm, did not keep him from preparing this concise, practical statement for Cabell's use in December.

Monticello Dec. 28. [18]22

If the remission of the principal debt, and an accomodation of the cost of the library cannot both be obtained, which would be most desirable? Without any question, the latter. Of all things the most important is the completion of the buildings. The remission of the debt will come of itself.... The great object of our aim from the beginning has been to make this establishment the most eminent in the United States, in order to draw to it the youth of every state, but especially of the South and West. We have proposed therefore to call to it characters of the first order of science from Europe as well as our own country; and, not only by their salaries, and the comforts of their situation, but by the distinguished scale of it's structure and preparation.... Had we built a barn for a College and log-huts for accommodations, should we ever have had the assurance to propose to an European Professor of that character to come to it? Why give up this important idea, when so near it's accomplishment that a single lift more effects it?... The opening of the institution in a half-state of readiness would be the most fatal step which could be adopted. It would be an impatience defeating it's own object....

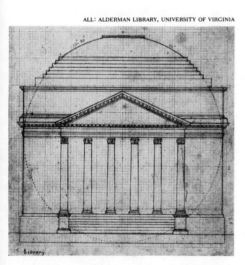

Elevation of Rotunda, which housed the library, as drawn by the Rector

Jefferson never completely recovered from the accident that cost him the use of his left arm. His senses were as keen as ever, but his physical stamina was severely limited. The year 1823 was not an easy one on other scores. The legislature had granted the Visitors another loan but did nothing to relieve them of the payment of old debts. The year was brightened by an appeal from James Monroe. Unlike Madison, Monroe had seldom sought Jefferson's advice, but in October he asked both ex-Presidents for their counsel on the latest diplomatic turn: Britain's suggestion that she and the United States issue a joint condemnation of the efforts of the Quadruple Alliance to reconquer the Spanish American colonies, which had won their freedom and independence. The fate of these new republics had long troubled Jefferson, and he had discussed their problems in a letter to Lafayette a decade earlier.

Monticello Nov. 30. [18]13

I join you sincerely, my friend in wishes for the emancipation of South America. That they will be liberated from foreign subjection I have little doubt. But the result of my enquiries does not authorise me to hope they are capable of maintaining a free government. Their people are immersed in the darkest ignorance, and brutalised by bigotry & superstition.... Their efforts I fear therefore will end in establishing military despotism in the several provinces.... But their future wars & quarrels among themselves will oblige them to bring the people into action & into the exertion of understandings. Light will at length beam in on their minds and the standing example we shall hold up, serving as an excitement as well as a model for their direction may in the long run qualify them for self government.

James Monroe by Thomas Sully, 1820

When Monroe wrote in October to ask whether the present situation warranted an exception to the rule of America's splendid diplomatic isolation, Jefferson answered in the affirmative.

Monticello Oct. 24. [18]23.

The question ... is the most momentous which has ever been offered to my contemplation since that of independance. That made us a nation, this sets our compass, and points the course which we are to steer thro' the ocean of time opening on our view.... Our first and fundamental maxim should be, never to entangle ourselves in the broils of Europe; our 2d. never to suffer Europe to intermeddle with Cis-Atlantic affairs. America, North & South, has a set of interests distinct from those of Europe, and peculiarly her own. She should therefore have a system of her own, separate and apart from that of Europe. While the last is laboring to become the dom-

Francis Walker Gilmer

icil of despotism, our endeavor should surely be to make our hemisphere that of freedom. One nation, most of all, could disturb us in this pursuit; she now offers to lead, aid, and accompany us in it.... With her then we should the most sedulously nourish a cordial friendship; and nothing would tend more to knit our affections than to be fighting once more side by side in the same cause. Not that I would purchase even her amity at the price of taking part in her wars. But the war in which the present proposition might engage us, should that be it's consequence, is not her war, but ours. It's object is to introduce and establish the American system, of ousting from our land all foreign nations, of never permitting the powers of Europe to intermeddle with the affairs of our nations. It is to maintain our own principle, not to depart from it.

This philosophy found official expression in December when the Monroe Doctrine was proclaimed. The independence of the two American continents had been declared. The next year, 1824, Jefferson brooded over the coming presidential elections. For the first time since 1800 Republican unity was in question; no fewer than four candidates competed for party support. The election was bound to reflect the growing division between North and South, free and slave states, and Jefferson wrote Lafayette of his fear that "the question will be ultimately reduced to the northernmost and southernmost candidate." Jefferson was busy that spring with the university. He compiled a catalogue of 6,860 volumes that should be purchased for the library—an astounding intellectual feat. News that the Virginia legislature had decided to forget the interest on the three loans freed enough income to allow the Visitors to recruit a faculty in earnest. Jefferson had difficulty attracting American scholars of the "first grade" for the professorships, and since he would not settle for second-rate men, was forced to look in Europe. Francis Walker Gilmer, described by Jefferson as "the best-educated subject we have raised since the Revolution," sailed to Britain to recruit teachers from Oxford, Cambridge, and Edinburgh with this letter of introduction to Richard Rush, the American minister in London.

Monticello Apr. 26. [18]24.

I have heretofore informed you that our legislature had undertaken the establishment of an University of Virginia.... and we propose to open it at the beginning of the next year. We require the intervening time for seeking out, and engaging Professors. As to these, we have determined to recieve no one who is not of the first order of science in his line; and as such in every branch cannot be obtained with us, we propose to seek some of them at least in the countries ahead of us in science, and preferably in Great Britain, the land of our own language, habits, and manners. But how to find out those who are of the first grade of science, of sober and correct habits and morals, harmonising tempers, talents for communication is the difficulty. Our first step is to send a special agent to the Universities of Oxford, Cambridge & Edinburgh, to make the selection for us....We do not certainly expect to obtain...men of the first eminence, established there in reputation and office, and with emoluments not to be bettered anywhere. But we know that there is another race, treading on their heels, preparing to take their places, and as well, and sometimes better qualified to fill them. These while unsettled, surrounded by a crowd of competitors, of equal claims and perhaps superior credit and interest, may prefer a comfortable certainty here to an uncertain hope there, and a lingering delay even of that. From this description we expect we may draw professors equal to those of the highest name.

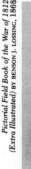

John Quincy Adams

In the autumn, Jefferson learned that the school would be honored by a visit from Lafayette. "What recollections, dear friend, will this call up to you and me! What a history have we to run over...," he wrote in October. Lafayette reached Monticello three weeks later and was the guest of honor at a banquet held in the unfinished Rotunda of the university. Because Jefferson was too weak to read the brief speech he had prepared, another guest delivered his tribute to "our benefactor in peace as well as in war." The speech concluded with a plea for the university: "Could I live to see it once enjoy the patronage & cherishment of our public authorities with undivided voice, I should die without a doubt of the future fortunes of my native state." That wish seemed near fulfillment, for Gilmer had returned from Europe with commitments from five British scholars; a sixth professor was found in New York City. Delays in the professors' arrival threatened the scheduled opening on February 1, but Jefferson seemed relieved that the event was at last in sight.

An indecisive vote in the Electoral College brought John Quincy Adams to the Presidency that month; Jefferson contented himself with a gracious note of congratulations to the new President's father. As one visitor remarked of Jefferson that winter, "in politics, his interest seems nearly gone." He was, he wrote John Adams, "comforted and protected from other solicitudes by the cares of our University." Slowly, but unmistakably Jefferson's health failed. An illness, variously described as urinary disease or diabetes, developed in the late winter of 1825, just as the university finally opened its doors to pupils and faculty. Despite his weakness, Jefferson sent word to Madison of the school's progress.

> Monticello Mar. 22. [18]25.
>
> Our Students are at present between 50. & 60, and are coming in 2. or 3. every day. We hear of many on the road who cannot come on, the Richmond and Frederick stages having ceased to run. Some of them hire horses and get on. The schools of antient & modern languages and Mathematics have a little over 30. each, Nat. Philosophy fewer, because few come well enough prepared in Mathematics to enter that school to any advantage. They are half idle all, for want of books, Hilliard's supply shipped from Boston . . . being not yet arrived.

The ailing Rector was not left in peace, however, as his dream of a university came to pass. Thomas Mann Randolph, Martha Jefferson's brilliant and charming husband, had become a victim of the mental instability that crippled so many members of his family. Randolph had served as Governor of Virginia from 1819 to 1822 but suffered financial difficulties and found it difficult to live in the shadow of his father-in-law. By 1825 he was completely alienated from his wife and children and tended to blame his wife's family for his financial disgrace. In June Jefferson tried unsuccessfully to placate the son-in-law he had welcomed so happily thirty-five years before.

Engraving of Monticello drawn for a mid-nineteenth-century magazine

> Monticello June 5. [18]25.
>
> Your situation is painful, but neither novel nor infrequent. It is indeed that of a great portion of our countrymen, brought on them, not by their own errors, but by that of our legislators, in subjecting the proportions between the money of the country, and it's other property to the gambling operations of money brokers. . . . I hope that to your other pains has not been added that of moment's doubt that you can ever want a necessary or comfort of life while I possess any thing. All I have is destined to the comfortable maintenance of yourself and the family, and to a future provision for them. I have no other use for the property. Abandon then, dear Sir, to the will of the law the afflicting concerns, which have been hitherto but sources of pain and labour to you. Restore yourself to the bosom of your family & friends.

In August, a friend noticed for the first time that Jefferson's memory failed occasionally. Even so, the "men and gentlemen" of the university plagued their aging Rector. On the evening of October 1 students rioted. When the Visitors met two days later to consider the situation, Jefferson rose to speak, but as one student recalled, "he had not gone far before his feelings overcame him, and he sat down, saying that he would leave to abler hands the task of saying what he wished to say." The guilty students were so moved that they stepped forward to confess. Jefferson recounted the story to Joseph Coolidge, husband of his granddaughter Ellen.

The descendants of Jefferson still possess this scrap of paper which announces the marriage of Ellen Wayles Randolph to Joseph Coolidge.

Engraving of the University of Virginia after an 1826 map, showing major buildings completed

Monticello Oct. 13. [1825].

The University had gone on with a degree of order and harmony which had strengthened the hope that much of self government might be trusted to the discretion of the Students of the age of 16. and upwards, until the 1st. instant. In the night of that day a party of 14. students, animated first with wine, masked themselves so as not to be known, and turned out on the lawn of the University, with no intention, it is believed, but of childish noise and uproar. Two professors hearing it went out to see what was the matter. They were received with insult, and even brick-bats were thrown at them. Each of them seised an offender, demanded their names (for they could not distinguish them under their disguise) but were refused, abused, and the culprits calling on their companions for a rescue, got loose and withdrew to their chambers. The Faculty of Professors met the next day, called the whole before them, and in an address, rather harsh, required them to denounce the offenders. They refused, answered the address in writing and in the rudest terms, and charged the Professors themselves with false statements. 50 others, who were in their rooms, no ways implicated in the riot and knowing nothing about it, immediately signed the answer, making common cause with the rioters, and declaring their belief of their assertions in opposition to those of the Professors.... The Visitors called the whole body of Students before them; exhorted them to make known the persons masked, the innocent to aid the cause of order, by bearing witness to the truth, and the guilty to relieve their innocent brethren from censures which they were conscious that themselves alone deserved. On this the fourteen maskers stepped forward and avowed themselves the persons guilty of whatever had passed, but denying that any trespass had been committed.

402

In this last year of Jefferson's life, even the most innocuous matter turned into a drain on his failing strength. In October, J.H.I. Browere visited Monticello to make a life mask of the former President. Browere had promised that the procedure would take only twenty minutes, but the operation involved hours of agony for Jefferson as the artist used "freely the mallet and chisel" to remove the plaster in which he had coated Jefferson's head. Jefferson remarked to Madison that "there became real danger that the ears would tear from the head sooner than from the plaster. I now bid adieu for ever to busts and even portraits." As his life was ending, Jefferson's letters were often directed to saying what had been too long unsaid and doing what he had left undone. In December, for instance, he sent an unusually explicit statement of his political views to Governor William Branch Giles. John Quincy Adams's first annual message alarmed Jefferson and other Old Republicans; indeed, Adams's policies would soon divide the party into Federal Republicans and Democratic Republicans. The President's obvious commitment to a federal program of internal improvements convinced Jefferson that "consolidation" had triumphed. He counseled patience and perseverance instead of armed resistance to such measures, but his letter to Giles betrayed his suspicion that dissolution of the Union might be necessary.

Browere's life mask of Jefferson

Monticello Dec. 26. [18]25.

Take together the decisions of the federal court, the doctrines of the President, and the misconstructions of the constitutional compact, acted on by the legislature of the federal branch, and it is but too evident, that the three ruling branches of that department are in combination to strip their colleagues, the State authorities, of the powers reserved by them and to exercise themselves all functions foreign and domestic.... And what is our resource for the preservation of the constitution? Reason and argument? You might as well reason and argue with the marble columns encircling them. The Representatives chosen by ourselves? They are joined in the combination; some from incorrect views of government, some from corrupt ones, sufficient, voting together, to outnumber the sound parts; and, with majorities only of 1, 2, or 3, bold enough to go forward in defiance. Are we then *to stand to our arms, with the hot-headed Georgian* [William H. Crawford]? No. That must be the last resource, not to be thought of until much longer and greater sufferings. If every infraction of a compact of so many parties is to be resisted at once, as a dissolution of it, none can ever be formed which would last one year. We must have patience and long endurance then with our brethren while under delusion; give them time for reflection and experience of consequences; keep ourselves in a situation to profit by the chapter of accidents; and separate from our companions only when the sole alternatives left are the dissolution of our union with them, or submission to a government without limitation of powers. Between these two evils, when we must make a choice, there can be no hesitation.

The next month Jefferson undertook a desperate project to provide for his family. Payments on Nicholas's debts and installments on his own mortgaged acres had drained his income each year. He had tried over and over again to sell land to wipe out his debts and establish some funds on which Martha and her children could draw after his death, but Jefferson found no buyers. Virginia's agriculture no longer seemed a wise investment to those who had seen so many planters struggle for years with falling prices and increased taxes. In January, 1826, Thomas Jefferson Randolph rode to Richmond with instructions to seek legislative authorization for a lottery in which the prize would be his grandfather's lands and slaves. Despite the aid of such devoted friends as Joseph Cabell, young Randolph met strong opposition; lotteries were rarely granted to individuals. Jefferson wrote to Cabell of his desire to "save the house of Monticello and a farm adjoining to end my days in and bury my bones." To his grandson, who had worked so long and valiantly to protect his interest, Jefferson sent his thanks.

Monticello Feb. 8. [18]26.

For myself I should not regard a prostration of fortune, but I am over whelmed at the prospect of the situation in which I may leave my family. My dear & beloved daughter, the cherished companion of my early life and nurse of my age and her children, rendered as dear to me as if my own from having lived with them from their cradle, left in a comfortless situation hold up to me nothing but future gloom. And I should not care were life to end with the line I am writing, were it not that ... I may yet be of some avail to the family. Their affectionate devotion to me makes a willingness to endure life a duty as long as it can be of any use to them. Yourself particularly, dear Jefferson, I consider as the greatest of the God-sends which heaven has granted to me. Without you, what could I do under the difficulties now invironing me? ... Perhaps however even in this case I may have no right to complain, as these misfortunes have been held back for my last days when few remain to

A ticket for the Jefferson Lottery

me.... And should this my last request be granted, I may yet close with a cloudless sun a long and serene day of life.

The legislature was generous neither to Jefferson nor to his university. On February 17 he wrote Madison of the vote against additional funds for completion of buildings at Charlottesville and the failure of his plan for a lottery. The letter grew in length and became Jefferson's valedictory to his trusted friend at Montpelier, his comrade and confidante for fifty years.

Extract of Jefferson's will (copied by his grandson Thomas Jefferson Randolph) giving "to my friend James Madison of Montpellier my gold mounted walking staff...."

Monticello Febr. 17. [18]26.

The friendship which has subsisted between us, now half a century, and the harmony of our political principles and pursuits, have been sources of constant happiness to me thro' that long period. And if I remove beyond the reach of attentions to the University, or beyond the bourne of life itself, as I soon must, it is a comfort to leave that institution under your care.... It has also been a great solace to me to believe that you are engaged in vindicating to posterity the course we have pursued for preserving to them, *in all their purity,* the blessings of self-government, which we had assisted too in acquiring for them. If ever the earth has beheld a system of administration, conducted with a single and steadfast eye to the general interest and happiness of those committed to it, one which, protected by truth, can never know reproach, it is that to which our lives have been devoted. To myself you have been a pillar of support thro' life. Take care of me when dead, and be assured that I shall leave with you my last affections.

Not long afterward, the lottery was finally approved by the legislature. When newspapers began to carry offers of tickets in the "Jefferson Lottery," however, private subscribers promised funds in his support, and the lottery was suspended. On March 19 Jefferson made his will, carefully drafting its provisions so that Martha's husband would be unable to touch the funds her father had fought so desperately to give her. A few days later, young Randolph prepared for a visit to Boston and Jefferson gave him a letter of introduction to Adams. Perhaps guessing that it was the last he would write his old friend, Jefferson drafted a touching note which Adams described as "a cordial to me."

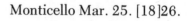

*Jefferson's design for tombstone
and the inscription he desired*

Monticello Mar. 25. [18]26.

Dear Sir

My grandson Th: Jefferson Randolph, being on a visit to Boston, would think he had seen nothing were he to leave it without having seen you.... Like other young people, he wishes to be able, in the winter nights of old age, to recount to those around him what he has heard and learnt of the Heroic age preceding his birth, and which of the Argonauts particularly he was in time to have seen. It was the lot of our early years to witness nothing but the dull monotony of colonial subservience, and of our riper ones to breast the labors and perils of working out of it. Theirs are the Halcyon calms succeeding the storm which our Argosy had so stoutly weathered. Gratify his ambition then by recieving his best bow, and my solicitude for your health by enabling him to bring me a favorable account of it. Mine is but indifferent, but not so my friendship and respect for you.

Th. J.

Jefferson's indifferent health failed further after his grandson's departure. Soon he could hardly walk and by the last week of June, he was confined to bed. To the end, nonetheless, he met his duties as elder statesman and symbol of America's heritage. On June 24 he replied to an invitation to attend the celebration of the fiftieth anniversary of the Declaration of Independence at Washington. In declining the honor, Jefferson labored carefully over the precise wording of what was to be his last public statement.

Monticello June 24. [18]26.

I should, indeed, with peculiar delight, have met and exchanged there, congratulations personally, with the small band, the remnant of that host of worthies, who joined with us, on that day, in the bold and doubtful election we were to make for our country, between submission, or the sword; and to have enjoyed with them the consolatory fact that our fellow citizens, after half a century of experience and prosperity, continue to approve the choice we made. May it be to the world, what I believe it will be ... the Signal of arousing men to burst the chains, under which Monkish ignorance and superstition had persuaded them to bind themselves, and to assume the blessings & security of self government.... All eyes are opened, or opening to the rights of man. The general spread of the light of science has already laid open to every view the palpable truth that the mass of mankind has not been born, with saddles on their backs, nor a favored few booted and spurred, ready to ride them legitimately, by the grace of god. These are grounds of hope for others. For ourselves let the annual return of this day, for ever refresh our recollections of these ri[ghts,] and an undiminished devotion to them.

T he anniversary of the Fourth of July obsessed Jefferson in his last days. On July 2 he lapsed into a coma, only to wake briefly on the evening of the third to ask: "Is it the Fourth?" His physician answered that it soon would be. Shortly before one o'clock on the afternoon of July 4, 1826, Jefferson died. Later that day John Adams passed away, leaving as his last words: "Thomas Jefferson survives." The next day Jefferson was buried in a quiet ceremony at Monticello. His grandson arranged for the simple marker his grandfather had designed. The stone was not to list a single office he had held, only "The following inscription, & not a word more 'Here was buried Thomas Jefferson Author of the Declaration of American Independance, of the Statute of Virginia for religious freedom, & Father of the University of Virginia.' because by these, as testimonials that I have lived, I wish most to be remembered."

These accomplishments reflected what Jefferson felt were the most important events of the long struggle he had led toward the triumph of republican principles. Certainly he could be forgiven the suspicion that the American nation of the second quarter of the nineteenth century would have little regard for his labors in public office. The private subscriptions did not fully materialize, and his daughter and grandchildren were left in want. Many of Jefferson's dreams would become real, however. Although Jefferson only freed five of his own slaves at his death, all slaves would eventually be freed, at great cost to the Union he cherished. Public education would become commonplace. And one hundred and fifty years after his death, those who fought impersonal, unresponsive government, those who defended the rights of conscience against bigotry and prejudice, and those who simply said that government must benefit the governed, not the governors, would call themselves "Jeffersonians."

A modest man who detested hero worship, Jefferson would have cared little that men fought for these principles in his name. His struggles were vindicated merely because the battle continued and because his example and words proved useful to later generations who carried on his jealous guardianship of the nation's honor and her citizens' rights. It was for this that Jefferson had risked his way of life and his family's estates: men were freer because he had lived. He needed no other monument.

Selected Bibliography

Adams, Henry. *History of the United States During the Administrations of Jefferson and Madison.* 9 vols. New York: Charles Scribner's Sons, 1891–93.

Berman, Eleanor D. *Thomas Jefferson among the Arts.* New York: Philisophical Library, 1947.

Boorstin, Daniel. *The Lost World of Thomas Jefferson.* New York: Holt, 1948.

Bowers, Claude G. *Jefferson and Hamilton: The Struggle for Democracy in America.* Boston: Houghton Mifflin, 1925.

Brodie, Fawn M. *Thomas Jefferson, An Intimate History.* New York: W. W. Norton, 1974.

Cabell, N.F., ed. *Early History of the University of Virginia, as Contained in the Letters of Thomas Jefferson and Joseph C. Cabell.* Richmond: J.W. Randolph, 1856.

Cappon, Lester J., ed. *The Adams-Jefferson Letters: The Complete Correspondence between Thomas Jefferson and Abigail and John Adams.* Chapel Hill: University of North Carolina Press, for the Institute of Early American History and Culture, 1959.

Cunningham, Noble E., Jr. *The Jeffersonian Republicans in Power: The Formation of Party Organization, 1789–1801.* Chapel Hill: University of North Carolina Press, 1957.

————. *The Jeffersonian Republicans in Power: Party Operations, 1801–1809.* Chapel Hill: University of North Carolina Press, 1963.

Dumbauld, Edward. *Thomas Jefferson: American Tourist.* Norman: University of Oklahoma Press, 1946.

Fleming, Thomas. *The Man from Monticello.* New York: Morrow, 1969.

Jefferson, Thomas. *The Commonplace Book of Thomas Jefferson: A Repertory of His Ideas on Government.* Edited by Gilbert Chinard. Baltimore: Johns Hopkins Press, 1926.

————. *Thomas Jefferson's Farm Book.* Edited by Edwin M. Betts. Princeton: Princeton University Press, for the American Philosophical Society, 1953.

————. *Thomas Jefferson's Garden Book, 1766–1824.* Edited by Edwin M. Betts. Philadelphia: American Philosophical Society, 1944.

————. *Family Letters of Thomas Jefferson.* Edited by Edwin M. Betts and J.A. Bear, Jr., Columbia: University of Missouri Press, 1966.

————. *Notes on the State of Virginia.* Edited by William Peden. Chapel Hill: University of North Carolina Press, 1955.

————. *The Papers of Thomas Jefferson.* Edited by Julian P. Boyd and others. 19 vols. to date. Princeton: Princeton University Press, 1950–.

————. *The Writings of Thomas Jefferson.* Edited by A.A. Lipscomb and A.E. Bergh. 20 vols. Washington: Thomas Jefferson Memorial Foundation, 1905.

————. *The Writings of Thomas Jefferson.* Edited by Paul Leicester Ford. 10 vols. New York: G. P. Putnam's Sons, 1892–99.

Kimball, Fiske. *Thomas Jefferson, Architect.* 2d ed. New York: Da Capo, 1968.

Koch, Adrienne and Peden, William, eds. *The Life and Selected Writings of Thomas Jefferson.* New York: Random House (The Modern Library), 1944.

Madison, James. *The Papers of James Madison.* Vols. 1–7, edited by William T. Hutchinson and William M.E. Rachal et al. Vol. 8–, edited by Robert A. Rutland and William M. E. Rachal et al. Chicago: University of Chicago Press, 1962–.

Malone, Dumas. *Jefferson and His Time.* 5 vols. to date: *Jefferson the Virginian; Jefferson and the Rights of Man; Jefferson and the Ordeal of Liberty; Jefferson the President: First Term, 1801–1805; Jefferson the President: Second Term, 1805–1809.* Boston: Little Brown, 1948–74.

Martin, Edwin T. *Thomas Jefferson, Scientist.* New York: Henry Schuman, 1952.

Padover, Saul K. *Jefferson.* New York: Harcourt, Brace & Co., 1942.

Peterson, Merrill D. *Thomas Jefferson and the New Nation.* New York: Oxford University Press, 1970.

————. *The Jefferson Image in the American Mind.* New York: Oxford University Press, 1960.

Randall, Henry S. *The Life of Thomas Jefferson.* 3 vols. 1858. Reprint. New York: Da Capo, 1972.

Randolph, Sarah N. *The Domestic Life of Thomas Jefferson.* New York: Harper & Bros., 1871.

Schachner, Nathan. *Thomas Jefferson, A Biography.* New York: Appleton-Century-Crofts, 1951.

Weymouth, Lally, ed. *Thomas Jefferson, The Man . . . His World . . . His Influence.* New York: G. P. Putnam's Sons, 1973.

White, Leonard D. *The Jeffersonians: A Study in Administrative History, 1801–1829.* New York: Macmillan, 1951.

Acknowledgments

Unless otherwise specifically credited below, all documents reproduced in this volume are from the Thomas Jefferson Papers, Library of Congress, Washington, D.C., the greatest collection of Jefferson documents in existence. The sources of other documents reprinted in this volume are as follows:

Alderman Library, University of Virginia, Charlottesville, page 397
Historical Society of Pennsylvania, Philadelphia, pages 280(middle), 399(bottom)–400
Houghton Library, Harvard University, Cambridge, Mass., page 402
Massachusetts Historical Society, Boston, pages 54(bottom), 285(bottom)–286(top)
National Archives, Washington, D.C., pages 66(bottom)–70
New-York Historical Society, New York, N.Y., page 250
New York Public Library, New York, N.Y., pages 268(bottom)–269, 326(top)
Pierpont Morgan Library, New York, N.Y., pages 234, 256(bottom)–257(top), 280(bottom)
United States Naval Academy Museum, Annapolis, Md., pages 347(bottom)–348

In addition, some documents were reprinted from the following published works:
Jefferson, Thomas. *Notes on Virginia.* London, 1787. Pages 18(bottom)–19, 78–79(center), 82–84, 88(bottom)–90, 107(bottom)–108, 132(bottom)–135, 148
La Rochefoucauld-Liancourt, François, A.F., Duc de. *Travels Through the United States of North America.* 2 vols. London, 1799. Pages 261(bottom)–262(top)
Randall, Henry S. *The Life of Thomas Jefferson.* 3 vols. New York, 1858. Pages 274(bottom)–275(top)
Randolph, Sarah N. *The Domestic Life of Thomas Jefferson.* New York, 1871. Page 381

The principal sources of information contained in the Introduction were the prefatory remarks written by Julian P. Boyd for Volume 1 of *The Papers of Thomas Jefferson,* an essay on the provenance of the Jefferson papers by Paul G. Sifton of the Library of Congress, and *The Jefferson Image in the American Mind* by Merrill D. Peterson.

The Editors wish to express their appreciation to the many institutions and individuals who have made available their pictorial materials for use in this volume. In particular the Editors are grateful to:
Alderman Library, University of Virginia, Charlottesville
American Antiquarian Society, Worcester, Mass.
American Philosophical Society, Philadelphia
Bibliothèque Nationale, Paris
The College of William and Mary, Williamsburg, Va.
Historical Society of Pennsylvania, Philadelphia
Independence National Historical Park Collection, Philadelphia
Library of Congress, Manuscript and Rare Book Divisions, Washington, D.C.
Maryland Historical Society, Baltimore
Massachusetts Historical Society, Boston
Musée Carnavalet, Paris
New-York Historical Society, New York, N.Y.
New York Public Library, New York, N.Y.
Princeton University Library, Princeton, N.J.
Thomas Jefferson Memorial Foundation, Charlottesville, Va.
Virginia Historical Society, Richmond
Yale University Art Gallery, New Haven, Conn.
Yale University Libraries, New Haven, Conn.

Finally, the Editors would like to thank Barbara Nagelsmith in Paris, John D. Knowlton in Washington, D.C., and Ruth W. Lester, Assistant Editor of *The Papers of Thomas Jefferson,* Princeton, for advice and assistance in obtaining pictorial material, Susan Sheldon for editing and proofreading, and Lynn Seiffer for research.

Index

142–47
Congress Hall (Philadelphia), **274**
Connecticut, 235, 285, 298, 347, 375
Connecticut Magazine, The, 271
Constitutional Convention of 1787, 76, 185–88, **188,** 189, 190, 290
Continental Army, 54, 94, 97–98
Continental Association, 52
Continental Congress
    First, 43–53, 54, 279–80
    Second, 34, 54–71, 72, 75
Continental currency, 93, 99
Convention of 1800, 330
Coolidge, Joseph, 402
Cooper, Thomas, 367
Copley, John Singleton, 154
Cornwallis, Lord Charles, 102
    Southern forces, 96, 98, **99,** 99, 103, 104, 105, 106–107
    surrender of, 136
Cosway, Maria Hadfield, **124,** 126, 172–76, **173, 175**
Cosway, Richard, 172
Cowpens, Battle of, 102, **103**
Crawford, William H., 403
Currie, Dr. James, 158–59

Dearborn, Henry, 325, 359, 372
Decatur, Lt. Stephen, 312
Declaration of the Causes and Necessity for Taking Up Arms (Dickinson and Jefferson), 54, 55–59
Declaration of Independence, 6, 62–71, **179,** 192, 307, 383
    adoption of, 70–71
    celebration of, **71,** 320, 406, 407
    in committee, 64, **65**
    debates on, 62–66
    draft of, **15, 65,** 66
    presentation of, **67, 68, 69**
Declaration of the Rights of Man, 203, 204
Democratic Republicans, 403
Democratic Societies, 255
Descartes, René, 83
Detroit, British post at, 99
"Dialogue between my Head and my Heart" (Jefferson), 172–76
Dickinson, John, 45, 55, 55–59, 63, 340
"Discourses on Davila" (Adams), 233
Doolittle, Amos, 271
Doolittle, Horace, 36
Douglas, William, 17
Du Pont de Nemours, Pierre Samuel, **335,** 335–36, 377–78
Du Simitière, Pierre, 53, 55
Dunmore, Lord, 42, 61, 62
    seal, **43**
Dusseldorf, art gallery at, 195

Election of 1792, 241–42
Election of 1796, 265, 268, 269–70
Election of 1800, 294–302, **307,** 325, 339, 344, 349, **387,** 399
Election of 1804, 343, 344–47, **345,** 349

Election of 1816, 392
Election of 1824, 400–401
Electoral College, 268, 300, 322, 400
Embargo Act of 1807, 368–77
    effect of, 374, 378
    enforcement of, 371–72
    opposition to, **320,** 372–77
    repealed, 376–77
Enlightenment, 22
Eppes, Elizabeth (sister-in-law), 140, 156
Eppes, Francis (brother-in-law), 140, 209
Eppes, John Wayles (son-in-law), **280,** 280, **354**
Eppes, Nicholas, 140
Essex Junto, 375–76
Estates General (France), 200–203, **201**
    Second Estate, 202
    Third Estate, 202–203

Fabbroni, Giovanni, 35–36
Farmers General (France), 162
Fauquier, Governor Francis, **22**
Federal Hall (New York City), **215**
Federal Republicans, 403
Federalist, The, 29
Federalists, 252, 258–59, 262, 264, 273, 277, 278, **281,** 281, 300–302. *See also* Elections.
    Alien and Sedition Acts, 284–86
    differences with Republicans, 280
    Hamilton and, 277, 297, 300
    intra-party quarrels, 294–95
    Jefferson administration and, 322, 323, 324, 325, 349, 359
        Adams's appointees, 325, **326,** 326–27, **327**
        attacks during 1802 campaign, 336
        Burr trial, 365
        fear of (cartoon), **324**
        judiciary, opposition in, 339–40, 365
    Mazzei letter, use of, 281
    in New England, 285
    in New York, 296, 297
Fenno, Joseph, 235, 239, 241
Fincastle County (Virginia), 74
First Principles of Government (Priestley), 29
Fleming, William, 27–28, **28**
Floridas, the, 314, 337, 352
    purchase of, 354–55
    cartoon of, **354**
Ford, Paul Leicester, 9
Forest, The (estate), 39–40
Fontainebleau, 165–66
Fox, Charles James, **357,** 357–58, 361
France, 149–208, 243, 244–47
    See also French Revolution.
    abolition of the monarchy, 242
    Bourbon power, disintegration of, 185–208
    Directory, 275, 276, 290
    famine, 201
    Jacobins, 242–43, 246

anti-Jacobin cartoon, **242**
Napoleonic Wars, 349
Paris mobs, **202**
peasants in, 166
quasi war with U.S. (1798), **284,** 284
rapprochement with (Adams administration), 276–77, 278, 279, 290, 292–93, 297
trade negotiations with America (1784–87), 149, 150–53, 156, 160–62, 176–77, 184
war with Great Britain (1793), 243, 265, 330
Franklin, Benjamin, 6, 10, 11, 63, 65, 65–66, 123, **129,** 135, **141,** 141, 148, 150, **159,** 212, 258, 282
    return to America, 156, 159
Franklin, William Temple, 141
Franks, David, 178
Frederic of Prussia, 153
French Revolution, 202–208, 225, 233, 242, 244
    badge worn by revolutionaries, **189, 244**
    beginning of, 189–90, 203
    fall of the Bastille, 203
    reign of terror, 242
French West Indies, 244
Freneau, Philip, 235, 239, 241
Fry, Joshua, 16
Funding controversy, 213–15, 225

Galileo, 83
Gallatin, Albert, 325, 328, **331,** 359, 372
    financial program of, 331–33, 348
Garde Nationale, 207
Gardening, 114, 170
Gaspee (schooner), 41
Gates, General Horatio, 96–97, 98, 102, 250
Gazette of the United States, 233, 235, 239, 241
Geismar, Baron de, 166
Gem, Dr. Richard, 206
General Advertiser (Philadelphia), 235
Genêt, Edmond Charles, 244–46
George III, King, **51,** 61–62, 66, 169
Georgia, 98
Germany, 195–96
Gerry, Elbridge, 277–78, **278,** 279, 283, 290–92
Ghent, Treaty of, 390
Giles, William Branch, 257, 261, 364–65, 375–76, 403–404
Gilmer, Francis Walker, **399,** 399–400
Gordon, William, 105–106
Governor's House (Richmond), proposed plan for, **95**
Governor's Palace (Williamsburg), 18–19, **19,** 22, 27
    list of articles for, **91**
Graff, Jacob, boardinghouse, **64**
Great Britain, 153, 168–71, 252, 398. *See also* American

your draughts will be most negoc[...]

necessaries for yourself & your me[...]

United States that these draughts [...]

are made prayable. I also ask if [...]

nation with which we have interco[...]

-plies which your necessities may [...]

~~retribution.~~ and our own Consuls in f[...]

~~hereby~~ instructed & required to be [...]

necessary for procuring your retur[...]

entire satisfaction & confidence to th[...]

Jefferson, President of the United S[...]

              for you
general credit with my own hand.

To

    Capt. Meriwether Le[...]